VBA
FOR
DUMMIES®
5TH EDITION

by John Paul Mueller

BICENTENNIAL
1807
WILEY
2007
BICENTENNIAL

Wiley Publishing, Inc.

VBA For Dummies,® 5th Edition

Published by
Wiley Publishing, Inc.
111 River Street
Hoboken, NJ 07030-5774
www.wiley.com

Copyright © 2007 by Wiley Publishing, Inc., Indianapolis, Indiana

Published by Wiley Publishing, Inc., Indianapolis, Indiana

Published simultaneously in Canada

No part of this publication may be reproduced, stored in a retrieval system or transmitted in any form or by any means, electronic, mechanical, photocopying, recording, scanning or otherwise, except as permitted under Sections 107 or 108 of the 1976 United States Copyright Act, without either the prior written permission of the Publisher, or authorization through payment of the appropriate per-copy fee to the Copyright Clearance Center, 222 Rosewood Drive, Danvers, MA 01923, (978) 750-8400, fax (978) 646-8600. Requests to the Publisher for permission should be addressed to the Legal Department, Wiley Publishing, Inc., 10475 Crosspoint Blvd., Indianapolis, IN 46256, (317) 572-3447, fax (317) 572-4355, or online at http://www.wiley.com/go/permissions.

Trademarks: Wiley, the Wiley Publishing logo, For Dummies, the Dummies Man logo, A Reference for the Rest of Us!, The Dummies Way, Dummies Daily, The Fun and Easy Way, Dummies.com, and related trade dress are trademarks or registered trademarks of John Wiley & Sons, Inc., and/or its affiliates in the United States and other countries, and may not be used without written permission. All other trademarks are the property of their respective owners. Wiley Publishing, Inc., is not associated with any product or vendor mentioned in this book.

For general information on our other products and services, please contact our Customer Care Department within the U.S. at 800-762-2974, outside the U.S. at 317-572-3993, or fax 317-572-4002.

For technical support, please visit www.wiley.com/techsupport.

Wiley also publishes its books in a variety of electronic formats. Some content that appears in print may not be available in electronic books.

Library of Congress Control Number: 2006936829

ISBN: 978-0-470-04650-0

10 9 8 7 6 5 4 3

5O/SS/RS/QW/IN

About the Author

John Mueller is a freelance author and technical editor. He has writing in his blood, having produced 71 books and over 300 articles to date. The topics range from networking to artificial intelligence and from database management to heads-down programming. Some of his current books include a Windows power optimization book, a book on .NET security, and books on Amazon Web Services, Google Web Services, and eBay Web Services. His technical editing skills have helped more than 50 authors refine the content of their manuscripts. John has provided technical editing services to both *Data Based Advisor* and *Coast Compute* magazines. He has also contributed articles to magazines like *DevSource, InformIT, Informant, DevX, SQL Server Professional, Visual C++ Developer, Hardcore Visual Basic, asp.netPRO, Software Test & Performance*, and *Visual Basic Developer*.

When John isn't working at the computer, you can find him in his workshop. He's an avid woodworker and candle maker. On any given afternoon, you can find him working at a lathe or putting the finishing touches on a bookcase. He also likes making glycerin soap and candles, which comes in handy for gift baskets. You can reach John on the Internet at JMueller@mwt.net. He is also setting up a Web site at http:// www.mwt.net/~jmueller/; feel free to look and make suggestions on how he can improve it. Check out John's weekly blog at http://www.amazon.com/gp/blog/id/AQOA2QP4X1YWP.

Dedication

This book is dedicated to Uncle Bob on his birthday; thanks for helping me understand the need to enjoy some time off.

Author's Acknowledgments

Thanks to my wife, Rebecca, for working with me to get this book completed. I really don't know what I would have done without her help in researching and compiling some of the information that appears in this book. She also did a fine job of proofreading my rough draft.

Russ Mullen deserves thanks for his technical edit of this book. He greatly added to the accuracy and depth of the material that you see here. I really appreciate the time he devoted to checking my code for accuracy. I also spent a good deal of time bouncing ideas off Russ as I wrote this book, which is a valuable aid to any author.

A number of people read all or part of this book to help me refine the approach, test the examples, and generally provide input that every reader wishes they could have. These unpaid volunteers helped in ways too numerous to mention here. I especially appreciate the efforts of Eva Beattie, who read the entire book and selflessly devoted herself to this project. Members of various newsgroups and the support staff from Microsoft were instrumental in helping me overcome obstacles. A number of other people, including Tom Rider and Chellingi Prasad, helped me in ways too numerous to mention. I'd love to thank by name each person who wrote me with an idea, but there are simply too many to name.

Finally, I would like to thank Kyle Looper, Nicole Sholly, Rebecca Whitney, and the rest of the editorial and production staff for their assistance in bringing this book to print. It's always nice to work with such a great group of professionals.

Publisher's Acknowledgments

We're proud of this book; please send us your comments through our online registration form located at www.dummies.com/register/.

Some of the people who helped bring this book to market include the following:

Acquisitions, Editorial, and Media Development

Project Editor: Nicole Sholly

Acquisitions Editor: Kyle Looper

Copy Editor: Rebecca Whitney

Technical Editor: Russ Mullen

Editorial Manager: Kevin Kirschner

Media Development Specialists: Angela Denny, Kate Jenkins, Steven Kudirka, Kit Malone

Media Project Supervisor: Laura Moss

Media Development Manager: Laura VanWinkle

Editorial Assistant: Amanda Foxworth

Sr. Editorial Assistant: Cherie Case

Cartoons: Rich Tennant (www.the5thwave.com)

Composition Services

Project Coordinator: Adrienne Martinez

Layout and Graphics: Carl Byers, Stephanie D. Jumper, Barbara Moore, Barry Offringa, Heather Ryan, Ronald Terry

Proofreaders: Susan Moritz, Dwight Ramsey, Techbooks

Indexer: Techbooks

Anniversary Logo Design: Richard Pacifico

Publishing and Editorial for Technology Dummies

    Richard Swadley, Vice President and Executive Group Publisher

    Andy Cummings, Vice President and Publisher

    Mary Bednarek, Executive Acquisitions Director

    Mary C. Corder, Editorial Director

Publishing for Consumer Dummies

    Diane Graves Steele, Vice President and Publisher

    Joyce Pepple, Acquisitions Director

Composition Services

    Gerry Fahey, Vice President of Production Services

    Debbie Stailey, Director of Composition Services

Contents at a Glance

Table of Contents

Introduction

· ·

*W*elcome to your first look at Visual Basic for Applications (VBA)! You might think that VBA is a secret code used by advanced computer users to intimidate the rest of us. Nothing could be further from the truth. VBA is all about doing things your way. When you want an application to perform a task in a certain way, use VBA to extend it. VBA makes *you* the boss. After you discover the wonders of VBA, you can customize a number of applications to make them work the way you want them to work.

VBA is a tool that empowers you to perform tasks you never thought possible in a fraction of the time that it takes to perform the task by hand. For example, you can add new toolbars, create custom reports, and perform special kinds of data analysis. When you write a VBA program, you become the master of your environment — someone who gets the job done quickly.

Over 500 readers of the previous edition of this book sent me e-mail, many of whom told me about their current projects. After reviewing those messages for this edition of the book, I can truly say that VBA is an amazing tool because you're doing amazing things with it. After seeing everything that people are doing with VBA, it's easy to say that this is the tool for everyone!

About This Book

VBA For Dummies, 5th Edition, is a reference book. You don't have to read it in any particular order, and you can skip anything that you don't find interesting. Readers who have VBA programming experience can skip to the advanced examples at the end of the book or explore new language elements as needed. That said, I did put the book into a logical order. When you begin at Chapter 1 and progress through the book chapter by chapter, you acquire a complete view of VBA, even if you've never used it.

This book contains many examples from my own library. I write VBA programs for all my applications that support it because I know that using VBA can save me time and effort. In addition, I write VBA programs for some of my consulting clients. This real-world approach to using VBA will help you get started quickly.

Some of the new examples are the result of my experiments with the new Ribbon interface. You'll find that the Ribbon adds a new dimension to working with VBA and that it breaks some of your older code. Fortunately, you'll find many of the answers for fixing your applications in this book.

Conventions Used in This Book

I always try to show you the fastest way to accomplish any task. In many cases, this means using a menu command, such as Tools➪Macro➪Visual Basic Editor. When you're working with the Ribbon, I'll tell you which tab to access first and then which feature to use on that tab.

I'm assuming that you've worked with Windows long enough to know how the keyboard and mouse work. You should also know how to use menus and other basic Windows features.

Whenever possible, I use shortcut keys to help you access a command faster. For example, you can also start the VBA Integrated Development Environment (IDE) by pressing Alt+F11.

This book also uses special type to emphasize some information. For example, entries that you need to type appear in **bold**. All code, Web site URLs, and onscreen messages appear in monofont type. Whenever I define a new word, you'll see that word in *italics*.

Because you use two applications when working with VBA, I always tell you to move from one application to the next. When a chapter begins, I assume that you're in the VBA IDE unless I tell you otherwise. All the commands in that chapter are for the VBA IDE until I specifically tell you to move to the host application. I also specifically tell you when it's time to move back to the VBA IDE.

What You Should Read

What you read depends on your level of experience — you need to know how to use at least one Microsoft Office application. It also helps to know something about VBA before you tackle the programs at the end of the book. With this in mind, you probably want to read Chapters 1 through 7 in order before you begin discovering other parts of the book.

You might have used VBA before and want to know only what you can add to your knowledge. The programs become progressively more complex and application specific as the book progresses. When you want to find out how to work with Word only, feel free to select Chapter 13. You might find Chapter 17 a good place to start because, in it, I tell you about interesting VBA resources that you might not know about. Of course, *all* the content in this book is great, and I hope that you eventually read it all.

Because Office 2007 is so different from previous versions, I provide a special chapter to address those changes. Although you'll find tips for working with the Ribbon interface spread throughout the book, anyone moving from toolbars and menus to the Ribbon will want to pay particular attention to Chapter 12.

What You Don't Have to Read

Most chapters contain some advanced material that interests only some readers. When you see one of these specialized topics, such as writing information to the Windows Registry, feel free to skip it. You can also skip any material marked with a Technical Stuff icon. This material is helpful, but you don't have to know it in order to use VBA. I include this material because I find it helpful in my programming efforts and hope that you will, too.

Foolish Assumptions

You might find it difficult to believe that I have assumed anything about you (after all, I haven't even met you yet!), but I have. Although most assumptions are indeed foolish, I made these assumptions to provide a starting point for the book.

I assume that you've worked with Windows long enough to know how the keyboard and mouse work and how to use menus and other basic Windows features. It's essential to know how to use at least one Office application. If you're working with a Ribbon example, I assume that you have spent time discovering how to use the Ribbon in a new Office 2007 application. Some portions of the book work with Web pages, and others use eXtensible Markup Language (XML); you need to know at least a little about these technologies to use those sections. You don't have to be an expert in any of these areas, but more knowledge is better.

How This Book Is Organized

This book contains several parts. Each part demonstrates a particular VBA feature and helps you build your VBA knowledge. In each chapter, I discuss a particular topic and include example programs that you can use to discover more about VBA on your own. You can find the source code for this book, along with Bonus Chapters, on the Dummies.com Web site at http://www.dummies.com/go/vbafd5e.

Part I: An Overview of VBA

The main purpose of this part of the book is to help you use the VBA IDE to write programs. In Chapter 1, I tell you about the various windows and other physical features of the VBA IDE. In Chapter 2, I tell you about the parts of a VBA program and show you various methods for running any VBA program you create. You also gain some experience with the Microsoft help files in this chapter.

Part II: Learning the Ropes

The main purpose of this part of the book is to help you understand the VBA language. VBA uses *statements* (commands) to perform work. Just like in any language, parts of these statements are very much like human language. In Chapter 3, I show you how to create various kinds of VBA program containers. In Chapter 4, you see how to store and manage data. Controlling a program is important (you don't want it to run amok), so in Chapter 5 you see examples of how to perform this task. We all know the results of buggy programs, so in Chapter 6 I show you how to avoid this problem. Finally, in Chapter 7, I demonstrate methods of interacting with the user.

Part III: Expanding Your VBA Horizons

The main purpose of this part of the book is to help you build your VBA knowledge. In Chapter 8, you see how to work with objects — an essential skill when you discover the benefits of writing programs to create documents automatically. In Chapter 9, I demonstrate how to use *arrays* and *collections,* which are special kinds of data storage containers that VBA uses. Storing information on disk is very important, so read Chapter 10 to discover how to access the disk drive. Microsoft is touting XML as the next best thing for Office users; see Chapter 11 for how to use XML files to your benefit.

Part IV: Programming for Applications

The main purpose of this part of the book is to help you become productive by using VBA with a particular application. However, before you begin reading about a specific Office application, in Chapter 12 I show you how to make some Office-specific changes by using VBA code. Make sure that you read Chapter 12 to understand how the Ribbon interface will affect your existing applications.

In this part, I discuss the three main Office applications: Word (Chapter 13), Excel (Chapter 14), and Access (Chapter 15). You probably don't use just one application, so in Chapter 16 I extend the idea of individual application programming into working with multiple applications by using a single program.

Part V: The Part of Tens

We all accumulate cool tips and techniques that other people find helpful. Chapter 17 tells about ten kinds of resources that you can use to make VBA better, easier to use, or simply more productive. Chapter 18 describes ten ways to upgrade your existing VBA code quickly.

The accompanying Web site

This book contains a lot of code, and you might not want to type it. Fortunately, you can find the source code for this book on the Dummies.com Web site at http://www.dummies.com/go/vbafd5e. The source code is organized by chapter, and I always tell you about the example files in the text. The best way to work with a chapter is to download all the source code for it at one time.

The Web site also has three Bonus Chapters: one on FrontPage, a second on Visio, and a third on ten cool things that you can do with VBA. The FrontPage chapter describes how you can use VBA to make FrontPage easier to use. In fact, you'll find an application that lets you create the initial part of a Web page automatically. Other programs show how to discover more about FrontPage features and demonstrate how to customize those features to meet specific needs, such as exchanging data between applications.

The Visio chapter describes how you can use VBA to automate some Visio drawing tasks. For example, you'll discover that you can create Visio drawings significantly faster by automating required setup tasks that you can't easily perform using a stencil or template. This Bonus Chapter relies on Visio 2007. Although many of the macros will work with older versions of Visio, you'll still want to use Visio 2007 to obtain the maximum benefit from this Bonus Chapter.

Icons Used in This Book

The tips in this book are timesaving techniques or pointers to resources that you should try in order to get the maximum benefit from VBA.

I don't want to sound like an angry parent or some kind of maniac, but you should avoid doing anything marked with a Warning icon. Otherwise, you could find that your program melts down and takes your data with it.

Whenever you see this icon, think advanced tip or technique. Skip these bits of information whenever you like.

This material usually contains an essential process or bit of material that you must know to write VBA programs successfully.

You'll see this icon whenever the book has Web content to present — the source code and Bonus Chapters that come with this book. You'll definitely want to download the Web content to get the most from this book and reduce the work required to use the book.

This icon helps you locate features that Microsoft has added to VBA as part of Office 2007. Use this icon to look for upgrade issues as well. Anyone who has existing VBA applications that they want to upgrade should look for this icon.

Where to Go from Here

It's time to start your VBA adventure! I recommend that anyone who has only a passing knowledge of VBA go right to Chapter 1. This chapter contains essential, get-started information that you need to write your first program.

Those who already know VBA might want to skip to Part IV to sink their teeth into some complex examples. You might want to check out the resources in Part V if you find your current VBA experience lacking. The VBA refresher course begins in Part II and ends in Part III. Start with the part that best suits your needs.

Part I
An Overview
of VBA

The 5th Wave   By Rich Tennant

Well heck—that's just darn impressive! And you say it's programmed to sew up and dress the incision afterward as well?

In this part . . .

You might wonder whether you need to visit this part of the book. This section of the book contains essential information that you need to use VBA effectively. In Chapter 1, I introduce all the windows and other graphical elements of the VBA Integrated Development Environment (IDE). In addition, you create your first program in this chapter. In Chapter 2, I describe the steps for creating a program and show you four methods to run it. This chapter contains the first permanent program for the book. The most important idea to take away from these initial chapters is that you can write programs by using VBA — it's not something that only advanced computer users can do.

Chapter 1

Getting to Know VBA

* *

In This Chapter

▶ Finding uses for Visual Basic for Applications (VBA) programs

▶ Discovering where VBA appears other than in Microsoft Office

▶ Using the VBA Integrated Development Environment (IDE)

▶ Writing a one-line program

* *

*H*ave you ever talked with someone about an application that you're using and said that you thought the vendor who created the application was clueless? The application is just too hard or too time consuming to use because the features are difficult to access. In a few cases, I'll bet you saw a feature that *almost* does what you want it to do . . . but not quite. Something that almost works is frustrating to use, and many of us have wished for a solution to the problem.

At some point, someone at Microsoft made something that fixes all these problems and more: Visual Basic for Applications (VBA). VBA is a simple programming language. By using VBA, you can have things your way — you can customize your applications to meet your needs and expectations. No longer are you a slave to what the vendors want. If you use an application that supports VBA, you can add new features — such as automated letter writing and special equation handling — to change things around to the way that you want. In short, it becomes your custom application and not something that the vendor thinks that you want.

VBA works with many applications, including the Microsoft Office applications. You use VBA to write programs to accomplish tasks automatically or change the application environment. Many people think that they can't write even simple programs. This book helps you understand that anyone can write a program. In fact, you write your first program in this chapter. Of course, first you find out the secret handshake for starting the VBA Editor. Using the VBA editor is just a little different from the word processors you've used in the past. Along the way, you see some interesting uses for VBA and just how many applications you can modify by using it.

Batteries Included — VBA Comes with Office

A good many people have written to ask me whether VBA really does come with Office. The answer is yes. All Office products support VBA, and you can use VBA to perform a wealth of tasks, many of which will seem impossible now. Older versions of Office provide a convenient method for accessing the VBA editor. Simply use the Tools➪Macro➪Visual Basic Editor command to display the VBA editor where you type your VBA commands and store them for later use.

One of the reasons for this section is that Microsoft no longer feels that the average user is smart enough to work with VBA. I find it amazing that the company keeps dumbing down its products and making them more difficult to use in the process, but it does. Newer versions of Office hide VBA from view. If you're using a product such as Word 2007, you actually need to look for VBA before you can use it. Don't bother to scour the new Ribbon interface because you won't find it there. The following steps help you reveal the VBA hidden in your copies of Word, Excel, and PowerPoint.

1. **Choose the Word, Excel, or PowerPoint button and click Word Options, Excel Options, or PowerPoint Options.**

   You see the Word Options (see Figure 1-1), Excel Options, or PowerPoint Options dialog box. All three dialog boxes are similar and have the VBA option in the same place.

2. **Check Show Developer Tab in the Ribbon.**

3. **Click OK.**

   Word, Excel, or PowerPoint displays the Developer tab, shown in Figure 1-2, which contains VBA options described in this book.

Depending on which Office 2007 product you use, you'll find the VBA options in different places. You already know that Word, Excel, and PowerPoint place these buttons on the Developer tab of the Ribbon. When working with Access, you'll find the VBA buttons located on the Database Tools tab of the Ribbon. The actual buttons look the same as those shown in Figure 1-2. Even though Outlook does use the new Ribbon interface, you'll find VBA on the Tools➪Macro menu, just as you always have.

Another way in which the Ribbon changes things is that you can no longer right-click a toolbar (because the toolbars don't exist) and choose Customize to add new menu entries. The Ribbon doesn't allow any changes without some programming on your part. Chapter 12 describes the process you use to add new buttons to the Ribbon. Any toolbars you created programmatically with VBA in the past now appear on the Add-Ins tab of the Ribbon, so even programmatically created toolbars have lost some of their effectiveness in Office 2007.

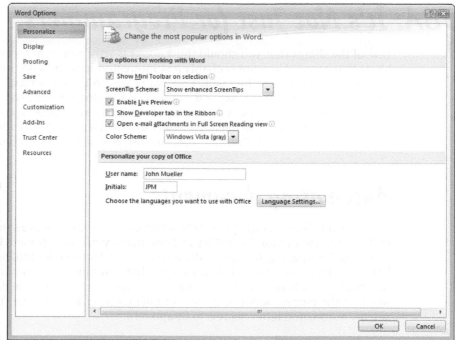

Figure 1-1:
The Word
Options
dialog box
helps you
configure
Word for
specific
needs.

Figure 1-2:
The
Developer
tab of the
Ribbon
contains the
features you
used to find
in the Tools
menu.

Interestingly enough, Microsoft didn't upgrade OneNote, Publisher, Visio, and Project to use the new Ribbon interface. Consequently, you access VBA using the same method you always have on the Tools➪Macro menu. In addition, you'll find that these products lack many of the new features that Microsoft is touting for its core Office products.

VBA: It's Not Just for Programmers

One of the things that you should think about is why you want to use VBA. I know that some of you are probably just interested in using VBA, but most of you need a good reason for taking time out of your busy schedules. It's important to think about what tasks you can use VBA to do. It won't take out the garbage or fold your laundry, but you can use it to write some types of letters automatically. With this in mind, you find out about a few things in this section that I've done with VBA. Knowing you, I'm sure you'll come up with more.

Automating documents

I hate writing letters, especially if the letter contains most of the same information that I wrote for the last letter. Sometimes you can automate letters by using mail merge, but that generally doesn't work too well for individualized letters. In these situations, I set up a form that contains the common information that I include in some letters but not in others. I check off the items that I need for the current letter, and VBA automatically writes it for me. You can see my automated letter secrets in Chapter 13.

Document automation isn't limited to word processing. You can also automate a spreadsheet. I have several programs that I've created for Excel. For example, whenever I get a new client for my business, I click a button, and VBA creates all the required client entries in Excel for me. Because Excel performs the task the same way every time, I can't forget anything and each client receives the same level of high-quality service. You can see techniques for creating automated Excel worksheets in Chapter 14.

If you have to move the data that you create in your word processor or spreadsheet to the Internet, VBA can help make the process nearly automatic. Chapter 16 contains everything that you need to know to move information from one Microsoft Office product to another without the usual modification and reformatting. In Bonus Chapter 1 on the Web site (at http://www.dummies.com/go/vbafd5e), you see how to create automated documents in FrontPage. Bonus Chapter 2 shows how to work with Visio. The Visio applications focus on automating drawing tasks, but you'll see other examples as well.

Customizing an application's interface

Sometimes an application feature just bugs you. You could turn it off if it bugs you that much, but that might not be an option if you need that function in your work. Use VBA to create a new version of the feature with everything that you need and nothing that you don't. For example, I never liked how Word performs a word count, so I created my own program to perform the task. Chapter 12 shows you some of my secrets for taming unruly interfaces.

Changing an application interface to your liking is easy. You can create a customized menu system or toolbars. You can move some interface elements out to a form or get rid of them completely. In addition, any interface change that you want to make is probably doable by using VBA. In addition, you don't necessarily have to use just one interface. You can create programs to change the interface as needed for the task that you're performing. For example, I have a program to switch between book, article, and client document-writing modes. Chapter 7 shows a number of interesting ways to use forms.

Performing calculations

One of the most common uses of special applications is to perform complex calculations. You can create many types of equations by using any of the Microsoft Office products. Sometimes, however, you need to change the data before you can use it or perform the calculation differently depending on the value of one or more inputs. Whenever a calculation becomes too complicated for a simple equation, use VBA to simplify things by solving the calculation problem using small steps rather than one big step. Chapters 4 and 14 show a number of ways to work with calculations.

Sometimes the number that you create using a calculation doesn't mean much — it's just a number until someone makes a decision. Some decisions are easy to make yet repetitive. Chapter 5 shows the methods that your application can use to make decisions automatically with VBA. Smart applications save you more time for playing that game of Solitaire.

Getting stuff from a database

I use Access to store a variety of information — everything from my movie collection to a list of clients that I work with regularly. You use databases to store information, although that doesn't help much if you can't get it out. Use VBA to get the information from your database in the form that you need it. For example, you can display that information on a form so that you can review it, or use that same data to create a report.

I love databases because they provide the most flexible method for storing repetitive information, such as a client list or any other kind of list that you can imagine. Don't assume that databases are so complicated that you'll never understand how they work. Most productivity databases are actually quite simple to use. All you need is a little easily understood VBA code to gain access to them. Chapter 15 shows you everything you need to know to work with productivity databases.

VBA even includes ways of creating temporary databases for those lists that you need only today. This can save you a lot of time and still force the computer to do the work for you. You can see these alternatives in Chapter 9.

Adding new application features

With all the features that vendors have stuffed into applications, you'd think that every possible need would be satisfied. However, I'm convinced that vendors never actually use the applications that they build. (A nifty new screen saver for Windows is not my idea of a necessary feature.) However, the window-sizing program that I really needed came from a third-party vendor.

Most of this book covers adding new application features. Discover how to add specific features by reading specific chapters. (See the preceding sections to find where.) If you read this book from cover to cover, you'll be able to use VBA to add just about any feature to any product that supports VBA. Your friends will be impressed and think that you're a genius. Maybe your boss will become convinced that you're the most valuable employee in the world and give you a large bonus. Reading this book could make you famous, but more importantly, it will make you less frustrated.

Making special tools

If you have to send information to other people who might not have Microsoft Office and they need the information formatted, you might have to work a long time to find a solution. Chapters 10 and 11 contain two methods for storing information in alternative formats. Chapter 10 uses the trusty text file, and Chapter 11 relies on eXtensible Markup Language (XML) files.

Having things your way

Sometimes I'd just like to scream. Microsoft seems to think that it knows precisely what I want — based on what people tell it. Who these other people are remains a mystery, but I wouldn't trust the person in the dark suit sitting next to you.

Fortunately, you can use VBA to help customize Microsoft's well-intentioned application features. If Word decides that it absolutely must display the information you don't want on startup, store your settings to disk and restore

them every time you launch Word. The use of automatically executing programs (see Chapter 2) can help you have things your own way. Chapter 10
shows you how to store your settings in text format, and Chapter 11 shows
you how to store them in XML format.

Other Products Use VBA, Too

Don't assume that VBA is good only if you're using Microsoft Office or a few
other Microsoft products. With VBA at your command, you can control a lot
of different applications. Go to the Microsoft site `http://msdn.microsoft.`
`com/vba/companies/company.asp` to see a list of companies that have
licensed VBA. You'll be amazed at the number of applications that you can
work with using VBA. Here are a few of my favorites:

✔ **Corel products (`http://www.corel.com/`):** Corel makes WordPerfect
   and Draw. *WordPerfect* is a word processing program that many legal
   offices still use. One of my first professional writing jobs required the
   use of WordPerfect. *CorelDRAW,* a drawing program that many professionals enjoy using, supports a wealth of features. All the line art in this
   book was originally drawn using CorelDRAW, and all my drawing setups
   are performed automatically by using VBA programs.

✔ **Micrografx iGrafx series (`http://www.micrografx.com/`):** This product can help you create flowcharts or organizational charts. Unlike a lot
   of drawing tasks, both flowcharts and organizational charts are
   extremely repetitive, making them a perfect place to use VBA.

✔ **IMSI TurboCad (`http://www.turbocad.com/`):** I love to work with
   wood, which means that I have to draw plans for new projects from time
   to time. TurboCad is the drawing program that I prefer to use. It's relatively inexpensive, and the VBA programs I've created for it automate
   many of the drawing tasks, such as creating ¾" boards.

VBA hasn't been around forever. If you drag out that old, dusty copy of
WordPerfect for DOS, you'll be disappointed because it doesn't support VBA.
The Microsoft vendor participant list doesn't tell you which version of a
product supports VBA for the most part, so you either have to check the
product packaging or ask the vendor.

A Room with a View

Many people approach VBA with the same enthusiasm and clarity of thought
with which the condemned person faces the gallows. When you work with an
application, you see what the developer wants you to see and not much more.
You're in the user room — the one without a view. Approach using VBA like

entering a new room: You now have a room *with* a view — you're the one who sees what will happen and when.

Looking at the Integrated Development Environment (IDE)

VBA is a visual programming environment. That is, you see how your program will look before you run it. Its editor is very visual, using various windows to make your programming experience easy and manageable. You'll notice slight differences in the appearance of the editor when you use it with Vista as compared to older versions of Windows. In addition, you might notice slight differences when using the editor with a core Office application — one that uses the new Ribbon interface. Figure 1-3 shows what this Integrated Development Environment (IDE) looks like when it's opened using Excel in Vista. No matter which Office product and version of Windows you use, the editor has essentially the same appearance (and some small differences), the same menu items, and the same functionality.

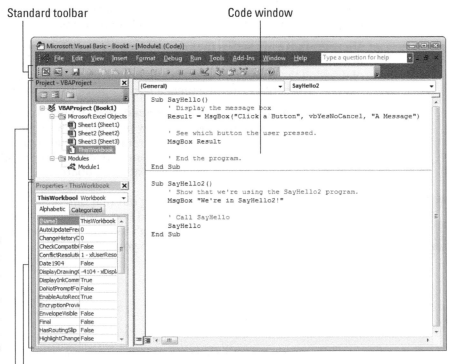

Figure 1-3: The VBA IDE is an editor for writing VBA applications.

An *IDE* is an editor, just like your word processor, spreadsheet, or database form. Just as application editors have special features that make them especially useful for working with data, an IDE is a programming editor with special features that make it useful for writing instructions that the application should follow. These instructions are *procedural code* — a set of steps.

As you can see from Figure 1-3, the VBA IDE consists of a menu system, toolbars, a Project Explorer window, a Properties window, and a Code window, to start with. The IDE can show other windows when it needs to, but these are the three windows that you see when you start VBA. Here's a brief summary of what each of the windows does. (The upcoming "Starting the Visual Basic Editor" section shows how to use them.)

- **Project Explorer:** This window contains a list of the items in your project, which contains all the document elements in a single file. Your application exists within a file that appears in the Project Explorer window.

- **Properties:** Whenever you select an object, the Properties window tells you about it. For example, this window tells you whether the object is blue or whether it has words on it.

- **Code:** Eventually, you have to write some code to make your application work. This window contains the special words that tell your application what to do. Think of it as a place to write a specialized to-do list.

Looking at the VBA Toolbox

You won't have to write code for every task in VBA. The IDE also supports forms, just like the forms that you use to perform other tasks. In this case, you decide what appears on the form and how the form acts when the user works with it. To make it easier to create forms, VBA provides the Toolbox, like the one shown in Figure 1-4, which contains controls used to create forms.

Figure 1-4:
Use the VBA Toolbox to add controls to forms you create.

Each Toolbox button performs a unique task. For example, clicking one button displays a text box, but clicking another displays a command button. The form features that these buttons create are *controls.* Chapter 7 shows you how to use all these controls, as well as how to add other controls when the controls that the Toolbox provides don't meet a particular need.

Looking at objects

You see the term *object* quite a bit while you read this book and use VBA to create your own applications. An object used in a program is very much like an object in real life. Programmers came up with this term to make programs easier to understand. Read on while I use the real-world example of an apple to explain what an object is in VBA — and to understand why objects are such an important part of VBA and how they make things easier.

Property values are up

When you look at an apple, you can see some of its properties: The apple is red, green, or yellow. VBA objects also have properties — for example, a button can have a *caption* (the text that users see when they look at the button). Some of the apple's properties are hidden. You don't know what the apple will taste like until you bite into it. Likewise, some VBA objects have hidden properties.

There's a method to my madness

You can do a number of things with an apple. For example, picking an apple from a tree is a method of interacting with the apple. Likewise, VBA objects have methods. You can move a button from one place to another with the Move method. *Methods* let the developer do something to the object.

And now, for a special event!

An apple usually changes color when it ripens. No one did anything to the apple; it turned ripe because it reached maturity. This is an *event*. Likewise, VBA objects can experience events. A user clicks a command button, and the command button generates a Click event. As a developer, you didn't do anything to the command button. The command button decides when to generate the event. In short, *events* let the developer react to changing object conditions.

Starting the Visual Basic Editor

How you start the Visual Basic Editor depends on the application that you're using. Newer versions of Office use a different approach than older versions.

In all cases, you see a Visual Basic Editor window, similar to the one shown in Figure 1-3. This section describes each of these variations.

Word 2007, Excel 2007, and PowerPoint 2007

Make sure that you enable the use of VBA by using the procedure in the "Batteries Included — VBA Comes with Office" section, earlier in this chapter. After you have the Developer tab displayed on the Ribbon, select it. Click Visual Basic on the left side of the Developer tab (refer to Figure 1-2). You'll see the Visual Basic Editor.

Access 2007

Access 2007 displays the Database Tools tab of the Ribbon whenever it's possible to use the Visual Basic Editor. Because you must have a database open and meet certain other conditions, you won't always see the Database Tools tab. When you do see this tab, select it and click Visual Basic. You'll see the Visual Basic Editor.

OneNote 2007, Publisher 2007, Visio 2007, Project 2007, and all older versions of Office

If you're using any of the products listed in the heading to this section, start the Visual Basic Editor by choosing Tools⇨Macro⇨Visual Basic Editor. When you execute this command, you'll see the Visual Basic Editor.

Security under Vista

Vista places extra security constraints on Office products. The User Access Control (UAC) makes it impossible to run some macros that would ordinarily work under previous versions of Windows. Even setting the macro security won't help, in some cases, depending on the security policies set by the administrator, your personal security settings, and the task the macro performs. In general, you want to sign your macros before you use them under Vista. See the "Adding a Digital Signature to Your Creation" section of Chapter 8 for details.

Setting macro security for Word 2007, Excel 2007, PowerPoint 2007, and Access 2007

Office 2007 sets the security bar very high. It's unlikely that you'll be able to run most of the macros in this book without changing your security settings. The following steps help you make the required changes:

1. **Select the Developer or Database Tools tab on the Ribbon.**

2. **Click Macro Security.**

   You see the Trust Center dialog box, shown in Figure 1-5.

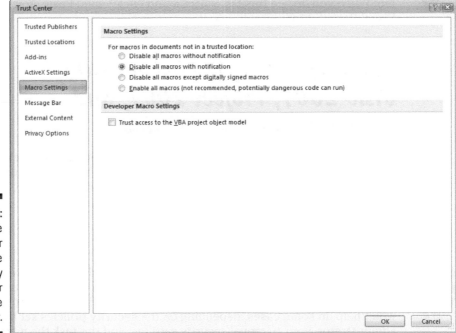

Figure 1-5:
Use the Trust Center to adjust the security settings for your Office product.

3. **Select Enable All Macros unless you plan to sign each of the macros in this book before running them.**

4. **Check Trust Access to the VBA Project Object Model.**

5. **Click OK.**

   You can now run macros, but with greatly reduced security. Make sure you change the settings back as soon as possible.

Setting macro security for OneNote 2007, Publisher 2007, Visio 2007, Project 2007, and all older versions of Office

Depending on which version of Microsoft Office you use and how you set it up at the beginning, the macro security feature might be set too high to allow you to use the examples in this book. To change the macro security level, use the following procedure.

1. **Choose the Tools⇨Options command.**

   The Microsoft Office application displays the Options dialog box.

2. **Select the Security tab.**

3. **Click Macro Security.**

   The Microsoft Office application displays the Security dialog box.

4. **Select the Security Level tab and choose the Low option.**

5. **Click OK twice to close the Security and Options dialog boxes.**

Using Project Explorer

Project Explorer appears in the Project Explorer window. You use it to interact with the objects that make up a project. A *project* is an individual file used to hold your program, or at least pieces of it. The project resides within the Office document that you're using, so when you open the Office document, you also open the project. See Chapter 3 for a description of how projects and programs interact. Project Explorer works much like how the left pane of Windows Explorer does. Normally, you see just the top-level objects, like the Excel objects shown in Figure 1-6.

Figure 1-6:
Use Project
Explorer to
work with
project
objects.

The objects listed in Project Explorer depend on the kind of application that you're working with. For example, if you're working with Word, you see documents and document templates. Likewise, if you're working with Excel, you see worksheets and workbooks. However, no matter what kind of application you work with, the way that you use Project Explorer is the same.

Figure 1-6 also shows some special objects. A project can contain forms, modules, and class modules. Here's a description of these special objects:

- **Forms:** Contain user interface elements and help you interact with the user. Chapter 7 shows how to work with forms.

- **Modules:** Contain the nonvisual code for your application. For example, you can use a module to store a special calculation. Most of this book contains modules.

- **Class modules:** Contain new objects that you want to build. You can use a class module to create a new data type. Chapter 8 shows how to work with objects.

To select an object so that you can see and change its properties, highlight it in Project Explorer. To open the object so that you can modify it, double-click the object.

Right-clicking everything

Project Explorer has a number of hidden talents, which you can find by right-clicking objects to see what you can do with them. For example, right-click the VBAProject (Book1) entry at the top of Figure 1-6 to see the context menu shown in Figure 1-7.

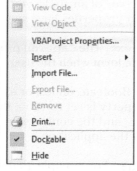

Figure 1-7:
Right-click
VBA objects
to display
context
menus.

It's amazing to see what's hidden on this menu. Don't worry about using all of the menu entries now. Each of the menu entries appears at least once and probably more often in the book. For example, Chapter 3 shows how to use the VBAProject Properties entry. The important thing to remember now is that most objects have context menus that you can access by right-clicking or using the Context Menu button on your keyboard.

Working with special entries

Sometimes you see a special entry in Project Explorer. For example, when you work with a Word document, you might see a References folder, which contains any references that the Word document makes. Normally, it contains a list of templates that the document relies upon for formatting.

In many cases, you can't modify the objects in the special folders. This is the case with the References folder used by Word document objects. The References folder is there for information only. To modify the referenced template, you need to find its object in Project Explorer. In this book, I don't discuss special objects because you normally don't need to work with them.

Using the Properties window

Most of the objects that you click in the VBA IDE have properties that describe the object in some way. The earlier "Property values are up" section of this chapter tells about properties if you haven't worked with them before. The following sections provide details about the Properties window (refer to Figure 1-3).

Understanding property types

A property needs to describe the object. When you look at an object, you naturally assume something about the information provided by a particular property. For example, when describing the color of an apple, you expect to use *red, yellow,* or *green.* Likewise, VBA object properties have specific types.

One of the most common property types is text. The Caption property of a form is text. The text appears at the top of the form when the user opens it.

Another common property type is a logic, or Boolean, value. For example, if a control has a Visible property and this property is set to True, the control appears onscreen. Set this property to False, and the control won't appear onscreen even though it still exists as part of the application.

Object properties can also have numeric values. For example, to describe where to place a control onscreen, set the Top and Left properties to specific numeric values. These values tell how many pixels are between the top and left corner of the screen and the top-left corner of the control.

In some cases, a property can display a drop-down list box from which you can choose the correct value. Other properties display a dialog box like the one for color, shown in Figure 1-8.

Figure 1-8:
Some properties display a dialog box to select the correct value.

Getting help with properties

Don't expect to memorize every property for every object that VBA applications can create. Not even the gurus can do that. To determine what a particular property will do for your application, just highlight the property and press F1, and, in most cases, VBA displays a Help window similar to the one shown in Figure 1-9.

The older versions of Office Help don't include quite as many features as shown in Figure 1-9. For example, you won't find an option to tell Microsoft whether the information is helpful. Notice also that the bottom of the Help window now contains a status bar that tells you whether the information you're seeing is static or taken directly from Microsoft's Web site. Finally, the Standard toolbar now includes a button that looks like a thumbtack. When placed in one position, the Help window always remains on top so that you can see it no matter what you might be doing. When placed in the second position, the Help window hides (like any other window) when you cover it with another window.

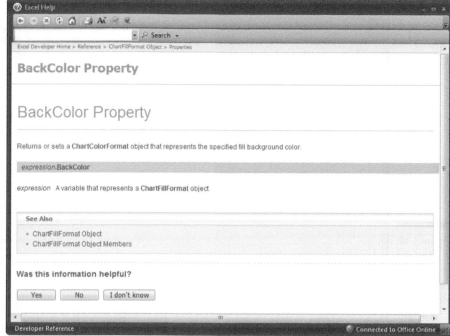

Figure 1-9:
Help
documents
the
properties
that VBA
supports.

Such help screens tell you about the property and how it's used as well as provide you with links for additional information. The additional information is especially important when you start changing the property values in your application code. For example, click the Example link, and the help system shows how to write code that uses that property. (You don't have to click the Example link when working with newer versions of Office — the example appears at the bottom of the help screen.)

Click the See Also link on help screens for more information about a topic, such as info about objects, properties, methods, and events associated with the topic. In some cases, you also get recommended ways to work with an object, property, method, or event. (You don't have to click the See Also link when working with newer versions of Office — the additional information links appear in the middle or bottom of the help screen.)

Using the Code window

The *Code window* is where you write your application code. It works like any other editor that you've used, except that you type in a special language: VBA. Figure 1-10 shows a typical example of a Code window with some code loaded. Notice that the Project Explorer window and the Properties window are gone — you can display them again by using the View➪Project Explorer

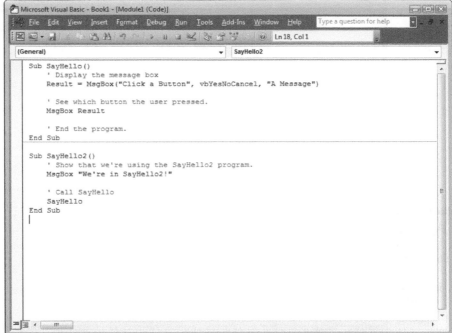

Figure 1-10:
Use the
Code
window to
modify your
program.

and View➪Properties Window commands. As an alternative, press Ctrl+R to display Project Explorer or F4 to display the Properties window.

Opening an existing Code window

Sometimes you won't be able to complete an application and need to work on it later. To open an existing Code window, find the module that you want to open in Project Explorer. Double-click the module entry, and the IDE displays the code within it with your code loaded.

The Code window also appears when you perform other tasks. For example, if you double-click one of the controls on a form, the Code window appears so that you can add code to the default event handler. VBA calls the *event handler* (special code that responds to the event) every time that the specified event occurs.

Creating a new Code window

When you start a new module within an existing document or template, open a new Code window by using either the Insert➪Module or Insert➪Class Module command. After you save this module or class module, it appears in Project Explorer (refer to Figure 1-3) with the other modules and class modules in your project.

Typing text in the Code window

When you type code, VBA checks what you type. If you make a major error, such as typing a word that VBA doesn't understand, you see an error message explaining what you did wrong (see Figure 1-11). If you don't understand the error, click the Help button for additional information.

Figure 1-11:
VBA
displays an
error
message
when you
make a
mistake.

While you type the code for your application, VBA also formats it. For example, if you type a keyword in lowercase letters, VBA changes it so it appears as shown in the help file. *Hint:* Keywords also appear in a different color so that you can easily identify them. This book contains examples of the common VBA keywords.

Finding more Code window features

The Code window has a context menu, just like other objects in VBA. When you right-click the Code window, you see a list of optional actions that you can perform. For example, you can obtain a list of properties and methods that apply to the object that you're currently using in the window. Chapter 3 shows how to use many of the special Code window features.

Getting help with code

Because it's hard to remember precisely how to use every function and method that VBA supports, use the VBA help feature. For any keyword that you type in the Code window, highlight the keyword and press F1, and VBA will look for help on the keyword that you selected.

Make sure that you select the entire keyword, or VBA might not find the information that you need. Double-click the keyword to ensure that you highlight the entire word.

Using the Immediate window

Although you can use the Immediate window for debugging applications, this window can actually help you learn about VBA and save you from having to write reams of code. You can execute statements one at a time. Use the View⇨Immediate Window command to display the Immediate window. This window normally appears at the bottom of the IDE, and it won't contain any information until you type something in it.

Creating a variable in the Immediate window

Most developers spend their days using the Immediate window to check their applications for errors. You can use the Immediate window to ask VBA about the value of a variable, for example. (A *variable* acts as a storage container for a value, such as Hello World.) This feature is always available in the VBA IDE, even if you aren't using VBA for anything at the moment. To try this feature, type **MyVal = "Hello World"** (don't forget the double quotes) in the Immediate window and then press Enter. Now type **? MyVal** and then press Enter. Figure 1-12 shows the output of this little experiment.

Figure 1-12:
Use the
Immediate
window to
check the
value of a
variable.

You asked VBA to create a variable named MyVal and assign it a value of Hello World. The next step is to ask VBA what MyVal contains by using the ? operator. Figure 1-12 shows that MyVal actually does contain Hello World.

Creating a one-line program

Experimenting with the Immediate window is one of the fastest ways to learn how to use VBA because you get instant results. You can also copy successful experiments from the Immediate window and paste them into the Code window. Using this method ensures that your code contains fewer errors than if you type it directly into the Code window.

If you've read the earlier section "Creating a variable in the Immediate window," you created a variable named MyVal. The variable still exists in memory unless you closed VBA. You can use this variable for a little experiment — your first program. Type **MsgBox MyVal** into the Immediate window and then press Enter. You see a message box like the one shown in Figure 1-13.

Congratulations! You just completed your first VBA application! The code that you typed asked VBA to use the MsgBox function to display the text in the MyVal variable. Click OK to clear the message box.

Figure 1-13:

Figure 1-13:
The
`MsgBox`
function
produces a
message
box like this.

Using Object Browser

VBA provides access to a lot of objects, more than you'll use for any one program. With all the objects that you have at your disposal, you might forget the name of one or more of them at some time. Object Browser helps you find the objects that you need. In fact, you can use it to find new objects that could be useful for your next project. Use the View⇔Object Browser command to display Object Browser, as shown in Figure 1-14. Normally, you need to filter the information in some way.

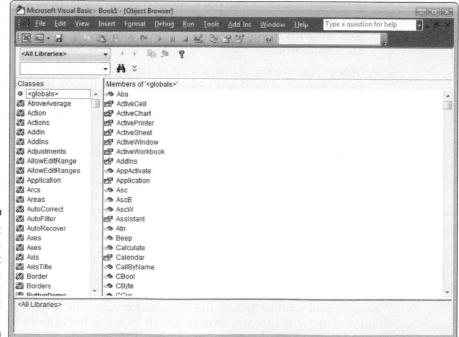

Figure 1-14:
View the
objects that
VBA makes
available
via Object
Browser.

Browsing objects

Object Browser contains a list of the contents of all projects and libraries loaded for the VBA IDE. You can view the list of projects and libraries by using the Project/Library drop-down list box. When you start Object Browser, this list box reads <All Libraries>, which means that you're viewing everything that VBA has to offer — usually too much for someone to make sense of it all.

Projects and libraries are different, but you won't normally need to worry about them to use the objects that they contain. A *project* is the VBA code contained in one of the files that you load into the application. In most cases, you use a project to store the code that you create. A *library* is external code contained in a Dynamic Link Library (DLL) file. The DLL contains support routines used by the application or VBA. This code is normally written by a developer using a language such as Visual Basic or Visual C++. You can't easily edit the code in a DLL.

The list of projects and libraries might look complicated at first, but you can narrow it to a few types of entries. Of course, you always see your project templates. In addition to project templates, you find these libraries in the list:

- ✓ **Application:** This library has the name of the application, such as Excel or Word. It also includes the features that the application provides for VBA users. For example, the Excel library has a Chart object, which contains a list of chart-related methods, properties, and events that Excel supports.

- ✓ **Office:** This library contains a list of objects that Microsoft Office supports. For example, this is where you find the objects used to support Office Assistant. Of course, if you're using an application other than Microsoft Office, you won't see this library. Your application might provide an alternative.

- ✓ **StdOLE:** This library contains some of the Object Linking and Embedding (OLE) features that you use in the application. For example, when you embed a picture into a Word document, this library provides the required support. You can use this library in your VBA applications, too, but the Office or application-related library usually provides access to objects that are easier and faster to use.

- ✓ **VBA:** This library contains special utility objects that VBA developers need. For example, it contains the MsgBox function, which I demonstrate in the earlier "Using the Immediate window" section of this chapter.

Whenever you want to browse the libraries for a specific object, limit the amount of material that you have to search by using the options in the Project/Library drop-down list box (*filtering* the content). This is a helpful technique when you perform searches as well.

Looking for names and features in Object Browser

When you remember . . . almost, but not quite . . . the name of a method or
other programming feature that you want to use, using the search feature of
Object Browser can make your life easier. Simply type the text that you want
to look for in the Search Text field (the empty box beneath All Libraries), and
then click the Search button (the one with a symbol that looks like binocu-
lars) in Object Browser. The Search Results field shown in Figure 1-15 shows
what happens when you look for MsgBox.

Whenever you choose (highlight) one of the entries in the Search Results
field, the bottom two panes change to show that entry. This feature helps you
locate specific information about the search result and see it in context with
other methods, properties, and events. Notice that the bottom pane tells you
more about the selection item. In this case, it tells you how to use the
MsgBox function.

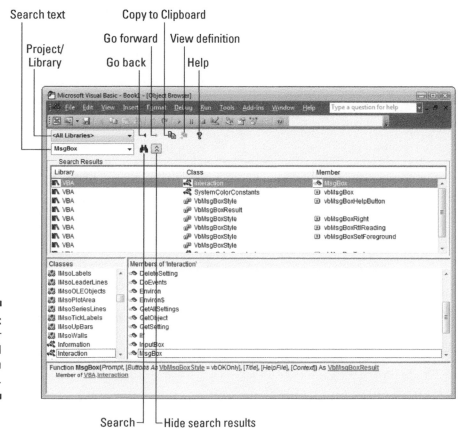

Figure 1-15:
Search for
the method
that you
want to use.

Cutting and pasting in Object Browser

Whenever you find a method, property, or event that you want to use in Object Browser, you can copy the information to the Clipboard by clicking the Copy to Clipboard button (the one with a symbol that looks like two documents) and then pasting that information directly into your application code. Using this feature means not only that you type less code, but also that you have fewer errors to consider.

Getting help in Object Browser

Sometimes the information at the bottom of the Object Browser display isn't enough to tell you about the element that you're viewing. When this happens, highlight the element that you want to know more about and press F1, and VBA displays the help screen for that element.

Chapter 2

Your First VBA Program

● ●

In This Chapter

▶ Creating an application plan

▶ Defining the steps to create an application

▶ Using different methods to run your application

▶ Getting and using code found in the help files

● ●

*I*n Chapter 1, I show you how to work with the VBA Integrated Development Environment (IDE). In that chapter, I also show you how to use the Immediate window to create one-line test programs. However, the programs that you create by using the Immediate window aren't the same as permanent programs (because Immediate window programs aren't permanent), and you'd find it difficult to perform useful work with them.

This chapter shows you how to move from the Immediate window into the Code window. The *Code window* is where you create programs of a lasting nature — the kind that you can use to perform the same task more than once. Because of the time required to write the code, it only pays to create an application that you can use more than once. The benefit of writing a program is that you can perform a repetitive task quickly.

One trick that you can use is to get hold of pre-made code whenever you can. I end this chapter by showing you one of the techniques that is used most often — stealing the code directly from Microsoft. (You'll see that it isn't really stealing, but, considering all you get for free, it's a steal in a sense.) The help files that come with VBA contain a lot of code that you can use in a number of ways. Microsoft knows that some developers want to use the code, so it tries to make the samples as flexible as possible.

Deciding What to Do

Whenever you decide to create a program, start with a plan. Just like a builder needs a plan to construct a house, you need a plan to construct your program. You can easily tell whether a builder decided to build a house without using a plan, and it's just as easy to determine when someone writes a program without using a plan. Application users can see that the application isn't well designed because it doesn't work as anticipated. The plan that you use doesn't have to be very complicated, but you do need to think about these questions:

- ✔ What will the program do?
- ✔ How will the program accomplish its task?
- ✔ When will the program run?
- ✔ Who will use the program?
- ✔ Why is the program important?

Professional developers use a number of complex and hair-raising methods to answer these questions. You work on much smaller programs, and you can normally answer the questions quite easily. Don't make this more complicated than you need to. You might answer the first question by saying, for example, that the program will count the number of words in a document.

The reason that you want to go through this planning process is to ensure that you've thought about the program you want to create. It's easier to answer the questions *before* you write any code than to fix the code later. Writing down your answers also helps you avoid making the program into something that you didn't intend. This problem is a common one for everyone; even developers with a lot of experience write programs that quickly grow beyond the original intent.

Another good reason to go through this planning process is to ensure that you actually need to write the program. By describing a program in unambiguous terms, you can seek help from other people. In many cases, you'll find that you won't need to write the application because

- ✔ Someone else has already written the program.
- ✔ You can obtain the program from a third-party vendor for less money than it would require for you to write the application.
- ✔ An update to the existing application includes the functionality of the program as a feature.

Steps to Create a VBA Program

Writing a program usually involves four steps. In this section, I tell you about the four steps while you create your first permanent program — one that you can run as often as you like. The permanent program displays a dialog box, just like the example in Chapter 1.

Step 1: Design the program

In the "Deciding What to Do" section, earlier in this chapter, I tell you how to plan your program. I also tell you what questions you should ask in preparation for writing the program. This step is actually part of the design phase, but most developers make it a separate step. Thinking through your application before you commit something to paper is important.

After you plan your application, you can use any of a number of techniques to design the program. Some people use the *flowcharting* technique, which uses special symbols to replace programming elements. Other people use specialized engineering software to do the job. You might read about these methods when you get more involved with VBA. However, the best way to design most simple applications is to use *pseudo-coding,* a method in which you write down a list of steps in your own words that say what you want VBA to do.

Using pseudo-code is a good way to think about how you want to write the code without getting too concerned about coding issues. This example displays a dialog box. The pseudo-code can be as easy as

```
Display the message box.
See which button the user clicked.
End the program.
```

Don't worry about being precise about the pseudo-code. The idea is to write a list of steps that you can understand before you begin writing code. If you don't understand what you want to do, it's unlikely that you can tell VBA how to do it. Pseudo-code is a method for putting your words into a form that you can convert to code later.

You can also add pseudo-code as comments to the VBA code that you write. In Chapter 3, I show you how to use comments in your code. Using your pseudo-code as a basis for comments that appear in your code helps you tell others about the thought process used to design the program. Never write a program that is devoid of comments because you might need to make changes later.

Step 2: Implement the design

The wording for this step is just a fancy way of saying that you need to write some code. You often hear programmers use the phrase "implement the design," and it also appears as commonly used jargon in many magazines.

Before you can write some code, you need to open the Visual Basic Editor in older versions of Office by using the Tools➪Macro➪Visual Basic Editor command. When working with Office 2007, all you need to do is click Visual Basic the Developer tab on the Ribbon. I'm using Excel for this example, but the same steps work in Access, Word, FrontPage, PowerPoint, and most other applications that support VBA. The only change is that your screen shots won't look precisely like mine when you use another product.

The first thing to do is create a Code window. To do that, use the Insert➪ Module command. The Visual Basic Editor creates a blank Code window where you can type your program. A blank Code window can be a scary experience, but you don't need to worry because you already have some text (the code snippet in the previous section, "Step 1: Design the program") to put into it. The Code window is a kind of container (an editor) where you create a Sub (or sub-procedure). The Sub contains your pseudo-code and, eventually, the code you write to implement the pseudo-code. (Chapter 3 describes the Sub in detail, so you don't need to worry about it for now.) Add a single-quote character (') in front of each pseudo-code statement to ensure that VBA knows that this is pseudo-code. All VBA comments begin with a single quote. Figure 2-1 shows how your Code window should look.

Figure 2-1:
The Code window starts blank, but you already have information to add to it.

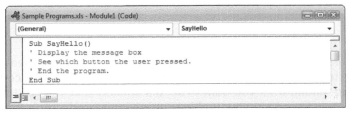

You can run the Sub shown in Figure 2-1, but it doesn't do anything. To make this example do something, add to it some code that VBA understands. This means converting the English statements, such as "Display the message box," into VBA. To display a message box, use the MsgBox function, which I describe in Chapter 1.

The MsgBox function is capable of doing more than the Chapter 1 example shows. First, the function can return a Result that shows which button the user selected. The Result variable holds the selection information so that you can use it in other ways. You can also tell MsgBox which buttons to display and to provide a title. Here's a more advanced version of the MsgBox function that I use in Chapter 1 — type this line directly beneath the 'Display the message box comment:

```
Result = MsgBox("Click a Button", vbYesNoCancel, "A
        Message")
```

This code tells VBA to display a message box with "Click a Button" as the text and "A Message" on the title bar. The message box includes the Yes, No, and Cancel buttons. After VBA displays the message box, it waits for the user to make a decision. When the user clicks one of the three buttons, VBA stores the choice in the Result variable. Wow, that's a lot for one piece of text to do!

The pseudo-code says that the code needs to detect which button the user pressed. You can use another message box to display the information like this:

```
MsgBox Result
```

This is the same technique that I use in Chapter 1. The only difference is that the information contained in Result relies on a user selection. You don't know in advance which button the user will select, but this code works no matter which button the user clicks.

The final piece of pseudo-code says that VBA should end the program. You do this with the End Sub statement shown in Figure 2-1. Whenever VBA runs out of instructions to process, it ends the program. Figure 2-2 shows what your code should look like now. Make sure that you save the code at this point by using the File⇨Save command.

Figure 2-2:
Writing code is easy when you use pseudo-code to describe it first.

Step 3: Test, test, test

It's time to run the application for the first time. The easiest way to run an application is to click the Run Sub/User Form button on the Standard toolbar in the Visual Basic Editor. (It's the one that looks like the Play button on a VCR.) Click the button to see the first message box. It should look like the one shown in Figure 2-3. If the program won't run, use the appropriate procedure in the "Starting the Visual Basic Editor" section of Chapter 1 to set macro security.

Figure 2-3: The first message box asks the user to click a button.

The message box contains the title, message, and buttons that you asked VBA to display in the code. Checking the contents of the message box to verify that it contains everything that you thought it would contain is *testing*. If you want to ensure that your program always works the way you originally designed it, you need to test as many features as possible.

Click Yes to see another message box like the one shown in Figure 2-4. Look at the code again. Notice that this message box contains the result (the return value) of the MsgBox function. The number 6 isn't very useful to humans, but it's quite usable for the computer. An actual program converts this number to something that humans can understand. For now, you know that clicking Yes produces a number 6.

Figure 2-4: The MsgBox function return value.

When you click OK, the program ends, and you don't see any other message boxes. This condition verifies that the last step of the pseudo-code is complete.

Don't assume that the testing process is over; there are two other buttons on the initial message box. Unless you test the buttons, you won't know that they work. Run the program again, but try the No button the second time and the Cancel button the third time.

The return value displayed in the second message box (refer to Figure 2-4) should change for each button. Clicking No should produce a value of 7, and clicking Cancel should produce a value of 2. If you don't see these values, your program has an error. Professionals call a programming error a *bug*.

Step 4: Swat the bugs

Bugs can appear when you test your program. Planning and writing your code carefully reduces the number of bugs, but everyone makes mistakes. It's often a matter of not understanding how a function works. Testing your programs helps you find the bugs. After you find the bugs, you have to look at your code and discover the coding errors that create the bugs.

Not every bug is even your fault — it could be an error in the documentation for the function. Microsoft is well known for committing mistakes of this sort and then telling everyone that they were intentional. (Microsoft is fond of calling these mistakes *undocumented features*.) You might find that a bug isn't actually in your program but is somewhere in VBA itself. Microsoft might tell you about these errors, but it often leaves them as surprises for you to discover.

Microsoft won't knock on your door to tell you that it made a mistake. You have to search for these errors on your own at a central Web site that Microsoft has set up. The Microsoft *Knowledge Base* is a special kind of search engine that helps you find information about problems with VBA and their associated fixes. You can find the Microsoft Knowledge Base at `http://search.support.microsoft.com/search/default.aspx`.

You must get rid of as many bugs as possible in your program. This task is so important that I devote an entire chapter to it: In Chapter 6, I provide details on how to locate and fix bugs in your program. Chapter 6 also tells you how to keep the user from making mistakes by detecting the error before the program does. The important idea for this chapter is that you need to fix bugs in your application; don't worry too much about the precise details for this task right now.

The origins of computer bugs

You might wonder why professionals call a programming error a *bug*. There are many versions of this story, but all of them begin in the early annals of computer history. At that time, computers were immense devices that could take up an entire building. Instead of the small chips used in today's computers, these older devices used switches and vacuum tubes. The story holds that one day a programmer of one of these massive machines experienced an error. After a long search, the programmer found an actual bug in one of the switches used to control the computer. The term stuck — all programming errors are now blamed on insects.

Four Ways to Run Your Program

Running your program from within the Visual Basic Editor is fine when you want to test it. However, the goal is to run it from the application and not have to open the Visual Basic Editor first. You have a lot of choices for running any VBA program — more than most people want to remember. VBA provides four common methods for running applications, but most VBA users never need to think beyond the first method, which is using the Macro dialog box.

Using the Macro dialog box

The Macro dialog box is the most common way to run a VBA program. Every time that you create a new Sub, it appears in the list of macros that you can run. You don't have to do anything special. This feature means that you can always access every program that you create by using this method, which is why it's the most popular method.

When working with older versions of Office, use the Tools⇨Macro⇨Macros command to display the Macro dialog box. When using newer versions of Office, click Macros on the Developer tab on the Ribbon to display the Macro dialog box, as shown in Figure 2-5. You can also display this dialog box by pressing Alt+F8 in Office applications. (Other applications use different key combinations.) Notice that Figure 2-5 shows the macro, SayHello, that appears in the earlier "Step 2: Implement the design" section of this chapter.

When you want to run the program, highlight it and then click the Run button. Try it now. You should see the same two dialog box sequences that you saw when you tested the program earlier in this chapter.

Figure 2-5:
Use the
Macro
dialog box to
access the
programs
that you
create.

You can also use this dialog box to perform other tasks. Highlight the macro name, and then click the Edit button; the application opens the Visual Basic Editor. The Code window displays the code associated with the program that you highlighted. You can also remove old programs by clicking the Delete button.

Notice the Macro Name field near the top of the Macro dialog box shown in Figure 2-5. This field normally contains the name of the macro that you've highlighted in the list. However, you can also use the Macro dialog box to create new programs. Type **SayGoodbye** in the Macro Name field, and the Macro dialog box enables the Create button and disables everything else, as shown in Figure 2-6. You can use this dialog box to create any new programs that you need.

Figure 2-6:
Typing a
non-existent
macro name
in the Macro
Name field
enables the
Create
button.

Using the quick-launch methods

It isn't always convenient or efficient to open the Macro dialog box to run the programs that you design. If you use the same program several times a day, opening the Macro dialog box can become a time-wasting event. What you need is a *quick-launch method* — a way to start the program that doesn't require you to open the Macro dialog box.

Defining a shortcut key

The Macro dialog box, shown in Figure 2-5, has one other use that helps you create quick-launch programs. Open the Macro dialog box by using the Tools⇨Macro⇨Macros command or by clicking Macros on the Developer tab on the Ribbon. Highlight the program that you want to launch quickly (SayHello, for this example). Click the Options button. Excel opens the Macro Options dialog box. Type **h** in the Shortcut Key field and **This is a simple program.** in the Description field. Your dialog box should look like the one shown in Figure 2-7.

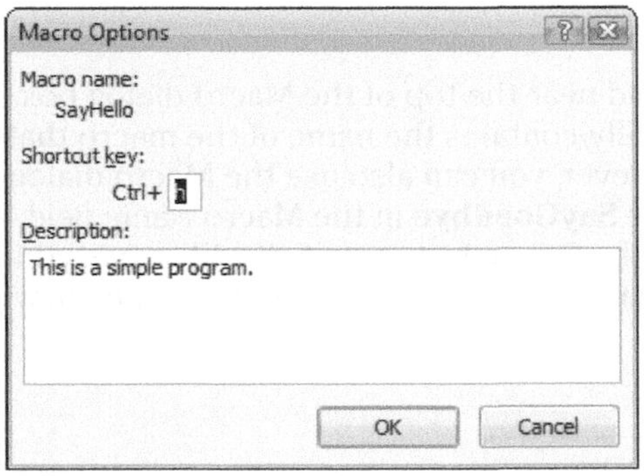

Figure 2-7:
Make a program quick-launch by using the Macro Options dialog box.

Click OK to close the Macro Options dialog box, and then click Cancel to close the Macro dialog box. When you press Ctrl+H, the program that you created earlier should run and display the same two dialog box sequences as before.

Defining a toolbar button

Using shortcut keys is fine when you don't have a lot of them to remember and you don't mind performing finger gymnastics. However, you don't have to limit yourself to keyboard shortcuts. If you're using an older version of Office or one of the newer versions with the standard toolbar interface, you can place a button on a toolbar that starts your program. When working with an Office 2007 product that sports the Ribbon interface, you can't easily add anything to the Ribbon, so this section isn't for you (see the "Working with the New Ribbon Interface" section of Chapter 12 for details on adding buttons to the Ribbon interface using VBA). Using this method means that all you have to remember to do is to look at the toolbar.

Many people place custom buttons on the same toolbars that the application uses for other purposes. This is fine if you don't mind seeing the toolbar grow longer and longer, right off the right side of the screen. It's better to create a custom toolbar so that you can show or hide the buttons associated with your programs when you need them.

To add a VBA program to a toolbar, you can begin by creating a custom toolbar for the task or selecting an existing toolbar. The SayHello example uses an existing toolbar, Standard, to speed things up. The Standard toolbar is provided with just about every Windows application that uses VBA, but you might need to use another toolbar. The following steps show how to add a program to your toolbar:

1. **Right-click in the toolbar area, and then choose Customize from the context menu that appears.**

   The Customize dialog box appears.

2. **Select the Commands tab and scroll through the Categories list until you find Macros.**

   Figure 2-8 shows that you have two options for adding macros to your toolbar — as a menu item or as a button.

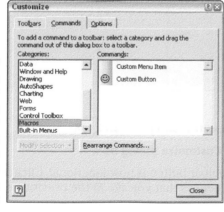

Figure 2-8: Add your program to the toolbar by using either a button or a menu item.

Use a button when you need to save space on a toolbar. However, make sure that you add a name to the button that explains what the button is used for, or else you might forget its purpose. Use a menu item to make the button's purpose easier to remember. Choosing the menu item option displays a new toolbar button. The new button has the name that you assigned to the button displayed on the toolbar, making it easier to see what the button does.

3. **To add a custom button, drag a Custom Menu Item object from the Customize dialog box to the Standard toolbar.**

   The application should add a new (blank) button to the toolbar.

4. **Right-click the new button on the toolbar, and then select the Name option. (This entry has a text box next to it.)**

5. **In the Name field, type** &Say Hello.

   This action assigns a name to the button. The ampersand (&) places an underline beneath the *S* in *Say.* A user can press Alt+S to access the button quickly when the toolbar is selected.

6. **Right-click the new button on the toolbar, and then select Assign Macro.**

   An Assign Macro dialog box appears, like the one shown in Figure 2-9.

Figure 2-9:
Use the
Assign
Macro
dialog box
to add a
macro to the
toolbar
button.

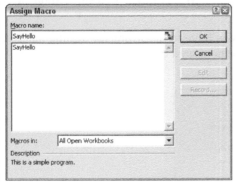

7. **Highlight the SayHello entry, and then click OK.**

8. **Click Close to close the Customize dialog box.**

   That's it! The Say Hello toolbar button is now functional. Click it to see the same two dialog box sequences that you see in the previous examples.

Defining a menu entry

You might use a program often enough to attach it to a regular program element but not often enough to take up space on a toolbar. In this case, you can use a menu to hold the quick-launch option when working with versions of Office that don't rely on the Ribbon interface. You use the same set of steps shown in the preceding "Defining a toolbar button" section to perform this task. The only difference is that you drag the custom button or custom menu item to the menu that you want to use instead of to a toolbar (Step 3).

Accessing the program from other VBA code

Never write a piece of code twice when you can write it once and use it everywhere. Saving time is one reason to use VBA, so saving time by writing VBA code is a good way to increase the benefits that you receive. In Chapter 3, I discuss many of the methods that you can use to reuse code. However, the first idea that you have to understand is that you can *call* (tell VBA to execute) any VBA program that you create from another program. Here's a simple example that you can add to the Code window:

```
Sub SayHello2()
' Show that we're using the SayHello2 program.
MsgBox "We're in SayHello2!"

' Call SayHello
SayHello
End Sub
```

Notice how this sample uses pseudo-code to describe what happens when you run the program. Remember that *pseudo-code* is a list of steps, written in a form that you can understand, that the program must perform. The first task is to prove that you executed the SayHello2 program by displaying a message box containing a message that doesn't appear in SayHello. The second task is to call SayHello. Make sure that you save your program at this point.

When you run this program, it displays three message boxes. The first one reads We're in SayHello2! The second and third message boxes look just like the ones you see for the SayHello program used throughout this chapter.

Executing the VBA program automatically

In rare cases, you need to write a VBA program that does something when you start the associated application or perform some other task, such as open a document. You should use this method of executing your programs automatically only if it serves a very special purpose. Using this technique to perform a setup that you only use once in a while doesn't make sense. If you set up something every day, it usually pays to make it a permanent part of the application configuration rather than run a program to make the changes.

The smartest VBA users avoid using this technique, for two reasons. First, many users have disabled automatic macro execution on their machines, which means that this technique won't work at all. The reason that people disable automatic macro execution is that some *crackers* (nefarious fiends who write viruses) have used automatic macro execution as a weapon in the past. (You can read more about macro viruses at `http://www.cert.org/advisories/CA-2001-28.html` — this is just one of over 400 sites I've found that discuss this problem.) Microsoft actually tells you how to remove these macros in the Knowledge Base article at `http://support.microsoft.com/?scid=kb;en-us;918064`. Second, the precise method for creating an automatically executing program varies by application. The technique used in Word might not work in Excel and vice versa.

The program used most often in this chapter is `SayHello`. The name that you give your program is important because it can have special effects on the application. When you name your program `AutoExec`, the application (Word, Excel, Access, and so on) automatically executes the macro whenever it's started. Table 2-1 contains a list of special program names that you can use to perform tasks automatically in some applications.

Table 2-1	Special Program Names That Automatically Execute
Name	**When It Runs**
AutoClose	When the user closes a document
AutoExec	When the application starts
AutoExit	When the application ends
AutoNew	When the user creates a new document
AutoOpen	When the user opens an existing document

Using Help to Your Advantage — Stealing Microsoft's Code

This book contains a lot of code — most of it very practical code that you can use today to improve your Microsoft Office experience. Even with as much as this book has to offer, you still won't find examples of every function that VBA has to offer. Fortunately, Microsoft does provide you with lots of sample code in the help files. In fact, you can even copy this code right out of the help file and use it for your next program.

To see the sample code associated with a function, open the help page to that function. You might want to highlight one of the MsgBox entries in the sample code for this chapter and then press F1. In Chapter 1, I describe some of the information on this page. However, notice the links at the top of the page. (Newer versions of Office include all the information inline, so you won't see the links.) Three of the most common links are See Also, Example, and Specifics. Click Example or scroll down to the bottom of the help page to see an example of the MsgBox function, like the one shown in Figure 2-10.

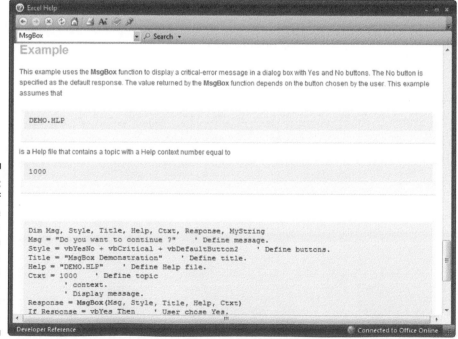

Figure 2-10: Copy any of the code that you need from the help file to reduce programming time and effort.

This code is a little complex given what you know from this chapter, but in this book I show you how to read and understand it. More importantly, you can highlight the code, right-click it, and then choose Copy from the context menu that appears. Paste the code into the Code window for your VBA program to use it.

Part II
Learning the Ropes

The 5th Wave   By Rich Tennant

"Can't I just give you riches or something?"

In this part . . .

Every adventure begins with a discovery phase. This part of the book is all about discovery. You consider all the elements that define VBA as a language. Good structure is the basis of most projects in life. When you build a house, you create the basic structure first and then add on to it. Chapter 3 is all about VBA program structure. You discover how to create a framework for the programs that you build later.

In Chapter 4, I help you understand how to manage data by using VBA. Data management is the single most important skill that a programmer can learn. This chapter also provides useful information about questions that VBA programmers ask most often, such as when to use + or & to concatenate strings (add them together).

In Chapter 5, I tell you how to control program flow by using several techniques. Controlling program flow lets you do things like make decisions. In Chapter 6, I show you techniques for debugging your program (removing errors). Debugging is an essential part of creating great applications. In Chapter 7, I help you discover the joys of creating a user interface.

Chapter 3

Writing Structured VBA Programs

• •

• •

*I*n Chapters 1 and 2, I concentrate on describing the basics of VBA programming without discussing an important element that VBA programs need — structure. Adding structure makes code easier to read and use. It's also a mandatory part of the development process.

There are a number of ways to look at structure in a program. Just as you use an outline to structure a presentation, you need to add structure to your program to make it work properly. Using structure in a program is like using a checklist with a large customer order — it helps you ensure that all the program elements are in place. The structure that you add to a program is like presenting numeric information with a graph — it makes the content of the program easier to see and understand.

In this chapter, I present various forms of structure. The obvious structuring element is physical. By using physical structure, you can divide your program into small pieces that are easy to write and understand. Many people divide programs into task-oriented pieces. It helps to use the Macro Recorder to see how you can create small tasks out of larger procedures, so this chapter discusses how to use the Macro Recorder to discover more about your specific program needs.

Another form of structure includes the concept of privacy. Consider who can see your program and how they can use it. *Scope,* which is the act of determining the range of program access, is important because you want to make some parts completely private and other parts completely public.

Finally, there are visual elements of structure. How you use white space when you write your program can make the difference between reading it and scratching your head. In Chapter 2, I discuss the use of comments in the form of pseudo-code, but you might find that you need additional comments to help someone truly understand your program (and to jog your memory when you need to make alterations).

Parts of a Program

The examples in Chapters 1 and 2 use some physical structure. You can't write a program, not even a simple one, without using at least a little structure because VBA needs that structure to understand what you want it to do. A VBA user can ignore the structure, but VBA can't. This chapter formalizes the meaning for each structural element.

Defining the parts of a program

A *program* is the highest level of physical structure. It contains everything needed to perform a given task. A program can cross module, class module, and form boundaries. (*Modules, class modules,* and *forms* are special containers for holding program code. You can save them as individual files for access later, but Office embeds them within an application document or template for use.) The concept of a program comes from the earliest use of computers. A program acts as a container for the code used to implement a set of features required by the operating system or the user.

Some people have a hard time understanding what a program is because modern software packages often define the term incorrectly. When you open a copy of Word, you're using a *program*. Conversely, Microsoft Office is a set of programs, or an *application suite*. Microsoft Office isn't a single program; it's a set of programs that includes Word, PowerPoint, Excel, and other individual programs. Likewise, when you open a copy of Notepad, that's a program. Notepad and Word each contain a set of features required by the user to perform a given task.

Programs also extend into other areas of computing. A single device driver (say, the driver that you installed for your mouse), is a program. The user interface that helps you configure the mouse is often a separate program. It's not part of the device driver even though it controls the device driver's actions. When you control Excel from Word, the two programs don't become a single unit. You're still using two programs to accomplish a single task.

Don't assume that a program equates to a project. (A *project* is the container used to hold the embedded modules, class modules, and forms associated with a given document.) You're not creating a new program when you create a new project. A *VBA project* can actually contain a number of VBA programs.

Every public Sub that a user can access by using the Macro dialog box (as I describe in Chapter 2) is a separate program. The SayHello program that I use in Chapter 2 is an example of a simple program that relies on a single Sub, but you can create programs of any complexity.

In Chapter 16, I demonstrate that a single program can cross project boundaries. All the examples in that chapter rely on the services of at least two Microsoft Office products to perform a single task. Even though the program is calling on the services of more than one Microsoft Office product, and it resides in more than one location, it's still a single program. Each example contains a set of features required by the user to perform a given task. The physical location and the use of external modules don't affect this definition.

Understanding the VBA programming blocks

A VBA program consists of building blocks. In fact, because programming is abstract, people tend to use physical examples to explain how things work. You still need to know about the abstract elements of VBA programming, or else you can't write a program. This section explains the basic constructs of VBA programming. In the upcoming "Taking the Lego Approach" section of this chapter, I use a physical example as a means of describing these abstract elements in detail. Consider only the four elements that I describe here:

- **Project:** The project acts as a container for the modules, class modules, and forms for a particular file. In Word, you normally see a minimum of three projects loaded into the Visual Basic Editor: the normal template, the document template, and the document. Excel users normally see just one project for the file that they have open.

- **Module, class module, and form:** These three elements act as containers for main programming elements such as class descriptions and procedures. A single project can have multiple modules, class modules, and forms in it. However, each of these elements requires a unique name.

- **Function and Sub:** The Function and Sub elements hold individual lines of code (also called *statements*). A Function returns a value to the caller, but a Sub does not. Microsoft Office provides access to code functionality through the Sub, not through the Function. Consequently, you must always provide access to your VBA program by using a Sub.

- **Statement:** Many people call an individual line of code a *statement*. The pseudo-code in Chapter 2 shows why. Each line of pseudo-code is a statement of what the application should do. The example in the "Step 2: Implement the design" section of Chapter 2 shows how these lines of pseudo-code are translated into code that VBA can understand. You're still making a statement when you use VBA code to perform a task — you're just doing it in VBA's language.

Using the Macro Recorder

The Macro Recorder lets you record keystrokes and actions that you perform as a VBA program. You can use it to record complete tasks, such as setting up a document, or for partial tasks, such as highlighting text and giving it certain attributes. The Macro Recorder can help you perform the following tasks:

- ✔ Create a macro based on your actions.
- ✔ Discover how Word performs certain tasks.
- ✔ Decide how to break your program into tasks.
- ✔ Help you create the basis for a more complex program.

The Macro Recorder isn't a complete solution for your VBA needs. For example, you can't use the Macro Recorder to create interactive programs without extra coding. The same holds true for programs that must change based on user input, the environment, or the data you're manipulating. All of these tasks require you to add more code. However, it's a good starting point for many structured programming tasks. You can get the basics down quickly using the Macro Recorder and then make changes as needed. The macro recording process follows the same basic steps no matter which version of Office you use:

1. Start the Macro Recorder.

2. Perform all of the steps that you normally perform to accomplish a task.

3. Stop the Macro Recorder.

4. Save the macro when the Office application prompts you.

5. Optionally, open the resulting macro and make any required changes.

Recording a macro using the Ribbon interface

Recording a macro with the new features provided by the Office 2007 Ribbon interface is easier than in past versions. Microsoft has added features that reduce the complexity of creating a macro. For example, when you press Alt, you see the number or letter you must press to perform a particular action in little boxes over each control on the Ribbon.

If you're used to using the mouse to perform most Office tasks, you may want to practice the keystrokes you need to use to record the macro several times. Recording the macro without mistakes makes it run faster and also makes it easier to edit the recorded macro later. The following steps describe how to record a macro using the Ribbon interface:

1. **Select the Developer tab.**

   Because Office 2007 doesn't display this tab by default, see the "Batteries Included — VBA Comes with Office" section of Chapter 1 for details on displaying it.

   You see the Developer tab, shown in Figure 3-1.

Figure 3-1:
The Developer tab contains most of the items you need to work with macros.

2. **Click Record Macro.**

   The Office application displays the Record Macro dialog box, shown in Figure 3-2.

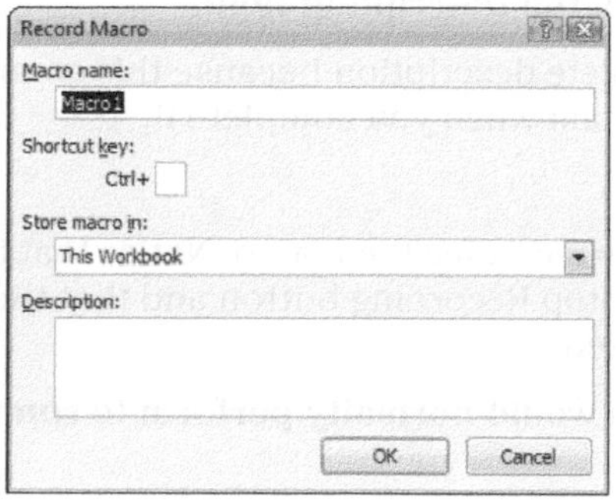

Figure 3-2:
Use the Record Macro dialog box to type details about your macro.

3. **Type a descriptive name for the macro.**

4. **Type a control-key combination for the macro when you want to access it from the keyboard.**

   Use this option only for major macros because you don't want to use up all of the available key combinations.

5. **Select a storage location in the Store Macro In field.**

   The storage locations vary by Office application. Here's an explanation of the locations for Excel:

   • **This Workbook:** Use this option when you want to store the macro within the local file. Anyone opening the file can access the macro.

   • **Personal Macro Workbook:** Use this option when you want to store the macro in a special workbook that contains all of your personal macros. This storage location makes the macro available to you at all times. It doesn't matter which workbook you open.

   • **New Workbook:** Use this option when you want to store the macro in a new workbook.

   The storage locations for Word are similar, as explained in the following list:

   • **Document:** Use this option to store the macro within the local file. Anyone opening the file can access the macro.

   • **Document Template:** Use this option to store the macro within the template used with the document. Anyone who creates a document that relies on the template can access the macro.

   • **All Documents (Normal.dotm):** Use this option to store the macro within the global template. Storing the macro here means that anyone opening a document of any kind can access the macro.

6. **Type a macro description in the Description field.**

   It's essential to type a complete description because this comment is the only one the macro will contain when you complete it.

7. **Click OK.**

   The Office application begins recording the macro. Notice that the Record Macro button changes to a Stop Recording button and that the button icon is now blue instead of red.

8. **Perform any tasks that you would normally perform to complete the task.**

   The Office application records all of your keystrokes. However, it doesn't record mouse movements. Consequently, you should avoid using the mouse and perform all tasks using the keyboard.

9. **Click Stop Recording.**

   The Office application finishes the macro.

You can view your new macro by clicking Macros on the Developer tab. The Macro dialog box shows the macros associated with the current document whether they appear locally or as part of an external document or template. The "Modifying the macro" section, later in this chapter, describes this dialog box in more detail.

Recording a macro using the menu interface

Older versions of Office and some Office 2007 products require that you use the menu interface to activate the Macro Recorder. The following steps describe how to record a macro using the menu interface:

1. **Choose Tools➪Macro➪Record New Macro.**

   The Office application displays a Record Macro dialog box similar to the one shown in Figure 3-2.

2. **Type a descriptive name for the macro.**

3. **Type a control-key combination for the macro when you want to access it from the keyboard.**

   Use this option only for major macros because you don't want to use up all of the available key combinations.

   Some older Office products include other options. For example, when working with an older version of Word, you can choose to associate the macro with either the keyboard or the toolbar, or both, by clicking the appropriate button and making the assignment.

4. **Select a storage location in the Store Macro In field.**

   (This is an Office 2007 feature; older versions always store the macro in the local document.)

   The storage locations vary by Office application. Here's an explanation of the locations for Visio:

   • **Active Document:** Use this option when you want to store the macro within the local file. Anyone opening the file can access the macro.

   • **Stencil:** Stores the file within the stencil file. Anyone using the stencil can access the macro no matter which document is opened.

5. **Type a macro description in the Description field.**

   It's essential to type a complete description because this comment is the only one the macro will contain when you complete it.

6. **Click OK.**

   The Office application begins recording the macro. You see the Stop Recording toolbar, shown in Figure 3-3. This toolbar includes options for stopping and pausing the macro recording. Pausing the recording lets you make changes that aren't required for the macro. Click Pause Recording a second time to start recording again.

7. **Perform any tasks that you would normally perform to complete the task.**

   The Office application records all of your keystrokes. However, it doesn't record mouse movements. Consequently, you should avoid using the mouse and perform all tasks using the keyboard.

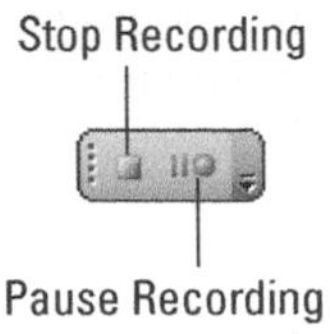

Figure 3-3:
Stop or
pause the
macro
recording
process as
necessary.

Stop Recording

Pause Recording

8. Click Stop Recording.

The Office application finishes the macro. The Stop Recording toolbar disappears.

You can see your new macro by choosing Tools⇔Macro⇔Macros. The Macro dialog box contains a list of the macros associated with the current document, whether they're local or part of another document, stencil, template, or other associated file.

Although this book proper doesn't contain much material on Visio or FrontPage, you'll find a Visio Bonus Chapter on the Dummies.com Web site. Visit www.dummies.com/go/vbafd5e to download both the source code and the Bonus Chapters (one for Visio and another for FrontPage).

Modifying the macro

Modifying a macro recorded using the Macro Recorder is much like modifying any other macro. The only differences are that you didn't write the initial code and the Macro Recorder doesn't add any comments for you. As an example, open the Excel macro created earlier in this chapter, in the "Recording a macro using the Ribbon interface" section. The following steps describe how to perform this task:

1. Open the Macro dialog box. When using the Ribbon interface, you click Macros on the Developer tab. When using the menu interface, choose Tools⇔Macro⇔Macros.

You see the Macro dialog box, shown in Figure 3-4.

2. Choose the macro you want to edit and then click Edit.

The Office application opens the Visual Basic Editor with the selected macro opened, as shown in Figure 3-5. (You may see other macros files opened as well.)

3. Add comments to the recorded macro so that you can retrace your steps later.

Figure 3-4:
The Macro
dialog box
contains a
list of
available
macros.

4. **Make any required macro changes.**

5. **Save the macro and close the Visual Basic Editor.**

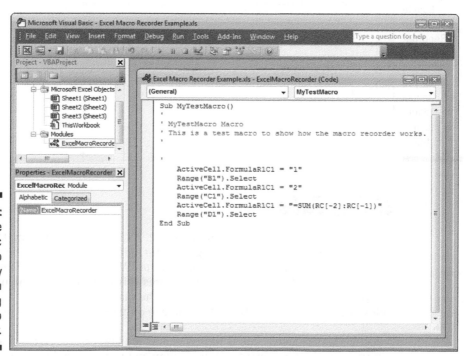

Figure 3-5:
You use the
Visual Basic
Editor to
modify any
macros you
create using
the Macro
Recorder.

It isn't necessary now to understand the macro shown in Figure 3-5. However, this macro begins by assigning a value of 1 to the worksheet cell at A1. Because the cursor was already in cell A1 when the macro recording started, this action doesn't appear in the macro. This omission points out one of the reasons you want to edit macros you create with the Macro Recorder. The macro then moves the cursor to cell B2 and assigns it a value of 2. Finally, the macro moves the cursor to cell C3 and enters an equation in it that sums the two numbers. You'd probably edit this macro by adding the missing cell reference for A1, adding comments, and removing the one extra statement, as shown in Figure 3-6.

Figure 3-6:
Editing
Macro
Recorder
output is
important
when you
want to use
the macro
for multiple
tasks.

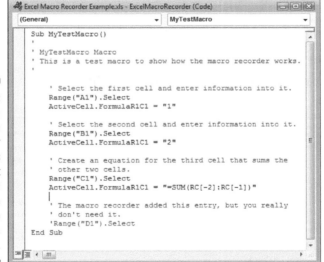

```
Sub MyTestMacro()
'
' MyTestMacro Macro
' This is a test macro to show how the macro recorder works.
'

    ' Select the first cell and enter information into it.
    Range("A1").Select
    ActiveCell.FormulaR1C1 = "1"

    ' Select the second cell and enter information into it.
    Range("B1").Select
    ActiveCell.FormulaR1C1 = "2"

    ' Create an equation for the third cell that sums the
    ' other two cells.
    Range("C1").Select
    ActiveCell.FormulaR1C1 = "=SUM(RC[-2]:RC[-1])"

    ' The macro recorder added this entry, but you really
    ' don't need it.
    'Range("D1").Select
End Sub
```

Using Subs

I use a sub-procedure, or Sub, in Chapter 2. A Sub is the easiest method of packaging code, and it's the only packaging method that appears in the Macro dialog box. In fact, the example in the "Writing Your First Function" section (later in this chapter) demonstrates this feature. Consequently, the one place where you always use a Sub is the main entry point for a program unless the program is a utility that you use only for programming purposes.

A second way to use a Sub is to perform a task and not receive a direct return value. You can use a Sub to display an informational message, such as the ones in Chapter 2. A Sub can modify information in a number of ways; it just can't return a value — only a `Function` can do that. However, you can use arguments as one method for modifying information by using a `Sub` (see the example in the upcoming "Writing Your First Function" section). A second method relies on global variables (see the example in the later "Defining the effects of scope" section).

Many VBA users also use the `Sub` as a means of breaking up code. Instead of creating code that goes on for miles and miles, using several `Sub`s can break up the code into page-sized pieces. Using this method makes the code a lot easier to read.

Using Functions

You might not see a use for the `Function` after spending some time working with the `Sub`. However, not every problem is a screw requiring the use of a screwdriver or a nail in search of a hammer. You use a `Function` for different problems than a `Sub` can answer. In most cases, there's definitely a correct answer to using a `Function` or a `Sub`. For example, you always use a `Sub` when you want to access program code from within the host application, and you always use a `Function` when you want to perform a calculation with a return result.

A `Function` always returns a value, which makes it different from a `Sub`. For this reason, you can write functions that contain code that you plan to repeat a lot within a program. To process a list of names, you might create a `Function` to process each name individually and then call that `Function` once for each name. The `Function` can provide the processed information as a return value. In Chapter 5, I describe how to create repeating code using structures such as `Do...Until`.

You can also use a `Function` for public code that you don't want to list in the Macro dialog box. You normally don't see a `Function` listed in the Macro dialog box — this dialog box usually lists only `Sub`s.

Modifying the project settings

So far, you've used VBA without configuring many of the options, and the examples have relied on defaults that VBA normally uses. Most of the VBA program levels have some type of configuration, including the project. In this section, I describe the various project-setting options.

To open the project settings, right-click the project in the Project Explorer window and then choose the Project Properties option from the context menu that appears. You see the Project Properties dialog box, shown in Figure 3-7. See the "Looking at the Integrated Development Environment (IDE)" section of Chapter 1 for a description of the Project Explorer window. (Note that I've already filled out the various options that I describe in the following sections.)

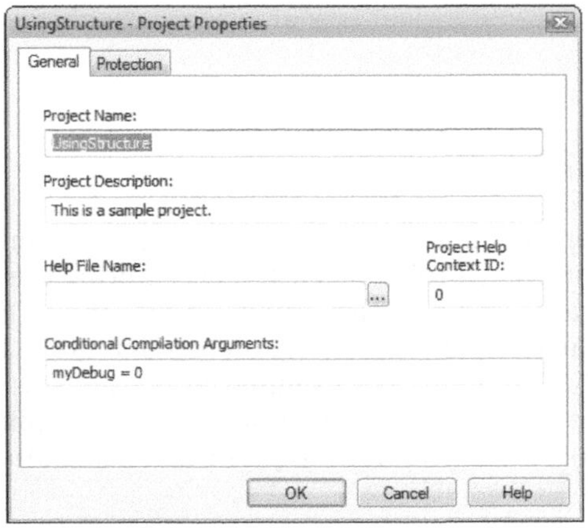

Figure 3-7:
Define basic information for your projects.

Describing your project

Describing your project makes it easier to track when you view it in the VBA IDE windows. Start by giving your project a meaningful name. It shouldn't be long, but calling your project *VBAProject* isn't very meaningful because it doesn't describe what the project does. The Project Name field, shown in Figure 3-7, has a meaningful project name for this chapter because the examples show how to add structure to your programs.

Although the Project Name field value shows up in a number of places, the Project Description field value shows up only in Object Browser. You can write a longer text description of the project so that it's easier to track each entry that Object Browser shows. Otherwise, you might have a hard time finding the project that you want.

Some people don't see help files as a necessary project description, but a *help file* is a detailed description of what your project can do. The Help File Name field tells where to locate the help file and which one to use. The Project Help Context ID field contains the number of the help topic that relates to the project. This entry normally contains the topic number of an overview page.

Adding conditional compilation

Conditional compilation is an essential feature for creating multiple versions of your program. Normally, VBA goes through your list of statements and performs them one at a time. However, using conditional compilations allows VBA to perform a task in one way while you write and test the program, and in another way when you finish it.

The most common use for this feature is to help debug a program. In Chapter 6, I show you how to use conditional compilation to debug your application. However, for now, just to have a little fun, you can create a very simple program that shows how this feature works. First, make sure that you type **myDebug = 0** in the Conditional Compilation Arguments field and then click OK. Then type the following program in a module (see the "Step 2: Implement the design" section of Chapter 2 for instructions on creating a module):

```
Public Sub CheckConditional()
    #If myDebug = 0 Then
        MsgBox "In Standard Mode"
    #Else
        MsgBox "In Debug Mode"
    #End If
End Sub
```

This program says that if myDebug is set to 0, the program should display a message box that reads In Standard Mode. If myDebug is set to any other value, the program should display a message box that reads In Debug Mode. Run the program, and you should see a message box that reads In Standard Mode.

Avoiding code-locking security issues

One consideration for code locking is that it can provide a false sense of security. Although code locking keeps novice users from modifying your code, it doesn't keep out dedicated crackers. The Internet contains offerings from many vendors who offer to unlock your Office documents for you when you lose the password. Unfortunately, the same application that can help you retrieve your documents when you forget the password can also give crackers access to it. The best policy to follow is to use code locking when you need to protect novice users from themselves, rather than as a means for protecting your investment in the code itself.

Open the Project Properties dialog box again. Change the Conditional Compilation Arguments field so that it reads **myDebug** = **1**. Click OK and then run the program again. The program displays a message box that reads In Debug Mode.

Locking your code

At some point, you might decide that you want to lock away your code forever so that no one can modify it. The Protection tab of the Project Properties dialog box, shown in Figure 3-8, helps you accomplish this task. Simply select the Lock Project for Viewing check box, and then supply the same password in both the Password and Confirm Password fields. Click OK to complete the process.

Figure 3-8:
Locking
your code
can keep it
safe from
prying eyes.

 Locking your project might seem like a good idea, but you should carefully consider whether to do so, for a number of reasons. The most important reason is that you can't unlock the project without the password. If you forget the password, the project might remain locked forever. The second reason is that locking your project doesn't prevent someone from viewing your code. The only thing that locking the project does is to prevent someone from modifying the code. Consequently, when you need to hide the code for some reason, VBA isn't the best tool for the job. (If hiding your code is essential, you need a native code compiler, such as Visual C++, or a product, such as Visual Studio Tools for Office [VSTO], that can integrate managed code solutions with Office products.)

Defining compiler options

When you first start VBA, it makes certain assumptions about how you want to write code. These assumptions might not be accurate, so Microsoft provides a way for you to tell VBA to do something else. The compiler options listed in Table 3-1 help you define how VBA works with your code. (A *compiler* reads your code and translates the words into instructions that Windows can understand.) You can add these options at the very beginning of a module, class module, or form, before any other code appears.

Table 3-1	Compiler Options for VBA
Option	*Description*
Option Base <Number>	Use this option to change how VBA numbers array elements. You can number array elements beginning at 0 or 1. In Chapter 9, I describe how to use arrays.
Option Explicit	Smart VBA programmers always add this compiler option to their code. This option tells VBA that you want to define variables before you use them. This option not only makes your code easier to read, but can also help you find typos in your code. Although the standard setting treats MyVar and MVar as two variables, this option forces VBA to question the misspelled version.
Option Compare <Method>	Use this option to change how VBA compares strings. When you're using the Binary technique, VBA considers *hello* and *Hello* different because the first form is in lowercase. Using the Text method means that VBA considers *hello* and *Hello* as the same word because it doesn't take into consideration the case of the letters. The Database technique, which is available only in Access, uses the database sort order for string-comparison purposes.
Option Private Module	Use this option to make a module private so that no other module can see what it contains. The concept of public and private is the object's scope. The upcoming section "Getting the Scoop on Scope" describes in greater detail what scope means.

The Option Explicit statement is so important that you should always add it to a program. Listing 3-1 is a short example of how this feature works.

Listing 3-1   Using Option Explicit to Reduce Errors

```
' Tell VBA to ensure we define variables.
Option Explicit

' This Sub will fail because it doesn't
' define the variable.
Public Sub OptionCheck()
    MyVar = "Hello"
    MsgBox MyVar
End Sub

' This Sub will succeed.
Public Sub OptionCheck2()
    ' Define the variable.
    Dim MyVar As String

    ' Add a value to the variable.
    MyVar = "Hello"

    ' Display a message box.
    MsgBox MyVar
End Sub
```

In both cases, the Sub defines a value for a variable named MyVar. The OptionCheck Sub fails because it doesn't define the variable before it uses it. VBA doesn't know anything about MyVar, so it can't use it. Look at the second Sub, OptionCheck2. This Sub works because it defines MyVar first and then assigns a value to it. Although using the Option Explicit statement might seem like a lot of work, it really does save time spent debugging typos in your program.

Taking the Lego Approach

It's easy to make writing a program harder than it needs to be by getting caught up in the abstract nature of code. The biggest mistake that you can make is to write one long program that goes on for pages and pages that no one can understand — not even you. Code that looks more like a copy of *War and Peace* rather than a simple set of instructions is usually called *spaghetti code.*

The Lego approach to writing code is one in which the programmer breaks up the program into easily understood modules and writes just one module at a time. Using this approach helps you write code that is easy to modify later and that most people can understand with ease. The Lego approach also makes it easy for you to move pieces of code when writing another program.

Creating an application plan

In Chapter 2, I describe how to use pseudo-code to write a program. The program in that chapter uses only one module because it's quite simple. Not every program that you create is that simple. Sometimes a program performs complex tasks, and you need to create an *overview,* or *application plan,* first. Think of the Lego approach again: Each block is separate, but you don't get the whole picture until you put the blocks together. The application plan shows how to put the blocks together to get a particular result. You have three sizes of blocks that you can use:

✔ Projects

✔ Modules, forms, and class modules

✔ Sub-procedures and functions

Think about the writing of a VBA program this way: You have a pile of blocks, and you have a picture of what you want to create in your mind. To make the creation a reality, you choose and add blocks that look like they fit. You can choose standard blocks from this book, the VBA help file, or online sites, such as FreeVBCode.com at `http://www.freevbcode.com/`.

You can use a number of techniques to create your application plan. I usually start with a list of major tasks, such as printing a report or finding a word. This isn't pseudo-code. You're not writing a procedure for VBA to follow. All that you're thinking about are the major tasks that VBA has to perform. Maybe your program performs only one major task. In that case, you might be able to get by with a single project, module, and sub-procedure, like in the example in Chapter 2.

Understanding the Lego approach

I call the method that I describe in this chapter *the Lego approach* because most people are familiar with this toy and it's an easy way to explain good programming technique. Some people use other names for this kind of programming. You might hear it called *modular programming,* for example, because it relies on modules to hold individual pieces of code. Don't confuse all these terms with object-oriented programming, which I describe in Chapter 8.

Defining the project

You may never need to define more than one project for a program. This is especially true of Access and Excel projects, in which everything needed to hold the data appears in one file in most cases. You can also place everything that you need into a single Word template if this is the only template that you need and the program is appropriate for use with more than one document.

However, think about Word for a moment, and you discover something about projects. Figure 3-9 shows a typical Project Explorer window setup. Notice that this window contains three projects: Normal, Project (Document1), and TemplateProject (LETTER).

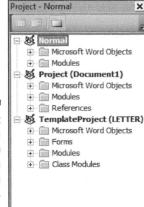

Figure 3-9:
A single
program
can span
more than
one project.

Word always loads the Normal template. (This template can have one of a number of different extensions, including DOT, DOTX, and DOTM in Office 2007.) Older versions of Word always use the Document Template (DOT) extension. Word 2007 can also use Microsoft's new XML format (DOTX) or macro-enabled format (DOTM). If you want to create macros for Word 2007, the best file format to use for compatibility is the DOT file, but you get the greatest flexibility and feature set by using the DOTM file. You can't store macros in the DOTX file.

You can also use a custom template. Custom templates contain special formatting and macros for a particular document type, such as a letter. As with the Normal template, custom templates come with DOT, DOTX, and DOTM extensions. You can never store macros in a DOTX file.

Finally, you also have the document, which also counts as a project. A document can have a DOC, DOCX, or DOCM file extension. You can store macros only in the DOC and DOCM file formats. In this case, I wrote a program for the individual document that uses template-specific sub-procedures and functions in the Letter template as well as generic utility sub-procedures and functions in the Normal template. You can see this example in Chapter 13. You might run into some situations like this when you create your Word programs, too.

Another situation in which you use multiple projects is when you create programs in which multiple applications have to work together. I have a program for Word that asks CorelDRAW to import a drawing and convert it into a form that Word can use. Word receives the converted drawing and places it in the current document. Word then asks Access to look up the drawing in a database. Access performs this task and returns a description of the drawing to Word, which then formats the description and places it under the drawing in the current document. If I had to perform this whole loop every time that I needed a drawing, it would take 20 minutes per drawing. My Word VBA program can perform the task in less than a minute, and the results are perfect every time.

Defining the program means figuring out how many building blocks you need in order to accomplish a task. You can take the simple approach and use just one project for many programs. However, don't make life difficult. If you need to use multiple projects, VBA makes it easy to use them.

Adding a module

Most of your beginning programs use a single module. However, good design begins with module definitions. You could create a huge module called *utility* that contains every utility program you've ever written, but it would be a mess. It's like the overstressed dresser drawer that hides the tie tack or other jewelry that you want to wear tonight: After you throw out all the contents of the drawer into the room, you finally find the one item that you were looking for. Instead of creating a single utility module, try creating a module for disk utilities and another for data manipulation. Be unique! Try arranging your modules to see what works best.

When your programming skills improve, you might want to interact with the user in some way. You might want to ask the user questions, for example. This task requires that you add a form to your program. Every form that you want to create requires a separate form addition to the program. Make sure that you create forms that ask for one kind of information — don't confuse the user by asking for all kinds of unrelated information on one form. (See Chapter 7 for a description of forms and how to use them.)

Working with objects means using classes. To create a special object, add a class module to your application. As when you're adding forms, you should add one class module for every new object that you want to create. Make sure that any object that you create performs only one task. (Chapter 8 demonstrates methods for working with objects.)

Designing procedures

Most of the example programs in this book rely on a single project and a single module. You might find that most (if not all) of your programs rely on just one of each of these blocks, too. When using this strategy, think about how to break your program into sub-procedures and functions. Use the information found in the earlier "Using Subs" and "Using Functions" sections in this chapter to determine which kind of module to use.

The important thing when working at the sub-procedure and function levels is to write code in convenient chunks. Use your sub-procedures and functions as containers to hold a certain kind of task. Think again about Legos. Every Lego is an individual unit. You need to write sub-procedures and functions so that you can break them apart easily — making each element an individual unit. The examples in this book show you various methods for breaking your code apart because this skill is one of the most important in programming.

It's easy to figure out how to break apart simple code. The MsgBox function that you've used so often is a good example. Look at how this function works: You send some information to it, and the function takes care of all the details for displaying the message box onscreen. You don't have to worry about how MsgBox accomplishes this task, and there aren't any weird conditions for using MsgBox.

Writing statements

After all the other organization is complete, you're left with one or more projects that contain one or more modules that contain at least a sub-procedure. All your Legos are put together, but they're empty. The statements that you write ultimately create the program. All the organization makes the task of writing the statements easier because you need to concentrate on only one task at a time.

In Chapter 2, I emphasize the importance of using an organized approach to writing statements. You begin by creating a pseudo-code procedure, and then you change that pseudo-code into statements that VBA can understand. This process provides two levels of organization for your program: code and documentation. However, there are two other forms of organization. In the upcoming "Creating Readable Code" section, I describe the importance of using white space to make your code readable. In the upcoming "Telling Others about Your Code" section, I show how to use comments to describe how your code works.

Writing Your First Sub

Most Microsoft Office products provide a Properties dialog box, similar to the one shown in Figure 3-10, that contains a Summary tab for documents. You can also find a variation of this Properties dialog box for most third-party products. The Summary tab can provide a lot of valuable information for your programs. You can find out basic statistics, such as the author's name and the company that created the document. The document information also includes statistics, such as the number of words that the document contains. See the BuiltinDocumentProperties help topic in the VBA help file for additional information.

Figure 3-10: Many applications include a Summary tab, like this one.

Unfortunately, Office 2007 products that rely on the Ribbon interface hide the Properties dialog box. The following steps describe how to display the Properties dialog box shown in Figure 3-10:

1. **Click the Office button to display the Office menu.**

2. **Choose Finish⇨Properties.**

   The Office product displays the standard proprieties list.

3. **Click Standard.**

   You see an Advanced option on the drop-down list that appears.

4. **Click Advanced.**

   The Properties dialog box shown in Figure 3-10 appears.

This is the first example where you work directly with an object. The property that you want to use is `BuiltinDocumentProperties`. This property is available for most of the Microsoft Office products, but it's attached to a different object in each one. When using Word, you find this property attached to both the `Word.Document` and `Word.Template` objects. Excel users find the property attached to the `Excel.Worksheet` object. Use Object Browser (press F2 to display Object Browser, if necessary), which I discuss in Chapter 1, to find this property for your product. Type **BuiltinDocumentProperties** in the Search text field and then click Search. Figure 3-11 shows typical results for Excel.

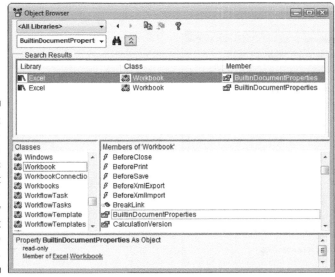

Figure 3-11: The documentation often tells you about an interesting property but not where to find it.

Notice the text at the bottom of Figure 3-11. The information includes the full object name for the property, which comes in handy when you write the code shown in Listing 3-2. Here's the code that you need in order to create this example in Excel. Change the `ActiveWorkbook` object to the object that your application supports, such as `Document` or `Template` in Word, when using another application.

Listing 3-2   Getting Author Information from a Document

```
Public Sub GetSummary()
    ' Declare a DocumentProperty object to hold the
    ' information.
    Dim MyProperty As DocumentProperty

    ' Set the DocumentProperty object equal to the author
    ' information.
    Set MyProperty = _
```

```
        ActiveWorkbook.BuiltinDocumentProperties("Author")

    ' Display a message box containing the property value.
    MsgBox MyProperty.Value, vbOKOnly, "Author Name"
End Sub
```

This example begins by declaring a variable named `MyProperty`. However, `MyProperty` is different from other variables because it's actually an object. This is a `DocumentProperty` object that can hold any document property, including the author or company name.

The next line of code sets `MyProperty` equal to the author information provided by the `BuiltinDocumentProperties("Author")` object. You can set one object equal to another if they're the same kind of object. It's like looking at two apples: You can say that one apple is like another, but you can't say that an apple is like an orange. In this case, you're storing the author information located in `MyProperty` in the `BuiltinDocumentProperties("Author")` object.

If a line of code is too long, you can continue it on the next line in VBA by adding an underscore, _, like the one shown in the code example. The underscore is a *continuation character*. You should add a continuation character when the text onscreen requires scrolling. It's easier to read the code if you don't have to scroll from side to side.

The last line of code displays the `Value` property of the `MyProperty` object. VBA already knows how to work with other variables that you have seen. An object usually requires special handling. In this case, you ask `MyProperty` what its value is and display it in a message box.

Run this program to see a dialog box containing the name of the document creator. In most cases, the creator is you. Try changing the Author field entry, shown in Figure 3-10, to something else. The output of the program changes to match whatever you type in this field.

Writing Your First Function

The example in the preceding "Writing Your First Sub" section is nice (refer to Listing 3-2), but you might want more than one piece of information. VBA users commonly rely on functions to perform repetitive tasks (see the earlier "Using Functions" section). That's what the example in this section shows.

Listing 3-3 uses a `Sub` named `GetSummary2` to call the `GetDocProperty` sfunction multiple times. In every case, a special variable stores the result. At the end of the program, `GetSummary2` displays all the information that the program has accumulated.

Listing 3-3 Using a Function to Retrieve Document Information

```
Public Sub GetSummary2()
    ' Declare a string to hold the output information.
    Dim DocumentData As String

    ' Store the name of the information.
    DocumentData = "Author Name: "

    ' Get the author name.
    DocumentData = DocumentData + GetDocProperty("Author")

    ' Add an extra line.
    DocumentData = DocumentData + vbCrLf

    ' Store the name of the information.
    DocumentData = DocumentData + "Company: "

    ' Get the company name.
    DocumentData = DocumentData +
        GetDocProperty("Company")

    ' Display a message box containing the property value.
    MsgBox DocumentData, vbOKOnly, "Summary"
End Sub

Private Function GetDocProperty(Name As String) As String
    ' Declare a DocumentProperty object to hold the
    ' information.
    Dim MyProperty As DocumentProperty

    ' Set the DocumentProperty object equal to the author
    ' information.
    Set MyProperty = _
        ActiveWorkbook.BuiltinDocumentProperties(Name)

    ' Return the information.
    GetDocProperty = MyProperty.Value
End Function
```

Listing 3-3 begins with GetSummary2. Much of what you see looks similar to previous examples. However, notice how the code works with DocumentData. The example builds the text output by adding the previous content of the string to itself. So, first DocumentData contains "Author Name: ", and then you add the actual author name to it by using GetDocProperty.

Another new addition is the use of a constant. The vbCrLf constant contains special characters that act the same as when you press Enter at the end of a line of text in a word processor.

The `GetDocProperty` function introduces several new ideas. The first idea is a return value. Functions can return a value to the caller. The second idea is the use of an argument. An *argument* is input to a `Sub` or `Function`. In this case, `Name` is the input to the `GetDocProperty` function.

The actual code within the `GetDocProperty` function looks the same as the example in the earlier "Writing Your First Sub" section. However, in this case, the code uses `Name` (a variable) as input to `ActiveWorkbook.Builtin DocumentProperties` instead of as a constant. Also, notice that the code makes the function equal to the `MyProperty.Value` property. This is how you return a value to the caller.

Getting the Scoop on Scope

You might think that the concept of scope is confusing and difficult to understand because you think that it's complex. Actually, *scope* is simply the range of what a program can see and how much it lets others know. When you look at the `MsgBox` function, you care about the inputs that you provide and the output that the function produces. These are the public (or visible) elements of the `MsgBox` function. You don't care too much about what happens inside the `MsgBox` function even though this information is important to the `MsgBox` function itself. These inner workings — the ones that you can't see — are the private (or invisible) elements of the `MsgBox` function.

There are two reasons that scope is important to you as a VBA user. First, if every part of a program could see every other part of a program, chaos would result because there would be too much information to track. Second, programs have to protect their data to ensure that it doesn't get damaged in some way. In short, you want to make some parts of your program visible so that people can use them, but leave other parts invisible so that they remain protected.

Understanding the purpose of scope

You've seen two keywords used for all the `Sub` and `Function` examples so far: `Public` and `Private`. These two keywords can affect other elements as well. You can use them to define the scope of variables or of classes. Scope has an effect on just about every kind of programming element that you use in this book, so it's important to understand how scope works:

- **Public:** Tells VBA that it should allow other program elements to see the affected elements
- **Private:** Tells VBA that it should hide the affected elements from other programming elements

Defining the effects of scope

The best way to learn about scope is to begin working with it. You can experiment with simple uses of scope to see how a change in scope affects your programs. The most important rule is that scope only affects everything outside the current block. That's right: The Lego example works here, too. (See the earlier section "Taking the Lego Approach.")

Making a module private by adding `Option Private Module` at the beginning of the module means that everything in that module is invisible to the outside world. Even if the module contains a `Public Sub`, only the other elements inside the module can see it — the `Public Sub` is invisible to everything outside the module. Likewise, when you're declaring a `Private Sub`, everything within the current module can still see it, but nothing outside the current module can.

Listing 3-4 demonstrates some of the basic elements of scope. Other examples in the book refine this concept, but this is a good starting point.

Listing 3-4   Using Global Variables

```
' Declare a private global variable.
Private MyGlobalVariable As String

Public Sub GlobalTest()
    ' Set the value of the global variable.
    MyGlobalVariable = "Hello"

    ' Display the value.
    MsgBox MyGlobalVariable

    ' Call the GlobalTest2 Sub.
    GlobalTest2

    ' Display the value on return from the call.
    MsgBox MyGlobalVariable
End Sub

Private Sub GlobalTest2()
    ' Show that the global variable is truly global.
    MsgBox MyGlobalVariable

    ' Change the value of the global variable.
    MyGlobalVariable = "Goodbye"
End Sub
```

Notice that `MyGlobalVariable` is private. You can't access this global variable outside the current module. However, both of the sub-procedures in this module can access the global variable.

As another example, `GlobalTest` is a public `Sub`, but `GlobalTest2` is private. To verify the use of scope in this case, open the Macro dialog box by using the Tools⇨Macro⇨Macros command. You see `GlobalTest` listed, but `GlobalTest2` doesn't appear in the list.

Type and run the example code in Listing 3-4 to see how the two `Sub` elements affect each other. You should see three dialog boxes. The first dialog box reads `Hello` because `GlobalTest` sets the value of `MyGlobalVariable`. The second dialog box also reads `Hello` because `MyGlobalVariable` is truly global. Even though the value of this variable was set in `GlobalTest`, `GlobalTest2` can read it. Finally, the third dialog box reads `Goodbye` because `GlobalTest2` has set `MyGlobalVariable` to another value.

Creating Readable Code

You might have noticed how the examples in this chapter use white space to make the code more readable. If you type all the statements for your program one right after the other, the code still works. VBA doesn't care about white space. However, you might care because code without white space is nearly unreadable.

Most VBA users rely on two kinds of white space. You've seen the first type in this chapter. Notice that every comment and statement pair in the code is followed by a blank line. This blank line tells anyone reading the code that he has reached the end of this particular statement or step in the procedure.

The second kind of white space is indention. The examples in this chapter indent the code within a `Sub` or `Function` to make the body of the `Sub` or `Function` clear.

Telling Others about Your Code

The pseudo-code technique that I describe in Chapter 2 is a good way to start documenting your code. However, at some point, you need to add information because simply reading the procedure presented by the pseudo-code might not be enough. You might want to add your name, a project title, and other forms of documentation to your code.

Writing basic comments

Comments can take a number of forms. The pseudo-code comment is the first kind of comment that everyone writes because it's the kind of comment that's most natural to use. Developers quickly move on to adding documentation comments, such as who wrote the program or when it was originally written and a list of updates made to code. Some developers move on to better comments at this point.

One of the more important comments that you can add to your code is why you chose to write the program in a certain way. Simply saying that the code performs a specific task isn't enough because you can usually perform the same task in several different ways. Telling why you made certain choices can reduce mistakes during code updates and serve as reasons for performing updates later, when your coding technique improves.

As a good programmer, you should also include mistakes that you make in the code as comments if you think that someone else might make the same mistake. These experiential comments have helped me in many situations because I actually end up using them for notes. When I start a new project, I look back at my notes for things that I should avoid.

Knowing when to use comments

Use comments wherever and whenever you think that you need them. You might think that comments are difficult to type and include only one or two paltry comments for each program that you write. You're correct — writing good comments can be time consuming and can be difficult because writing them makes you think yet again about the code. However, the programs with the fewest comments usually generate the most head scratching during an update. In fact, I've seen a few situations where the lack of comments in code actually caused a company to start writing the code from scratch during an update rather than pay someone to spend the time relearning what the old code meant.

Understanding how to create a good comment

A *good* comment is one that you can understand. Don't use fancy terms — write everything in plain terms that you can understand. When you feel that you need to explain something, feel free to do it. Good comments should answer the six essential questions: who, what, where, when, why, and how. Make sure that your comments are complete and that they fully answer any questions that someone reading your code might have.

Chapter 4

Storing and Modifying Information

*I*n this chapter, I refine the concept of a variable by describing variable types and how you can modify their content. Understanding how a computer stores information is very important. Computers don't see information the same way that you do — many methods of representing information that seem obvious to you are invisible to the computer.

As far as the computer is concerned, everything is a series of bits that it has to move around. Data types were invented, sometimes by trial and error, to make the bits easier for humans to understand. For example, when you see the letter C on the display, all that the computer sees is a series of 8 bits that form a special number. Interpretation of this number as the letter *C* is for your benefit. Understanding that everything is a series of bits makes this chapter easier to understand.

When you begin to realize that you're in control — that you decide how to organize and interpret the bits the computer is moving around for you — you've taken a large step in understanding how VBA works. VBA helps you tell the computer how you want the bits moved around. In the following sections, I describe various ways in which you can interpret and modify the bits that the computer stores for you.

Understanding Variables and Constants

VBA provides many levels of data interpretation. Some data interpretations help you make your program reliable, others make it run faster, still others provide accuracy, and a few make the data easier to interpret. One of the two big distinctions is between variables and constants. You can modify a *variable* anytime the program can actually access it. A *constant,* however, retains the same value all the time. You use variables as storage containers for data that changes, and you use constants for data that doesn't change. Variables are more flexible than constants are, but constants make your program run faster, so each type of storage has its place.

Making the declaration

All data in a VBA program looks like a series of bits to the computer. The computer doesn't understand the difference between a constant and a variable — VBA provides this distinction for your benefit. You use different methods to mark variables and constants in your program.

Variables have a scope and a data type. See the "Defining the Data Types" section, later in this chapter, for data type descriptions and how to use them. See the "Getting the Scoop on Scope" section of Chapter 3 for scope issues. Declare variables with both scope and data type so that VBA knows how to work with them. Constants can also have a scope, but they don't have a data type associated with them. A special constant type, #Const, lets you define conditional constants — those that help you tell the compiler how to compile an application. Listing 4-1 shows some examples of variable and constant declarations.

Listing 4-1   Examples of Variable and Constant Declarations with Scope

```
Option Explicit

' This variable is visible to other modules.
Public MyPublicVariable As String
' This variable is visible only to this module.
Private MyPrivateVariable As String
' Using Dim is the same as making the variable private.
Dim MyDimVariable As String

' A constant is only used for conditional compilation.
#Const MyConditionalConstant = "Hello"
' This constant is visible to other modules.
Public Const MyPublicConstant = "Hello"
' This constant is visible only to this module.
Private Const MyPrivateConstant = "Hello"

Public Sub DataDeclarations()
```

```
     ' Only this Sub can see this variable.
     Dim MyDimSubVariable As String

     ' Only this Sub can see this constant.
     Const MySubConstant = "Hello"
End Sub
```

Begin by looking at the variables in Listing 4-1. The example includes three declarations, along with their associated comments. Always include comments with your declarations so that you know what purpose the variable serves. The variable declarations rely on `Public` and `Private` for scope as well as on a data type keyword following the variable name to define the data type. All the variables in this example are strings (or text), but VBA supports many other data types. Using the `Dim` keyword makes a variable private. However, actually using the word `Private` is clearer, so that's what you should use in your code.

The next three declarations in Listing 4-1 are for constants. Notice that the first constant declaration is for conditional compilation. This kind of declaration always uses the `#Const` keyword. You can use this declaration in place of the Conditional Compilation Arguments field entry (see the "Adding conditional compilation" section of Chapter 3 for details). You can't define this type of constant as private or public because VBA hides the value from other modules.

The other two kinds of constant declaration do rely on `Public` or `Private` for scope. Notice that you do include the keyword `Const` to mark the value as a constant. The constant has a name and a value assigned to it. However, notice that it doesn't have a data type because you can't assign a data type to a constant. VBA stores constants as a series of bits by using the type of the information that you provide. Because you can never change the value of a constant, the question of data type isn't important. The fact that a constant doesn't have a data type is one reason that it improves application performance and is more efficient to store.

The next section of Listing 4-1 contains a `Sub` that includes both a constant and a variable declaration. Variables or constants defined within a `Sub` or `Function` are private to that `Sub` or `Function`. Consequently, VBA requires that you use the `Dim` keyword in this case. Notice that the constant still includes the `Const` keyword but lacks a `Private` or `Public` keyword for the same reason.

Knowing which storage type to use

At first, it might seem like you should always use variables so that you can always access the data and change it. Variables do provide flexibility that constants don't provide, and you can use variables more often than not to store your data. However, constants also have distinct advantages, including

✔ **Speed:** Using constants can make your application faster. Constants require less memory, and VBA can optimize your program to perform better when you use them.

✔ **Reliability:** Constants have a reliable value. If a constant has a specific value when you start the program, that value remains until the program ends.

✔ **Ease of reading:** Most VBA users rely on constants to make their programs easier to read. The vbCrLf constant shown in the examples in Chapter 3 is the same no matter how many programs you create. Every developer who sees this constant knows that VBA adds what amounts to pressing Enter (adding a carriage return and line feed combination) when you use the constant in an application.

There are other reasons to use constants in place of variables. For example, Object Browser makes it easy to work with constants. Whenever you highlight a constant in Object Browser, you see the value associated with that constant, as shown in Figure 4-1. Notice that the entry at the bottom of Object Browser tells you that the highlighted entry is a public constant with a value of "Hello".

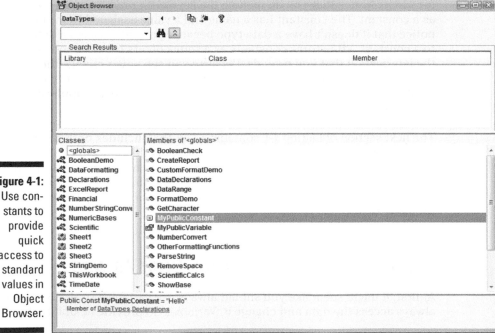

Figure 4-1: Use constants to provide quick access to standard values in Object Browser.

To see this constant for yourself, load the code example for this chapter. You can download the code from the Dummies.com Web site at http://www.dummies.com/go/vbafd5e. Choose View⇨Object Browser or press F2 to display Object Browser. Select DataTypes in the Library field, as shown in Figure 4-1. Highlight <globals> in the Classes list, and highlight MyPublicConstant in the Members list.

Even though you don't need to know about them now, VBA supports one additional constant type: enumerated constants. An *enumerated constant* provides a list of values, and you select one value from the list to use in your application. The "Using enumerated constants" section of Chapter 8 demonstrates the use of this constant type. Enumerated constants help document objects that you create and make them easier to use. Using enumerated constants also reduces the potential for error when someone uses an object that you create.

Defining scope

Listing 4-1 demonstrates that variable and constant scope rules work about the same. Always use Private to keep a variable or constant hidden from the outside world. Use Public to provide access to the variable or constant outside the current module. Any variable or constant that you define within a Sub or Function is always private to that Sub or Function. See the "Getting the Scoop on Scope" section of Chapter 3 for additional information.

Defining the Data Types

A *data type* is a method of defining data to make it easier to work with in a program. The computer still sees the data as a series of bits, but VBA works with different data types in different ways. The computer can see the binary value, 1000001b, but it doesn't do anything special with that value. VBA can see this binary value as the number 65 or the letter *A* depending on the data type that you assign to the value. The data type is important in understanding the value and working with it. Using a data type also ensures that the program follows certain rules. Otherwise, the data could become corrupted because the program could mishandle it.

Although a variable in general is simply a box for storing data, you can think of these data types as special boxes for storing specific kinds of data. Just as you would use a hatbox to store a hat and not a car engine, you use these special box types to store particular kinds of data. For example, you use a string to hold text, not logical (true/false) values.

VBA supports a number of standard data types, including Byte, Boolean, Integer, Long, Currency, Decimal, Single, Double, Date, String,

`Object`, and `Variant`. In addition to using the defined data types, you can create user-defined data types so that you can mark the information as needed for your program. A user-defined data type gives you the power to extend the VBA interpretation of data. (The computer still looks at the data as binary information.) Each of the data type descriptions that follows has a different purpose, and you can work with the data type in a variety of ways.

Using strings for text

The first data type that I discuss in this chapter is one that you've already seen in the message box examples: the string. When you create a message box, you use a string as input. The string is the most useful and most-often used data type in VBA.

In this chapter, I discuss only the essential string functions. VBA provides a rich set of string manipulation functions. You can discover more about these functions in the Working with Strings help topic. (Always access VBA help topics from within the VBA Integrated Development Environment [IDE] by using the Help➪Microsoft Visual Basic Help command or by pressing F1.)

Understanding strings

Programmers often use fancy terms for things that the average person easily recognizes. Strings are simply text, just like the text that you're reading now.

A *string* is a sequence of characters. The characters aren't always printable but can include control characters that determine how the text appears onscreen. A string can also include special characters, such as punctuation, or even special features, such as a circumflex or an umlaut. Although a string can contain all these elements, the main content of a string is always text.

Adding strings together with + or &

Sometimes you'll want to concatenate two or more strings to make a longer string. *Concatenation* is the process of adding strings together. For example, you might want to add a person's first name to their last name to create their full name. Often, you need to take information from more than one place and join it together to create a new kind of information. You'll see many examples of concatenation as the book progresses.

Concatenation is so important that VBA provides a number of ways to do it. The two most popular methods are using the + (plus sign) or the & (ampersand) symbol. Here are examples of both concatenation techniques:

```
MyVar = "A" & "B"
MyVar = "A" + "B"
```

In most cases it doesn't matter whether you use the + or the &. The & is the traditional symbol, so you'll see it used most often. However, it's important to realize that the + and & aren't precisely the same, even though they normally work the same. When in doubt, use the &.

The + is actually a math operation; it adds two items together. When you add two strings, VBA concatenates them as long as there are actually two values to add. Using the + symbol can help you achieve a performance benefit, especially when you need to add many strings together. The performance benefit occurs because VBA performs fewer checks.

The & is the safer symbol and the one you should use in situations where the + doesn't work. For example, when you try to add a string that contains information to a string that doesn't contain anything (a null string), the result is a null string. (You must use the `Variant` data type to create a null string; discover more about this data type in the "Working with variant data" section of the chapter.) However, when you concatenate the two strings by using the &, the result is a string with a blank (for the null) attached.

You must also use the & when you want to place text within an Excel or other application calculation. Using `= "Hello" + "Goodbye"` results in an error, but using `= "Hello" & "Goodbye"` concatenates the two strings.

Use of the + assumes that the two data types are the same or that you're adding a string to a `Variant` that contains a string. The *Variant* data type can contain anything or nothing (null). You must use & to concatenate dissimilar data types, such as a string to a number.

Sometimes you'll use the & and the + together to achieve a particular result. For example, you might experience a situation where you don't know in advance whether a particular variable will contain a null or a string. An address might contain a second address line, or it might contain a null value. If you use & for all of the concatenation tasks, the output will contain a blank line. However, using the + correctly displays the data without a blank line. Listing 4-2 shows an example of how to use & and + together.

Listing 4-2 Adding versus Concatenating Strings

```
Public Sub AddVersusConcatenate()
    ' Create three strings for testing.
    Dim Address1 As String
    Dim Address2 As Variant
    Dim OtherInfo As String

    ' Place a value into the strings.
    Address1 = "123 First Street"
    OtherInfo = "Somewhere, NV 12345"
```

(continued)

Listing 4-2 *(continued)*

```
    ' Place a Null value into the second address line.
    Address2 = Null


    ' Concatenate the string to a null.
    Dim ConString As String
    ConString = Address1 & vbCrLf & _
                Address2 & vbCrLf & _
                OtherInfo

    ' Display the result. You see a blank line for the
    ' null.
    MsgBox ConString

    ' Add the string to a null.
    Dim AddString As String
    AddString = Address1 & vbCrLf & _
                (Address2 + vbCrLf) & _
                OtherInfo

    ' Display the result. You see no blank line.
    MsgBox AddString

    ' Show that the results are correct when Address2
    ' contains a value.
    Address2 = "Apt 3G"
    AddString = Address1 & vbCrLf & _
                (Address2 + vbCrLf) & _
                OtherInfo
    MsgBox AddString
End Sub
```

When you run this code, the first MsgBox call displays the output with a blank line between Address1 and OtherInfo because Address2 is Null. However, the second MsgBox call displays the data correctly because it relies on + for concatenation.

Now that you've seen the first two cases showing a Null value, it's time to see what happens when Address2 contains a string. The code places a value into Address2, re-creates the AddString value, and displays the message box again. This time, the Address2 value appears between Address1 and OtherInfo, just as it should.

The + can improve performance in other ways. For example, when you need to check for a null in a variable, you can use the + instead of the & to improve performance. Because of the way + works, you don't need to use the IsNull() function to verify that a variant contains a null value before you process it.

Using character codes

Strings can contain a number of elements. In previous examples, I show you strings that contain control character constants such as vbCrLf. This constant actually contains two control characters: a carriage return and a line feed. The carriage return sends the cursor back to the beginning of the line; the line feed places the cursor on the next line. The result of using both control characters together is the same as pressing Enter on the keyboard.

Strings can also use a special function, Chr, to create special characters. You can combine this function with the Character Map utility (normally available on the Start⇨Programs⇨Accessories menu) to produce any character that you need for your program. Figure 4-2 shows a typical Character Map display. (Vista doesn't include Character Map in the list of applications. To access Character Map in Vista, choose Start⇨Run. Type **Charmap** in the Open field of the Run dialog box and click OK.)

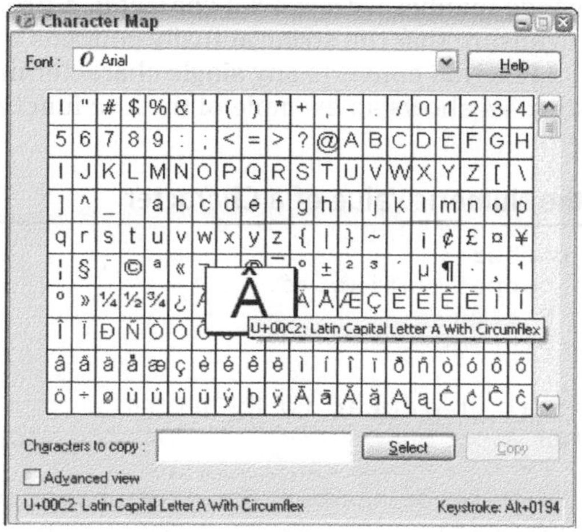

Figure 4-2: Character Map displays all the printable characters available for a particular font.

When you hover the mouse over a character, the balloon help displays the Unicode character number in hexadecimal or base 16 (see the upcoming "Defining hex and octal values" section for details). Selecting the character displays the Unicode number in the lower-left corner of the Character Map dialog box and displays the character in a larger size. Listing 4-3 shows the Chr function in use.

Listing 4-3   Creating Special Characters

```
Public Sub ShowCharacter()
    ' Declare the string.
    Dim MyChar As String
```

(continued)

Listing 4-3 *(continued)*

```
    ' Tell what type of character the code displays.
    MyChar = "Latin Capital Letter A with Circumflex: "

    ' Add the character.
    MyChar = MyChar + Chr(&HC2)

    'Display the result.
    MsgBox MyChar, vbOKOnly, "Special Character"
End Sub
```

This program displays a capital letter *A* with a circumflex when you run it. Notice how the code uses the `Chr` function. The hexadecimal value from Character Map appears as `&HC2`. The `&H` denotes a hexadecimal value, and the `C2` is the number of the character.

You can also get the Unicode number for a special character. A program might use this number to ensure that the string actually contains the requested value. The `Asc` function converts any single character into its numeric equivalent. Listing 4-4 shows an example of the `Asc` function.

Listing 4-4   Getting the Numeric Value of a Character

```
Public Sub GetCharacter()
    ' Declare the output variables.
    Dim MyChar As String
    Dim CharNum As Integer

    ' Add the special character to MyChar.
    MyChar = Chr(&HC2)

    ' Determine the Unicode number for the character.
    CharNum = Asc(MyChar)

    ' Display the result as a decimal value.
    MsgBox "Character " + MyChar + _
           " = Decimal Value " + CStr(CharNum), _
           vbOKOnly, _
           "Special Character Decimal Value"
End Sub
```

The program shows that the capital letter *A* with a circumflex has a decimal value of 194. This value equates to the hexadecimal value of `C2h` shown in the code. Note that when you see a lowercase *h* follow a number, the number is a hexadecimal value. VBA always writes hexadecimal numbers with a leading `&H`, such as `&HC2`. This program also includes the `CStr` function, which accepts an expression, such as a number, as input and outputs a string. See the upcoming "Defining hex and octal values" section for more information on the `CStr` function.

Removing excess space

Some strings come with extra baggage in the form of spaces that you don't need. The spaces can appear at either end of the string or at both ends. VBA provides three essential functions for removing excess space:

- ✔ **LTrim:** Removes the excess spaces from the left side of the string
- ✔ **RTrim:** Removes the excess spaces from the right side of the string
- ✔ **Trim:** Removes excess spaces from both ends of the string

You can combine these three functions with other string functions to produce specific information. Listing 4-5 shows the LTrim, RTrim, and Trim functions in action. It also demonstrates how to combine these three functions with other functions to produce new information.

Listing 4-5   Removing Spaces from a String

```
Public Sub RemoveSpace()
    ' Declare a string with spaces.
    Dim IStr As String

    ' Declare an output string.
    Dim Output As String

    ' Add a string to IStr
    IStr = "     Hello     "

    ' Show the original string length.
    Output = "Original String Length: " + CStr(Len(IStr))

    ' Get rid of the spaces on the left.
    Output = Output + vbCrLf + _
            "LTrim Length: " + CStr(Len(LTrim(IStr))) + _
            " Value: " + Chr(&H22) + LTrim(IStr) +
        Chr(&H22)

    ' Get rid of the spaces on the right.
    Output = Output + vbCrLf + _
            "RTrim Length: " + CStr(Len(RTrim(IStr))) + _
            " Value: " + Chr(&H22) + RTrim(IStr) +
        Chr(&H22)

    ' Get rid of all the extra spaces.
    Output = Output + vbCrLf + _
            "Trim Length: " + CStr(Len(Trim(IStr))) + _
            " Value: " + Chr(&H22) + Trim(IStr) +
        Chr(&H22)

    ' Display the result.
    MsgBox Output, vbOKOnly, "Trimming Extra Spaces"
End Sub
```

The program begins by creating a string that has extra spaces on both ends. It then performs four steps to create an output string that demonstrates the various string features. The first step determines the current string length by using the Len function. However, the Len function outputs a number, so the code uses the CStr function to convert the number to a string. Notice how the Len function acts as input to the CStr function. You can *nest* functions like this to produce special effects.

The three function strings work the same. The code first computes the output string size and places it in the Output string. It then removes the excess spaces and places this value into the Output string as well.

Notice that the code uses Chr(&H22) in several places. This function and value produce a double quote. Because VBA uses the double quote to show the beginning and end of a string value, this is one of the few ways that you can add a double quote to your string. In this case, the double quote shows the beginning and end of the string so that you can better see the space removal feature.

Getting the data you need

Strings can contain more information than you actually need or can contain it in a form that you can't use. You might use a string to provide storage for several pieces of information that you need to send to another location. When the string arrives at its destination, the receiving program unpacks the individual data elements from the string.

All these actions rely on some form of *parsing,* which is the act of removing and interpreting sub-elements from a storage element, such as a string. You can create a single string that contains Hello World and separate it into two pieces, Hello and World, by using parsing. A program could store these separate elements and use this technique for various purposes.

The three functions that you use to extract information from a string are Left, Right, and Mid. As their names suggest, you use the first to extract the left side of the string, the second to extract the right side, and the third to extract the middle. These three functions require location information and input on where to start and stop extracting information. You use the InStr and InStrRev functions to find this information. Listing 4-6 shows some of the techniques that you can use to parse a string.

Listing 4-6   Finding Information in Strings by Using Parsing

```
Public Sub ParseString()
    ' Create a string with elements the program can parse.
    Dim Mystr As String

    ' Create an output string.
    Dim output As String
```

```
' Fill the input string with data.
Mystr = "A string to parse"

' Display the whole string.
output = "the whole string is: " + Mystr

' Obtain the first word.
output = output + vbCrLf + "The First Word: " + _
         Left(Mystr, InStr(1, Mystr, " "))

' Obtain the last word.
output = output + vbCrLf + "The Last Word: " + _
         Right(Mystr, Len(Mystr) - InStrRev(Mystr, "
         "))

' Obtain the word string.
    output = output + vbCrLf + "The Word String: " + _
             Trim(Mid(Mystr, _
                      InStr(1, Mystr, "string"), _
                      Len(Mystr) - InStr(1, Mystr,
         "to")))

'Output the result.
    MsgBox output, vbOKOnly, "parsing a String"
End Sub
```

The code begins by creating two variables: one to hold the input data and a second to hold the output data. The input string has a simple phrase that code can parse. The first parsing task is easy: Locate the first word in the phrase. To perform this task, the Left function retrieves text starting at the first character and continuing until the first space. The InStr function returns the position of the first space as a number.

The second parsing task is more complicated. The Right function returns the right end of the string. The InStrRev function returns the number of characters from the beginning of the string to the last space. The Len function returns a value of 17 (the length of the string), and InStrRev returns 12 (the number of characters from the beginning of the string to the last space). The result is 5. Count the number of letters in *Parse* (the last word in the string) — it contains five characters. The Right function returns *Parse* in this case.

The third parsing task is to look for the word *String* in MyStr. The example code shows that you can perform nesting as needed. The nesting begins with the Trim function, which removes any extra characters. The Mid function requires three arguments for this example. The first is the string that you want to work with. The second is the starting position. Notice that the code uses the InStr function, but it searches for *String* and not a space this time. The third is the length of the string. The length of the string is still 17, and the position of *To* within the string is 10, for a total of 7 characters. The 7 characters include the word *String* and the space that follows, which is the reason for using the `Trim` function.

Using numbers for calculations

Numbers form the basis for a lot of the information computers store. You use numbers to perform tasks in a spreadsheet, to express quantities in a database, and to show the current page in a document. Programs also use numbers to count things such as loops, to determine the position of items such as characters in a string, and to check the truth value of a statement. Finally, VBA uses numbers in myriad ways, such as determining which character to display onscreen or how to interact with your code.

Understanding the numeric types

You look at numbers as a single entity — a number is simply a number. The computer views numbers in several different ways. The reason for this diversity of viewpoints is that the processor actually works with different kinds of numbers in different places: one for integer values (those without a decimal point) and another for floating-point values (those with a decimal point). At one time, the math coprocessor that was used to work with money and numbers with decimal points was a separate chip within the computer. Today a single processor performs both integer and floating-point (real) number calculations. The four basic number types include

- **Integer:** This is a number without a decimal. An *integer* can hold any whole number, such as 5, but not a number with a decimal, such as 5.0. Although these two numbers are the same, the first is an integer, and the second isn't.

- **Real:** A *real* number is one that contains a decimal point. The decimal portion doesn't have to contain a value. The number 5.0 is a perfectly acceptable real number. A real number is stored in a completely different format than an integer. (The storage technique only matters to the processor — you don't need to know it to use VBA.)

- **Currency:** Financial calculations usually require special accuracy. Even a small error can cause problems. The *currency* numeric type stores numbers with extreme precision but at an equally large cost in both processing time and memory use.

- **Decimal:** Computers normally store information by using a base 2, or binary, format. You use a base 10, or decimal, format for working with numbers. Small errors can occur when converting from one numbering system to the other and accumulate to create huge errors. The *decimal* numeric system stores numbers in a simulated base 10 format, which eliminates many computing errors. However, this system requires more memory and processing time than any other numeric type.

Computers also determine a numeric type based on the amount of memory that the data requires. VBA supports three integer types, including Byte (1 byte of storage), Integer (2 bytes of storage), and Long (4 bytes of storage). The extra memory stores larger numbers: 0 to 255 for Byte; –32,768 to 32,767 for Integer; and –2,147,483,648 to 2,147,483,647 for Long. See the Data Type Summary help topic for additional details. Listing 4-7 is an example that demonstrates various data types.

Listing 4-7   Demonstrating the Differences in Data Type Ranges

```
Public Sub DataRange()
    ' Declare the numeric variables.
    Dim MyInt As Integer
    Dim MySgl As Single
    Dim MyDbl As Double
    Dim MyCur As Currency
    Dim MyDec As Variant

    ' Define values for each variable.
    MyInt = 30 + 0.00010001000111
    MySgl = 30 + 0.00010001000111
    MyDbl = 30 + 0.00010001000111
    MyCur = 30 + 0.00010001000111
    MyDec = CDec(30 + 0.00010001000111)

    ' Display the actual content.
    MsgBox "Integer:" + TwoTab + CStr(MyInt) + _
            vbCrLf + "Single:" + TwoTab + CStr(MySgl) + _
            vbCrLf + "Double:" + TwoTab + CStr(MyDbl) + _
            vbCrLf + "Currency:" + vbTab + CStr(MyCur) + _
            vbCrLf + "Decimal:" + TwoTab + CStr(MyDec), _
            vbOKOnly, _
            "VBA Data Types"
End Sub
```

The first few variable types use standard declarations. However, notice that you can't declare the decimal data type directly — you must declare it as a Variant in VBA. See the upcoming "Working with variant data" section for more information about the Variant type. The code assigns each variable the same value. Notice that the code must use the CDec function to insert a decimal value into the Variant.

The output shown in Figure 4-3 demonstrates something interesting about the numeric data types. Each type silently dropped any decimal data that it couldn't hold. This is just one of many reasons why you have to carefully consider the numeric data type that you use.

Defining hex and octal values

Using base 10 numbers is natural. You usually don't worry about anything other than base 10 numbers. However, computers use base 2, or binary, numbers. The switch in the circuitry is either on or off — 1 or 0.

Figure 4-3:
Seeing
the actual
content of
the numeric
types
demon-
strates
their range.

Working in binary is quite difficult because even small numbers require many digits. Using either octal (base 8) or hexadecimal (base 16) numbers is easier, so computers group the output of their switches to work in these two bases, even though the computer itself still sees just binary numbers. Both octal (also abbreviated as *oct*) and hexadecimal (also called *hex*) convert directly to base 2. The binary bit positions convert easily to these other two bases, so VBA doesn't even support binary numbers directly.

Generally, the need to work with other bases is obvious. The VBA documentation might provide values in hex for you to use in your program. You might have to convert a number from one base to another because a program supports only a specific base. Your program might also rely on *flags,* which are essentially on or off indicators based on the value of a specific bit within a number.

Most people don't work well with other bases of numbers. We just don't use them often enough. To keep yourself from going crazy, you can use the calculator that comes with Windows. Switch to scientific mode by using the View➪Scientific command. Figure 4-4 shows what the Calculator program looks like. To convert a number by using this program, click the initial base of the number (Hex, Dec, Oct, or Bin), type any number that you need to convert to another base into the input area, and then click the base that you want to see as output. The result is shown in the input area where you typed the original number.

Figure 4-4:
The
Calculator
provides
a fast and
easy method
for
converting
between
numeric
bases.

VBA also provides a number of helpful functions and formatting features that you can use to work with other bases. Listing 4-8 is an example of all these features in action.

Listing 4-8   Converting between Numeric Bases

```
Public Sub ShowBase()
    ' Define the three number bases.
    Dim OctNum As Integer
    Dim DecNum As Integer
    Dim HexNum As Integer

    ' Define an output string.
    Dim Output As String

    ' Assign an octal number.
    OctNum = &O110

    ' Assign a decimal number.
    DecNum = 110

    ' Assign a hexadecimal number.
    HexNum = &H110

    ' Create a heading.
    Output = vbTab + vbTab + vbTab + "Oct" + _
            vbTab + "Dec" + _
            vbTab + "Hex" + vbCrLf

    ' Create an output string.
    Output = Output + "Octal Number:" + _
            vbTab + vbTab + Oct$(OctNum) + _
            vbTab + CStr(OctNum) + _
            vbTab + Hex$(OctNum) + _
            vbCrLf + "Decimal Number:" + _
            vbTab + vbTab + Oct$(DecNum) + _
            vbTab + CStr(DecNum) + _
            vbTab + Hex$(DecNum) + _
            vbCrLf + "Hexadecimal Number:" + _
            vbTab + Oct$(HexNum) + _
            vbTab + CStr(HexNum) + _
            vbTab + Hex$(HexNum)

    ' Display the actual numbers.
    MsgBox Output, _
            vbInformation Or vbOKOnly, _
            "Data Type Output"
End Sub
```

The code begins with three integers. It then assigns values to each of these integers. Notice that the octal number is set by using the &O prefix (that's the letter *O* and not a zero), and the hex number is set by using the &H prefix.

This example also adds a new constant to your list. The vbTab constant adds a tab character to the output string. (See the Visual Basic Constants help topic for a complete list of VBA constants.) Notice that this example provides both a header and some data in the dialog box, which shows how to display data in a tabular format.

Whenever you want to convert a number to a string, you need to use a conversion function. This example shows the three common conversion functions for octal (Oct$), decimal (CStr), and hex (Hex$) numbers. Run this program to see how the functions interact. Notice that you can see the header and each of the numbers in different bases.

Performing conversions between numbers and strings

Most display features, such as the MsgBox function and forms, require strings, even for numbers. When you work with numeric data, you convert the data to a string. The preceding "Defining hex and octal values" section shows some techniques for converting numbers to strings (and vice versa), but this example is only the beginning. Listing 4-9 demonstrates some of the essential string-to-number and number-to-string conversion functions.

Listing 4-9   Converting between Numbers and Strings

```
Public Sub NumberConvert()
    ' Create some variables for use in conversion.
    Dim MyInt As Integer
    Dim MySgl As Single
    Dim MyStr As String

    ' Conversion between Integer and Single is direct
    ' with no data loss.
    MyInt = 30
    MySgl = MyInt
    MsgBox "MyInt = " + CStr(MyInt) + _
        vbCrLf + "MySgl = " + CStr(MySgl), _
        vbOKOnly, _
        "Current Data Values"

    ' Conversion between Single and Integer is also direct
    ' but incurs data loss.
    MySgl = 35.01
    MyInt = MySgl
    MsgBox "MyInt = " + CStr(MyInt) + _
        vbCrLf + "MySgl = " + CStr(MySgl), _
        vbOKOnly, _
        "Current Data Values"

    ' Conversion between a String and a Single or an
    ' Integer can rely on use of a special function. The
    ' conversion can also incur data loss.
    MyStr = "40.05"
```

```
    MyInt = CInt(MyStr)
    MySgl = CSng(MyStr)
    MsgBox "MyInt = " + CStr(MyInt) + _
            vbCrLf + "MySgl = " + CStr(MySgl), _
            vbOKOnly, _
            "Current Data Values"

    ' Conversion between a Single or Integer and a String
    ' can rely on use of a special function when making a
    ' direct conversion. The conversion doesn't incur any
    ' data loss.
    MyInt = 45
    MySgl = 45.05
    MyStr = MyInt
    MsgBox MyStr, _
            vbOKOnly, _
            "Current Data Values"

    ' You must use a special function in mixed data
    ' situations.
    MyStr = "MyInt = " + CStr(MyInt) + _
            vbCrLf + "MySgl = " + CStr(MySgl)
    MsgBox MyStr, _
            vbOKOnly, _
            "Current Data Values"
End Sub
```

The code begins by declaring an Integer, a Single (a real number), and a String. Although the code relies on these three data types, the principles shown apply to any of the data types. Notice that you can perform direct conversion between numeric types without relying on a function. An integer value can always convert to a real number without data loss. Be careful about going the other way, though, because you can run into problems with data loss. The conversion process drops the decimal value but uses proper rounding, as do the CInt and CLng functions.

Conversion from a string to a numeric value might not require the special functions shown in the code. Use the conversion functions, as shown (CInt for Integer conversion and CSng for Single conversion), to ensure that VBA converts the data correctly. Try changing the source code so that it reads MyInt = MyStr — it works as normal in this case, but this behavior isn't guaranteed.

The code also shows that you can assign a numeric value directly to a string as long as that's the only assignment that you make. Always use the correct conversion function when you work with mixed data types. Read the Type Conversion Functions help topic to see other data conversion functions.

Using Boolean values to make decisions

The Boolean type is the easiest to use and understand. This type is used to indicate yes or no, true or false, and on or off. You can use this type to work with any two-state information. It's commonly used to represent data values that are diametrically opposed. Chapter 5 shows how to use Boolean values to make decisions. Listing 4-10 shows several conversion techniques that you can use with Boolean values.

Listing 4-10   Making Decisions with Boolean Values

```
Public Sub BooleanCheck()
    ' Create a Boolean data type.
    Dim MyBool As Boolean

    ' Set MyBool to True
    MyBool = True

    ' Display the native value.
    MsgBox "MyBool = " + CStr(MyBool), _
           vbOKOnly, _
           "Native Value"

    ' Display the numeric value.
    MsgBox "MyBool = " + CStr(CInt(MyBool)), _
           vbOKOnly, _
           "Numeric Value"

    ' Make MyBool equal to a number. Only the number
    ' 0 is False; everything else is True.
    MyBool = CBool(0)
    MsgBox "MyBool = " + CStr(MyBool), _
           vbOKOnly, _
           "Converted Numeric Value"
End Sub
```

The code begins by declaring a Boolean variable and setting its value. As with numeric variables, you can assign a Boolean variable directly to a string as long as that's the only thing that you do. When working in a mixed data type environment, such as the one shown in the code, you must use the appropriate function (such as CStr) to perform the conversion.

The Boolean type isn't numeric — it's logical . . . simply a decision value. You can convert it to a number, as shown in the example code. The value is always –1 for True values and 0 for False values.

VBA also lets you convert a numeric value to a Boolean type by using the CBool function shown in the code. Any value that you store in the Boolean, other than 0, equates to True. Converting the Boolean back to a number still shows –1 for True values and 0 for False.

Using scientific values for math calculations

VBA provides a number of math functions normally used for scientific calculations. You can use the Atn, Cos, Sin, and Tan functions for trigonometric calculations. The Abs and Sgn functions help you work with the sign of a number. Listing 4-11 shows some of the math functions in action.

Listing 4-11 Performing Scientific Calculations

```
Public Sub ScientificCalcs()
    ' Define an input value.
    Dim MyInt As Integer
    MyInt = 45

    ' Create an output string.
    Dim Output As String

    ' Display the trigonometric values for a 45 degree
    ' angle.
    MsgBox "The original angle is: " + CStr(MyInt) + _
            vbCrLf + "Arctangent is: " + CStr(Atn(MyInt)) + _
            vbCrLf + "Cosine is: " + CStr(Cos(MyInt)) + _
            vbCrLf + "Sine is: " + CStr(Sin(MyInt)) + _
            vbCrLf + "Tangent is: " + CStr(Tan(MyInt)), _
            vbOKOnly, _
            "Trigonometric Values"

    ' Change the sign of the number using Sgn and Int.
    ' Add the value to Output each time.
    Output = "The sign of 0 is: " + CStr(Sgn(0))
    MyInt = -45
    Output = Output + vbCrLf + _
            "The sign of " + CStr(MyInt) + " is: " + _
            CStr(Sgn(MyInt))
    MyInt = Abs(MyInt)
    Output = Output + vbCrLf + _
            "The sign of " + CStr(MyInt) + " is: " + _
            CStr(Sgn(MyInt))
    MsgBox Output, vbOKOnly, "Using Sgn and Abs"
End Sub
```

The code begins by defining an input value. The VBA documentation leads you to believe that you can use a Double only as input to the trigonometric functions. This example shows that you can use any numeric type as long as the value that it contains is correct. The code builds an output string for the first message box by using the various trigonometric functions.

The second portion of the example begins by showing the output of the Sgn function when you supply a value of 0. The output is 0 to show that the number is neither positive nor negative. The input value is set to a negative value for the next part of the Output string construction, so the Sgn function returns -1. Finally, the code uses the Abs function to remove the sign from MyInt and calls on Sgn once again to show that the value is indeed positive.

The Math Functions help topic contains more information on the math functions that VBA supports. The Derived Math Functions help topic contains additional examples of how to combine the math functions to produce specific results.

Using currency values for money calculations

Money usually requires special handling on a computer because you don't want to introduce rounding or other errors. Even small incremental errors can result in large errors if they accumulate over time. The Currency data type provides special handling for money calculations but at a slight performance hit because the Currency data type requires additional memory and processing cycles.

Along with the Currency data type, VBA provides a number of special functions for calculating common monetary values. These are the same special functions available to you in your Excel spreadsheet. For example, you still have access to the Pmt function. The main concern when working with monetary values in a VBA program is to ensure that you use the Currency data type as needed. Listing 4-12 shows how the Currency data type and the Pmt function work together.

Listing 4-12   Working with Monetary Values

```
Public Sub ShowPayment()
    ' Create the required variables. All non-monetary
    ' values use the Double type to ensure accuracy. The
    ' monetary values use the Currency data type.
    Dim Rate As Double
    Dim Periods As Double
    Dim PresentValue As Currency
    Dim FutureValue As Currency

    'Calculate the monthly payment on a mortgage.
    Rate = 0.005             ' 6 Percent divided by 12
         Months
    Periods = 60             ' 5 years
    PresentValue = 120000    ' $120,000.00 loan
    MsgBox CStr(Pmt(Rate, Periods, PresentValue)), _
```

```
        vbOKOnly, _
        "Mortgage Output"

    ' Calculate the monthly payments required to build
    ' a savings account to 120000.
    Rate = 0.0025          ' 3 Percent divided by 12
        Months
    Periods = 240          ' 20 years
    PresentValue = -5000   ' $5,000 current savings.
    FutureValue = 120000   ' $120,000.00 savings in 20
        years
    MsgBox CStr(Pmt(Rate, Periods, PresentValue, _
              FutureValue)), _
        vbOKOnly, _
        "Savings Output"
End Sub
```

The code shows two examples. The first determines the minimum amount that you would need to pay each month on a 5-year loan of $120,000.00 compounded at a 6 percent interest rate. The second example shows how much you would need to pay into a savings account each month to have $120,000.00 saved at 20 years when starting with $5,000 in the account and a 3 percent interest rate from the bank. Running the example shows that the mortgage payment is $2,319.94 per month and that the savings rate is $337.79 per month.

Using date and time values

Tracking time and date in your program can be important. Client contact entries in Access usually require the date that the client was last contacted. A spreadsheet might require dates for each entry in a ledger. It's helpful to include dates in Word documents so that you know the last time that someone accessed or changed it. You might need to know how long a task takes or have an indicator of when time has elapsed.

Both date and time variables rely on the Date data type. This data type contains both date and time information. However, you can separate the information as needed. You can also assign date and time independently to the variable by using the Date and Time functions or assign both date and time by using the Now function. These are the same functions that you use to perform this task within a spreadsheet.

As with a spreadsheet, you can work with time values individually. Listing 4-13 demonstrates various time functions. Notice that you can control individual elements, making it easy to change just what you need.

Listing 4-13   Keeping Track of the Time

```
Public Sub ShowTime()
    ' Create a time variable.
    Dim MyTime As Date

    ' Obtain the current time.
    MyTime = Time

    ' Display the hours, minutes, and seconds.
    MsgBox "The current time is: " + _
            vbCrLf + "Hours: " + CStr(Hour(MyTime)) + _
            vbCrLf + "Minutes: " + CStr(Minute(MyTime)) + _
            vbCrLf + "Seconds: " + CStr(Second(MyTime)), _
            vbOKOnly, _
            "Current Time"
End Sub
```

VBA provides access to the whole time value by using the Time function.
You can also use the Hour, Minute, and Second functions for specific information. Not shown in the example is how you can set the current time by
using Time on a line by itself and supplying a time value such as Time =
#1:0:0# (for 1 a.m.). In this case, Time acts as a property rather than as a
statement and accepts input in any valid format, such as #1 PM# for 1 p.m.
(or 1300 military time). Notice that time and date values always appear
within the # symbol rather than with the double quotes used for strings.

Using dates is similar to using time in a program. Listing 4-14 demonstrates
that you can use the Date function directly instead of placing the information
in a variable. The listing also shows how to set the date (provided that you
have sufficient security rights on the workstation that you use).

Listing 4-14   Displaying Date Values

```
Public Sub ShowDate()
    ' Create a date variable.
    Dim MyDate As Date

    ' Obtain the current date.
    MyDate = Date

    ' Set the date.
    Date = #1/1/1980#

    ' Display the Day, Month, and Year.
    MsgBox "The current date is (DD/MM/YYYY): " + _
            CStr(Day(Date)) + "/" + _
            CStr(Month(Date)) + "/" + _
            CStr(Year(Date)), _
            vbOKCancel, _
            "Modified Date"
```

```
    ' Reset the date.
    Date = MyDate

    ' Display the Day, Month, and Year.
    MsgBox "The current date is (DD/MM/YYYY): " + _
           CStr(Day(MyDate)) + "/" + _
           CStr(Month(MyDate)) + "/" + _
           CStr(Year(MyDate)), _
           vbOKCancel, _
           "Actual Date"
End Sub
```

The code begins by creating `MyDate` and using it to store the current date information. The next step is to change the date by using `Date` as a property. As when you're using `Time`, you can modify `Date` by using any valid date format. You must have sufficient security to perform this task. If the program fails, ask your network administrator whether you have time- and date-setting privileges. The code creates a message box to demonstrate that the date change actually occurred. You can verify this change by looking at the clock area of the Taskbar Notification area.

After you click OK, the code continues by resetting the date to its original value. Again, the code displays a message box to show that the change has actually occurred. Notice how the code relies on the `Day`, `Month`, and `Year` functions to display both message boxes.

Working with variant data

The earlier "Understanding the numeric types" section demonstrates one use of the `Variant` data type: A `Variant` can hold any data type, including objects. The earlier "Adding strings together with + or &" section shows another use of the `Variant` data type: `Variant` variables can hold nothing (a null value) or a string. A program can use a `Variant` when VBA doesn't provide direct support for a data type (such as the `Decimal` type); when the type of information that the program user will provide is unknown when you write the program; or when the native data type doesn't support a certain kind of storage, such as a null string. In short, a `Variant` is the universal data type for VBA.

VBA does track the data type of the `Variant` variables that you create. In Chapter 6, I demonstrate how you can see this information while debugging the program. The data type names begin with `Variant` and end with the native data type. Thus, a `Date` stored in a `Variant` would appear as a `VariantDate` data type.

You can also use the Variant type as a means for data conversion. Place a date within a Variant, such as 1/1/80, and you can convert it to a String or an Integer. The Integer value for this date normally appears as 29221 when using the default Windows settings. You can use the Integer value as input to the Date function to convert the number back into a Date and then place the result back into the Variant.

About now, you may think that the Variant data type is the best data type to use for all situations, and it's definitely the right choice in many situations. However, all of the added functionality that the Variant data type supports comes with a price. Variant variables consume more memory than any other data type because the Variant data type must support all data types equally well. In addition, the Variant data type slows application performance because VBA must first discover how to interact with the Variant variable. Because a Variant variable is essentially undefined, you'll also find it harder to debug applications that use them, and the VBA automation won't work as well with Variant variables. Many security problems that you could locate using other data types are completely hidden when using Variant variables because the data type plays a part in making your applications more secure (for example, you can't place a string in a number). In short, the Variant data type does solve a host of problems, but adds a significant number of problems of its own.

Presenting data in a pleasing format

Most programs can use the default formatting that VBA provides for output. However, you might need some way to present the data in another way, such as a short or long date (04/24/06 or 24 April 2006). It's important to know how to format data so that you can create astounding reports and concise analysis.

Using the Format function

The Format function is the most common way to change the appearance of data. This function accepts any valid expression as input. You can also supply an expression that defines how to format the data. The Named Date/Time Formats help topic describes predefined formats for date and time, and the Named Numeric Formats help topic describes numeric formats. Listing 4-15 demonstrates some of the common, named formats for time and date.

Listing 4-15   Changing the Format of a Date

```
Public Sub FormatDemo()
    ' Create the date variable.
    Dim MyDate As Date
```

```
        ' Fill MyDate with the current date and time.
        MyDate = Now

        ' Display the date using standard formats.
        MsgBox "Standard Format =" + vbTab + CStr(MyDate) + _
               vbCrLf + "Long Date =" + vbTab + _
               Format(MyDate, "Long Date") + _
               vbCrLf + "Short Time =" + vbTab + _
               Format(MyDate, "Short Time"), _
               vbOKOnly, _
               "VBA Named Formats"
End Sub
```

The program displays the standard date/time format, the long date format, and the short time format. You get the raw format by using the `CStr` function. The `Format` function requires the `MyDate` variable and a string containing the named format as input.

Creating custom formatting

Named formats don't always provide the output that you need. In these cases, you can create your own formatting by using custom strings. The elements of these strings are described in three help topics: User-Defined Date/Time Formats, User-Defined Numeric Formats, and User-Defined String Formats. (Press F1 in the VBA IDE to access help.) Listing 4-16 shows how you can create a custom date-and-time string.

Listing 4-16   Defining a Custom Date Format

```
Public Sub CustomFormatDemo()
    ' Create the date variable.
    Dim MyDate As Date

    ' Fill MyDate with the current date and time.
    MyDate = Now

    ' Display the date using standard formats.
    MsgBox "Custom Date/Time = " + _
           Format(MyDate, "dd mmmm yyyy Hh:Nn:Ss"), _
           vbOKOnly, _
           "VBA Custom Formats"
End Sub
```

The essential difference in this example is the string input for the `Format` function. This example tells VBA that you want a date/time display that uses a day with a leading 0, the full month name, and a four-digit year. The time appears as hours, minutes, and seconds — all of which have a leading 0 when needed.

Working with other formatting functions

VBA provides four custom formatting functions: `FormatNumber`, `FormatDateTime`, `FormatCurrency`, and `FormatPercent`. These functions don't do anything that you can't do with the `Format` function. The reasons why some VBA users rely on these functions is that their names make clearer the purpose of the formatting and using them requires less typing.

All four functions return a string, just like the `Format` function. The only input that you must provide is the expression that you want formatted. The default settings return a formatting string that relies on the regional settings that the user has set for the computer. You can override these settings by specifying the optional arguments provided for each function.

Working with Operators

Operators determine how VBA works with two variables and what result it produces. The examples in this chapter use operators to add numbers and *concatenate* (add) strings. In both cases, your code uses the + operator to perform the task. However, the result differs. When you're using numbers, the result is a summation, such as `1 + 2 = 3`. When you're using strings, the result is a concatenation, such as `Hello + World = Hello World`. VBA groups operators into four areas:

- **Arithmetic:** Operators that perform math operations, such as addition (+), subtraction (−), division (/), and multiplication (*)

- **Comparison:** Operators such as less than (<), greater than (>), and equal (=) that compare two values and produce a Boolean result

- **Concatenation:** Operators such as & and + that are used to add two strings together

- **Logical:** Operators such as `Not`, `And`, `Or`, and `Xor` that are used to perform Boolean operations on two variables

The Operator Summary help topic explains in detail each of these operator categories and the associated operators. The examples in this book demonstrate how to use the various operators, such as the + (plus) operator, shown in Listing 4-15.

VBA also assigns operators a *precedence,* or order of use. When your code contains the equation `MyVal = 1 + 2 * 3`, VBA performs the multiplication first and then the addition to receive a value of 7 because multiplication has a higher precedence than addition. However, the equation `MyVal = (1 + 2) * 3` has a result of 9 because parentheses have a higher precedence than multiplication. The rules that VBA uses for precedence are the same rules that you learned in math class. See the Operator Precedence help topic for more information.

Applying What You Know to Design an Excel Report

All the examples up to this point in the book have worked with abstract (or demonstration) code. *Abstract code* is practical for presenting concepts, but you wouldn't actually add it to a document because it doesn't perform useful work. The reason that you use VBA is to accomplish useful work.

The example in this section relies on code to create an Excel report. You begin by typing the entries shown in Figure 4-5. These entries serve as a basis for the report.

The report contains data entries. It also has a summary when the code executes. Listing 4-17 provides the code to use.

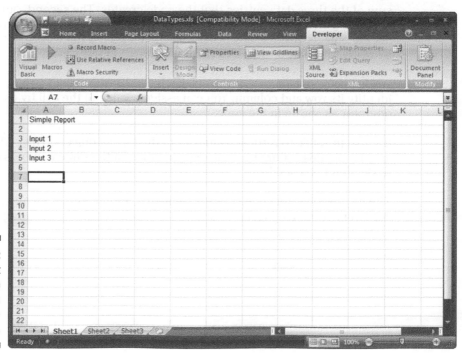

Figure 4-5:
The report example begins with a few simple entries.

Listing 4-17 Designing an Excel Report

```
Public Sub CreateReport()
    ' Create some output variables.
    Dim DataSum As Integer
    Dim Output As String

    ' Begin by adding data to the report.
    Sheet1.Cells(3, 2) = 1
    Sheet1.Cells(4, 2) = 2
    Sheet1.Cells(5, 2) = 3

    ' Create a sum of the cell content.
    DataSum = Sheet1.Cells(3, 2) + _
              Sheet1.Cells(4, 2) + _
              Sheet1.Cells(5, 2)

    ' Create an output string.
    Output = "The sum of the three numbers is: " + _
             CStr(DataSum)

    Sheet1.Cells(7, 1) = Output
End Sub
```

The code begins by declaring two variables. The first, DataSum, holds the sum of the three data entries that the code creates. The second, Output, contains a string that holds the report summary. The worksheets in an Excel file are objects, just like any other object. You access the worksheet objects by using the name assigned to them — Sheet1 in this case.

Worksheets contain Cells objects. Each Cells object uses two numbers to identify its row and column. You can assign a value to the cell by using the = operator as shown in the code.

It's also possible to retrieve values from the Cells objects. The code shows how to use this feature to create a summation of the three numbers entered as data on the worksheet.

The last two lines of code create a summary statement that includes the summation in DataSum. Figure 4-6 shows the result of running this program.

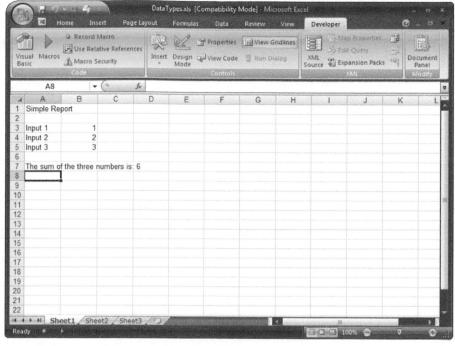

Figure 4-6:
The Excel
report is
simple but
demon-
strates that
you know
enough to
perform
simple
tasks.

Chapter 5

Creating Structured Programs

● ●

In This Chapter

▶ Using the `If...Then` statement

▶ Using the `Select Case` statement

▶ Using `Do` loops

▶ Using `For Next` loops

▶ Using the `GoTo` statement

● ●

*S*tructures help organize your VBA code so that it can perform more tasks more efficiently. Special *statements* can help organize the code so that it accomplishes tasks based on decisions or performs the same task multiple times. In this chapter, I demonstrate how to use the special statements used to make decisions, perform tasks more than once, or redirect control to another area of the program. The result of using these statements is increased program structure, which makes controlling program execution easier.

These statements also improve program flexibility. A program that uses the right statements can perform a wider variety of tasks and take into account outside conditions, such as the day of the week or the current state of the computer. Statements that control program flow are essential to writing programs that need less input from you and perform more tasks automatically. For example, VBA can help you create Word documents that automatically reflect special days, such as a business anniversary, or Excel reports where VBA automatically tracks business quarters.

Exercising Control with Structures

Few programs use all the statements in the program file all the time. You might want the program to perform one task when you click Yes and another task when you click No. The statements for both tasks appear in the code, but the program executes only one set of statements.

To control program execution, the developer adds special statements — such as the If...Then statement — that show the beginning and end of each task and also decide which task to execute. You might think that letting the computer decide which task to execute would cause the developer to lose control of the program. However, the developer hasn't lost control of the program, because the decision-making process is predefined as part of the program design.

Most developers refer to the beginning and ending statements for a task as a *control structure* because the statement combination adds control to a program. When you see the If...Then statement with its accompanying End If statement in code, the two statements combine to form an If...Then structure.

Because the program contains more than one task, it has more than one path of execution. When you add control structures, the number of execution paths increases exponentially. For example, a program with one control structure has two paths of execution, but a program with two control structures has four paths. As you can imagine, the task of debugging the application becomes harder when you add control structures, so designing your program carefully is important.

You can also *nest* control structures. A program might require multiple decision points to address a specific need. For example, the program might need to decide whether you requested an apple or an orange. When you select an apple, the program then might have to decide between a yellow, green, or red apple. The program can't make the second decision without the first, so the second decision is nested within the first.

Making a Decision with the If...Then Statement

Most programs require decision-making code. When you need to make the same decision every time that you perform a task and the outcome of the decision is always the same, then making the decision is something that you can tell VBA to do for you by using the If...Then statement. Decision-making code has several benefits:

- ✔ **Consistency:** The decision is made by using the same criteria and in the same manner every time.

- ✔ **Speed:** A computer can make static decisions faster than humans can. However, the decision must be the same every time, and the decision must have the same answer set every time.

✔ **Complexity:** Requesting that the computer make static decisions can reduce program complexity. Fewer decisions translate into ease of use for most people.

All forms of `If...Then` statements can use any expression that equates to a Boolean value, including a variable of the `Boolean` data type. The term *expression* refers to any equation or variable that VBA can interpret as a means of determining when it should perform the tasks within the `If...Then` structure. The expression `2 > 1` is true, so VBA would perform the tasks within the `If...Then` structure. You can also use variables for an expression such as `A = B`. Anything that equates to a Boolean value can be used as an expression for the `If...Then` statement.

Using the If...Then statement

The `If...Then` statement is the simplest form of decision-making code. This statement tells VBA to perform a task if a condition is true. If the condition isn't true, VBA ignores the statements within the `If...Then` structure.

The example in this section checks the highlighted text in a document. To test the `If...Then` statement in VBA, create a Word document. Type **Hello**, press Enter, and then type **Goodbye**. Then double-click the word *Hello* to select the text. The code in Listing 5-1 shows how a simple `If...Then` statement works. (You can find the source code for this example on the Dummies.com site at `http://www.dummies.com/go/vbafd5e`.)

Listing 5-1   Using an If...Then Statement for Decisions

```
Public Sub IfThenTest()
    ' Create a variable for the selected text.
    Dim TestText As String

    ' Get the current selection.
    TestText = ActiveWindow.Selection.Text

    ' Test the selection for "Hello."
    If TestText = "Hello" Then

        ' Modify the selected text to show it's correct.
        TestText = "Correct!" + vbCrLf + "Hello"
    End If

    ' Test the selection for end of line.
    If TestText = Chr(13) Then

        ' Modify the selected text to show the control
```

(continued)

Listing 5-1 *(continued)*

```
        ' character.
        TestText = "End of line selected!"
    End If

    ' Test the selection for a space.
    If TestText = Chr(32) Then

        ' Modify the selected text to show the space.
        TestText = "Space selected!"
    End If

    ' Display the selected text.
    MsgBox TestText
End Sub
```

The code begins by creating a variable to hold the selected text. It then shows how to use a new object, `ActiveWindow`. The `ActiveWindow` object is useful for a number of tasks, but in this case you use it to get hold of the selected text, if any. If you don't have any text selected, the resulting message box may simply display an OK button without any additional information.

The first `If...Then` structure determines whether you select the word *Hello*. If so, the statement `TestText = "Correct!" + vbCrLf + "Hello"` executes. Otherwise, VBA ignores the statement and moves on to the next test.

The second `If...Then` structure determines whether the cursor is at the end of the line. This test tells you two things about selections. First, VBA always sees at least one character selected. If you haven't selected anything, `ActiveWindow.Selection.Text` returns the next character in line. Second, the `vbCrLf` constant does have two control characters in it. The code tests for `Chr(13)` or a carriage return because that's always the first character in the `vbCrLf` sequence. If you set the cursor at the end of the line, VBA modifies `TestText` as shown in the code.

The third `If...Then` structure checks for a space. Although it isn't always essential to check for spaces, in this case viewers will see a blank dialog box when they place the cursor immediately before a space in the line of text. Making this additional check reduces the risk that the user will see something unexpected. You should always try to include checks such as this one in your code. Unfortunately, you won't always find all of these difficult scenarios immediately, which is why you should ask other people to check your applications for potential problems.

The final line of code shows whatever `TestText` contains. Unless you select *Hello* or the end of the line, the message box contains the selected text. Try out the example code by using various selections, or set the cursor at the end of the line, and you can see the usefulness of this feature.

Using the If...Then...Else statement

The `If...Then...Else` statement makes one of two choices. If the expression controlling the statement is true, VBA executes the first set of statements. On the other hand, if the expression is false, VBA executes the second set of statements.

The example in this section determines whether two numbers are equal or whether one is greater than the other. To test the `If...Then...Else` statement, create a new Excel worksheet. The code relies on input from the worksheet for test purposes. Figure 5-1 shows the setup and some sample input.

The code used for this example makes three checks: equal to, greater than, and less than. Listing 5-2 shows the code that you need in order to make these three checks. (You can find the source code for this example on the Dummies.com site at `http://www.dummies.com/go/vbafd5e`.)

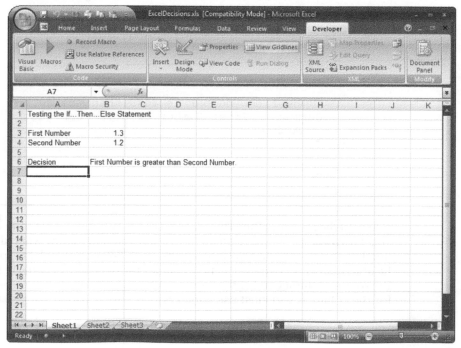

Figure 5-1: Use this worksheet to compare the value of two numbers.

Listing 5-2   Using the If...Then...Else Statement for Comparisons

```
Public Sub CompareNumbers()
    ' Create variables to hold the two numbers.
    Dim Input1 As Double
    Dim Input2 As Double

    ' Create an output string.
    Dim Output As String

    ' Fill the variables with input from the worksheet.
    Input1 = Sheet1.Cells(3, 2)
    Input2 = Sheet1.Cells(4, 2)

    ' Determine if the first number is greater than or
    ' equal to the second number.
    If Input1 >= Input2 Then

        ' Determine if they are equal.
        If Input1 = Input2 Then

            ' Tell the user they are equal.
            Output = "The values are equal."

        Else

            ' The first number must be greater than the
            ' second.
            Output = "First Number is greater than " + _
                    "Second Number."

        End If

    Else

        ' The first number is less than the second.
        Output = "First Number is less than Second
            Number."

    End If

    ' Place the output on the worksheet.
    Sheet1.Cells(6, 2) = Output
End Sub
```

The code begins by getting the contents of the two input cells from the work-sheet. Always use a `Double` data type when you don't know what kind of number that you might type into a worksheet, because this data type is more flexible than an `Integer`. The first number for the `Cells` property is always the row, and the second is the column. Although the worksheet uses letters for the columns, you must use numbers.

You might find it confusing to continually convert between column letters and numbers when working with large worksheets. To avoid this problem, you can define global constants with the numbers. A Column_A constant would equal 1 and so on. Using this technique can make your code easier to read when you use large worksheets.

The first If...Then statement checks whether the first number is greater than or equal to the second. You might wonder why the code doesn't simply check for equality. Using this technique reduces the amount of code that you have to write. Notice that the second If...Then statement immediately chooses between equality and greater than. It relies on a nested If...Then...Else structure to choose between two values for the Output string. This is a good example of how to use nesting within your programs.

If the first If...Then statement is false, the Else statement immediately executes. Notice how the use of nesting saves VBA two checks. When you use individual If...Then statements, VBA must make three decisions every time that it compares the two numbers. Using the nested If...Then...Else structure shown in the code reduces the number of decisions to one.

The final line of code outputs the comparison results to the worksheet. Try various numbers, and you can see how the nested decision technique works.

Using the If...Then...ElseIf statement

When making multiple comparisons, you can use the If...Then...ElseIf statement to make the code easier to read. Using this format can also reduce the number of decisions that VBA must make, which ensures that your code runs as quickly as possible. Listing 5-3 shows an alternative form of the example in the preceding "Using the If...Then...Else statement" section. (You can find the source code for this example on the Dummies.com site at http://www.dummies.com/go/vbafd5e.)

Listing 5-3   Using the If...Then...ElseIf Statement for Comparisons

```
Public Sub CompareNumbers2()
    ' Create variables to hold the two numbers.
    Dim Input1 As Double
    Dim Input2 As Double

    ' Create an output string.
    Dim Output As String

    ' Fill the variables with input from the worksheet.
```

(continued)

Listing 5-3 *(continued)*

```
    Input1 = Sheet1.Cells(3, 2)
    Input2 = Sheet1.Cells(4, 2)

    ' Determine if the first number is greater than
    ' the second number.
    If Input1 > Input2 Then

        ' Tell the user the first number is greater.
        Output = "First Number is greater than " + _
                "Second Number."

    ' Determine if they are equal.
    ElseIf Input1 = Input2 Then

        ' Tell the user they are equal.
        Output = "The values are equal."

    Else

        ' The first number is less than the second.
        Output = "First Number is less than Second
            Number."
    End If

    ' Place the output on the worksheet.
    Sheet1.Cells(6, 2) = Output
End Sub
```

The first thing that you should notice is that this code avoids nesting, which makes it easier to read. VBA will see the first If...Then statement and determine whether Input1 is greater than Input2. If the first statement is true, VBA sets the value of Output and leaves the structure. However, if the first statement is false, VBA checks the ElseIf statement. Finally, if the first two statements are false, VBA executes the statements within the Else part of the structure. You can use as many ElseIf statements as you need to check every possible condition in your code.

This code is almost as efficient as the first version — it requires just one decision for greater than, two for equality, and three for less than. The ease of reading might become more important to you when the complexity of your programs increases, so this is a perfectly acceptable way to write your code. In short, this example demonstrates that there's usually more than one way to write a program, many of which work fine; the choice of which method to use depends on your personal tastes.

Using the IIf function

You might need to make a decision in a single line of code instead of the three lines (minimum) that other decision-making techniques require. The IIf function is a good choice when you need to make simple and concise decisions in your program. It has the advantage of providing decision-making capability in a single line of code. Listing 5-4 shows an example of the IIf function in action. (You can find the source code for this example on the Dummies.com site at http://www.dummies.com/go/vbafd5e.)

Listing 5-4   Using IIf to Make Inline Decisions

```
Public Sub IIfDemo()
    ' Create variables to hold the two numbers.
    Dim Input1 As Double
    Dim Input2 As Double

    ' Create an output string.
    Dim Output As String

    ' Fill the variables with input from the worksheet.
    Input1 = Sheet1.Cells(3, 2)
    Input2 = Sheet1.Cells(4, 2)

    ' Use nested IIf functions to check all three
    ' conditions.
    Output = IIf(Input1 = Input2, _
                "The values are equal.", _
                IIf(Input1 > Input2, _
                    "First Number is greater.", _
                    "Second Number is greater."))

    ' Place the output on the worksheet.
    Sheet1.Cells(6, 2) = Output
End Sub
```

This example begins by getting the input from the worksheet. It also creates an Output string.

The IIf function requires three arguments, none of which is optional. The first argument is an expression. The second is a single-line statement of what to do if the expression is true, and the third is a single-line statement of what to do if the expression is false.

The first IIf function determines whether Input1 is equal to Input2. If the expression is true, the first IIf function returns The values are equal. to Output. Otherwise, the first IIf function calls the second IIf function.

The second IIf function determines whether Input1 is greater than Input2. If it is, the second IIf function returns First Number is greater. to the first IIf function, which returns it to Output. Likewise, if the expression is false, the second IIf function returns Second Number is greater.

You can see that this technique could easily become impossible to read and is nearly impossible to comment. However, it uses only one line of code. The nearest contender appears in the preceding "Using the If...Then...ElseIf statement" section and requires seven lines of code.

Making a Choice by Using the Select Case Statement

You can use the If...Then...Else or If...Then...ElseIf statement to meet all decision-making needs. However, using these statements can quickly make your code hard to read when you need to make a lot of decisions in rapid succession. Using these statements is required when you want to perform complex expression checking. VBA provides the Select Case statement as an easier-to-read choice when making a single selection from a list of choices. If you know that a variable contains one of several choices and all you need to check is the choice, using the Select Case statement makes sense.

Using the Select Case statement

The Select Case structure begins with the Select Case statement and ends with an End Case statement. You provide a variable that the Select Case statement can use for selection. Within the Select Case structure are Case *clauses,* or values that the Select Case structure uses for comparison. When the value of a clause matches the value of the input variable, the Select Case structure performs all tasks required by that clause.

In this section, I use examples of the Select Case statement to make a choice of which room to use to store a product. You could easily make this example into a database program, but this section uses a spreadsheet for ease of explanation. Figure 5-2 shows the two input columns used for this example along with typical output in the third column.

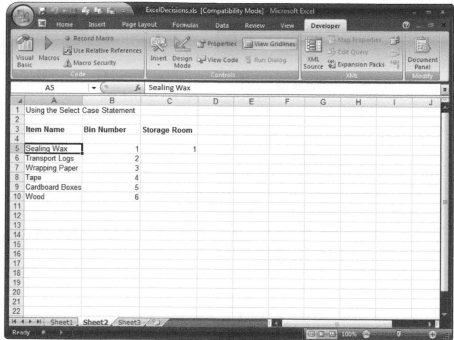

Figure 5-2:
Make a
choice by
using this
worksheet
and its
associated
program.

This decision-making process uses the Bin Number column as input to a
Select Case structure. Each clause assigns a number based on a particular
number or a range of numbers. Listing 5-5 shows the code that you need in
order to make the choices. (You can find the source code for this example on
the Dummies.com site at http://www.dummies.com/go/vbafd5e.)

Listing 5-5   Using a Select Case Statement for Multiple Decisions

```
Public Sub MakeChoice()
    Dim CursorPosition  As Integer   ' Current row
            selection.
    Dim BinValue As Integer          ' Bin for selected
            row.
    Dim Output As Integer            ' Storage room number.

    ' Determine if the user has selected more than one
    ' row.
    If ActiveWindow.RangeSelection.Rows.Count = 1 Then

        ' Get the cursor position.
```

(continued)

Listing 5-5 *(continued)*

```
        CursorPosition = ActiveWindow.RangeSelection.Row
    Else

        ' Tell the user to select only one cell.
        MsgBox "Select only one cell!", _
               vbExclamation Or vbOKOnly, _
               "Selection Error"

        ' Exit the Sub without further processing.
        End
    End If

    ' Get the selected bin number.
    BinValue = Sheet2.Cells(CursorPosition, 2)

    ' Select a choice of storage room based in the bin.
    Select Case BinValue
        Case 1
            Output = 1
        Case 2
            Output = 2
        Case 3 To 4
            Output = 1
        Case 5 To 6
            Output = 3
    End Select

    ' Store the number in the worksheet.
    Sheet2.Cells(CursorPosition, 3) = Output
End Sub
```

This example demonstrates some new techniques. The code begins by checking the number of rows that you select. If you select only one row, the code retrieves this value by using the `ActiveWindow.RangeSelection.Row` property. You can also get hold of the column number by using the `Column` property, or the row and column by using the `Address` property.

When you select more than one row, it's hard for the program to know which row to work with. The code displays an error message and then exits without performing further processing by using the `End` statement. This is the first time that you've used *error trapping* in a program, which means figuring out that an error will happen before it can cause problems. See Chapter 6 for more information on debugging and error trapping.

The next step is to retrieve the Bin Number entry by using the row information contained in `CursorPosition`. The `BinValue` variable acts as input to the `Select Case` statement. Notice how this statement uses `Case` clauses to determine which action to take. You can provide a single value, a range of values, or a list of values separated as commas. The final step is to place the `Output` value in the worksheet.

Using the Case Else clause

A `Select Case` statement should normally contain the optional `Case Else` clause to ensure that you handle all cases, even those that you don't expect when you write the program. Adding this clause requires little time and adds an important error-trapping feature to your program. You could easily change the program from the previous section to include a `Select Case` statement like the one shown in Listing 5-6. (You can find the source code for this example on the Dummies.com site at `http://www.dummies.com/go/vbafd5e`.)

Listing 5-6   Handling Unforeseen Decisions with Case Else

```
' Select a choice of storage room based in the bin.
Select Case BinValue
    Case 1
        Output = 1
    Case 2
        Output = 2
    Case 3 To 4
        Output = 1
    Case 5 To 6
        Output = 3
    Case Else
        ' Tell the user to select only one cell.
        MsgBox "Provide a Bin Number between 1 and 6", _
               vbExclamation Or vbOKOnly, _
               "Bin Number Input Error"

        ' Exit the Sub without further processing.
        End
End Select
```

The older version of the code could cause problems when you type a non-existent bin number. This version provides an error message telling you what range of numbers to use. It exits before the code has a chance to create an error condition.

Performing a Task More than Once by Using Loops

Many tasks that you perform require more than one check, change, or data manipulation. You don't change just one entry in a worksheet; you change all the affected entries. Likewise, you don't change just one word in a document; you might change all occurrences based on certain criteria. Databases require multiple changes for almost any task.

Loops provide a method for performing tasks more than one time. You can use loops to save code-writing time. Simply write the code to perform the repetitive task once and then tell VBA to perform the task multiple times.

When using loops, you decide how the code determines when to stop. You can tell the loop to execute a specific number of times or to continue executing until the program meets a certain condition.

Using the Do While...Loop statement

A `Do While...Loop` statement keeps performing a task until a certain condition is true. The loop checks the expression first and then executes the code within the structure if the expression is true. You use this loop to perform processing zero or more times. A `Do While...Loop` works especially well if you can't determine the number of times that the loop should execute when you design your program.

One example of a file that could require zero or more changes is a Word document. You might need to format certain words in a specific way for each file, but you have no idea which words you'll use or whether you'll use them at all. The code in Listing 5-7 shows a technique for checking specific words and formatting them. You could easily adapt this program to meet your formatting needs. (You can find the source code for this example on the Dummies.com site at `http://www.dummies.com/go/vbafd5e`.)

Listing 5-7   Modifying Words by Using a Do While...Loop Statement

```
Public Sub ChangeWords()
    Dim CurrentWord As Long ' Current word selection.
    Dim TotalWords As Long  ' Total number of words

    ' Get the total number of words.
```

```
        TotalWords = ActiveDocument.Words.Count

        ' Select the first word in the document.
        ActiveDocument.Words(1).Select
        CurrentWord = 1

        ' Keep selecting words until we run out.
        Do While CurrentWord < TotalWords

            ' Make a change based on the word.
            Select Case Trim(ActiveWindow.Selection.Text)
                Case "Hello"
                    Selection.Font.Italic = True
                Case "Goodbye"
                    Selection.Font.Bold = True
                Case "Yes"
                    Selection.Font.Color = wdColorGreen
                Case "No"
                    Selection.Font.Color = wdColorRed
            End Select

            ' Move to the next word.
            CurrentWord = CurrentWord + 1
            ActiveDocument.Words(CurrentWord).Select
        Loop
End Sub
```

The code begins by getting the word count for the active document — the one currently selected for editing. The program uses this number to determine when to stop making changes. The `ActiveDocument.Words` document has a number of other interesting uses (such as those shown in the example code), so you should keep it in mind when working with Word.

The next task is to select the first word in the document. You do this by telling `ActiveDocument.Words` which word to select and then using the `Select` method as shown. It's also important to keep track of the current word selection, so the code sets `CurrentWord` to 1. This variable uses the `Long` data type because `ActiveDocument.Words.Count` can return a `Long` value. VBA won't tell you whether you use the wrong data type — you must verify the data type needs by viewing the return data type from method calls and properties.

The `Do While...Loop` structure compares the `CurrentWord` value with the `TotalWords` value. If `CurrentWord` is less than `TotalWords`, it executes the statements contained within the structure.

Notice how the code uses a `Select Case` statement to choose between word choices. This `Select Case` statement also lacks a `Case Else` clause because it doesn't rely on user input. This is one example where the `Case Else` clause can't contribute anything to error trapping or default processing. This example also introduces techniques for modifying the font characteristics of text in a document.

The next two lines of code are especially important. First, the code updates `CurrentWord`. You must do this, or else the loop will continue forever because `CurrentWord` is always less than `TotalWords`. Not updating the `CurrentWord` value results in an endless loop — a common source of bugs in programming code. The second statement moves the selection to the next word in the document by using the updated `CurrentWord` value. Note the order of the statements. You must update `CurrentWord` first and then move to the next word in the text. Figure 5-3 shows the document used to test this program with the interesting formatting in place.

Using the Do...Loop While statement

The `Do...Loop While` statement works the same as the `Do While...Loop` statement. The difference is that this statement always executes once because the expression used to verify a need to loop appears at the end of the structure. Even if the expression is false, this statement still executes at least one time. You can use this statement when you want to ensure that a task is always completed at least one time.

Using the Do Until...Loop statement

The `Do Until...Loop` statement continues processing information until the expression is false. You can view the `Do While...Loop` statement as a loop that continues while a task is incomplete. The `Do Until...Loop` statement continues until the task is finished. The subtle difference between the two statements points out something interesting: They rely on your perspective of the task to complete. These two statement types are completely interchangeable. The big difference is how you define the expression used to signal the end of the looping sequence.

Using the Do...Loop Until statement

The `Do...Loop Until` statement is the counterpart of the `Do Until...Loop` statement. This statement examines the expression at the end of the loop, so it always executes at least once even if the expression is false.

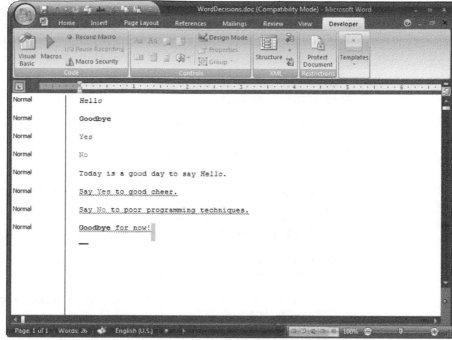

Figure 5-3:
Create
programs
that help
you perform
repetitive
tasks,
such as
formatting
text.

Using the For...Next statement

The For...Next statement is very handy for performing a task a specific number of times. As long as you can determine how many times to do something in advance, this is the best looping option to use because there's less chance of creating an infinite loop. You can create absurdly large loops, but they eventually end.

The Sub created in the earlier section "Using the Select Case statement" and augmented in other areas of this chapter works fine for determining the storage room for a single entry. Figure 5-2 shows multiple entries, however, so creating a method for processing all of them would make it easier to assign storage rooms to a new worksheet. The code shown in Listing 5-8 does just that — it makes changing all rows possible with a single program execution. (You can find the source code for this example on the Dummies.com site at http://www.dummies.com/go/vbafd5e.)

Listing 5-8   Changing Datasheets with the For...Next Statement

```
Public Sub ChangeAllRooms()
    Dim ActiveRows As Integer     ' Number of active rows.
    Dim Counter As Integer        ' Current row in process.

    ' Select the first data cell in the worksheet.
    Range("A5").Select

    ' Use SendKeys to select all of the cells in the
    ' column.
    SendKeys "+^{DOWN}", True

    ' Get the number of rows to process.
    ActiveRows = ActiveWindow.RangeSelection.Rows.Count

    ' Reset the cell pointer.
    Range("C5").Select

    ' Keep processing the cells until complete.
    For Counter = 5 To ActiveRows + 5

        ' Call the Sub created to change a single cell.
        MakeChoice3

        ' Move to the next cell.
        Range("C" + CStr(Counter)).Select
    Next
End Sub
```

The SendKeys function works with the active window. Unlike with many of the other examples in this book, you must run this example from the Excel worksheet. Make sure that the Excel worksheet is open, open the Macro dialog box by clicking Macros on the Ribbon or choosing Tools⇨Macro⇨Macros, highlight ChangeAllRooms, and click Run. If you run this particular macro from within the Visual Basic Editor, you'll experience an error.

Of course, the need to run the macro in the active window begs the question of how to debug a macro that has this particular problem. You'll run into it relatively often when a macro has to perform tasks with the active window but could just as easily perform the task in the Visual Basic Editor. You need to use two techniques in this case. First, never set breakpoints on the SendKeys function. Second, use message boxes as often as possible to report the content of variables and potential errors.

This example shows several new functions that you can use. The code begins by selecting the first data row in the worksheet. This selection is important because you want to start at the very beginning of the entries.

The `SendKeys` function call comes next. This function is interesting because it helps you duplicate keystrokes that you normally make in the worksheet using code. The advantage of this method is that after you get used to the special characters, you can make writing a program very similar to using the program normally. This example sends a Shift (+), Ctrl (^), down-arrow (+^{DOWN}) sequence to the worksheet to select the entire column. The SendKeys Statement help topic provides full documentation of this function. You can also find other `SendKeys` examples in other parts of this book.

The `SendKeys` function is extremely useful. However, don't use it in place of functions that VBA supplies for specific tasks. Using `SendKeys` can make your code difficult to read and can also slow execution of the program.

By using the `ActiveWindow.RangeSelection.Rows.Count` property, the code determines how many rows it must process. The code places this value in `ActiveRows` for later use. Unfortunately, now the worksheet has a range of rows selected rather than a single cell. The code calls on the `Range("C5").Select` method to select a single cell again.

The `For...Next` statement requires three inputs as a minimum. You must provide a counter variable so that the statement knows the current count. The second variable sets the counter to a specific value. This value can be any integer. The code uses 5 in this case because that's the first data row in the worksheet. The third input is the ending count. `Counter` equals `ActiveRows + 5` when the loop completes.

The worksheet is ready to receive the first storage room value, so the code calls `MakeChoice3`. This is an augmented version of the code in the earlier "Using the Select Case statement" section of this chapter. `MakeChoice3` modifies a single cell at a time, so when it returns, only the first data cell has a storage room value in it. The `Range("C" + CStr(Counter)).Select` method call moves the cell pointer to the next storage room cell. The code continues until all the cells have appropriate storage room numbers.

Using the For Each...Next statement

The `For Each...Next` statement is similar to the `For...Next` statement in operation. However, this statement doesn't rely on an external counter. The statement uses an object index as a counter. The advantage of using this statement is that you don't have to figure out how many times to perform the loop — the object provides this information. The disadvantage of using this statement is that you lose a little control over how the loop executes because the counter is no longer under your control.

You can use this statement for a number of purposes, but generally it's easier and faster to use the `For...Next` statement for standard code. You must use the `For Each...Next` statement with arrays and collections. See Chapter 9 for details on using arrays and collections.

Redirecting the Flow by Using GoTo

You might run into situations where the existing program flow doesn't work, and you have to disrupt it to move somewhere else in the code. The `GoTo` statement provides a means of redirecting program flow. Used carefully, the `GoTo` statement can help you overcome specific programming problems.

Unfortunately, the `GoTo` statement has caused more problems (such as creating hard-to-understand code and hiding programming errors) than any other programming statement because it has a great potential for misuse. Novice programmers find it easier to use the `GoTo` statement to overcome programming errors rather than to fix these problems. Always use the `GoTo` statement with extreme care. Designing your code to flow well before you write it and fixing errors when you find them are both easier than reading code with misused `GoTo` statements.

Using the GoTo statement correctly

The `GoTo` statement provides the essential service of helping you redirect program flow. Before you use the `GoTo` statement, ask yourself whether there's some other means of performing the redirection, such as using a loop. If there isn't any other way to perform the programming task efficiently, using a `GoTo` statement is acceptable. Listing 5-9 shows an example of correct `GoTo` usage. It's an update of the example shown in the earlier "Using the Select Case statement" section of this chapter. (You can find the source code for this example on the Dummies.com site at `http://www.dummies.com/go/vbafd5e`.)

Listing 5-9   Using the GoTo Statement

```
' The restart point.
RestartCheck:

' Determine if the user has selected more than one row.
If ActiveWindow.RangeSelection.Rows.Count = 1 Then

    ' Get the cursor position.
```

```
        CursorPosition = ActiveWindow.RangeSelection.Row
Else

    ' Tell the user to select only one cell.
    Result = MsgBox("Select only one cell!" + vbCrLf + _
                    "Choose the first row in the range?", _

                    vbExclamation Or vbYesNo, _
                    "Selection Error")

    ' Determine if the user selected Yes.
    If Result = vbYes Then

        ' Modify the selection.
        Range("A" + _

            CStr(ActiveWindow.RangeSelection.Row)).Select

        ' Try the check again.
        GoTo RestartCheck
    End If

    ' Exit the Sub without further processing.
    End
End If
```

This version of the code extends the error trapping found in the earlier "Using the Select Case statement" section of this chapter. The original version correctly identifies an error condition, but then it rudely ends without helping you fix the problem. Rude programs make people mad, so it's best to provide some helpful assistance when you can.

Notice that the message box now displays a message that gives you a chance to fix the error. Result is a VbMsgBoxResult data type, and it stores the button click information.

When you click Yes, the code changes the current selection by using the Range function. Notice how the code converts the numeric ActiveWindow. RangeSelection.Row property value to a string and combines it with a column letter for the Range function. After the code moves the selection point, it uses the GoTo statement to return to a point before the row selection check in the code. Because there's only one row selected now, the check is completed successfully.

Avoiding misuse of the GoTo statement

Many programmers misused the GoTo statement so severely in the past that most books tell you not to use it at all. Misuse of the GoTo statement leads to buggy code that is hard to read. In addition, GoTo statements can hide poor program design. However, the GoTo statement can also accomplish useful work, so the goal is to avoid misuse of the GoTo statement and concentrate on useful tasks. Here are some ways to avoid misusing the GoTo statement:

- ✔ **Loops:** Never use a GoTo statement as a loop replacement. The statements used for loops signal others about your intent. In addition, standard loop statements contain features that keep bugs, such as endless loops, to a minimum.

- ✔ **Exits:** Avoid using a GoTo statement as a means of exiting a program. You can always use the End statement for that task.

- ✔ **Program flow problems:** If you detect problems with the flow of your program, check your pseudo-code and design documents again. Make sure that you implement the design correctly. The design might require change as well. Don't assume that the design is correct, especially if this is a first attempt.

Chapter 6

Trapping Errors and Squashing Bugs

*E*ven the best programmer in the world makes mistakes. It's part of the human condition. Don't be surprised when a bug creeps into your well-designed and well-implemented VBA program. Bugs are the gremlins of the computer industry — they're insidious and evil.

Fortunately, you can hunt down bugs and squash them. You can also prevent bugs from occurring in the first place by coding your VBA program carefully. The goal of this chapter is to help you understand what you can do to prevent bugs in your VBA program and what to do when they get in anyway.

You won't figure out how to write perfect programs because no one does. As a result, you use *error trapping* to detect bugs and do something about them before they can cause problems. In the cases where you can't detect the bugs, you use *error handling* to fix the problems that the bugs cause and to help your VBA programs recover.

Knowing the Enemy

Users look at bugs as non-entities devoid of any characteristics. All a user knows is that a bug causes the program to crash and lose data. You can't afford to have that perspective. Bugs have personalities, in that they vary by

- ✔ Type
- ✔ Cause
- ✔ Effect
- ✔ Severity
- ✔ Other factors that you include in your personal classification system

Locating a bug means knowing about its personality so that you can find it quickly. It helps to classify the bug by type. Each bug type has a different method for prevention and troubleshooting. You can classify bugs into the following four types:

- ✔ Syntax
- ✔ Compile
- ✔ Run-time
- ✔ Semantic

The best way to find bugs is to know your coding style. Keeping notes helps you understand patterns in your programming so that you can correct techniques that lead to bugs. More importantly, understanding your personal style helps you develop techniques for finding bugs based on past mistakes. Knowing what you did in the past helps you locate and squash bugs today.

Understanding syntax errors

Syntax errors are the easiest errors to avoid but are also some of the hardest errors to find. A *syntax error* can include a spelling mistake, misuse of punctuation, or misuse of a language element. When you forget to include an `End If` for an `If...Then` statement, it's a syntax error.

Typos are common syntax errors. They're especially hard to find when you make them in variable names. For example, VBA views `MySpecialVariable` and `MySpecialVaraible` as two different variables, but you might miss the typing error. Adding `Option Explicit` to the beginning of every module, form, and class module that you create eases this problem. (See the upcoming "Understanding compile errors" section for details on using `Option`

`Explicit`.) You can rely on VBA to find most variable typos when you add this simple statement to your code. In fact, this statement should become a standard part of every program that you create.

You can easily miss some of the subtle aids to locating syntax errors if you don't view carefully enough the tasks that the Integrated Development Environment (IDE) performs. The balloon help shown in Figure 6-1 for the `MsgBox` function provides a cue that you could miss. VBA displays the balloon help shown in the figure only when it recognizes the function name that you type. When you don't see the balloon help, it's a cue that VBA doesn't recognize the function name and that you need to look at your code. Unfortunately, this feature works only where VBA normally displays balloon help — it doesn't work when you type property names.

Figure 6-1:
Balloon help
helps locate
syntax
errors in
your code.

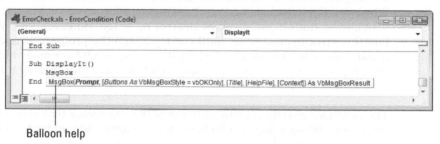

Balloon help

No matter what you do, a few syntax errors can slip by and cause bugs in your program. You can look at the errors for hours and not actually see them because you've worked with the code for so long. Asking someone else to look at your code often helps because that person isn't familiar with the code. Make sure that you ask someone with the same level of programming skills that you have (or better) to ensure that they understand your code.

Syntax errors also include errors in *logic* (the construction of expressions in your program). You can create a loop that processes the loop structure statements once too often or not often enough. An `If...Then` statement can use an expression that works most of the time but isn't quite right, so it doesn't produce the correct result all the time. Code with logic errors runs because VBA doesn't know that the expression is incorrect. The only way to find this kind of syntax error is to debug the program. See the upcoming "Time for a Bug Hunt" section for details.

Understanding compile errors

The VBA *compiler* is actually a syntax checker. Unlike compilers used by other languages, the VBA compiler doesn't produce a freestanding module that you can execute outside the Office environment. VBA uses the compiler to look for errors that prevent the program from running properly. You might create an `If...Then` statement and not include the corresponding `End If` statement. The compiler runs constantly, so VBA finds some mistakes almost immediately after you make them.

VBA uses the compiler to find many of the syntax errors that you make and displays an error message. You can try this feature. Open a new project, create a `Sub` (the name isn't important), and type **MsgBox()**. Then press Enter. VBA displays a message box stating that it was expecting an equals sign (=). When you use parentheses after `MsgBox`, VBA expects that you want to include a result variable to hold the result, such as `MyResult = MsgBox("My Prompt")`. You should also notice that the errant line of code appears in a highlight color, which is normally red.

Missing elements are another syntax error that VBA finds with relative ease. When you fail to include an `End If` statement for an `If...Then` statement, VBA always finds it and displays an error message. However, VBA doesn't find this error in most cases until you try to run the program. In addition, it doesn't show the errant `If...Then` statement — VBA normally highlights the `End Sub` or `End Function` statement instead, thus making this error a little harder to find.

The compiler also finds many of the punctuation errors that you can make in your code. When a line of code becomes too long and you try to move to the next line without adding a continuation character, the compiler notices the error and tells you about it. (See the "Writing Your First Sub" section of Chapter 3 for a description of the continuation character.) The compiler also notes missing periods between elements of a statement or missing parentheses from function calls (when needed).

When you add `Option Explicit` to your code, the compiler checks variables for a number of problems. You could try to assign a string value to an integer. VBA allows you to make this error when you type the code. However, when you try to run the code, the compiler sees the type mismatch and tells you about it. The compiler can detect many variable errors that would go unnoticed otherwise, thus making your code less likely to contain errors.

Understanding run-time errors

A *run-time error* happens when something outside your program is incorrect. A disk access request can fail, or you can type the wrong information. Your VBA code is correct, but the program still fails because of this external error. Run-time errors are the reason why many large companies, such as Microsoft, run beta programs. (A *beta program* is a vendor-sponsored method of getting a program before its developers have finished it for the purpose of testing

---

Difficult-to-diagnose run-time errors

Sometimes VBA actually creates problems for you when it comes time to diagnose bugs. The SendKeys() function is one example. You can see this function in use in Listing 5-8. The biggest problem with the SendKeys() function is that it works in only the active window. If you have the Visual Basic Editor displayed when you call SendKeys(), VBA sends the SendKeys() output to the Visual Basic Editor rather than to the active Office window, as you might expect. Consequently, a procedure that you write that normally works perfectly well suddenly fails because of a poor implementation of the SendKeys() function by Microsoft.

The best way to overcome this kind of problem is to place debugging code in your Sub or Function. Use the MsgBox() function to display a message containing the SendKeys() information immediately before the actual SendKeys() call in your code. For example, you might add a MsgBox() call like this:

```
' Use SendKeys to select all
    of the cells in the
    column.
MsgBox "Select all of the
    cells in the column."
SendKeys "+^{DOWN}", True
```

Using this technique lets you keep the focus on the Office application, yet also helps you determine what actions are taking place in the background. Although this solution is less than perfect, it's probably the best solution in most cases because you can change the debugging statements as needed. Of course, you can add MsgBox() calls after SendKeys() as well when needed, but the important location is before you make the call so that the focus is in the right place when the actual SendKeys() call is made.

---

and evaluation.) A large base of users can help you find run-time errors that depend on particular machine configurations or specific kinds of user-entry techniques.

You can trap run-time errors or change the program flow to ensure that they don't happen. In Chapter 5, I show several forms of error trapping. See the upcoming "Prevention Is Better than a Cure" section of this chapter for additional examples. The remainder of this book contains yet more examples of error trapping because this is an important topic. Error trapping helps your program overcome errors that you can't predict when you write a program.

Understanding semantic errors

A particularly difficult error to find and understand is the *semantic error*, which happens when the VBA code and logic are correct but the meaning behind the code isn't what you intended. For example, you could use a Do...Until loop in place of a Do...While loop. Even if the code is correct and you use the correct logic, the code doesn't produce the result that you expected because the meaning of a `Do...Until` loop is different from the meaning of a `Do...While` loop.

The meaning that you assign to your code has to match the words that you use to write the code. Just as a good book uses precise terms, a good program relies on precise statements to ensure that VBA understands what you want to do. The best way to avoid semantic errors is to plan your application carefully, use pseudo-code to "pre-write" the design, and then convert the pseudo-code to VBA code. When you skip steps in the process, you can introduce semantic errors because you don't communicate your ideas well to VBA.

Introducing semantic errors in subtle ways is easy. Writing an equation the wrong way can result in output errors. When you use the wrong equation to determine the next step in a loop, the problem becomes worse because the error looks like a syntax or run-time error. The steps between loops and the expression used to make a decision are very important. The most common error is leaving a parenthesis out of an equation. For example, VBA interprets $1 + 2 * 3$ as 7 but $(1 + 2) * 3$ as 9. A missing parenthesis is easy to miss when you frantically search for an error.

Prevention Is Better than a Cure

Avoiding an error is always easier than trapping or handling it later. However, any form of prevention is better than letting the error occur without any intervention at all. Whenever your program experiences an unhandled error, it stops running (crashes). Here are some reasons why you want to handle errors rather than just let them happen:

- You can provide specific error information.
- Programs can recover from many errors.
- Programs can reduce or prevent data loss.
- You can include special handling that tracks the error for later debugging.
- The host application (such as Office) can help reduce the effects of the error.
- The operating system can help with some errors and reduce the effect of others.

Avoiding run-time errors

Run-time errors can include many unforeseen events. You can't handle all run-time errors in your program. For example, a storm that removes power from the computer isn't something that you can control. You need an uninterruptible power supply (UPS) attached to the computer to handle that error. Even so, such an error can result in data loss.

However, you can avoid other kinds of run-time errors. Input errors are one of the most common run-time problems that you face when working with VBA. In Chapter 5, I show some techniques for avoiding run-time errors caused by improper input. You can also use these techniques:

- ✔ Check every input for data type, length, value, and meaning.
- ✔ Provide easy-to-understand prompts for your application.
- ✔ Make the prompts and error messages as specific as possible.
- ✔ Offer to fix the problem automatically whenever possible.
- ✔ Offer to retry the operation after you correct the error.
- ✔ Reduce the chances of error by providing complete context-sensitive help that includes examples and other resource information.

Checking the input is the most important task that your program can perform. If the program needs a word as input, don't accept a number. Ensure that the length of the input matches expectations. This check is especially important to avoid *buffer overrun,* which is a condition where the program receives too much input. Buffer overrun errors often make the news as security breaches. If possible, look for specific values. Even if you don't have specific input values, check for strange characters or values that seem out of place. It's also possible in some cases to examine the meaning of the input. A street address usually requires a street number and name. When you want to ensure that the address information is correct, try looking for this information in the input.

Program resource problems are the second-most common source of run-time errors. You might not have enough space on the hard drive to save a file, or the program might not find a file that it needs. Checking for the resource before you need it helps avoid the associated run-time error. If the resource is something that you can fix, such as a lack of hard drive space, include code that allows you to perform this task and then ask the program to check again.

Errors can also creep into your applications when you don't include required library references. A *library* is code that resides outside of your application. The code might appear in many forms, but the form doesn't really matter. All you're concerned about is the functionality that the library provides. You'll see library references used in many places in this book. For example, when you work with the hard drive, you need to add a new library to your application. The following section of this chapter describes how to add a reference to a library. If you don't include all the library references that your application requires, the application displays a run-time error.

Recovering from an error

Recovering from an error is important. Adding recovery code means that you can count on your program to help you overcome problems with the system and keep your data safe. You can add two kinds of recovery code to your program:

✔ Code that recovers before the error happens

✔ Code that recovers after the error happens

It's always better to detect an error and recover from it before the error actually happens. You can always recover from a resource error, such as lack of hard drive space, before the error happens. Likewise, you can always recover from input errors by making the required checks and asking for the correct input. The only time you must wait for the error to happen is when you can't predict the error, such as a sudden loss of power.

A common run-time error is lack of hard drive space. To add a drive-checking feature to your program, you need to add a new library to your program. Use the Tools⇨References command to display the References dialog box, as shown in Figure 6-2. Notice that the Microsoft Scripting Runtime check box is selected. Look for this entry in your dialog box and select it. Click OK. The new library is ready for use.

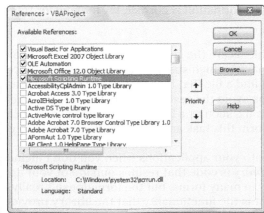

Figure 6-2:
Use this dialog box to add a new library to your program.

The Microsoft Scripting Runtime Library has many powerful features that I explore in detail in other parts of this book. The feature that you use in this section (see Listing 6-1) demonstrates how to check for disk space and recover from an error when the disk drive doesn't have enough space. (You can find the source code for this example on the Dummies.com site at `http://www.dummies.com/go/vbafd5e`.)

Listing 6-1   Determining the Amount of Free Disk Space

```
Public Sub DriveTest()
    ' Create a variable to hold the free space.
    Dim FreeSpace As Double

    ' Create a reference to the file system.
    Dim MyFileSystem As FileSystemObject

    ' Create a reference for the target drive.
    Dim MyDrive As Drive

    ' Create a dialog result variable.
    Dim Result As VbMsgBoxResult

    'Provide a jump back point.
DoCheckAgain:

    ' Fill these two objects with data so they show the
    ' available space on drive C.
    Set MyFileSystem = New FileSystemObject
    Set MyDrive = MyFileSystem.GetDrive("C")

    ' Determine the amount of free space.
    FreeSpace = MyDrive.AvailableSpace

    ' Make the check.
    If FreeSpace < 1000000000 Then

        ' The drive doesn't have enough space. Ask what to
        ' do.
        Result = MsgBox("The drive doesn't have enough " +
            _
                        "space to hold the data. Do you" +
            _
                        " want to correct the error?" + _
                        vbCrLf + _
                        Format(FreeSpace, "###,###") + _
                        " bytes available, " + _
                        "1,000,000,000 bytes needed.", _
```

(continued)

Listing 6-1 *(continued)*

```
                        vbYesNo Or vbExclamation, _
                        "Drive Space Error")

      ' Determine if the user wants to correct the
      ' error.
      If Result = vbYes Then

            ' Wait for the user to fix the problem.
            MsgBox "Please click OK when you have freed" +
            _
                  " some disk space.", _
                  vbInformation Or vbOKOnly, _
                  "Retry Drive Check"

            ' Go to the fallback point.
            GoTo DoCheckAgain
      Else

            ' The user doesn't want to fix the error.
            MsgBox "The program can't save your data " + _
                  "until the drive has enough space.", _
                  vbInformation Or vbOKOnly, _
                  "Insufficient Drive Space"

            ' End the Sub.
            Exit Sub
      End If
   End If
End Sub
```

The code begins by creating some variables. The `FileSystemObject` object contains information about every drive that you can access from your machine. The `Drive` object contains information about a specific drive. The code uses the `Set` keyword with objects. You `Set` a variable equal to an object. See Chapter 8 for details on using objects.

The code places the amount of space available into `FreeSpace` and compares it with the space needed to hold the information. You might have to change the value in the `If...Then` statement to match your drive. Make the number larger than the space that your drive has available.

One interesting issue to note is that `FreeSpace` is a `Double`. Using earlier versions of VBA, you would use a `Long`, and it would provide more than sufficient space. Because hard drives are getting larger, you actually need a `Double` to make the `AvailableSpace()` method work. If you used a `Long` today, you'd very likely see an error message because a `Long` isn't large enough to hold the number required to express the amount of available drive space. Office 2007 has updated variables wherever the old variable isn't large enough to hold the expected data values. Consequently, you might find that some of your old macros have broken because the data type has changed.

Because the drive doesn't have enough space, the code displays an error message. The message shown in the code might seem long and complicated, but it provides all the information needed to make a decision. It tells what's wrong, provides you with a choice of actions, and contains specifics about the amount of space needed. Notice the use of the Format function for the message. It shows how to use a custom formatting string to display the free space with comma separators but without a decimal point.

If you say that you want to fix the drive space error, the code presents a message box that tells you to click OK when it's okay to make the change again. The code uses the GoTo statement to redirect execution to the drive space check again.

On the other hand, if you decide not to fix the error, the program tells you the result of the action. It then exits the Sub without doing anything else. This step is important. Otherwise, the program attempts to save the file, and the error occurs.

Understanding error handlers

Error handlers are your option of last resort in dealing with bugs. You use an error handler to work with any errors that you can't trap. The important thing to remember is that the error has happened — you can't prevent it at this point. The best that you can do is to display a message box saying that the error happened and to tell whether your program can recover from the error.

When your program can't recover, it should fail gracefully. However, failing gracefully shouldn't be a standard option — always try to recover from the error. A program that fails gracefully performs the following tasks:

- ✓ The program doesn't rely on the standard VBA message. It uses a custom message that contains detailed failure information instead.

- ✓ The user is always informed about the consequences of the failure, possible fixes, and whom to contact (when necessary).

- ✓ The reporting information should also appear in the Windows Event Log when necessary to ensure that the administrator sees the error. VBA doesn't support this feature directly.

- ✓ If possible, the program includes you as part of the reporting loop so that you can keep track of bugs in your application.

✔ The host application doesn't fail (and cause data loss) because of an error in the program.

✔ Instead of using default error handling, the program provides robust error handling that leaves the operating system in a stable state.

Writing your own error-handling code

Adding an error handler to your program is a two-part process. First, you must tell VBA that you've included an error handler. Otherwise, VBA uses the default error handler, even when error-handler code appears in the program. Second, you must provide the error-handling code. Listing 6-2 shows an example of a Sub that uses error handling. (You can find the source code for this example on the Dummies.com site at http://www.dummies.com/go /vbafd5e.)

Listing 6-2   Defining a Custom Error Handler

```
Public Sub ErrorHandle()
    ' The variable that receives the input.
    Dim InNumber As Byte

    ' Tell VBA about the error handler.
    On Error GoTo MyHandler

    ' Ask the user for some input.
    InNumber = InputBox("Type a number between 1 and " + _
                    "10.", "Numeric Input", "1")

    ' Determine whether the input is correct.
    If (InNumber < 1) Or (InNumber > 10) Then

        ' If the input is incorrect, then raise an error.
        Err.Raise vbObjectError + 1, _
                "ErrorCheck.ErrorCondition.ErrorHandle", _

                "Incorrect Numeric Input. The number " + _

                "must be between 1 and 10."
    Else
        ' Otherwise, display the result.
        MsgBox "The Number You Typed: " + CStr(InNumber), _

                vbOKOnly Or vbInformation, _
                "Successful Input"
    End If

    ' Exit the Sub.
```

```
    Exit Sub

' The start of the error handler.
MyHandler:

    ' Display an error message box.
    MsgBox "The program experienced an error." + vbCrLf + _

        "Error Number: " + CStr(Err.Number) + vbCrLf + _

        "Description: " + Err.Description + vbCrLf + _
        "Source: " + Err.Source, _
        vbOKOnly Or vbExclamation, _
        "Program Error"

    ' Always clear the error after you process it.
    Err.Clear
End Sub
```

This example introduces a few new VBA features that you haven't seen in previous examples. Notice the use of the `GoTo` statement. You can use a number of forms of `On Error`, but the `GoTo` form shown here is the most common. Another common form is `On Error Resume Next`, which tells VBA to ignore the line of code with a problem and continue with the next line. The problem with this second form is that you haven't really handled the error. It remains unreported and could cause a severe crash later.

Never use the `On Error GoTo 0` statement. This statement turns off error handling, which means that errors go unhandled and VBA doesn't even tell you about them. This setting can cause a range of problems, including application failure and data loss.

The `InputBox` function is an interesting way to get hold of one piece of information. This example uses the `InputBox` function for testing, which is the most common way that I've seen it used. In general, you never use the `InputBox` function in a program because you normally need more than one input. The first argument prompts for information, the second contains a default value, and the third provides a title for the dialog box. You can also include arguments for placement of the dialog box onscreen and provide a help context.

Notice the `InNumber` data type. Using this data type ensures that you can't input a letter or special character without generating an error. If you try to input the wrong information, VBA detects the error and generates an error number 13 (type mismatch). The `Byte` data type also limits the acceptable input range. If you overflow the buffer by using a number that's too large, VBA generates error 6 (overflow). You can detect these errors in your error handler and take appropriate action.

The `If...Then` statement performs a special task. This is one method for performing a range check — something that you should do for every instance of input that you receive from a user. The check ensures that the input is within a specific range. If the input isn't within the specified range, the code uses the `Err.Raise` function to generate an error. User-defined errors fall within a specific range, so you should always add your custom error number to `vbObjectError` to ensure that the number is within the proper range. All error numbers must be less than 65,535.

Whenever you define a *custom error* (one that you define), you should tell yourself exactly where the error occurred. I always include the filename, the module name, and the `Function` or `Sub` name. Notice that the description information for this error is complete and descriptive. Just because Microsoft provides ambiguous information doesn't mean that you have to follow its bad example. Always include descriptive error messages so that you have a good idea of what went wrong.

The error handler begins at the `MyHandler` label. The handler shows the various `Err` object properties that you can access to determine the source and cause of an error. The example could easily include a retry feature, but I chose to keep things simple. See the earlier "Recovering from an error" section for details on a retry feature.

The last statement might not look like much, but it's very important. Always clear errors after you handle them, by using the `Err.Clear` method. If you don't, VBA might think that the error is still a problem and fail again.

Reporting errors

It's essential to report program errors. You can't overcome problems with your program when you don't know about them. In addition, knowing about errors makes it possible to create a recovery plan. Here are some techniques that you can use to report errors:

- ✔ **Message box:** Many of my examples in this chapter use message boxes, which is the standard method that most programs use.

- ✔ **Text file:** You can create a text file with error information. A formatted text file — one that uses tabs to separate individual entries — can act as input to a database. See Chapter 10 for details on working with disk files.

- ✔ **Windows Event Log:** You can use a Windows Event Log entry to hold the error information. The Event Log uses a standard format for error messages. It's the place where a network administrator looks for errors.

- ✔ **E-mail:** You can create an e-mail message with error information about your program. See Chapter 16 for details on working with Outlook from a VBA program.

Saving and Restoring Code

Some VBA code is generic, which means that you can use it in more than one place. Keeping this code in a separate module that you move from application to application is always a good idea. When you use generic modules, you write the code once and then you always have it when you need it. This section describes how to export modules from one application and import them into another.

Exporting a module from a program

When you work with VBA, you might create some modules that you want to use in other places. This means exporting your module to a BAS (BASIC) file. (Forms rely on the FRM file, and class modules rely on the CLS file.) The following steps tell you how to perform this task.

1. **Highlight the module, form, or class module that you want to export from a program in the Project Explorer window.**

2. **Right-click the entry and then choose Export File from the context menu that appears.**

   You see the Export File dialog box.

3. **Choose a location for the module, form, or class module and then click Save.**

   VBA exports the file.

Importing a module in a program

The library that you build while you write VBA programs is an important resource because it reduces the need to write new code. Every time that you need to reuse existing code, you can import the module by using the following procedure:

1. **Right-click anywhere in the Project Explorer window and then choose Import File from the context menu that appears.**

   You see the Import File dialog box.

2. **Locate the BAS, FRM, or CLS file that you want to import.**

3. **Highlight the file and then click Open.**

   The module appears in the Project Explorer window in the appropriate folder.

Time for a Bug Hunt

You aren't alone when you have a bug to find in your program, because the VBA IDE provides a special tool called a debugger. The *debugger* is a built-in feature that you access by using a special Debug toolbar. Figure 6-3 shows the Debug toolbar. Add it to your IDE by right-clicking the toolbar area and then choosing Debug from the list of available toolbars.

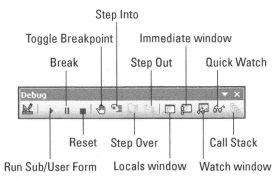

Figure 6-3:
Use the Debug toolbar to access debugger features.

Executing a break

Whenever you open your program in the VBA IDE and execute it from there, the program is in debug mode. Using debug mode lets you stop the program and see what it's doing at any particular moment. Stopping the program can help you not only find bugs but also discover more about VBA and how to use it. You can use this feature to view other people's code to see how they perform programming tasks.

Before you can stop execution of your program, you need to tell VBA where to stop. A stop within a VBA program is a *breakpoint.* To add a breakpoint to your code, highlight the stopping point and then click Toggle Breakpoint on the Debug toolbar. When you click Run Sub/User Form, VBA automatically stops at the point that you selected.

When your program has a natural stop, such as in a form or at an `InputBox` statement, you can also click Break on the Debug toolbar to stop the program. (See the earlier "Writing your own error-handling code" section for an example of the `InputBox` statement.) The Break button differs from the Reset button because it only pauses execution. Clicking Reset always stops the program, and you have to restart it from the beginning.

Another way to execute a break is to use the Debug.Assert method. You can use any Boolean expression with this method. If the expression is true, program execution continues as normal. However, if the expression is false, the program breaks so that you can examine the value. This form of break is helpful when you know that a program should have variables with a certain range of values.

Whenever you execute a break, the program is temporarily stopped. Click Run Sub/User Form to start the program from the current stopping point. As far as the program is concerned, it never stopped.

Taking individual steps

Whenever you execute a break in a running program, the debugger enables the Step Into, Step Over, and Step Out buttons (refer to Figure 6-3). You use these three buttons to take individual steps within the program — to execute one line of code at a time. The reason why you want to do this is to see the effect of each statement on the program data. When you think that a statement changes a string in a certain way, you can prove it to yourself by viewing the effect of that particular statement.

You use the Step Over button in most cases because you want to see the effects of statements in the current Sub or Function. Clicking Step Over moves from line to line in the current code. The code still executes in any Function or Sub called from the current Function or Sub, but you don't see it. The code executes in the background.

When you suspect that the called Function or Sub has an error, use the Step Into button to go into that Function or Sub from the current location. The IDE moves the cursor from the current position to the called Function or Sub so that you can see the code while it executes. You still view one line at a time when using this button. The difference is that you see the called code in addition to the Function or Sub of interest.

When you debug a called Function or Sub, you might decide that there really isn't an error in that section of the code. Instead of stepping through one statement at a time until you return to the calling code, you can use the Step Out button to return immediately. VBA still executes all the code in the called function — it just happens in real time rather than one line at a time.

Viewing the data tips

When you execute a program break, you can view the current value of variables in several ways. The easiest way is to use the data tips feature, shown in Figure 6-4. (See the upcoming "Using the Locals Window" and "Using the Watches Window" sections for other techniques.) To see this view, simply hover the mouse over any variable, even an object.

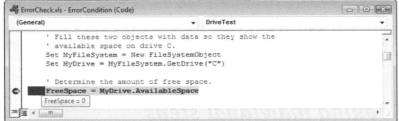

Figure 6-4:
Rely on
data tips
whenever
possible to
see the
value of a
variable.

Using the Immediate window to your advantage

The Immediate window is a valuable debugging tool. You can display the Immediate window by clicking the Immediate Window button on the Debug toolbar (refer to Figure 6-3). In Chapter 1, I show how you can actually create a mini-program by using the Immediate window. It can perform simple assignments, and you can use it to determine the value of a variable.

The Immediate window can act as an output screen. The most common way to use the Immediate window as an output is the `Debug.Print` method. Here in Listing 6-3 is some code showing how to use this valuable debugging method. (You can find the source code for this example on the Dummies.com site at `http://www.dummies.com/go/vbafd5e`.)

Listing 6-3   Using the Debug Object

```
Public Sub UseDebug()
    ' The variable that receives the input.
    Dim InNumber As Byte

    ' Ask the user for some input.
    InNumber = InputBox("Type a number between 1 and " + _
                        "10.", "Numeric Input", "1")

    ' Print the value of InNumber to the Immediate window.
    Debug.Print "InNumber = " + CStr(InNumber)

    ' Stop program execution if InNumber is not in the
    ' correct range.
```

```
Debug.Assert (InNumber >= 1) And (InNumber <= 10)

' Display the result.
MsgBox "The Number You Typed: " + CStr(InNumber), _
    vbOKOnly Or vbInformation, _
    "Successful Input"
End Sub
```

Notice how this sample uses the `Debug.Print` and the `Debug.Assert` methods in combination. The `Debug.Print` method outputs the current values to the Immediate window, and the `Debug.Assert` method checks for a specific input range. When the range is incorrect, the program breaks, and you can see the errant value in the Immediate window.

Using the Locals Window

The Locals window shows all the variables that the current code segment can see. You can see variables defined within the current `Sub` or `Function` as well as global variables. You display the Locals window by clicking the Locals Window button on the toolbar. Figure 6-5 shows a typical example of the Locals window.

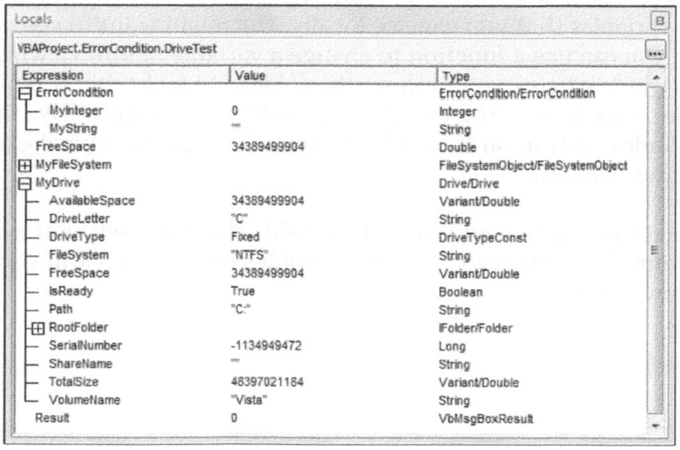

Figure 6-5:
Use the Locals window to see visible variables.

The Locals window displays three kinds of information: variable name, value, and data type. You can see two global variables at the top of Figure 6-5. Immediately below the global variables is `FreeSpace`, a local `Double`. The current value is the amount of space on the C drive of my system.

Two objects appear next in the list. Normally, just the object name appears in the list. Click the plus sign next to the name, and you see the object properties and their values. Notice that the `MyDrive.AvailableSpace` property matches the `FreeSpace` value because I stopped the program immediately after the drive space assignment. (See the earlier "Recovering from an error" section for details.)

Objects can contain other objects. `MyDrive` is a `Drive` object that contains a `RootFolder` object. Notice the plus sign next to `RootFolder` in Figure 6-5. Click this plus sign, and the Locals window shows the contents of the second object. You can continue looking through a hierarchy of objects until you reach the last one contained within the original object.

The Locals window is also handy for playing what-if scenarios with your program. The `DriveTest` program always fails because the check value is too high. You can double-click the Value field of the `FreeSpace` entry to change its value to 1,000,000,001. The check passes now because `FreeSpace` is one more than the check value. Try this test; the program exits without error.

Using the Watches Window

The Watches window works similarly to the Locals window, but has a different purpose. The Locals window shows variables in their raw format and only the variables that you can see locally. You might want to see other variables, or you can use a function to change a variable before viewing it. The Watches window helps you perform these kinds of tasks, but it requires a little more work to use. You can display the Watches window by clicking the Watch Window button on the toolbar. Figure 6-6 shows a typical example of the Watches window.

Notice that this window adds a Context field. This field tells you where a variable is defined. Because you can use variables from any location, knowing where they come from is important.

Figure 6-6:
The Watches window tracks variables and expressions.

Adding a new watch expression

The easiest way to add a watch expression is to highlight the expression in your code and then drag it to the Watches window. VBA automatically enters all the correct information for you — you don't need to do anything but look at the value. You can also highlight the expression and click the Quick Watch button on the toolbar. When you use this method, you see a Quick Watch dialog box that tells you about the new watch expression. Click Add to add the new watch or click Cancel to change your mind.

Using the Add Watch window

A watch expression might be more complex than a single variable or even an expression in your code. Look at the first expression shown earlier, in Figure 6-6. This expression doesn't come from the code — I created it by using the Add Watch dialog box. The Add Watch dialog box (see Figure 6-7) gives you full control over the expression. To display the Add Watch dialog box, highlight any expression in your code, right-click the selection, and then choose Add Watch from the context menu that appears.

Figure 6-7:
The Add Watch dialog box helps you modify existing expressions or create new ones.

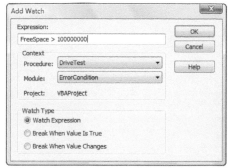

You can modify an expression by changing the content of the Expression field. For example, as you can see in Figure 6-6, I first highlighted the FreeSpace entry in the code and then added the CStr part of the expression. You can also use the Add Watch dialog box to change the context of a watch expression. It might help to have access to global variables in every procedure and not just in the current procedure. A common local variable could also appear in more than one Sub or Function.

Notice the three options in the Watch Type group. VBA assumes that you want to create a watch expression. That's what you get when you create a quick watch or use the drag-and-drop method. You can also set a watch to cause the program to break when the value is true or when it changes. Creating a break condition is one of the more interesting ways to use the Watches window.

Chapter 7

Interacting with the User

- -

- -

*V*BA utility programs can usually perform their jobs without much input. However, a VBA program that helps you perform a task usually needs some type of input. A *form* provides fields where you can enter or read additional information, objects (such as labels) that display information, and controls (such as command buttons) that help you interact with the form.

You might need a form that asks about the machine environment or how to interact with the data. Forms can also provide formatted output in ways that a message box can't. You can include fields on the form that format data and present it in a useful manner. You use forms constantly in Windows, in the form of dialog boxes and data entry windows.

This chapter provides an overview of VBA forms. You can also find forms in most of the remaining chapters of this book. VBA forms can include complex concepts, but the best forms are simple and easy to use. The examples in this chapter concentrate on the idea of simplicity. Other chapters build on this base and demonstrate special kinds of forms.

Understanding Forms

It's easy to think of forms as blobs with controls attached because so many examples of bad form design are available. Well-designed forms consider a number of requirements, such as how the information flows from one area to the next. A form also needs prompts that are easy to understand and a pleasing presentation. You might think that designing such a form is hard, but if you follow the same strategy as you do with other areas of programming, you can create great forms with relative ease.

Using forms creatively

Good design begins when you consider how your application uses the information that appears on the form and how you want to interact with it. A form that presents every piece of information that you might ever need sounds good until you try to use it. A form should contain focused information that easily fits on any display that you use. You might find that you need to design a series of forms that appear in sequence.

Another consideration is clutter. Even if you create a focused form, it might contain too much nonessential information. That's why you see Details and Properties buttons of various kinds on forms. When you need to see the details, you can click the button to present another form or expand the existing form. Otherwise, you can ignore the details and provide just the essentials.

Add informational forms to your program as needed. When a program completes a task, the program should tell you about it. A message box that says "I'm done" might seem appropriate, but often it's a nuisance. The exception to this rule is when the user is actually waiting for confirmation that the application has completed a task, in which case you should display the message box. Otherwise, you can include program statistics or other helpful information as part of an informational field or a status bar. I often build statistical forms into my programs so that I can monitor performance. When I see that the program isn't performing as expected, I know that I need to look for potential problems. I often fix the problem long before it becomes a work-stopping issue.

The important issue to consider is that a form is an interaction between a person and the program running on the computer. If the form that you design doesn't evoke a response, perhaps you haven't used the form creatively enough. You should be able to look at a form and have a good idea of its purpose. Each control (such as a pushbutton) should provide a *ToolTip* (the little window that pops up when you hover the mouse over the control) that helps anyone using the form to understand the intent of that control. Finally, context-sensitive help and other forms of visual aid should make difficult forms easy to understand.

Designing a form for your application

When you use the Forms Designer, you can easily get the idea that the VBA Integrated Development Environment (IDE) is somehow performing magic on your behalf by creating forms visually. A form is simply a specialized kind of code, and you use code to perform a number of tasks in this book. Forms are simply an extension of what you do when you perform any other task. The only difference is that a form is visual: It presents information onscreen in a form that the user can see.

To begin this example, you need to add a few references that VBA doesn't provide. Use the Tools⇨References command to display the References dialog box. Select the Microsoft Visual Basic for Applications Extensibility 5.3 and Microsoft Windows Common Controls (any version is fine) libraries, as shown in Figure 7-1. Make sure that you also have selected the other references shown.

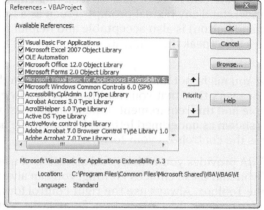

Figure 7-1:
Adding
these
references
can make
it easy
to create
your own
dynamic
forms.

Anyone who has used VBA for a while will notice that the version numbers of the libraries in Figure 7-1 are for Office 2007. However, the interesting fact is that the Visual Basic Editor didn't require any changes to use the new libraries. The editor automatically used the updated libraries when I loaded this code from the previous edition of this book for updating.

The easiest way to design a form is by using the IDE. In the upcoming "Using the Basic Controls" section of this chapter, you see this traditional method of form design in action. A form that you design using these tools is static — you decide how it looks during the design phase of your program.

Considering the form layout

The way that you design your form is important. When you use a well-designed form, you feel good about the program. A form with a good layout is easy to use and understand. Here are some design elements that you should consider for your form (all of which appear in examples in this chapter):

✔ **Flow:** The controls on a form should naturally flow from one element to the next. For example, you should place the fields on the form so that someone performing a task, such as typing an address, types the name first, the company second, the address third, and so forth. Make sure that the tab order follows the flow you provide. You can change the tab order by choosing View⇨Tab Order.

✔ **Prompts:** Forms should always have prompts for every field. Some forms in applications that you use probably have blank fields that don't contain any information. Unless you hover the mouse over the field, you don't know the field's purpose.

✔ **Decoration:** Gaudy forms make people ill, but you can still embellish the forms that you create. A company logo or other form of simple decoration makes a drab form nicer to use. An icon that enhances the user's ability to understand any textual prompts (such as a Delete icon on a Delete command button) is also acceptable and helpful when you must support users who speak the application's language as a second language.

✔ **Accelerator keys:** You might not like moving your hand from the keyboard to the mouse every time that you want to select a new control. In fact, many people find this requirement difficult or impossible. Using accelerator keys (shown as underlined letters) lets someone use just the keyboard to access the controls on your form.

✔ **Control choice:** VBA provides you with a good selection of useful tools in the Toolbox. If you find these choices limiting, you can always add new controls to the Toolbox. Always use the right control for the job. Not every data-entry task requires a `TextBox`. Some tasks require a `ListBox`, a `ComboBox`, a `CheckBox`, or an `OptionButton` control. (See the upcoming Figure 7-2 for a list of standard controls.)

✔ **Flexibility:** A form requires some level of flexibility to display properly on every system. You might need to use your program on a system with a smaller display, which means that you might have to resize the form. If you use a laptop, you might have to use the high-contrast setting to see the display, which means that the characters are larger and that the form might not display correctly.

Using the Basic Controls

VBA provides a good set of basic controls, as shown in Figure 7-2. You might use VBA to create a number of programs and never need anything more than the basic control set. In fact, the basic control set meets just about every need, and you seldom see anything other than these controls used in Windows programs.

Click the Select Objects button (refer to Figure 7-2) whenever you want to select any object on a form. VBA selects this button by default. It also picks the Select Objects button after you add a new control to a form.

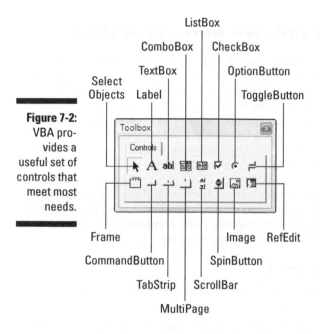

Figure 7-2:
VBA pro-
vides a
useful set of
controls that
meet most
needs.

Adding controls to the form

Before you can add controls to a form, you need a form. Right-click anywhere in the Project Explorer window and then choose Insert↔UserForm
from the context menu that appears. After you add the form, make sure that
you give it an easily remembered name by changing the `Name` property in
the Properties window. Use the `Caption` property to change the text on the
title bar.

The easiest and least error-prone method of adding a control to a form is to
select the control in the Toolbox and then click the area of the form where
you want the control to appear. The mouse cursor points to the upper-left
corner of the control. The cross cursor makes it easy to place the control
accurately. You might need to organize the controls after you add them
because it isn't easy to add the controls precisely. See the upcoming
"Making your form pretty" section for details.

Another method for adding controls to a form is to drag the control from
the Toolbox and then drop it on the form. The reason why this method is
less precise is that you don't always see the control's location. The IDE displays a box showing the outline of the control, so you do see the basic layout
when using this method.

Understanding the two parts of a form

Forms, and the controls they hold, provide the visual portion of a user interface. This is the part of the form interface that the user sees, but it isn't much good without some code. You need code to tell VBA what to do when the user interacts with the form. Any user interaction is an *event,* and the code you build is an *event handler.* Consequently, when you create a form, you work with two windows. The first is a UserForm window, where you address the visual elements; the second is the Code window, where you add code to handle user events, such as clicking a command button.

When you add a new form to an application, the Visual Basic Editor opens the UserForm window immediately and displays the Toolbox so that you can add controls. However, it doesn't display the Code window. You can use any of the following techniques to open the Code window:

- ✔ Choose View➪Code or press F7.
- ✔ Right-click the UserForm entry in Project Explorer and choose View Code from the context menu.
- ✔ Right-click the control you want to work with and choose View Code from the context menu.

The last option on the list not only displays the Code window but also creates a handler for the default event for that control. All standard VBA controls have a default event. For example, the CommandButton control uses the Click event, which occurs when the user clicks the command button. Even the form has a default event, Click, so this last option always results in the creation of an event handler. The default event depends on the action that the user is most likely to perform. See the later "Handling form events" section of this chapter for more information about events.

Using the Label control to display text

You use the Label control to display text onscreen. A Label is for informational purposes. Although you can copy the content of a Label, you can't change it directly. The most common use for labels is to identify other controls and to provide accelerator key access to them. (See the upcoming "Modifying the form and control properties" section of this chapter for details on adding an accelerator key.) Labels also act as output for read-only text.

Figure 7-3 shows a simple form with two labels. The first label has Message Text in the Caption property. The label uses M as the Accelerator property value, so the M in Message Text is underlined. When you press Alt+M, VBA selects the TextBox control associated with the first label.

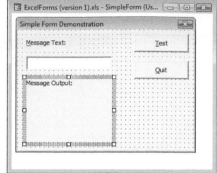

Figure 7-3:
Labels
identify
other
controls
or con-
tain output.

The second label contains `Message Output:` in the `Caption` property. This label receives the output from the `TextBox` when you click the Test button. Here's some sample code that shows the `btnTest_Click` event handler. (You can find the source code for this example on the Dummies.com site at `http://www.dummies.com/go/vbafd5e`.)

```
Private Sub btnTest_Click()
    ' Move the information from the TextBox input to the
    ' label output.
    lblOutput.Caption = "Message Output: " + vbCrLf + _
                        txtInput.Text
End Sub
```

VBA executes this code whenever you click the Test button. The name of the control is `btnTest`, and the name of the event is `Click`, so the name of the Sub is `btnTest_Click`. The result of this code is that `lblOutput`, the output label, contains the text that it originally contained plus the contents of the `TextBox` control, `txtInput`.

You might wonder why I begin the control names in this example with `lbl`, `txt`, or `btn`. The most important reason why I use this naming strategy (or *notation*) is that VBA sorts the controls for me so that I can quickly find the one that I want. For example, Figure 7-4 shows the object list in the Properties window. Notice that using the notation makes it easy to find the controls.

Getting user input with text boxes

The `TextBox` control makes it possible to request information from the user. This control doesn't have a `Caption` property because it doesn't provide any visual identification. You should always use the `TextBox` control with a `Label` control, as shown in Figure 7-4, so that everyone can see what kind of input the `TextBox` is supposed to get.

Figure 7-4:
Use a
standard
notation
for control
names.

You use the `Text` property to access the content of the `TextBox` control.
Even if you type a number, the `TextBox` control treats it like a string. VBA
automatically performs a conversion between a numeric variable and the
`TextBox` control for you in many cases. For example, the code in Listing 7-1
works just fine. (You can find the source code for this example on the
Dummies.com site at `http://www.dummies.com/go/vbafd5e`.)

Listing 7-1   Using the Text and Caption Properties

```
Private Sub btnTest_Click()
    ' Create the input variable.
    Dim InputValue As Integer

    ' Tell VBA about the error handler.
    On Error GoTo NotANumber

    ' Get the string value and place it in the numeric
    ' variable.
    InputValue = txtInput.Text

    ' Tell the user what they typed.
    lblOutput.Caption = InputValue

    ' Exit the Sub.
    Exit Sub

    ' Handle non-numeric input.
NotANumber:
    MsgBox "You must type a number!"
End Sub
```

The example code places the value contained in the `txtInput.Text` property into `Input`. VBA performs the conversion automatically as long as the user types a number. If you use this technique, always provide error handling, as shown in the example code after the `NotANumber` label. Otherwise, if the user types something other than a number, the program displays an error message.

The conversion process works in both directions. Notice that the `lblOutput.Caption` property accepts `InputValue` as acceptable input. If you decide to add text to the output value, you still need to use the `CStr` function to convert the number to a string. Otherwise, VBA displays a type mismatch error.

Executing tasks with command buttons

Command buttons are the main form of action. The default event (action) is a click. Whenever you click the button, it generates a special message known as an *event*. See the later "Handling form events" section for details on events and how they work.

Like the `Label` control, the `CommandButton` control has a `Caption` property so that you can type text that appears on the button face when you start the program. In addition, you can use the `Accelerator` property to make it easy to access the button by using an Alt+key combination. The example in this section uses three command buttons to perform three different tasks. Figure 7-5 shows the output of the example.

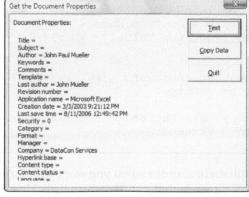

Figure 7-5:
Command buttons help you choose actions to perform with your program.

Listing 7-2 shows the code that you need to create this example. (You can find the source code for this example on the Dummies.com site at http://www.dummies.com/go/vbafd5e.)

Listing 7-2   Using the Clipboard to Copy Data

```
Private Sub btnCopy_Click()
    ' Create a Clipboard storage object.
    Dim ClipData As DataObject
    Set ClipData = New DataObject

    ' Place the text in lblOutput in the Clipboard.
    ClipData.SetText lblOutput.Caption

    ' Place the object on the Clipboard.
    ClipData.PutInClipboard
End Sub

Private Sub btnQuit_Click()
    'End the program.
    End
End Sub

Private Sub btnTest_Click()
    ' Create a string to hold the data.
    Dim Output As String

    ' Create a document property holder.
    Dim DocProp As DocumentProperty

    ' Handle properties that the application doesn't
            support.
    On Error Resume Next

    ' Start creating the output string.
    For Each DocProp In _
    ActiveWorkbook.BuiltinDocumentProperties
        Output = Output + DocProp.Name + " = " + _
                CStr(DocProp.Value) + vbCrLf
    Next

    ' Display the output onscreen.
    lblOutput.Caption = Output

    ' Enable the Copy Data button.
    btnCopy.Enabled = TrueEnd
Sub
```

VBA puts your code in alphabetical order when you work with forms, which changes the appearance of the code, but not the actual flow. This technique makes it easier to find a particular Sub. However, it can also make it more difficult to follow the expected flow of the program. The code begins with btnTest_Click because btnCopy is disabled when you start the program.

The "Writing Your First Sub" section of Chapter 3 shows how to retrieve just one value from the BuiltinDocumentProperties collection. This example shows how to use the `For Each...Next` statement to retrieve all the values available for an application.

Notice that `btnTest_Click` uses the `On Error Resume Next` statement. This program shows one of the few times where that statement is the correct one to use. Not every application supports every built-in property. If you try to retrieve the value of a built-in property that the application doesn't support, VBA generates an error. Because there's nothing that you should do to correct the error, resuming with the next statement is the correct error-handling strategy.

After the code retrieves all the built-in document properties, it places the information in the `lblOutput.Caption` property, which displays the information onscreen. The code also enables `btnCopy` by setting its `Enabled` property to true.

The `btnCopy_Click` sub-procedure introduces the `DataObject` type. You might need to interact with the Clipboard when writing an application. This object is what you use to perform the interaction. The `DataObject` methods help you retrieve information from the Clipboard, place information on the Clipboard, and format Clipboard data.

Working with the Clipboard is normally a two-step process. To place data on the Clipboard, the code must place it in the `DataObject` first by using the `SetText` method. The next step uses the `PutInClipboard` method to move the data from the `DataObject` to the Clipboard. To get data from the Clipboard, follow the opposite procedure. Use the `GetFromClipboard` method to place the text on the Clipboard into the `DataObject` and then use the `GetText` method to move the data from the `DataObject` to a variable.

Every program that you create should include some means of ending. A dialog-box–based program, like the one in this section, normally includes a Quit or an Exit button. A configuration dialog box normally relies on the OK or Cancel button to perform cleanup and then exit. The `btnQuit_Click` sub-procedure for this example performs a simple task — it uses the `End` statement to end the program.

Saying yes or no with check boxes and toggle buttons

The `CheckBox` and `ToggleButton` controls are Boolean — controls with a true or false value. The implication of each control is different. A `CheckBox` control normally indicates yes or no. On the other hand, a `ToggleButton` control indicates an on or off condition. You can use the controls as you see fit, but this is the normal way to work with them.

Both controls use the `Click` event to indicate a change in status. In addition, both controls use the `Value` property to show their status (checked or toggled). Each control maintains its status information automatically — you don't have to do anything special. This feature is useful when you're creating various types of toggled setups in addition to the more mundane task of providing input to a form.

The example in this section displays a message box each time you click the check box or toggle button. Listing 7-3 shows the code that you need to create this example. (You can find the source code for this example on the Dummies.com site at `http://www.dummies.com/go/vbafd5e`.)

Listing 7-3   Using Check Boxes

```
Private Sub cbChecked_Click()
    ' Verify the checked status.
    If cbChecked.Value Then
        ' Display a message.
        MsgBox "CheckBox Checked"

    Else
        ' Display a message.
        MsgBox "Checkbox Cleared"
    End If
End Sub

Private Sub tbCBEnable_Click()
    ' Check the state of cbChecked.
    If tbCBEnable.Value Then
        ' Disable cbChecked.
        cbChecked.Enabled = True

        ' Change the caption.
        tbCBEnable.Caption = "CheckBox Enabled"

    Else
        ' Enable cdChecked.
        cbChecked.Enabled = False

        ' Change the caption.
        tbCBEnable.Caption = "CheckBox Disabled"
    End If
End Sub
```

When the program starts, `cbChecked` is disabled and `tbCBEnable` is in the non-depressed state. Click the CheckBox Disabled button, and the code calls `tbCBEnable_Click`. This sub-procedure checks the status of the `tbCBEnable.Value` property to determine which course of action to take. In both cases, it changes the state of `cbChecked` by using the `Enabled` property and the `ToggleButton Caption` property. The code doesn't need to consider the `Value` property because the control changes it automatically.

After the CheckBox is enabled, you can click it. This time, the code calls the cbChecked_Click sub-procedure. The code checks the cbChecked.Value property and displays the appropriate message box. Again, the control automatically changes the value, so you don't have to keep track of it.

You could easily exchange the roles of the controls in this case. There's no reason to avoid using the ToggleButton as a yes/no indicator or the CheckBox as an on/off toggle. However, when you build your application, you need to consider how the visual presentation affects you. Although the two controls work precisely the same, the ToggleButton does present as an on/off switch and the CheckBox does present as a yes/no indicator.

Making choices with option buttons and frames

You never use the OptionButton control alone. This control always appears in a group. A group of OptionButton controls lets you make one selection from a list of selections. Only one OptionButton control is selected at any given time, so selecting one automatically deselects all the other buttons.

Because the OptionButton controls work in a group, you have to tell VBA which controls belong to which group, especially if a form contains more than one group. You can create groups in one of two ways. The first technique is to add the same string to the GroupName property of each memory of the group. The advantage of using this method is that it requires less space and can make your program work faster. In addition, this method is transparent, so any background image you use on the form shows through.

The second method is to place the OptionButton controls in a Frame control. To use this technique, you must create the Frame control first and then place the OptionButton controls within the Frame control. The advantage of using this method is that it's less error prone (the first method depends on you typing the same string each time and not making a typo), and you can visually see which buttons belong in the same group. Frames can also provide special visual effects, such as a sunken control group.

Unfortunately, a group of OptionButton controls still acts as individual controls. You have to monitor each control separately.

 One way to monitor option button groups is to create a global variable and use the Click event of each control to change it. This method provides a slight performance boost because you don't have to determine which OptionButton is selected when you want to perform a task — the status is always known. The disadvantages of this method are that it requires slightly more code and a little more memory, and the global variable could be a source of errors. Listing 7-4 shows an example of using the global variable approach. (You can find the source code for this example on the Dummies.com site at `http://www.dummies.com/go/vbafd5e`.)

Listing 7-4   Using Global Variables with Option Buttons

```
Private ColorSelect As String
Private NumberSelect As String

Private Sub btnStatus_Click()
    ' Create an output string.
    Dim Output As String
    Output = "The selected color is: " + ColorSelect + _
            vbCrLf + _
            "The selected number is: " + NumberSelect


    ' Display the result.
    MsgBox Output
End Sub

Private Sub obBlue_Click()
    ' Change the ColorSelect value.
    ColorSelect = obBlue.Caption
End Sub

Private Sub obGreen_Click()
    ' Change the ColorSelect value.
    ColorSelect = obGreen.Caption
End Sub

Private Sub obOne_Click()
    ' Change the NumberSelect value.
    NumberSelect = obOne.Caption
End Sub

Private Sub obRed_Click()
    ' Change the ColorSelect value.
    ColorSelect = obRed.Caption
End Sub

Private Sub obThree_Click()
    ' Change the NumberSelect value.
    NumberSelect = obThree.Caption
End Sub

Private Sub obTwo_Click()
    ' Change the NumberSelect value.
    NumberSelect = obTwo.Caption
End Sub

Private Sub UserForm_Initialize()
```

```
          'Set the initial global values.
          ColorSelect = obRed.Caption
          NumberSelect = obOne.Caption
     End Sub
```

Using global variables means that you have to set them to some initial value.
The `UserForm_Initialize` sub-procedure performs this task when you
start the program. When you click each `OptionButton` control, VBA calls
the appropriate `Click` event handler. The event handler changes one of the
two global variables, `ColorSelect` or `NumberSelect`, as appropriate. Click
the Status button, and VBA calls the `btnStatus_Click` sub-procedure. Notice
that this sub-procedure has little work to do because the program tracks the
option button status.

Another approach is to use a series of `If...Then...ElseIf` statements to
determine which `OptionButton` control is selected by using the `Value`
property. Listing 7-5 shows a sample of the selection process that uses this
second method.

Listing 7-5   Making Selections with Option Buttons

```
Private Sub btnElseIfSelect_Click()
    ' Create an output string.
    Dim Output As String
    Output = "The selected color is: "

    ' Determine the color value.
    If obRed.Value Then
        Output = Output + "Red"
    ElseIf obGreen.Value Then
        Output = Output + "Green"
    Else
        Output = Output + "Blue"
    End If

    ' Add the number string.
    Output = Output + vbCrLf + "The selected number is: "

    ' Determine the number value.
    If obOne.Value Then
        Output = Output + "One"
    ElseIf obTwo.Value Then
        Output = Output + "Two"
    Else
        Output = Output + "Three"
    End If

    ' Display the result.
    MsgBox Output
End Sub
```

The code begins by determining the status of the color option buttons. It uses the `Value` properties to perform this task. After the code determines the color option status, it creates that part of the `Output` string and moves on to the number values. The code uses the same procedure as before to determine the number option status.

Both of these techniques display the same output. The difference between the two techniques is where they perform their work. If you use the first technique, you write more code to gain a performance advantage. The second method requires just one sub-procedure and no global variables but can result in a performance hit.

Choosing options with list boxes and combo boxes

You use `OptionButton` controls when you want to create a *static* list — one that doesn't ever change. The `ListBox` and `ComboBox` controls help you create *dynamic* lists — lists that can change while the program runs or from session to session. The list of options doesn't have to change, but knowing that you have the option is helpful.

Both controls require that you *populate* (fill) them with information. The easiest method is to use the `AddItem` method. Use this method when you populate the control with the same information each time that the program starts. You can also create an array and add the array to the `List` property. The advantage of this second method is that you can pass different arrays to a function or sub-procedure when the list content requirements change. (See Chapter 9 for details on using arrays.)

You need to consider differences in these two controls when you're designing an application. The `ComboBox` is smaller, but it displays only the selected option. To see all the options, you have to click the down arrow. The `ListBox` is a bit more accessible because it displays many (but not necessarily all of the) options at once.

The default `ComboBox` setting also lets the user type in a value other than those presented. This makes the `ComboBox` more flexible, but it also means that you have to deal with input errors. Set the `MatchRequired` property to `True` if you want the `ComboBox` to limit the input to the choices that you provide. A `ListBox` always limits input to the choices that you provide, so there's never a chance for input that causes a program error.

The advantage of using a `ListBox` is that you can set the `MultiSelect` property to allow the user to make more than one choice. This feature lets you limit the input choices while allowing multiple inputs. Use the `Selected` property to determine which entries are highlighted. The `Value` property is always `Null` (set to nothing) when you allow multiple selections.

Both of these controls require less code than the `OptionButton` control to perform approximately the same task. Listing 7-6 shows an example of both the `ComboBox` and the `ListBox` in action. (You can find the source code for this example on the Dummies.com site at `http://www.dummies.com/go/vbafd5e`.)

Listing 7-6   Working with List Boxes and Combo Boxes

```
Private Sub btnStatus_Click()
    ' Create an output string.
    Dim Output As String
    Output = "The selected color is: " + _
             comboColors.Value + vbCrLf + _
             "The selected number is: " +
         listNumbers.Value

    ' Display the result.
    MsgBox Output
End Sub

Private Sub UserForm_Initialize()
    ' Populate the ListBox control.
    listNumbers.AddItem "One"
    listNumbers.AddItem "Two"
    listNumbers.AddItem "Three"
    listNumbers.AddItem "Four"
    listNumbers.AddItem "Five"
    listNumbers.AddItem "Six"

    ' Select the default value.
    listNumbers.Value = "One"

    ' Populate the ComboBox control.
    comboColors.AddItem "Red"
    comboColors.AddItem "Green"
    comboColors.AddItem "Blue"
    comboColors.AddItem "Yellow"
    comboColors.AddItem "Orange"
    comboColors.AddItem "Purple"

    ' Select the default value.
    comboColors.Value = "Red"
End Sub
```

The code begins in the `UserForm_Initialize` sub-procedure. You must populate the two controls by using the `AddItem` method. Setting the `Value` property to one of the values that you provide selects that value in the list.

The `btnStatus_Click` sub-procedure retrieves the current selections that use the control's `Value` property. It displays a message box containing essentially the same information as the `OptionButton` example in the preceding "Making choices with option buttons and frames" section.

Although this code performs essentially the same task as the `OptionButton` code, it requires far less code. In fact, this code actually provides more input choices than the `OptionButton` example.

Adding controls to the Toolbox

You might find that you need other controls in order to create your program. Windows provides a wealth of controls that you can use. The Toolbox that VBA provides has only a few essential controls in it — you can always add more by using the following procedure:

1. **Right-click anywhere on the Controls page of the Toolbox, and then choose Additional Controls from the context menu that appears.**

   You see the Additional Controls dialog box, shown in Figure 7-6.

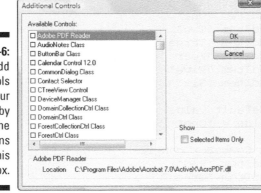

Figure 7-6:
Add controls to your Toolbox by using the options in this dialog box.

2. **Select the control that you want to add to your Toolbox by placing a check mark next to its entry.**

3. **Click OK.**

   VBA adds the selected control to your Toolbox.

The Toolbox can get crowded after you add a few controls to it. You can add pages to the Toolbox by right-clicking outside the existing pages and then choosing New Page from the context menu that appears. Getting rid of a page is as easy as selecting that page, right-clicking outside the page area, and then choosing Delete Page from the context menu that appears. It's also easy to move and rename pages by using context menu entries.

Using the Forms You Create

Forms are useful only if they're usable. This means modifying the form and control properties to provide a pleasant appearance. You should change certain properties every time that you create a form to ensure that everyone can use it easily. Arranging the content of the form onscreen is important, as is making sure that the form operates correctly. Finally, you need to know how to handle events that the form generates to ensure that you see the expected results.

Modifying the form and control properties

In previous sections of this chapter, you discovered properties that you can change on your form or control to get specific results. Whenever you select the form or a control that it contains, the Properties window changes to match the selection.

You might look at the enormous list of properties provided with the form and controls and wonder how you can memorize them all. The fact is that you don't have to memorize any of them. To see what task a property performs, highlight that property and then press F1. VBA provides property-specific help.

Some properties provide exceptional value from a user perspective. Always define the Accelerator property for your controls. This property lets someone use the keyboard, rather than the mouse, to access the control. It's an essential property if you want to make your program accessible to those with special needs.

When you use a Label control to provide accelerator key access for a control that doesn't include a Caption property, make sure that the TabIndex property value for the Label is one less than the control that it references. For example, if a TextBox has a TabIndex value of 5, the associated Label should have a TabIndex value of 4. Otherwise, the accelerator key doesn't work as anticipated.

Another important property is ControlTipText. Type a description of the control's purpose in this property. When you hover the mouse over the control, VBA displays the text that you typed as balloon help. This kind of help is a halfway point between the prompt that you type and the context-sensitive help that your program should provide. It gives additional information without opening the help file.

Every control should have a `Caption` property entry. If the control doesn't provide a `Caption` property (such as a `TextBox` control), make sure that you add a `Label` to act as a prompt for the control.

Making your form pretty

Creating a neat appearance for your form is important. You want to use a form that looks nice because the appearance of the form affects the attitude of those who use it. VBA provides a number of options in the Format menu for making your form look nice. These same options appear on the UserForm toolbar in button form (see Figure 7-7).

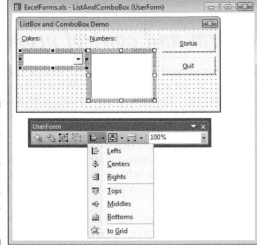

Figure 7-7:
Make your form look nice by using the Designer window features.

Notice that some of the buttons on the UserForm toolbar have down arrows associated with them. Click the down arrow, and you see a list of potential button functions for that button. Select the option that you want to use.

Aligning controls begins when you select two or more controls on the same form, as shown in Figure 7-7. Use a Ctrl+left-click to select each control in turn. The last control that you select acts as the guide for aligning the other controls, so make sure that the last control is in the position that you want to use for the other controls. If you want to align the tops of the controls, choose the Format➪Align➪Tops command. You can perform tasks such as centering individual controls by using the Format➪Center in Form menu options.

Creating a connection between forms and modules

Generally, you need to make some type of connection between a form and a module to display the form. The user can only access Subs contained in a module through the Macro dialog box. Consequently, the code you include with a form should affect only the handling of data locally to that form. When you want to interact with the user programmatically, you use a module. The example in this section shows how to display a form from a module. You'll see a number of other examples of interactions between forms and modules as the book progresses.

Displaying a form onscreen is easy. Access the form by simply using its name, and use the Show method to display it, as shown in Listing 7-7.

Listing 7-7   Displaying a Form

```
Public Sub ShowAForm()
    ' Use the Show method to show a form.
    ' You can perform other tasks using a modeless form.
    ButtonDemo.Show vbModeless

    ' A modal form requires that you complete the task
    ' with that form before you proceed to other tasks.
    NumericText.Show vbModal
End Sub
```

The problem that many developers face is deciding between a modal form and a modeless form. Always use a *modeless* form if you want to display other forms or perform other tasks while the current form is displayed. Use a *modal* form when you want to ensure that any tasks for the current form are complete before you display another form.

The example code shows both kinds of forms. You can try to select the ButtonDemo form, but you won't be able to do it. The NumericText form insists that you complete tasks with it before you do anything else. As soon as you finish working with the NumericText form, the program completes. VBA displays modeless forms and essentially forgets about them.

Validating user input

Always validate user input. The main source of security problems and many types of application errors is user input. If the user doesn't provide the correct input, your program doesn't run no matter how much effort you put into it. In addition, many security exploits rely on poor program validation. A *buffer overrun,* one of the well-known causes of security problems, is simply a failure to check input. Validating user input means that you should do the following:

✔ **Always ensure that the input uses the correct data type.**

✔ **Always check the range of numeric information.** If you want numbers between 1 and 5, don't let the user input anything else.

✔ **Always check the value of text input whenever possible.** If you're expecting an address, look for elements in the text that make up an address.

✔ **Never allow the user to input special characters unless you actually need the special characters to make the input work.**

✔ **Keep input simple enough that the user knows what you want and it's easy to check.** For example, use separate entries for city, state, and zip code in a contact management program.

Handling form events

Events are a part of most objects. Whenever the system, a user, or an external input interacts with your program, it's likely to generate an event. For example, when you click a button, it generates a `Click` event. An *event* is simply a way of saying that something has happened.

Forms and every control that they contain support a number of events. Look at the top of the Code window, and you see two Combo Boxes. The first is the Object list. It contains a list of every object associated with the current form. Figure 7-8 shows an example of this list. The UserForm entry is the actual form object.

Figure 7-8:
Use the
Object list
to select
objects
associated
with the
current
form.

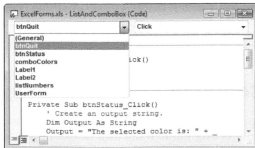

Whenever you select an object, VBA automatically creates a sub-procedure for the default event that the object supports (the `Click` event in many cases). You can remove this entry if you're interested in writing code for some other event.

The second Combo Box is the Procedure list. Figure 7-9 shows an example of this list box. The Procedure list contains a list of events associated with the current object. This list changes when you change entries in the Object list.

Figure 7-9:
Use the
Procedure
list to select
events
associated
with the
current
object.

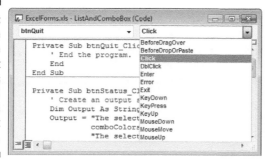

When you look through the Procedure list, notice that some entries are in bold. A bolded entry is one that you've added to the program. The entries shown in normal text are events that you can choose to handle but haven't so far. To add a new event handler to the program, simply select the entry from the Procedure list. VBA adds the event `Sub` to your code — type your code within this `Sub` to handle the event.

Part III
Expanding Your VBA Horizons

The 5th Wave   By Rich Tennant

COMPUTER SCIENCES LAB

"I'm sure there will be a good job market when I graduate. I created a virus that will go off that year."

In this part . . .

This is the part of the book where you move from knowing the language to using the language for beneficial work.

In Chapter 8, I show how VBA can use objects to model program elements. (For example, VBA sees every document that you create as an object with its own, unique features.) Arrays and collections in VBA share similar characteristics to real-world collections. Chapter 8 also shows you how to sign your work so that others know that the application is from you and not from someone else.

In Chapter 9, I help you understand the value of the individual elements and the collection as a whole. You can't perform many tasks with Office without using collections; this exceptionally useful programming technique appears everywhere.

In Chapter 10, I demonstrate techniques for using disk storage. Microsoft considers XML the next storage technology that everyone will want to use.

In Chapter 11, I describe how XML can benefit you and how to use it within VBA.

Chapter 8

Object-Oriented Programming

*I*f you've followed each chapter of the book to this point, you've used objects to perform tasks. For example, forms and all the controls that they contain are objects. The Clipboard also requires use of an object. In short, objects are an essential part of working with VBA because they reduce the amount of code that you have to write.

In this chapter, I describe the underlying mechanisms behind objects. You can create your own objects by using VBA to design classes, which are essentially object blueprints. In fact, you can create these objects and share them with other people who might need to use the same features. Using and creating objects by designing classes makes your VBA programming experience better.

Understanding Classes

A *class* is a description of an object: It's the blueprint that VBA uses to build an object when you request one. The class isn't the object; it's merely the set of building instructions for the object. You can use the class to visualize what the object will look like, but you can't use a class to perform any tasks. Once

VBA builds the object using the class, it doesn't look at the class any more unless it wants to build another object. This differentiation between classes and objects is important to remember because many information sources confuse the two concepts. You need to keep them separate to better understand how objects work. The sections that follow describe classes and objects in detail.

Understanding object-oriented programming concepts

At one time, developers had to worry about every variable, construct, and step in their code. Procedural languages use step-by-step instructions to tell the computer how to perform a task. Many developers continue to use procedural languages because they find them easy to use and understand. Object-oriented programming (OOP) hides implementation details from the developer. All the developer needs to know is that an object accomplishes a specific task; how the object performs the task is up to the object's developer. The act of hiding the working details of an object is called *encapsulation*.

The idea behind using objects is that you don't worry about how the information you type gets turned into executable code. This concept may sound really odd to anyone who's used to working with a procedural language, but that's the way it is. I had similar difficulties when I moved from assembler and C to C++. It took some time for me to learn that although the object code does get translated into executable code in some way, the whole reason for using objects is to create an *abstraction* so that you worry less about the actual underlying code than you do about the task the object is supposed to perform. The object creator takes care of the internal workings of the object.

Using classes also benefits the developer because it's possible to inherit all of the features of another class. *Inheritance* is the act of creating a new class based on the content of a parent class. For example, you might already have a class called Dog and want to create a new class called BorderCollie. Because a border collie is a kind of dog, you can inherit the feature of the Dog class into the new BorderCollie class.

Class theory can become quite complex, but you really don't need to worry about the complexities when working with VBA. You can find all kinds of OOP topics online that discuss everything from the intricacies of good class definition to whether OOP is really better than procedural code. If you really want to know the low-level concepts behind OOP, one of the best places to begin is Wikipedia (http://en.wikipedia.org/wiki/Object-oriented_programming).

Understanding properties, methods, and events

All classes include some comment elements. Because a class is essentially a black box that accepts input and provides output, you need some way to interact with it. Classes provide three common constructions that help you interact with them: properties, methods, and events. The following list describes each of these constructions.

- ✔ **Properties:** A property provides a means to access data within the object. Unlike a variable, a property can include code that controls the interaction with the object data. The property might check the data type of the incoming request or format the outgoing data in some way. Properties can provide read/write access so that you can change the object data as well as use it in your own code. However, a class developer can also choose to make a property read-only or write-only.

- ✔ **Methods:** A method provides a means of asking the object to perform a task. As with a Function or Sub, a method can return a value and accept data as input. Unlike with a Function or Sub, you need not worry about the inner workings of the method. Your only concern is that you must provide certain input to obtain specific output. In some cases, you will find methods that accept no input and provide no output but still perform a task. For example, a Refresh() method may tell the object to refresh its data. Methods always perform a task, but need not work with data (from an external perspective) to do it.

- ✔ **Events:** An event is the object's way of interacting with the outside world. An event signals that something has happened. A user might have clicked a button, or the status of a text box might have changed. The events that an object signals depend on the communication that the class designer chooses to provide. Even when an object signals an event, however, nothing takes place in your code unless you create an event handler, a special Sub or Function, to do something with the event.

Defining classes

You might want to think of a class as a substitute for a Function or a Sub, but classes are separate. A Function or Sub always describes a *procedure* — a list of steps. A *class* describes a thing. You can visualize a file because it's a thing. That's why VBA uses classes to describe the file system and uses objects to work with individual file system elements, such as a drive. Although you might read that objects are substitutes for procedures, the two kinds of programming have definite places in your programmer's toolbox. Make sure that you work with both as needed.

To build an object, you tell VBA to *instantiate* (create an instance of) the object. All the code required to build the object appears in the class. As a VBA user, you create the class and not the object. Here's a simple example of the two-step process used to instantiate an object:

```
' Create a reference to the file system.
Dim MyFileSystem As FileSystemObject

' Create a reference for the target drive.
Dim MyDrive As Drive

' Fill these two objects with data so they show the
' available space on drive C.
Set MyFileSystem = New FileSystemObject
Set MyDrive = MyFileSystem.GetDrive("C")
```

VBA creates the object, `MyFileSystem`, based on the blueprint provided by the `FileSystemObject` class. Likewise, VBA creates the object, `MyDrive`, based on the `Drive` class.

Telling VBA that you want to create these two objects by using the `Dim` statement is not the same as instantiating them. The `Set` statement instantiates the object. You `Set` an object equal to the blueprint contained within a class.

You can instantiate objects by using a number of techniques — the previous example shows two of them. In the first case, `MyFileSystem` is instantiated by using the `New` keyword and the name of the class, `FileSystemObject`. In the second case, `MyDrive` is instantiated based on an existing object contained within the `MyFileSystem` object. The `GetDrive` method tells VBA which `Drive` object to use within the `MyFileSystem` object.

Considering class types

Classes come in two varieties: components and controls. A *component* is a class that describes an object without a user interface. The `FileSystem Object` class is a component. It shows VBA how to create an object that lacks a user interface. You usually create components with VBA. All the examples in this book (such as the upcoming Listing 8-1) show how to create components.

A *control* is a class that describes an object that includes a user interface or affects the user interface. The `CommandButton` class is a control because it includes a user interface. Don't assume that every control provides a viewable piece of the user interface. When you use the `Timer` class, it's still a control (even if it doesn't have a user interface) because it interacts with the user and affects the user interface. It's very hard to create controls with VBA. You should use another language — such as Visual Basic (not VBA), Visual

C++, or Visual C# — when you want to create special controls for your VBA program.

 Note that the `Timer` class might not appear with VBA, but you can read about it at `http://msdn.microsoft.com/library/en-us/vbcon98/html/vbcontimercontrol.asp`. This control is so incredibly useful that you might want to download the version that appears at Programmers Heaven (`http://www.programmersheaven.com/download/29614/download.aspx`) even if VBA includes the standard `Timer` control. The Programmers Heaven version provides better control over the timing interval and can provide long-term timing.

Using classes to improve your applications

VBA generally relies on a combination of classes and procedural code to create an application. The previous chapters of this book have demonstrated that you can create applications in VBA that rely entirely on procedural code, but these applications are limited. In some cases, you must use objects to interact with the host application. For example, when you want to interact with the Ribbon in Word, you must use an object to do it. All of these objects rely on classes that are built into the host application.

Once you begin seeing the power of classes, you can decide whether to create classes of your own. There isn't a right or wrong position to take on using classes of your own, despite what you might hear other people say. Many developers create complex VBA applications without ever building a class. It's a matter of personal preference.

The advantages of using classes are many. The biggest advantages, however, are that classes hide details that you might not want to think about as you create an application, and you can easily reuse class code to create other classes. The biggest disadvantages of using classes are that you do pay a small performance and resource penalty, and modifying applications with classes can become complex. A developer can lose contact with the code in the application and then have to relearn it when it comes time to make a change.

Designing a Basic Class

Because a class is a blueprint for an object, you need to have some idea of what you want to build. The best classes are ones that answer specific needs that you have. A class requires a specific look and feel. VBA includes this look and feel as part of the objects that it creates from the class.

It helps to look at existing classes when you think about your own class, to see what other people have done. All the controls provided with VBA make a good starting point because you can play with them in code to see how Microsoft designed a particular feature. You should also examine VBA objects, such as the ones used in the examples in this book. Control and component examples are readily available for your use as patterns for your own class. (See the "Locating Just the Right Code" section of Chapter 17 for ideas on where to find examples.) Here's a list of the items that you should consider copying:

- ✔ **Property, method, and event names:** Use recognizable (similar) names for properties, methods, and events. For example, don't call your Click event a Pushed event, because no one will know what you mean.

- ✔ **Mandatory features:** It's easy to forget to include a feature in your class. Existing classes can help you create a complete list of mandatory features, such as a Caption property, so that nothing is left out.

- ✔ **Design style:** Your control provides unique features and functionality. However, it helps to look at the way other people design classes, especially their visual elements. For example, something as simple as providing a True/False drop-down list box for Boolean properties is very helpful.

- ✔ **Visual aids:** A class can provide visual aids, such as special dialog boxes for some types of information. Look at other classes for ideas on how you can add visual aids to your class that make it easier to use.

- ✔ **Privacy:** You might find it tempting to expose every feature to anyone who might use it. However, that approach can lead to problems because objects are only supposed to expose necessary elements. Use other classes as examples of what you should keep hidden in your own class.

The example in this section shows how to create a simple class. The component encapsulates the MsgBox function and makes it easier to use by helping you see the options clearly. More importantly, the example demonstrates how to construct properties, methods, and events for this simple class.

Defining properties

A *property* describes a feature of the object, such as its color, the caption, a method of presentation (such as sunken or etched), or some other characteristic. Don't assume that a property has to describe a physical characteristic of the object. A filename is a perfectly acceptable property. A property is a special kind of object-specific data.

Property construction methods

VBA provides three kinds of construction methods for properties. You can choose to use one or all three methods. A property requires at least one of the methods described in this list:

✔ **Let:** The Let method helps you set the value of a property. Use it when the property has a standard data type as an input value.

✔ **Set:** Use the Set method when you create objects that contain other objects. For example, a FileSystemObject contains Drive objects. To access these objects, you must use the Set method and not the Let method.

When creating an object within an object, you're essentially creating a pointer to a location in memory; but unlike in C or other low-level languages, the location isn't important. Within the referenced object are properties that hold values that affect the operation of the object. You don't care how the object works with the property. All you know is that if you set the Caption property of a control, you'll see that text displayed somehow onscreen. Other properties work the same way — they affect the operation of the object in some documented way. The property is yet another kind of indirect pointer, so you need some way to dereference that pointer and work with the data that it points to. That's where Let and Get come into play. Use Let to set a property in a referenced object to a specific value. Use Get to obtain the value of a property within the referenced object.

✔ **Get:** The Get method returns the stored property value to the caller. The method that you use for objects is different from other data types, but you can return any property value by using this method.

When you create a property, you decide not only the name and data type, but also its accessibility. The accessibility is read only (using the Get method), write only (using the Set or Let method), or read/write (using the Get method along with the Set or Let method).

Properties have scope, just like everything else in VBA. Besides Public and Private, a property can also have a special Friend scope. The Friend scope is a step between Public and Private. Everything within the current project can see the property, but nothing outside the current project can. The Friend scope is useful for local configuration. Any part of the local project — the part of the program that controls the functionality of the object — can configure the property, but your other projects can't see it.

You can also add the Static keyword to properties. Always add the Static keyword when you want the property to maintain its value between calls but not when you want to make sure that the property resets to the default value. The Static keyword is important when you want the object to maintain its settings.

Here in Listing 8-1 is an example of two of the read/write properties used for this example. The example actually contains several properties, but these two represent standard data type and object coding. (You can find the source code for this example on the Dummies.com site at http://www. dummies.com/go/vbafd5e.)

Listing 8-1   Creating Object Properties

```
Private UseIcon As VbMsgBoxStyle
Private NewIcon As Image

Public Static Property Let Icon(Value As IconTypes)
    ' Change the value of the message icon based on the
    ' input value.
    Select Case Value
        Case Critical
            UseIcon = vbCritical
        Case Question
            UseIcon = vbQuestion
        Case Exclamation
            UseIcon = vbExclamation
        Case Information
            UseIcon = vbInformation
    End Select
End Property

Public Static Property Get Icon() As IconTypes
    ' Return the value of the message icon.
    Select Case UseIcon
        Case vbCritical
            Icon = Critical
        Case vbQuestion
            Icon = Question
        Case vbExclamation
            Icon = Exclamation
        Case vbInformation
            Icon = Information
    End Select
End Property

Public Static Property Set SpecialIcon(Value As Image)
    ' Set the custom icon value. Make sure the user has
    ' supplied a valid image.
    If Not Value Is Nothing Then
        Set NewIcon = Value
    End If End Property

Public Static Property Get SpecialIcon() As Image
    ' Return the custom icon value.
    Set SpecialIcon = NewIcon
End Property
```

The first property, Icon, uses a standard data type. In this case, it's an enumerated data type that ensures that you provide the correct values. See the "Using enumerated constants" section, later in this chapter, for details on using enumerated types. Notice that the code transfers the input value to the private UseIcon variable only after it checks the input for correctness. When you work with a non-enumerated data type, it pays to include an Else Case clause that displays a message with correct input values. Using an enumerated type means that you don't have to include this feature.

Notice that UseIcon is a variable that is based on the VbMsgBoxStyle enumeration. An enumeration is a special kind of data structure that contains special values — it's based on the enum data type, so the UseIcon variable lets you select one of the enumeration values. Using an enumeration simply makes the code easier to read.

The second property, SpecialIcon, requires an object as input. This means that you must use the Set and Get methods rather than the Let and Get methods that the first property uses. Data-type checking is less intense in this case because VBA always provides a type mismatch error message if you provide the wrong value.

NewIcon is an object based on the Image class. The Image class describes how to build a container for holding an image, such as a bitmap. The NewIcon object actually holds the image that you provide as input to the SpecialIcon property.

Notice that you still have to check for empty objects that don't contain anything. The code shows how to perform this task by using the Is Nothing keyword sequence. When you require specific kinds of input for objects, you need to check object property values as well. This example doesn't perform this task, but it's something that you should consider for complex properties. For example, an image should have a valid Picture property value.

Property conversion considerations

When you choose to encapsulate a function to make it easier to use, you can run into situations where there isn't a direct conversion between the function and the object version. The MsgBox function includes the vbMsgBoxHelpButton style. This feature works better as a Boolean property, so you use the following code to create a property for it:

```
Public Static Property Let HelpButton(Value As Boolean)
    ' Should the example use the vbMsgBoxHelpButton style?
    UseHelpButton = Value
End Property

Public Static Property Get HelpButton() As Boolean
    ' Return the vbMsgBoxHelpButton value.
    HelpButton = UseHelpButton
End Property
```

The code for this property is very simple. It simply passes the `UseHelp Button` value back and forth. Notice that the comment for the `Let` method includes a reference to the `vbMsgBoxHelpButton` style. (Whenever you convert a function or other real-world entity into an object, try to preserve the original information in the comments that you write.) This comment helps you remember that this property replaces the `vbMsgBoxHelpButton` style.

Property naming considerations

You normally want to use the same names for properties in your object that other programmers use for their objects. This technique makes it easier for you to remember the purpose of a property. However, you also want to avoid confusion. If a property doesn't provide precisely the same functionality, it's better to use a different name. For example, the `MsgBox` function provides the `vbMsgBoxRight` style to allow flush-right text alignment. You might think that you should use the `TextAlign` property found in other objects, such as the `Label` control. However, the `TextAlign` property allows left, center, and right text alignment, so using this name for the example could prove confusing because the `MsgBox` function doesn't allow center alignment. The example uses a `Boolean` value and a different name for the property, as shown here:

```
Public Static Property Let RightAlignText(Value As
        Boolean)
    ' Should the example use the vbMsgBoxRight style?
    UseRightAlignment = Value
End Property

Public Static Property Get RightAlignText() As Boolean
    ' Return the vbMsgBoxRight value.
    RightAlignText = UseRightAlignment
End Property
```

Notice that the property name is very specific. The name makes it clear that left alignment is the default and that you can only choose right alignment as an option.

The `MsgBox Context` argument does precisely match the `HelpContextID` property used by many existing objects, so the example does use that name for the property. I ran into a problem with the `MsgBox Prompt` and `Title` arguments. Theoretically, both arguments should appear as part of the `Caption` property. When you set the `Caption` property of a `UserForm`, you set the title bar text. Likewise, the `Caption` property sets the text that appears in a `Label` control. The example uses the `Caption` property for the `Prompt` argument and uses a `Title` property for the `Title` argument. Because you use the `Prompt` argument more often, setting it equal to the `Caption` property makes sense.

Defining methods

Methods help you interact with an object by defining the form of interaction. The example in this chapter has only one method, Show. After you configure a message box for use, you want to show it onscreen, so the name is appropriate. The UserForm control also uses this name for the same purpose.

A method can rely on a Public Sub if it doesn't return a value, or a Public Function if it does. You call a method by using the same technique that you would with a Sub or Function. The difference is that a method is associated with a specific object and relies on the property values contained within that object. This difference means that when you call a method, you don't have to supply every value that the method needs to perform a task — the object supplies many (if not all) of the required arguments. Listing 8-2 contains the Show method code for this example.

Listing 8-2   Creating an Object Method

```
Public Function Show() As VbMsgBoxResult
    ' Create a variable to hold the message box result.
    Dim Result As VbMsgBoxResult

    ' Create and build the option list.
    Dim Options As VbMsgBoxStyle
    Options = UseIcon
    Options = Options Or UseButtons
    Options = Options Or UseDefault
    Options = Options Or UseModal

    ' Each of the Boolean values requires conversion to a
    ' style equivalent.
    If UseForeground Then
        Options = Options Or vbMsgBoxSetForeground
    End If
    If UseRightAlignment Then
        Options = Options Or vbMsgBoxRight
    End If
    If UseRightToLeft Then
        Options = Options Or vbMsgBoxRtlReading
    End If

    ' The help button requires special handling.
    If UseHelpButton Then
        ' Verify the user has supplied all required
        ' help information.
        If TheHelpFile = "" Then
            ' If the help filename is missing, the message
            ' box can't display help. Raise an error to
        tell
```

(continued)

Listing 8-2 *(continued)*

```
                ' the user about the problem.
                Err.Raise vbObjectError + 1, _
                        "SpecialMsg.Show", _
                        "You must provide a HelpFilename " +
                _
                        "property value to use the Help " +
                _
                        "button in a message box."
            Else
                ' The user has provided all required help
                ' information, so set the help button option.
                Options = Options Or vbMsgBoxHelpButton
            End If
        End If

        ' Determine if the message box will display help.
        If ((TheHelpFile = "") And (Not UseHelpButton)) Then
            ' Display a message box without help.
            Result = MsgBox(ThePrompt, Options, TheTitle)
        Else
            ' Display a message box that includes help.
            Result = MsgBox(ThePrompt, Options, TheTitle, _
                    TheHelpFile, TheHelpContext)
        End If

        ' Raise the Click event so the caller can react to it.
        RaiseEvent Click(Result)

        ' Return a result.
        Show = Result
End Function
```

The `MsgBox` function provides access to a number of styles. It's easy to forget how many styles until you start looking at code like this. The code creates an `Options` variable that contains all the style options that you've set up through object properties. It selects an icon, a button set, a default button, and a modality type (application or system). These options always appear in the list, and the `Class_Initialize` method sets them to default values. (See the upcoming "Defining initialization" section for details.) The `Options` variable can also contain a number of optional settings. The code checks the Boolean values, such as `UseForeground`, to determine whether you want to include these optional styles. It then adds the actual style to the `Options` variable.

Notice that the `UseHelpButton If...Then` statement includes error handling. See the upcoming "Adding Error Handling to Classes" section for a description of class error handling. In this case, the class determines whether you've assigned a help file to the message object. If not, clicking the Help button causes an error. The `MsgBox` function doesn't protect you from this error, but the `SpecialMsg` class does.

The code uses one of two methods for displaying the message box. When you don't define help, it passes just the prompt, the style options, and the title to the MsgBox function. When you do define help, the code also passes the help filename and the help context to the MsgBox function.

At this point, the Show method pauses. It waits for you to click one of the buttons on the message box. After you click one of the buttons, control returns to the Show method.

The code calls the RaiseEvent method next. See the following "Defining events" section for more information about events. In this case, the code raises the Click event to show that you've clicked a button. Notice that the Click event receives the return value from the MsgBox function call. Finally, the Show method also returns the result to the caller. Using this approach lets you react to a message box return value as either a method call return or an event, which increases the flexibility of the MsgBox function. You can also choose to ignore the return value.

Defining events

Events are an essential part of most classes. They signify that you've done something to the control. The example provides two kinds of events, but the actual number that you can create is unlimited. Anytime that an action occurs, you can *fire* (raise) an event. However, most classes limit their events to a user action or a change in data.

The example code in the preceding "Defining methods" section shows one way to fire an event. You use the RaiseEvent method to perform this task. Before you can fire an event, you must define it. Events are always public, but you should include the Public keyword to ensure that your event works with future versions of VBA and that you avoid making the code hard to read. Here are some examples of event declarations:

```
' Define an event that occurs when the user clicks a
            button.
Public Event Click(Result As VbMsgBoxResult)

' Define events for various property changes.
Public Event ChangeButton(Result As ButtonTypes)
Public Event ChangeIcon(Result As IconTypes)
```

The event declarations always include the Event keyword and the event name. The example uses Click as an event name because that's what other VBA objects use for this particular event. Arguments are optional. All three of the declarations use single arguments in this case. I prefer to include information that I think I might need later as part of the event declaration rather than get that information by using other means.

Monitoring data change is an important event. You might need to perform verification or to modify other object settings when a data change occurs. For example, when you decide to change the button style, you also need to check the default button setting to ensure that it falls within the desired range. Listing 8-3 shows a typical example of a data modification event.

Listing 8-3   Creating an Object Event

```
Public Static Property Let Buttons(Value As ButtonTypes)
    ' Change the value of the message button based on the
    ' input value.
    Select Case Value
        Case OKOnly
            UseButtons = vbOKOnly
        Case OKCancel
            UseButtons = vbOKCancel
        Case AbortRetryIgnore
            UseButtons = vbAbortRetryIgnore
        Case YesNoCancel
            UseButtons = vbYesNoCancel
        Case YesNo
            UseButtons = vbYesNo
        Case RetryCancel
            UseButtons = vbRetryCancel
    End Select

    ' Raise an event to show the button type has changed.
    RaiseEvent ChangeButton(Value)
End Property
```

Notice in this code and in the code in the earlier "Defining methods" section that the `RaiseEvent` method isn't called until after the action takes place. Always raise the event after you verify that it has occurred. Otherwise, you might react to an event that hasn't taken place yet (and might not take place at all).

Using enumerated constants

The example uses a number of enumerated constants. These constants serve to limit the number of acceptable input values. They also act as reminders of the acceptable inputs. Listing 8-4 contains an example of a public enumeration.

Listing 8-4   Using Constants in an Object

```
' This enumeration shows the button types.
Public Enum ButtonTypes
    OKOnly = 0
    OKCancel = 1
```

```
        AbortRetryIgnore = 2
        YesNoCancel = 3
        YesNo = 4
        RetryCancel = 5
End Enum
```

You assign values to each of the constants within the enumeration. The values don't have to follow any particular order, and you don't have to start with 0. It helps to order the enumeration in some way. The example uses the help topic order to make it easier to compare the help files with the values that the code contains. You can also order the entries alphabetically or in order of usage frequency. When a class uses an enumeration for a particular value, VBA displays the acceptable values.

Look at the `MsgObj.Buttons` line of code shown in Listing 8-6. When you type = at this line, you see a list of acceptable values for that property. The list contains the acceptable button values for the example. The advantage of this technique is that you don't have to remember the individual values, and the probability of providing an incorrect value drops dramatically. Always use enumerated constants, when you can, to reduce errors and typing time.

Defining initialization

Every class should provide property and local variable initialization. Adding initialization ensures that your class won't fail because of a lack of input. In addition, initialization can help you create objects with less code because many of the values are already defined. The `Class_Initialize` method performs all the initialization tasks for any class. See Listing 8-5 for the initialization code used for the example.

Listing 8-5   Initializing a Class

```
Private Sub Class_Initialize()
    ' Set the initial prompt.
    ThePrompt = "Hello World"

    ' Define a simple title.
    TheTitle = ""

    ' Don't include a default help file or context.
    TheHelpFile = ""
    TheHelpContext = 0

    ' Initialize the variables.
    ' Use the Information icon.
```

(continued)

Listing 8-5 *(continued)*

```
        UseIcon = vbInformation

        ' Display only the OK button.
        UseButtons = vbOKOnly

        ' Make the first button the default button.
        UseDefault = vbDefaultButton1

        ' Ensure the message box is application modal. The
            user
        ' must clear the message box before doing anything
            else
        ' with the application.
        UseModal = vbApplicationModal

        ' Don't display a help button.
        UseHelpButton = False

        ' It's not essential that the message box always
            appear
        ' in the foreground.
        UseForeground = False

        ' Left-align the message box text.
        UseRightAlignment = False

        ' Display the text in left-to-right order.
        UseRightToLeft = False

        ' Initialize the special icon, but don't load a
            picture.
        Set SpecialIcon = New Image
End Sub
```

The code shows that initialization is simply the task of assigning values to every variable. However, the code also demonstrates some subtleties that you should consider. The MsgBox function has only one required input: a prompt. The code defines a value for ThePrompt because it's a required input. The Show method works even when you simply instantiate the object and make the method call.

The title, help filename, and help context are all optional MsgBox function arguments, so the code doesn't define a value for them. The empty string ensures that the variable is usable, but nothing else.

Variables such as UseIcon must use one of the enumerated values. In this case, the initialization process sets the variable to use the default value that the MsgBox function uses or the value that you use most often. For example, the MsgBox function doesn't require that you provide an icon, but the object does provide one for the sake of onscreen appearance.

Setting the Instancing property

You can create two kinds of classes for your program: private and public. The default setting is private, which means that no one outside the program can see the class or create objects from it. When you create a class that's so special that there's no chance that you can use it outside the current program, this is the setting that you should use.

You'll use most of the classes that you create in multiple programs. You should set the Instancing property of these classes to Public. Figure 8-1 shows the Instancing property in the Properties window.

Figure 8-1:
Modifying
the
Instancing
property for
class usage.

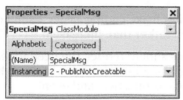

The not-creatable portion of this property value means that other VBA programs can use objects contained within your class, but only if your class creates them. In the case of the example, this means that other programs can use the SpecialIcon object, but they can't create the SpecialIcon object directly. The SpecialMsg class must create the SpecialIcon object, and then the caller can assign a value to that object.

Creating useful classes

You might wonder why a class that encapsulates the MsgBox function would be useful. This class is useful for a number of reasons. The most important is that it makes using the MsgBox function less of a memory teaser. The MsgBox function provides a wealth of style options, but trying to memorize them all is a waste of time. Creating a class that eliminates the memory gymnastics for you saves time and effort.

Using the class also reduces the chance of error. Each property provides access to mutually exclusive styles. You can combine multiple icon types when using the MsgBox function like this:

```
MsgBox "Hello", vbCritical Or vbInformation
```

The result is a message box that doesn't display any icon. The class version eliminates this problem. You can choose only one icon, and you don't have to remember the icon choices.

The class form of the MsgBox function also makes setups easier. You can use this class to set up certain types of message boxes that you use regularly at the beginning of the program. For example, you can use it to set up an error message box. When an error occurs, you can quickly set the Caption property and use the Show method to display the message box. The idea is that the error message box is consistent and easy to use.

The example class in this chapter shows the three reasons to encapsulate functions and also the three things that you should consider when you're creating new objects. The following list summarizes these three elements:

- **Ease of use:** A class should always make coding easier. Useful classes reduce the programming burden rather than increase it.

- **Reduced learning curve:** A class should reduce the need to memorize things or to figure out odd programming techniques. A class should provide easy-to-understand methods, properties, and events.

- **Enhanced reliability:** A well-designed class provides error handling not found in a function. The class should sensibly restrict actions that result in coding errors. It should also check inputs to ensure that the information is correct.

Using Your New Object in an Application

The SpecialMsg class is ready for use in an application. You can use it in place of the MsgBox function . . . and in some places where the MsgBox function simply won't work. For example, you can't ask the MsgBox function to generate events, but the SpecialMsg class does. The code in Listing 8-6 shows an example of the SpecialMsg class in action.

Listing 8-6   Testing the New Object

```
Private WithEvents MsgObj As SpecialMsg

Private Sub btnTest_Click()
    ' Instantiate the special message box.
    If MsgObj Is Nothing Then
        Set MsgObj = New SpecialMsg
    End If
    ' Assign some property values.
    MsgObj.Caption = "This is a message object."
    MsgObj.Title = "Special Message"
```

```
    MsgObj.Buttons = YesNoCancel
    MsgObj.Icon = Question

    ' Display the message box.
    MsgObj.Show
End Sub

Private Sub MsgObj_ChangeButton(Result As ButtonTypes)
    ' Show the new button type.
    lblButtonType = Result
End Sub

Private Sub MsgObj_Click(Result As VbMsgBoxResult)
    ' Show the return value.
    lblReturnValue = Result
End Sub
```

Notice that the example declares the `MsgObj` object as `Private WithEvents`. The `WithEvents` statement is important because it tells VBA that you want the object to handle events. When you leave out this statement, the object doesn't respond to any events declared in the class.

The example uses a standard form with Test and Quit buttons to test the class. The form also contains two labels for displaying output values from the class. The `btnTest_Click` sub-procedure instantiates the object, performs all the required setups, and then displays the message box by using the `Show` method.

Changing the button type automatically generates a `ChangeButton` event. The example handles this event by displaying the new button type in `lblButtonType`. Like with most event handlers, the sub-procedure is private and uses a combination of the object name and the event, `MsgObj_ ChangeButton`.

The example also handles the `Click` event. The `MsgObj_Click` sub-procedure produces the same result as the output of the `Show` method. Which technique you use in your code depends on the results that you want to achieve.

Because you can't directly access a form by using the Macro dialog box, you also need to create some simple code to display the form. Create a new module for your application and create a simple `Sub` to show the form, as shown here:

```
Sub ShowMsgBox()
    ' Display the special message box.
    SpecialMsgTest.Show
End Sub
```

Adding Error Handling to Classes

Classes have to provide exceptionally robust error handling so that they're reliable. The earlier "Defining methods" section shows one type of error handling that you can add to a class. Keeping track of property interactions before you perform a task such as displaying the message box is important.

You can add other forms of error handling to your class. Tracking actual input values is another good form of error handling when you can't use enumerated constants. It's also important to monitor property values based on other input values. Here's an example of code (see Listing 8-7) that monitors the DefaultButton property based on the number of buttons that the message box has. The code ensures that the default button is a button that actually exists on the message box.

Listing 8-7   Providing Error Handling in an Object

```
Public Static Property Let DefaultButton(Value As
        DefaultButtonTypes)
    ' Change the value of the message icon based on the
    ' input value.
    Select Case Value
        Case Button_1
            UseDefault = vbDefaultButton1
        Case Button_2
            If ((UseButtons = vbOKOnly) And _
                (Not UseHelpButton)) Then
                ' Can't have a single button setting if
                ' there is no Help button, so raise an
                ' error.
                Err.Raise vbObjectError + 2, _
                "SpecialMsg.DefaultButton", _
                "The selected default button value is " +
                _
                "incorrect. Choose a default button " + _
                "that matches the message box settings."
            Else
                ' Set the default button value.
                UseDefault = vbDefaultButton2
            End If
        Case Button_3
            If ((UseButtons = vbOKOnly) Or _
                (((UseButtons = vbOKCancel) Or _
                (UseButtons = vbRetryCancel) Or _
                (UseButtons = vbYesNo)) And _
                (Not UseHelpButton))) Then
                ' This setting doesn't support a single
                ' button option at all. It also doesn't
                ' support any of the double button options
```

```
                             ' if there is no Help button. Raise an
            error
                             ' if any of these conditions is true.
                             Err.Raise vbObjectError + 2, _
                             "SpecialMsg.DefaultButton", _
                             "The selected default button value is " +
            _
                             "incorrect. Choose a default button " + _
                             "that matches the message box settings."
                    Else
                             ' Set the default button value.
                             UseDefault = vbDefaultButton3
                    End If
            Case Button_4
                    If Not UseHelpButton Then
                             ' Can't have four buttons if there is no
                             ' Help button, so raise an error.
                             Err.Raise vbObjectError + 2, _
                             "SpecialMsg.DefaultButton", _
                             "The selected default button value is " +
            _
                             "incorrect. Choose a default button " + _
                             "that matches the message box settings."
                    Else
                             ' Set the default button value.
                             UseDefault = vbDefaultButton4
                    End If
        End Select
End Property
```

The logic that you use for error handling can become quite complex. There's
no error handling for a `DefaultButton` value of `Button_1` because you
can't create a message box with no buttons (every message box has at least
one button). Only one setting results in a message box with just one button.
When you create a message box with `vbOKOnly` and leave out the Help
button, there's only one button on the message box. The `Case Button_2`
clause checks for this possibility and generates an error message when you
ask for the second button as a default on a message box with only one button.

The `Case Button_3` error-handling logic is especially complex. When you
encounter a situation where the logic becomes this complex, it pays to take the
problem apart, solve the individual pieces, and then put the pieces together. A
message box has three buttons when you request the `vbYesNoCancel` option.
The message box also has three buttons when you request the `vbYesNo`
option and a Help button. The message box never has three buttons when
using the `vbOKOnly` option — even adding the Help button increases the
number of buttons to only two. The code uses all these criteria to look for

situations where the message box won't have three buttons. When the message box lacks the proper number of buttons, the code produces an error.

The `Case Button_4` error-handling logic demonstrates a situation where you can turn something very complicated into something very simple. None of the button options has more than three buttons. Therefore, the only time you can set the default button to the fourth button is when there's a Help button. The code looks for this button. When you don't include it, the code generates an error.

Using the With Statement

VBA does provide an interesting feature that makes it easier to write code for an object. The `With` statement tells VBA that you plan to perform a number of tasks by using the same object. Every dotted statement within the structure applies to that object. Using this technique reduces the amount of code that you have to type and can reduce the chance of typos. Listing 8-8 shows an example of the `With` statement in use.

Listing 8-8   Using an Alternative Object-Testing Technique

```
Private Sub btnTest2_Click()
    ' Instantiate the special message box.
    If MsgObj Is Nothing Then
        Set MsgObj = New SpecialMsg
    End If
    ' Assign some property values.
    With MsgObj
        .Caption = "This is a message object."
        .Title = "Special Message"
        .Buttons = YesNoCancel
        .Icon = Question

        ' Display the message box.
        .Show
    End With
End Sub
```

Notice that this code is similar to the code in the earlier "Using Your New Object in an Application" section. The only difference is that you don't have to type `MsgObj` so many times. The code works precisely the same as before, and you get the same prompts as before. This is a personal-taste coding technique. You don't lose anything by not using it, and you don't gain anything significant when you do.

Adding a Digital Signature to Your Creation

You might eventually want to send your class to someone else. In some cases, this means sending the entire project to them. Whenever you send your project to someone else, make sure that you sign it so that the recipient knows that you actually created it.

Obtaining a digital signature

A digital signature isn't anything special in its own right. You can create a digital signature quite easily and use it to sign your VBA projects. The magic in a digital signature is in the trust it provides. Consequently, you need to sign your projects with a digital signature that people can trust. In most cases, this means obtaining a digital signature from a third-party Certificate Authority (CA), such as VeriSign. You can find a list of CAs at `http://msdn.microsoft.com/library/?url=/library/en-us/dnsecure/html/rootcertprog.asp`.

Creating a test digital signature

Not everyone will want to buy a digital signature from a third party. If you create VBA applications exclusively for your own use, buying a digital signature is a waste of time and money. In addition, you might not want to use a third-party digital signature for testing. To receive full benefit from a third-party certificate, you must keep it secret. For these reasons and more, you'll probably want to create a test or personal certificate at some point. The following steps describe how to perform this task:

1. **Choose Start⇨Programs⇨Microsoft Office⇨Microsoft Office Tools⇨ Digital Certificate for VBA Projects.**

   You see the Create Digital Certificate dialog box.

2. **Type a name for your certificate in the Your Certificate's Name field.**

3. **Click OK.**

   You see a success message.

4. **Click OK.**

   The test certificate is ready to use.

Applying the digital signature to a project

After you have a digital signature, you need to apply it to your project. Use the following steps to sign your creation:

1. **In the VBA Integrated Development Environment (IDE), choose Tools⇨Digital Signature.**

   You see a Digital Signature dialog box, like the one shown in Figure 8-2.

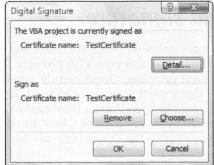

Figure 8-2:
Verify the signature status of your project.

2. **Click the Choose button.**

   You see a Select Certificate dialog box.

3. **Highlight a certificate in the list and then click OK.**

   VBA signs the target project using your certificate.

4. **Click OK to close the Digital Signature dialog box.**

Chapter 9

Working with Arrays and Collections

. . . .

In This Chapter

▶ Using arrays within a program

▶ Using collections within a program

▶ Creating new data types

▶ Defining collections within a program

. . . .

*T*o this point in the book, all the data types you've used have one thing in common — they store a single data element. When you create an integer, it holds a single number. Placing a new number within the integer removes the old value. However, the real world doesn't work this way. A computer can have more than one disk drive. Your contact database contains more than one name. A mailbox can contain more than one piece of mail. You need a method of storing more than one piece of information in a single variable so that you can model the real world in your programs. VBA provides two methods of doing this: arrays and collections.

Arrays provide a way for your programs to store more than one item in a single container. Think of the array as a large box with a bunch of small boxes inside. Each small box can store a single value. You decide how many small boxes the array can hold when you create the array. Use arrays when you need to store a number of related items of the same data type.

Collections always relate to a group or series of objects that are combined in a single container. In most cases, a main object contains one or more sub-objects. For example, an Excel `Application` object contains a `Workbooks` collection, and a `Workbook` object contains a `Sheets` collection. The `Application` can contain one or more `Workbooks`, and an individual `Workbook` can contain one or more `Sheets`. A Word `Section` object can contain a `HeadersFooters` collection. Microsoft Office and many third-party products are packed with object collections that you can access from VBA.

In this chapter, I also demonstrate how you can create your own data types. A *data type* is a way to mark information so that you can understand it better. The computer doesn't care about data types. VBA uses data types to enforce certain data behaviors, but it doesn't really understand them. The use of a data type is for your benefit so that you can understand the information better.

Using Arrays for Structured Storage

An *array* is a list of items. When you write a list of tasks to perform for the day, you create an array. The piece of paper is a single container that holds a number of strings, each of which is a task that you have to perform. Likewise, you can create a single piece of paper in your VBA program — an array — and use that array to hold multiple items.

Understanding array usage

You can define arrays by using several techniques. However, all these techniques use the same basic approach. Listing 9-1 contains an example that demonstrates the essential array usage process. (You can find the source code for this example on the Dummies.com site at `http://www.dummies.com/go/vbafd5e`.)

Listing 9-1   Creating and Using an Array for String Data

```
' Tell VBA to start all arrays at 0.
Option Base 0

Public Sub SingleDimension()
    ' Define an output string.
    Dim Output As String

    ' Define a variant to hold individual strings.
    Dim IndividualString As Variant

    ' Define the array of strings.
    Dim StringArray(5) As String

    ' Fill each array element with information.
    StringArray(0) = "This"
    StringArray(1) = "Is"
    StringArray(2) = "An"
    StringArray(3) = "Array"
```

```
    StringArray(4) = "Of"
    StringArray(5) = "Strings"

    ' Use the For Each...Next statement to get each array
    ' element and place it in a string.
    For Each IndividualString In StringArray

        ' Create a single output string with the array
        ' array elements.
        Output = Output + IndividualString + " "
    Next

    ' Display the result.
    MsgBox Trim(Output), _
            vbInformation Or vbOKOnly, _
            "Array Content"
End Sub
```

Notice that the code begins with an `Option Base 0` statement. This statement tells VBA whether you want to start counting array elements at 0 or 1. The default setting is 0. Most programming languages use 0 as the starting point, which is why Microsoft made 0 the default for VBA. However, older versions of Visual Basic (including VBA) use 1 as the starting point. When you want to ensure that your program works in every environment, include the `Option Base` statement.

The code for `SingleDimension` begins with some variable declarations. Notice the `StringArray` declaration. When you want to create an array, you follow the variable name with a pair of parentheses that contains the number of elements. You can also create an empty array by leaving out the number, but then you need to use the `ReDim` statement to set the number of elements later. See the upcoming "Understanding the array types" section for details.

Because the array begins at 0 and not at 1, you can actually store six items in an array that is defined as having five elements. The number that you include in the declaration is always the top element number of the array and not the actual number of elements.

The code that follows the array declaration fills each of these elements with a string. Notice the use of numbers in the statement. This number is an *index*. You use the index to access individual members of the array, just as you use letters or numbers to access individual apartments in an apartment complex. The statement `StringArray(1) = "Is"` places the word `Is` in the second array element by using an index of 1. You can always access an individual element by using its index.

This example shows how to use a `For Each...Next` statement to access each array element in turn. Notice that you don't need to use an index in this situation because the `For Each...Next` statement keeps track of it for you. The `IndividualString` variable is a `Variant` — the only acceptable type when using a `For Each...Next` statement. You don't have to convert `IndividualString` when you add it to `Output` because VBA tracks it as a `Variant/String`. Check out this statement in the Debugger, and you can see how it works.

The final statement displays a message box containing the value of `Output`. This message box presents the list of the strings originally added to the array. Notice that the output is a single string that the code created from the individual array elements.

Understanding the array types

You can classify arrays in several ways. The first method is by the kind of data that the array holds. A `String` array is different from an `Integer` array. An array always keeps the array data type unique. Using a `Variant` data type lets you mix data types within an array. You should use this technique carefully because it can lead to bugs that are difficult to debug.

A second method is to define the number of array dimensions. A *dimension* is the number of directions in which the array holds information. A simple list, such as the one in the earlier "Understanding array usage" section, is a single-dimensional array. A table that consists of rows and columns is a two-dimensional array. You can create arrays with any number of dimensions.

Listing 9-2 shows an example of a two-dimensional array that holds the result of a calculation. Note that this is the first example to mix forms into the program, and it also shows how to use the `ReDim` statement. (You can find the source code for this example on the Dummies.com site at `http://www.dummies.com/go/vbafd5e`.)

Listing 9-2   Creating and Using a Two-Dimensional Array

```
' Define some data exchange values for the
' GetArrayDimensions form.
Public Input1Value As Integer
Public Input2Value As Integer
Public ClickType As VbMsgBoxResult

Public Sub TwoDimension()
    ' Create an array to hold the calculation results.
    Dim CalcResult() As Integer
```

```
    ' Create some loop variables for the calculation.
    Dim Loop1 As Integer
    Dim Loop2 As Integer

    ' Create an output string for the display.
    Dim Output As String

    ' Display a form to obtain the array dimensions.
    GetArrayDimensions.Show

    ' Determine which button the user clicked.
    If ClickType = vbCancel Then

        ' If the user clicked Cancel, exit.
        Exit Sub
    End If

    ' Redimension the array.
    ReDim CalcResult(Input1Value, Input2Value)

    ' Perform the calculation.
    For Loop1 = 1 To Input1Value
        For Loop2 = 1 To Input2Value
            CalcResult(Loop1, Loop2) = Loop1 * Loop2
        Next
    Next

    ' Create a heading.
    Output = "Calculation Results" + vbCrLf + _
             "In Tabular Format" + vbCrLf + vbCrLf

    ' Define the column heading values.
    For Loop1 = 1 To Input2Value
        Output = Output + vbTab + CStr(Loop1)
    Next

    ' Define the rows.
    For Loop1 = 1 To Input1Value
        Output = Output + vbCrLf + CStr(Loop1)
        For Loop2 = 1 To Input2Value
            Output = Output + vbTab + _
                    CStr(CalcResult(Loop1, Loop2))
        Next
    Next

    ' Create a message box to show the result.
    MsgBox Output, vbInformation Or vbOKOnly, "Results"
End Sub
```

The program declares three public variables. These variables hold the results from the dialog box created to ask you how many values to compute. This technique is regularly used to get information.

The `TwoDimension` sub-procedure begins by declaring some variables. Notice that it doesn't define the number of elements in `CalcResult` — the code only tells VBA that it's an array.

The code displays a dialog box containing one input text box for each dimension using the `GetArrayDimensions.Show` method. The program uses this dialog box to get the array dimensions.

This dialog box has several interesting features to consider. First, unlike the standalone dialog boxes in Chapter 7, this dialog box interacts with a sub-procedure. Consequently, you can't simply end the dialog box — the code within the dialog box has to report back to the calling sub-procedure in some way. This is the reason for creating the global `Input1Value`, `Input2Value`, and `ClickType` variables. Listing 9-3 shows the essential code from the Two-Dimensional Array Dimensions dialog box.

Listing 9-3   Creating a Form to Interact with a Two-Dimensional Array

```
Private Sub btnOK_Click()
    ' Change the click type.
    ArrayTypes.ClickType = vbOK

    ' Check the two input values.
    txtInput1_Change
    txtInput2_Change

    ' End the form.
    Me.Hide
End Sub

Private Sub txtInput1_Change()
    ' Verify the user has input a number greater than 1.
    If Val(txtInput1.Text) = 0 Then
        ' If not, display an error message box.
        MsgBox "Type a numeric value greater than 1."

        ' Return the text to an acceptable value.
        txtInput1.Text = "5"
    Else
        ' Otherwise, store the numeric value.
        ArrayTypes.Input1Value = CInt(txtInput1.Text)
    End If
End Sub
```

The `txtInput1_Change` sub-procedure monitors any change to the `txtInput1` control. (The `txtInput2` control has a similar event handler associated with it.) The If...Then statement verifies that you have input a number by using the Val function to compare the number with 0. You can't use the CInt function because it generates a type mismatch error when you type a letter or special character. Typing an incorrect character generates an error message and returns the value to something correct. A correct entry places the integer value into the Input1Value variable in the ArrayTypes module (the one with the sub-procedure).

The btnOK_Click sub-procedure sets the ClickType variable in the ArrayTypes module to vbOK. Likewise, clicking Cancel sets the ClickType variable to vbCancel. The code then calls Me.Hide. The special keyword Me refers to the current object. The Hide method removes the form from sight but not from memory.

When you want to remove an object from memory, you use the Unload method and supply the object name. This method works only if VBA is done using the object. Likewise, when you want to load an object into memory (but not display it), use the Load method. This method works only when VBA has memory and other resources available to load the object.

When the GetArrayDimensions UserForm completes (you click OK or Cancel), control returns to the TwoDimension sub-procedure. The code checks the ClickType value. Click Cancel, and the sub-procedure exits.

At this point, the code has the information needed to *dimension* the array (that is, make it a certain size), so it uses the ReDim statement to change the CalcResult dimensions. Changing the dimensions erases the content of the array unless you include the Preserve keyword. A double loop serves to address the two dimensions of the CalcResult array. The calculation is simple multiplication, but you can perform any task in the loop.

After the array is filled with data, it's time to create an output string. The code uses simple assignment to create a heading, generates the row heading using a single loop, and then uses a double loop to create the output information. The final statement displays an output message box containing a table of the information.

Copying data from one array to another

You might need to copy data from one array to another. For example, you can base a new array on the content of an existing array. It's also safer to make changes to a copy of an array rather than to change the original and potentially damage the data. Listing 9-4 shows an example of code that you can use to copy one array to another. (You can find the source code for this example on the Dummies.com site at http://www.dummies.com/go/vbafd5e.)

Listing 9-4 Copying an Array

```
Public Sub ArrayCopy()
    ' Create a loop variable.
    Dim Counter As Integer

    ' Create an original array of strings and a copy.
    Dim OriginalArray(4) As String
    Dim CopiedArray(5) As String

    ' Create an output variable.
    Dim Output As String

    ' Fill the array with data.
    OriginalArray(0) = "This"
    OriginalArray(1) = "is"
    OriginalArray(2) = "the"
    OriginalArray(3) = "original"
    OriginalArray(4) = "array!"

    ' Copy the data.
    For Counter = 0 To UBound(OriginalArray)
        CopiedArray(Counter) = OriginalArray(Counter)
    Next

    ' Modify some data elements.
    CopiedArray(3) = "copied"
    CopiedArray(4) = "array"

    ' Add a new element.
    CopiedArray(5) = "too!"

    ' Create the first part of the output string.
    Output = "The first string:" + vbCrLf
    For Counter = 0 To UBound(OriginalArray)
        Output = Output + OriginalArray(Counter) + " "
    Next

    ' Create the second part of the output string.
    Output = Output + vbCrLf + "The Second String:" +
        vbCrLf
    For Counter = 0 To UBound(CopiedArray)
        Output = Output + CopiedArray(Counter) + " "
    Next

    ' Display the results.
    MsgBox Output, vbInformation Or vbOKOnly, "Results"
End Sub
```

The code begins by creating two arrays and filling the original array with information. Copying the OriginalArray elements to the CopiedArray elements comes next. Follow this process in the Debugger, and you see that the two arrays are the same except that the CopiedArray has one extra element. Notice how the code uses the UBound function to determine the last element of the array. Use the LBound function to determine the lower boundary of the array subscripts.

At this point, the code modifies CopiedArray. First, the code changes the content of two of the elements. Second, it adds information to the last element. These changes don't affect the original array. If an error occurs, you can always reconstruct CopiedArray by using OriginalArray as a starting point. The message box that the code constructs shows that the original array is the same, but the copied array is different.

Using Collections to Create Data Sets

You can view a collection as an advanced form of an array. Like an array, a *collection* maintains a list of items in one package. Because these items are related in more than a superficial way, such as a group of worksheets, many people refer to the list of items as a *data set*. Using a collection is different from an array, however, and you might find that you like using them better than arrays. A collection has some advantages, such as not requiring the ReDim statement, but is a little more complicated to use. This section explains these differences in detail and shows how to use collections in a program.

Understanding collection usage

If you've followed the book to this point, you've used collections in previous chapters. For example, the "Recovering from an error" section of Chapter 6 relies on a collection to retrieve information from a specific hard drive. The FileSystemObject object contains a collection of Drive objects. The example in the "Designing a form for your application" section of Chapter 7 also relies on collections. This example adds control objects to the Controls collection of the UserForm object. VBA uses a lot of collections — you can't escape their use.

The easiest way to understand a collection is to create one of your own. You can create collections and add them to a class that you create or use them by themselves. VBA doesn't place any restrictions on how you use collections. Listing 9-5 shows an example of a simple collection. It creates the collection and then provides the means for adding, removing, and listing elements in the collection. (You can find the source code for this example on the Dummies.com site at http://www.dummies.com/go/vbafd5e.)

Listing 9-5   Creating and Using a Simple Collection

```
' Declare the collection.
Private MyCollection As Collection

Private Sub btnAdd_Click()
    ' Add a new item.
    MyCollection.Add _
        InputBox("Type a new item.", "Add Item", "Hello")

    ' List the items.
    ListItems
End Sub

Private Sub btnDelete_Click()
    ' Define variables to hold the selection.
    Dim UserInput As String
    Dim Selection As Integer

    ' Define an error handling result variable.
    Dim Result As VbMsgBoxResult

    ' Get the input from the user.
RetryInput:
    UserInput = InputBox("Type an existing item number.", _
                         "Remove Item", _
                         "1")

    ' Validate the input.
    If Val(UserInput) > 0 And _
       Val(UserInput) < MyCollection.Count + 1 Then

        ' Use good input to delete a value.
        Selection = CInt(UserInput)
    Else
        ' Display an error message.
        Result = MsgBox("Type a number greater than 1 " + _
                        "and less than or equal to the " + _
                        "number of elements.", _
                        vbExclamation Or vbRetryCancel, _
                        "Input Error")

        ' Allow for a retry.
        If Result = vbRetry Then
            GoTo RetryInput
        Else
            Exit Sub
```

```
              End If
      End If

      ' Delete the existing item.
      MyCollection.Remove Selection

      ' List the items.
      ListItems
End Sub

Private Sub UserForm_Initialize()
      ' Initialize the collection.
      Set MyCollection = New Collection
End Sub

Public Sub ListItems()
      ' Create the listing variable.
      Dim Element As Variant

      ' Clear the current list.
      lblCollection.Caption = ""

      ' Display each element in turn.
      For Each Element In MyCollection
            lblCollection.Caption = lblCollection.Caption + _
                                    Element + vbCrLf
      Next

      ' Determine whether to enable the Delete button.
      If MyCollection.Count > 0 Then
            btnDelete.Enabled = True
      Else
            btnDelete.Enabled = False
      End If
End Sub
```

This is a standalone form program. The code declares MyCollection as a private global variable so that all the sub-procedures can access it. The UserForm_Initialize sub-procedure initializes the collection.

The example provides two CommandButtons for changing the collection: Add and Delete. The Delete button is disabled at program startup because you can't delete a non-existent element from the collection without producing an error. Consequently, the first button that you click is Add. The btnAdd_Click event handler displays an InputBox that requests string input. After making the addition by using the Add method, the code calls the ListItems sub-procedure.

The `ListItems` sub-procedure provides a convenient place to put common code for the event handlers. You should use this type of sub-procedure with common code for programs that you create. The code begins by creating a `Variant` to hold individual collection members. It also sets the `lblCollection.Caption` to `""` (nothing) in order to erase the current content from the display. Notice the use of the `For Each...Next` statement to fill the `lblCollection.Caption` property with new data.

It's important to check the status of the collection to ensure that the program enables or disables `btnDelete` as appropriate. The `If...Then` statement compares the number of collection items using the `Count` method with 0. When the `If...Then` statement is true, the collection is empty, and the code disables `btnDelete`. Otherwise, the code enables `btnDelete`.

The `btnDelete_Click` event handler requires some error handling to ensure that the program operates as expected. You can add any string desired to the collection, but you can't enter just any information during a deletion because incorrect input causes an error.

Knowing when to use a collection

Throughout this chapter, I show examples of both arrays and collections. The examples demonstrate that the techniques for using each storage technique are different, but the results can be the same in many cases. For example, you can store strings equally well in a collection or an array. You can also access the information by using similar techniques. It might be difficult to determine which method to use. In some cases, it doesn't matter — it's a matter of personal taste.

Consider both advantages and disadvantages when you make your decision. Here's a list of the things that you should consider:

✔ Arrays have a slight performance advantage and use less memory to store the same information.

✔ Collections are more flexible than arrays — they can grow and shrink as needed.

✔ Arrays are easier to conceptualize, and you might find them easier to use.

✔ Collections excel at storing objects, and they work well with complex data types.

✔ Arrays can appear in multiple dimensions — there's no limit. (Collections are limited to a single list.)

✔ Collections are self-contained, so you don't have to memorize a list of external functions to work with them.

Although you can use either an array or a collection in some situations, you must use a specific option in other cases. For example, arrays are the only solution when you need to perform complex matrix math because collections are simple lists and don't include the concept of dimensions. On the other hand, when you want to include a list of objects within an object, you must use a collection. However, you can use either solution when you want to create a list of simple items, such as names.

The `InputBox` places the information that it receives in `UserInput`. An `If...Then` statement compares the `UserInput` with specific numeric values. When you type a character or a special symbol, it's the same as typing a 0 — the `Val` function returns a 0 for non-numeric input. The `If...Then` statement also compares the `UserInput` with the upper limit of the collection entries by using the `Count` method. If the input meets the criteria, the code places the integer part of the input into `Select` by using the `CInt` function.

When an input error occurs, the code displays a message box that tells you about the correct input and asks whether you want to try again. An `If...Then` statement compares your button click with `vbRetry` and takes appropriate action.

The deletion process relies on the `Remove` method. You must supply an integer value that reflects the index of the entry that you want to remove. A collection can also use *keys* — strings that stand in for the actual values. You can see a demonstration of this technique in the upcoming "Adding keyed data to the collection" section. The event handler ends with a call to `ListItems`.

Adding keyed data to the collection

You can normally create collections without keys, and they work fine. A collection that relies on user input is an exception. It's easier to get string input from users than to ask them to count down a row of entries to provide a number. Database collections provide opportunities to use keyed entries. In fact, many predefined collections use keyed entries to make it easier for you to develop programs with them.

This example shows an Access contact database. It uses keys to make finding an entry easier. The database contains only three fields: a contact name, the telephone number, and the last date of contact. To use this example, you must add a reference to the Microsoft DAO 3.6 Object Library. Listing 9-6 shows the code for this example. (You can find the source code and associated database for this example on the Dummies.com site at `http://www.dummies.com/go/vbafd5e`.)

Listing 9-6   Using Keyed Data with a Collection

```
Public Sub DisplayContacts()
    ' Create a loop counter variable.
    Dim Counter As Integer
    Counter = 1

    ' Create a recordset object.
    Dim CurrentData As DAO.Recordset
```

(continued)

Listing 9-6 *(continued)*

```
    ' Create the collection variable.
    Dim ContactList As Collection
    Set ContactList = New Collection

    ' Create the output variables.
    Dim Element As Variant
    Dim Output As String

    ' Get the current data.
    Set CurrentData = _
        Application.CurrentDb.OpenRecordset("Contacts")

    ' Create the collection from the data.
    While Not CurrentData.EOF

        ' Get the information and place it in the user
        ' data type.
        ContactList.Add _
            CurrentData.Fields("Name").Value, _
            "Name" + CStr(Counter)
        ContactList.Add _
            CurrentData.Fields("Telephone").Value, _
            "Telephone" + CStr(Counter)
        ContactList.Add _
            CurrentData.Fields("LastContact").Value, _
            "LastContact" + CStr(Counter)

        ' Update the Counter.
        Counter = Counter + 1

        ' Move to the next database record.
        CurrentData.MoveNext
    Wend

    ' Create an output string by getting the values from
    ' the collection.
    For Counter = 1 To (ContactList.Count / 3)

        ' Access the collection elements by name.
        Element = ContactList("Name" + CStr(Counter))
        Output = Output + Element

        Element = ContactList("Telephone" + CStr(Counter))
        Output = Output + vbTab + Element

        Element = ContactList("LastContact" +
            CStr(Counter))
        Output = Output + vbTab + CStr(Element) + vbCrLf
```

```
      Next

      ' Create the message box.
      MsgBox Output, vbInformation, "Contact List"
End Sub
```

The code begins by defining and initializing some variables. Notice the `CurrentData` declaration. It's a `DAO.Recordset`, not the default `ADODB.Recordset` object. When you use the default, the program fails with a type mismatch error. This example points out one of the problems that you can encounter when working with objects. Make sure that you use specific object references as necessary.

You can use a number of methods to get hold of the Contacts table in the example database. The easiest method is to use the `Application.CurrentDb.OpenRecordset` method. This method includes constants that determine how VBA opens the recordset. For example, you can tell VBA that you want to read only the recordset by using the `dbReadOnly` constant. See the OpenRecordset Method help topic for additional information.

The code uses a `While...Wend` structure to retrieve the individual data elements. Notice the use of a string to access the `Fields` collection, which acts as the first argument for the `ContactList.Add` method. The second argument for the `Add` method used to add a new item to the `ContactList` collection is the string key that you can use to access it. When you look at `ContactList` in the Debugger, you see that it contains a single list of entries. Make sure that you use the `CurrentData.MoveNext` method to select the next record at the end of the loop, or else the database never reaches the end of the file (the `EOF` property set to `True`).

In this case, the code relies on a `For...Next` loop to create the output string. The collection isn't in a configuration where one element equals one database record — the code requires three elements for each database record. The code shows how you can create a loop to compensate for this fact.

The `For...Next` loop expression isn't actually optimal in this case. I use this presentation to make the example clearer. Notice the `ContactList.Count / 3` portion of the expression. VBA has to calculate that value during every loop. Calculating the value outside the loop would save time and make this program faster.

Accessing predefined collection items

VBA uses collections quite often. For example, the `Fields` collection of a database is a collection of `Field` objects. Likewise, the `Drives` collection contains multiple `Drive` objects.

REMEMBER

You should notice something interesting about the relationship between collections and objects. Microsoft usually uses an s at the end of the name to denote a collection, such as the Drives and Fields collections.

The balloon help that you see when you type an object name normally contains methods and properties for that object. It can also contain other objects and collections. When you look through the list of items, anything plural is normally a collection.

You see another clue when you double-click a property and then press F1 to display help. VBA help not only tells you that the item is a collection, but usually also displays a hierarchical chart to show where the collection fits within the object hierarchy and what types of items the collection can contain.

The Debugger can also help you ferret out collections. The Watches window, shown in Figure 9-1, shows how the CurrentData Recordset object holds the Fields collection, which contains multiple Field objects. (Type **CurrentData.Fields** in the Expression field of the Add Watch dialog box to obtain the view shown in Figure 9-1.) You can click the plus sign next to each item to see each field and its current content. Look especially in the Type column, where you can see the data type used for each item in the collection.

Figure 9-1:
Use the
Debugger
to see
predefined
collections.

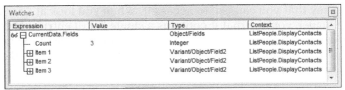

Another place to acquaint yourself with collections is in the Object Browser. The Help file is useful only when you know what you're looking for. The Debugger is also problematic because you have to build something to see what it contains. The Object Browser is different. When you know what you need but not what to call it, you can select the library in question and browse.

Figure 9-2 shows the DAO library used for the example in the preceding "Adding keyed data to the collection" section. This figure shows three collections and the objects that they contain: Errors, Fields, and Groups. When you find something interesting, highlight it, and then press F1. When you know what you're looking for, help can be useful.

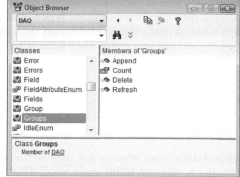

Figure 9-2:
Browse
for the
collections
that you
need to use
in your
program.

Defining Your Own Data Types

A VBA *user-defined data type* is nothing more than a list (collection) of data elements that you want to use together. You aren't really creating a new data type — at least not one that you could identify as a unique entity, such as a `String` or an `Integer`. In this section, I show how to benefit from user-defined data types and demonstrate their use.

Understanding user-defined data types

Creating a user-defined type means defining the data that you want to use together and deciding which native data types work best. The example in the earlier "Adding keyed data to the collection" section uses a database connection to get hold of data and place it in a collection. The implementation (the actual coding) in that example is difficult because you have to make three entries in the collection for each database record. Here's a user-defined type that places all the information in one entry. (You can find the source code for this example on the Dummies.com site at `http://www.dummies.com/go/vbafd5e`.)

```
' Define a user type.
Public Type APerson
    Name As String       ' The person's name.
    Telephone As String ' The contact telephone number.
    LastContact As Date ' The date of last contact.
End Type
```

You create a user-defined type by using the `Type` keyword followed by the name of the new data type. The structure contains native data types. Each variable also has a name. VBA helps you create user-defined types of any complexity. They can include arrays, other user-defined types, and even objects. However, you always want to make the user-defined type as simple as possible and document it fully so that you remember later what it does.

Knowing when to create your own data type

Before you create a user-defined data type, always ask whether any existing type (including objects and collections) can fulfill your need. After you know that you have to create a user-defined type, make sure that you think about the purpose that the user-defined type fulfills.

A user-defined data type can save time and effort by letting you declare all the data elements that you normally use together for a task in one place. It can also group data so that you don't have to perform finger gymnastics to locate your data. However, the main reason to create a user-defined type is to make your program easier to understand. A well-defined data type can make your code simpler and keep the number of code lines to a minimum.

Accessing and manipulating data

The example in the earlier "Adding keyed data to the collection" section works well because it doesn't have to work with complex data. A program that modifies multiple tables and 20 or 30 fields might not work so well by using the technique shown in that section. (It would work, but it wouldn't be fun to program.) By using the new data type that you just created, you can make the programming example in the "Adding keyed data to the collection" section easier to understand.

The example in this section relies on a user-defined data type. It builds an object on that data type and then adds the object to a collection. This example shows how to create your own collections to make working with your data faster and easier.

Defining an individual contact

When you decide to create your own collection, begin with the individual object. Make sure that you know what one copy of an object looks like before you create multiple copies of it. See Chapter 8 for a complete object creation demonstration.

```
' Create an instance of this type.
Private ThePerson As APerson

Public Property Get Name() As String
    ' Get the current user name.
    Name = ThePerson.Name
End Property

Public Property Let Name(Value As String)
    ' Set the new user name.
    ThePerson.Name = Value
End Property
```

The object for this example essentially maintains a reference to the user-defined data type and exposes the individual elements as properties. The listing shows the user-defined type declaration. Notice that the declaration doesn't vary from that used for native data types.

The code consists of three pairs of property declarations — one for each variable in the APerson data type. Each property provides both read and write capabilities. Although this is an object, the individual variables aren't objects, so you use the Let and Get methods of exposing them.

Defining a collection of contacts

After you have a single object to use, it's time to create a collection of them. A collection doesn't have to implement the methods and properties found in the Collection class, but it helps if it does. It pays to look at the collections in VBA for ideas on which methods and properties you can implement. Always implement the Item property because you need it for most of your code. Listing 9-7 shows an example of a typical collection.

Listing 9-7   Manipulating Data in Collections

```
' Declare the collection.
Private PersonCollection As Collection

Public Sub Add(Item As Person, _
               Optional Key As String, _
               Optional Before As Integer, _
               Optional After As Integer)

    ' Determine whether there is a Key.
    If Not Key = "" Then

        ' Determine whether there is a Before value.
        If Before > 0 Then
```

(continued)

Listing 9-7 *(continued)*

```
                ' Add an entry with a Key and Before value.
                PersonCollection.Add Item, Key, Before

        ' Determine whether there is an After value.
        ElseIf After > 0 Then

                ' Add an entry with a Key and After value.
                PersonCollection.Add Item, Key, , After

        Else

                ' The entry is just an Item and a Key.
                PersonCollection.Add Item, Key
        End If
    Else
        ' Determine whether there is a Before value.
        If Before > 0 Then

                ' Add an entry with a Before value.
                PersonCollection.Add Item, , Before

        ' Determine whether there is an After value.
        ElseIf After > 0 Then

                ' Add an entry with an After value.
                PersonCollection.Add Item, , , After

        Else

                ' The entry is just an Item.
                PersonCollection.Add Item
        End If
    End If
End Sub

Public Property Get Count() As Long
    ' Return the current collection count.
    Count = PersonCollection.Count
End Property

Public Sub Remove(Index As Variant)
    ' Remove the requested item.
    PersonCollection.Remove Index
End Sub

Public Property Get Item(Index As Variant) As Person
    ' Return the requested item.
    Set Item = PersonCollection.Item(Index)
```

```
End Property

Private Sub Class_Initialize()
    ' Initialize the collection.
    Set PersonCollection = New Collection
End Sub
```

Notice that the code begins by creating a Collection object. You could also use the Implements statement to implement the Collection class, but this technique is easier. The Class_Initialize method initializes PersonCollection so that other methods can use it.

The Add method is the most complex sub-procedure that you write for a collection in most cases. The reason for the complexity is that this method has so many optional arguments. In addition, when you supply a Before argument, you can't supply an After argument — the two are mutually exclusive. The code divides the task of determining what to do into a Key or no Key decision. It then decides whether you supplied a Before or After argument, or neither, and takes the appropriate action. Look through the Add method code, and you see that each decision results in a different Add method-calling syntax.

The Count property returns the PersonCollection.Count property. You never need to add error-handling code to this property because it's read only. Never make this property read/write. You don't want someone using the collection to change the count.

The Remove method makes a direct call to the PersonCollection.Remove method. You could add range checking to this method by using the same techniques that I use in previous examples. The PersonCollection.Remove method raises an error when you supply an incorrect value. Notice the use of a Variant for this method so that it can accept a string or an integer as input.

The Item property is also read only. Again, you should never make this property read/write. Always use the Add method to add new entries to the collection. Notice that this method returns an object, so you have to use the Set statement.

Creating a default property

No matter which collection you look at, Item is the default property or function. Figure 9-3 shows that Item uses a special symbol. The explanation for Item in the lower pane of the Object Browser window also says that this is the default property of the Fields collection. The only problem is that VBA doesn't provide a direct method for you to create a default property or method for your class.

Figure 9-3:
Create a
default
Item
property or
method
to ensure
that your
collection
works
properly.

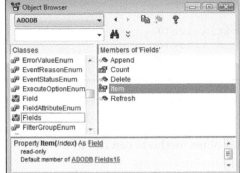

You have to use a little-known and somewhat undocumented method of adding a default property to the example. When you look at the Persons.cls file in the source code, you see that the code actually looks like the code in Listing 9-8:

Listing 9-8   Creating a Default Property Declaration

```
Public Property Get Item(Index As Variant) As Person
' Tell VBA this is the default property.
Attribute Item.VB_UserMemId = 0

    ' Return the requested item.
    Set Item = PersonCollection.Item(Index)
End Property
```

However, the first line of code doesn't appear in the IDE. VBA forces you to use a simple but odd procedure to add this line of code. Simply use the following procedure to add this line of code:

1. **Right-click the Persons entry in the Project Explorer window, and then choose Export File from the context menu that appears.**

   You see the Export File dialog box.

2. **Click Save to save the file as Persons.cls.**

   VBA exports the file.

3. **Open the file in any text editor, such as Notepad.**

   Never use Word for this task because it can add control characters.

4. **Type Attribute Item.VB_UserMemId = 0 as the first entry for the Item property.**

5. **Save the Persons.cls file and then exit the editor.**

6. **Right-click the Persons entry in the Project Explorer window, and then choose Remove Persons from the context menu that appears.**

   VBA asks whether you want to export Persons before you remove it.

7. **Click No.**

   VBA removes the class module.

8. **Right-click anywhere in the Project Explorer window, and then choose Import File from the context menu that appears.**

   VBA displays the Import File dialog box.

9. **Highlight the Persons.cls file and then click Open.**

   VBA imports the updated file. It appears that nothing has changed. The code looks the same as before. However, the unseen Attribute entry has changed.

10. **Open Object Browser and view the updated Persons class.**

    You notice that Item is now the default property for this class.

Developing the test program

The test program in Listing 9-9 is similar to the one used in the earlier section "Adding keyed data to the collection" (refer to Listing 9-6). You can find it in the source code as DisplayContacts2 (on the Dummies.com site at http://www.dummies.com/go/vbafd5e). The new example in Listing 9-9 still begins by creating variables, and it opens the same recordset.

Listing 9-9   Updating the Key Data Collection Example

```
' Create the collection from the data.
While Not CurrentData.EOF

    ' Define a new element.
    Set Individual = New Person

    ' Get the information and place it in the user
    ' data type.
    Individual.Name = _
        CurrentData.Fields("Name").Value
    Individual.Telephone = _
        CurrentData.Fields("Telephone").Value
    Individual.LastContact = _
        CurrentData.Fields("LastContact").Value

    ' Add the information to the collection.
    ContactList.Add Individual, Individual.Name
```

(continued)

Listing 9-9 *(continued)*

```
        ' Move to the next database record.
        CurrentData.MoveNext
    Wend

    ' Create an output string by getting the values from
    ' the collection.
    For Counter = 1 To ContactList.Count
        ' Get the current element.
        Set Individual = ContactList(Counter)

        ' Access the collection elements by name.
        Output = Output + Individual.Name + _
                vbTab + Individual.Telephone + _
                vbTab + _
                CStr(Individual.LastContact) + vbCrLf
    Next
```

The code is easier to understand now because you can quickly identify the data elements, and each collection entry is equal to a single database record. Notice that you create a single `Person` object (`Individual`) to store the information. A single call to the `Persons` collection object, `ContactList`, adds all the information at once.

Creating the output is also easier. A single call to `ContactList` places the information in `Individual`. The `Output` string uses information from this single object to create an entry for the message box. Notice that you don't need any strange math for the expression in the `For...Next` loop.

Chapter 10

Working with Disk Files

In This Chapter

▶ Working with data storage by using various techniques

▶ Interacting with the data found in data storage files

▶ Using data storage to perform tasks such as saving program settings

*Y*ou use disk storage every time that you work with an application. Disk storage is the most convenient and least expensive means of permanently saving data on a computer system. Permanent storage means that the information on the disk drive remains there after you turn off the computer.

Modern drives include everything from internal hard drives to flash disk thumb drives that you place in USB ports. In general, VBA disk storage is limited to devices you can access as standard hard drives unless you're willing to turn to exotic programming techniques not discussed in this book. Standard hard drive access includes flash disks and rewriteable CD-RW/DVD-RW drives, but doesn't include media you must burn. You may also find it difficult to use online (Internet) storage that requires special processing. Windows Vista promises to make many forms of media that are hard to access under Windows XP and earlier operating systems accessible using the same techniques you use with an internal hard drive, so you may have other options when working with Vista. Consequently, you need not limit VBA to an internal drive; you can easily place your data on a removable drive and carry it with you.

Disk storage can hold several kinds of information. The program that you use to write VBA code is an executable file — it contains information but not user data. The documents that you save are user data. The program that you use to work with VBA already supports the documents that you want to use. However, you might want to save information in other formats, which is one reason to write a VBA program that works with disk storage.

A third kind of disk storage is settings. Some applications use initialization (INI) files exclusively. In fact, Microsoft has begun recommending using something other than the Registry or Active Directory to store your settings to make applications easier to move from one machine to another. Using INI or eXtensible Markup Language (XML) files works perfectly for this purpose. (Chapter 11 discusses using XML with VBA in detail.) Most new applications rely heavily on the Registry for setting storage options, and some applications use server storage in the form of Active Directory. All three forms of settings storage are viable, but the INI or XML file is the easiest method to use from VBA.

This chapter demonstrates various methods for working with disk files. You might find that you want to store data in a new format or save program settings after you see how easy it is to work with disk files.

Using Disk Storage

Placing information on disk is an essential task for most applications. The data that an application creates is the main reason why you have an interest in it. However, the application already handles data storage for you, so you don't need to consider this use for disk files in your program. You might think that that's the extent of the data storage needs for your program, but it isn't. Your program also has valuable data that it must maintain.

Application configuration information

When a user interacts with your program, you might want to retain any settings that the user makes. It's always a good idea to store the user interface settings so that they're restored every time the user starts the program.

You can also store usage information. For example, when you open a Word document, you can press Shift+F5 to return to your previous editing location in the document. Microsoft stores that information between writing sessions so that you can resume your work quickly.

The easiest place to store these settings is on disk in an INI file. However, you can also use a plain-text file, if you want. You might find the text file easier to understand and use than an INI file. It's important to choose a convenient location for the information. Here are places that you should consider:

✔ **User folder:** Place user-specific information in the user's folder, which is normally the `\Documents and Settings` (older versions of Windows) or `\Users` (Vista) directory of the machine. Every user has a personal directory, and you can create a subdirectory in that folder for your program. Using this technique lets users have their own settings.

✔ **Document folder:** When a series of settings applies to a specific document and not to a particular user, it pays to use a document folder for configuration storage. Using this technique ensures that any custom document settings are stored with the document.

✔ **Project folder:** A setting can affect all documents in a particular project. You can store the configuration settings with the project to ensure that everyone working with the project can access the configuration settings. Using a project folder also ensures that the settings remain safe because the same security settings that keep the data safe keep your configuration file safe.

✔ **Workgroup folder:** Your program can affect how the members of a workgroup interact. When everyone uses the same settings, you want to be sure that the settings are in a central place. The question to ask yourself, in this case, is whether the settings are truly necessary. You might want to consider writing your program so that it uses those settings by default rather than stores the settings in a file.

Data translation

Data translation is a task that you might have to perform from time to time. You might have to transfer information to another system, or you might simply require the information in another form. Before you break out the VBA Integrated Development Environment (IDE), though, make sure that the application doesn't provide the required translation for you. Most applications install with just the most popular data conversion choices and support many others. In addition, a vendor often creates new translation options for its application that you can download from a Web site.

After you know that you need to translate the data, try to choose an easy format. Pure text is the easiest method of transferring information between two programs. Unfortunately, pure text lacks formatting information. The content is still intact, but notes and other information that you added in the application might not appear with the data. In some cases, transferring the content is the best you can hope to achieve, but you should look for other options.

Data storage

You might find that you have program data storage needs. This information is in addition to the data that the program normally tracks. For example, you might want to create a log file that contains activities performed by your program so that you can detect errors or security problems. It also helps to create performance logs when you suspect that your program doesn't work as fast as it could.

Program data storage should appear in a format that's convenient for you because you're the only one who will see it. You should try to store the information by using the program itself. This is relatively easy to do with a program such as Word or Excel. In some cases, you might want to go to the extra trouble of creating the document by using indirect programming of another application. See Chapter 16 for details on this technique. Finally, you can use an informational Event Log entry to store the information.

When no other technique will work (or other techniques are just too inconvenient), you can always rely on a simple text file to store the program information. The problem with using text files for complex data is that you can't format them, and they can't contain information in easy-to-use formats, such as graphs. The best reason to use a text file is that it's an easy and convenient method for storing text information.

Working with Settings

Many applications, including Windows, use INI files to store information. The INI file has a standard format that is easy to work with. View any of the INI files in the Windows folder, such as `Win.INI` or `System.INI`, and you see two kinds of entry. The first is the section entry, which is surrounded by square brackets, such as the `[fonts]` section in the `Win.INI` file. The second kind of entry is a key-and-value pair. The key comes first and is separated from the value by an equals sign.

You might need to create an INI file for your program. The INI file provides the means for storing settings and restoring them later. The `Dictionary` object provides the perfect means for working with INI settings because it uses a key-and-value pair for storing information. The example in this section shows how to read and write an INI file.

Writing an INI file

It pays to create one `Dictionary` object for each section of your INI file. Using the objects in this way makes it easy to quickly locate the information that you need. The trade-off is that you have more objects to work with, and your program will experience a small performance hit. Listing 10-1 contains the code that you need to use a `Dictionary` object to write to an INI file. (You can find the source code for this example on the Dummies.com site at `http://www.dummies.com/go/vbafd5e`.)

Listing 10-1   Using a Dictionary Object

```
Public Sub WriteDictionary()
    ' Create a variable to hold the data.
    Dim DataString As Variant

    ' Create the dictionary for user settings.
    Dim UserSetting As Dictionary
    Set UserSetting = New Dictionary
    UserSetting.Add "Greeting", "Hello"
    UserSetting.Add "Language", "English"

    ' Create the dictionary for application configuration.
    Dim AppConfig As Dictionary
    Set AppConfig = New Dictionary
    AppConfig.Add "ShowHelpMenu", "True"
    AppConfig.Add "AllowChanges", "True"

    ' Create the configuration file.
    Dim TheConfig As TextStream
    OpenWriteConfig "DictionaryDemo", "Data.INI",
            TheConfig

    ' Write the UserSetting Dictionary.
    TheConfig.WriteLine "[UserSetting]"
    For Each DataString In UserSetting
        TheConfig.Write DataString
        TheConfig.Write "="
        TheConfig.WriteLine UserSetting.Item(DataString)
    Next

    'Write the AppConfig Dictionary.
    TheConfig.WriteLine "[AppConfig]"
    For Each DataString In AppConfig
        TheConfig.Write DataString
        TheConfig.Write "="
        TheConfig.WriteLine AppConfig.Item(DataString)
    Next

    ' Close the configuration file.
    TheConfig.Close
End Sub
```

The code begins by creating two `Dictionary` objects — one for each section of the INI file. It fills these objects with data for the example. In your program, you fill the `Dictionary` objects with your program settings or other data.

The code calls the `OpenWriteConfig` sub-procedure next. This special function that I wrote looks almost exactly the same as the beginning code in the earlier "Writing to the file" section. When this call returns, `TheConfig` points to a `TextStream` that the code can use for writing.

It's important to provide a section header for each of your `Dictionary` objects, or else you can't parse the file later. The code writes this heading first, and then it writes the individual key/value pairs by using a `For Each...Next` statement. You can create a single routine to perform this task, but using the technique shown in the code is actually easier to understand and is self-documenting to a point. As always, make sure that you close the configuration file before you exit the sub-procedure.

It's time to look at the `OpenWriteConfig` sub-procedure in a little more detail. Listing 10-2 shows this code.

Listing 10-2   Opening a Configuration File for Writing

```
Public Sub OpenWriteConfig( _
    AppName As String, _
    Filename As String, _
    ByRef Output As TextStream)

    ' Define the path variable.
    Dim DataPath As String

    ' Create a path string for the file. Start with the
    ' default program settings path. Add a special folder
    ' for this program.
    DataPath = Application.UserLibraryPath + AppName + "\"

    ' Create a file system object.
    Dim FS As FileSystemObject
    Set FS = New FileSystemObject

    ' Verify the path exists.
    If Not FS.FolderExists(DataPath) Then
        ' If not, create it.
        FS.CreateFolder DataPath
    End If

    ' Create a text file object.
    Set Output = FS.CreateTextFile(DataPath + Filename)
End Sub
```

The code begins by determining the location of the user folder. It then adds the application name to the path to locate the folder for this application. You can use this same code no matter what user setting file you open. Creating a connection to other common folder types follows a similar pattern.

At this point, you need to create a `FileSystemObject` and use it to determine whether the application folder exists. If the folder doesn't exist, you must create it before you can write data to it. The example uses the `FS.CreateFolder` method to create the new folder.

Finally, the code creates a text file to hold the data that the application saves. Because an INI file is essentially a text file, you work with it as a text file by using FS.CreateTextFile(). When the call is completed, Output contains a pointer to the new file.

You might wonder why the application separates the code in the OpenWriteConfig sub-procedure from the rest of the code. Generally, you do this to make the code a little more generic. You can use OpenWriteConfig to open any file necessary for this application. In fact, the sub-procedure is so generic that you can use it as is with any application.

Reading an INI file

Reading the INI file is a little more difficult than writing to it. The problem is that you have straight text and don't know whether someone has changed the file in some way. Parsing straight text means reading key values and acting on them. (*Parsing* is the act of reading each word individually and determining what that word means in the context of the task at hand.) Listing 10-3 contains the code that you need in order to read an INI file.

Listing 10-3   Reading an INI File with a Dictionary

```
Public Sub ReadDictionary()
    ' Create an individual data element.
    Dim DataElement As String

    ' Create a dictionary selector.
    Dim Selector As Dictionary

    ' Create a string indexer.
    Dim Index As Long

    ' Create the dictionary for user settings.
    Dim UserSetting As Dictionary
    Set UserSetting = New Dictionary

    ' Create the dictionary for application configuration.
    Dim AppConfig As Dictionary
    Set AppConfig = New Dictionary

    ' Try to open the configuration file.
    Dim TheConfig As TextStream
    If Not OpenReadConfig("DictionaryDemo", "Data.INI",
            TheConfig) Then
```

(continued)

Listing 10-3 *(continued)*

```
            ' Exit the sub if not successful.
            Exit Sub
        End If

    ' Read the file into the dictionaries.
    While Not TheConfig.AtEndOfStream

        ' Read the data element.
        DataElement = TheConfig.ReadLine

        Select Case DataElement
            ' Set the selector for AppConfig.
            Case "[AppConfig]"
                Set Selector = AppConfig

            ' Set the selector for UserSetting.
            Case "[UserSetting]"
                Set Selector = UserSetting

            ' Fill the selected dictionary with data.
            Case Else
                Index = InStr(1, DataElement, "=")
                Selector.Add Left(DataElement, Index - 1), _

                            Mid(DataElement, Index + 1)
        End Select
    Wend

    ' Close the configuration file.
    TheConfig.Close
End Sub
```

The code begins by creating the two `Dictionary` objects that you need in order to hold the information. It also creates a special `Dictionary` object named `Selector` and a few variables that it needs in order to parse the file content.

The program begins by opening the configuration file and creating the `TextStream` by using the `OpenReadConfig` function. This function is very similar to the beginning code for the example in the earlier "Reading from the file" section. When the function returns, it's `True` if it opened the file. If the return value is `False`, the `ReadDictionary` sub-procedure exits because there's no file information to parse.

Notice how this example uses the `AtEndOfStream` property. This use is more common than the use shown in the earlier "Reading from the file" section. The `While...Wend` loop continues reading data until there's no more data to read. Each iteration of the loop selects an action based on the content of DataElement.

Notice the Set Selector = AppConfig statement. This statement does more than you might think. It actually makes Selector and AppConfig equal so that any changes made to Selector also appear in AppConfig. This technique provides a generic reference when parsing the key/value pairs in the file. The routine doesn't have to do anything special because the correct Dictionary object is already selected.

The final piece of coding to consider is the key/value pair parsing. The INI file stores them as two strings separated by an equals sign. The information appears on a single line. Using the string manipulation functions shown separates the two values so that the code can add them to the appropriate dictionary.

Now it's time to discuss the OpenReadConfig function. As with OpenWrite Config, this is a generic function for working with files. Listing 10-4 shows how this function looks.

Listing 10-4   Opening a Configuration File for Reading

```
Public Function OpenReadConfig(AppName As String, Filename
        As String, ByRef Output As TextStream) As
        Boolean
   ' Define the path variable.
   Dim DataPath As String
   DataPath = Application.UserLibraryPath + AppName + "\"

   ' Create a file system object.
   Dim FS As FileSystemObject
   Set FS = New FileSystemObject

   ' Determine whether the file exists.
   If Not FS.FileExists(DataPath + Filename) Then

      ' Tell the user there are no config settings.
      OpenReadConfig = False

      ' Exit the Sub without reading the file.
      Exit Function
   End If

   ' Create a text file object.
   Set Output = FS.OpenTextFile( _
      DataPath + Filename, ForReading)
```

(continued)

Listing 10-4 *(continued)*

```
        ' Determine whether there is data in the file.
    If Output.AtEndOfStream Then

        ' Tell the user the file is empty.
        OpenReadConfig = False

    Else

        ' Tell the user the file was opened successfully.
        OpenReadConfig = True
    End If
End Function
```

The function begins by creating a path to the user's settings. It then checks for the existence of the user file. Notice that in this case the function exits rather than creates the file. In many cases, you don't want to create a file when you're opening it for reading.

When the file does exist, the code opens the file for reading by using `FS.OpenTextFile()`. Notice the special `ForReading` argument. If you don't specify this value, `FS.OpenTextFile()` uses the default settings.

The next check ensures that the data file actually contains information. When `Output.AtEndOfStream` is true, the file is empty and the function returns to the caller with `False`. Otherwise, the return value is `True`.

Chapter 11

VBA Programming with XML

● ●

In This Chapter

▶ Defining the features of Word Markup Language (WordML)

▶ Designing your first XML document

▶ Working with XML data

▶ Creating an XML document

▶ Using eXtensible Style Language Transformation (XSLT) to modify presentation

● ●

The *eXtensible Markup Language* (XML) is a special way of marking text so that it contains both information and context. Using this technique means that the recipient knows not only the information but also the meaning behind the information. For example, if you see *12.99* in a text file, you don't know what it means. It's a number, but that's all you know. However, by adding context to the number, you can say that the number means 12 dollars and 99 cents.

XML began on the Internet as a means to make information exchange possible. You can use XML to exchange data with others, even if they don't have the same program or even the same operating system that you do. The only requirements are that both machines can read text and that you have a program that can understand the XML.

This chapter describes how you can use XML to enhance the documents that you create with Office. Although you can manually perform many of the tasks that I describe in this chapter, using VBA to perform them makes sense because the actions are both lengthy and repetitive. In addition, you must perform some XML tasks, such as defining precise output content, with VBA because there's no manual alternative. This chapter also shows how to write programs that can interpret the XML. This final task is important because you can then use XML to send information in any format needed.

Getting the scoop on XML

XML has become such a significant part of the computer environment that you probably use it every day, possibly without even knowing it. The Internet has a considerable number of resources to help you understand XML better. For example, the W3C Schools site at `http://www.w3schools.com/xml/` provides a complete XML tutorial, and you can discover XML namespaces at `http://www.zvon.org/index.php?nav_id=172&ns=34`.

Many people already know enough about XML to use it effectively, but they need a reference to make XML easier to use. One of the better reference resources appears on the ZVON Web site at `http://www.zvon.org/xxl/xmlSchema2001Reference/Output/index.`

`html`. However, make sure that you also look at the references at `http://www.zvon.org/xxl/xmlSchemaReference/Output/index.html` for complete information. The annotated XML reference at `http://www.xml.com/axml/axml.html` is handy for seeing the specification and expert commentary side by side.

If you need a full text on XML, get *XML All-in-One Desk Reference For Dummies,* written by Richard Wagner and Richard Mansfield (and published by Wiley). This text provides, in a series of seven books, everything you need in order to work with XML. You'll also find complete coverage of XML-related technologies, such as XSLT (described later in this chapter).

Comparing WordML with Saved XML

When you save a Word document either manually or programmatically, you can save it as an XML document. However, not all XML documents are created equal. Figure 11-1 shows a Word Save As dialog box set up to save a document as XML.

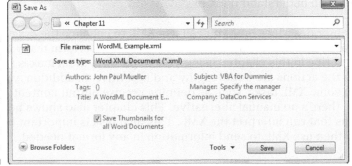

Figure 11-1: Save your document as XML by using the Save As dialog box.

This dialog box shows the default setup, which is to save the document by using WordML (Word Markup Language) and not as standard XML. Using WordML preserves the information in your document in an XML file that Word can understand. Figure 11-2 shows a Firefox view of the information in a simple Word document.

For those of you who are aware that both Firefox and Internet Explorer can open an XML file, the two applications have a significant difference. Notice the `<?mso-application progid="Word.Document"?>` processing instruction at the top of Figure 11-2. This instruction tells Internet Explorer to open a copy of Word to process the file. Consequently, when you open the file by using Internet Explorer, what you see is a copy of Word open, which means that you don't see the underlying XML. Internet Explorer is the only application that appears to perform this automatic processing, so you can use any other XML viewer or browser that supports XML to look at the Word XML file.

You might think this document is complex, but it isn't too hard to understand if you take it apart one piece at a time. For example, if you open the `<pkg:part pkg:name="/docProps/core.xml">` element, you see a list of document-information entries, such as the name of the author and the company. Every entry that appears in the Document Properties dialog box also appears as part of this element. You can also see elements devoted to the document properties (such as the document view and default tab stop settings), fonts, and styles.

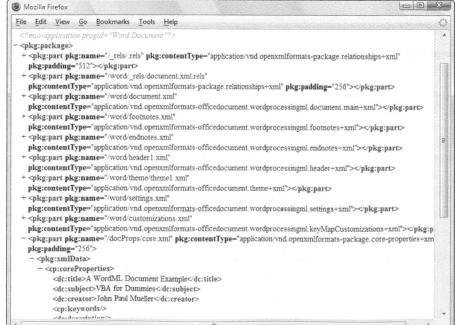

Figure 11-2:
Use Firefox to discover important information about your WordML file.

If you have used the WordML output in the past, you'll notice significant differences in the WordML that Word 2007 outputs. For example, Word 2003 places the document information in the `W:DOCINFO` element. The content that used to appear in the `W:BODY` element now appears in the `<pkg:part pkg:name="/word/document.xml">` element. The change in format means that any eXtensible Stylesheet Language Transformations (XSLT) processing you performed with Word 2003 WordML won't work with the Word 2007 version.

When you need the Word 2003 version, make sure that you select Word 2003 XML Document, as shown in Figure 11-3, rather than XML Document, as shown in Figure 11-1. The output is closer than the Word 2007 version, but you still face a few naming and namespace problems. For example, the `W:DOCINFO` element appears as `o:DocumentProperties`, even though the `W:BODY` element is the same.

Figure 11-3:
Use the special Word 2003 setting for saving XML in a compatible state.

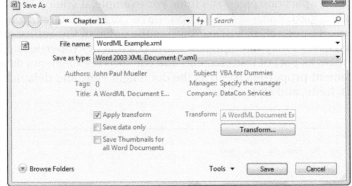

The sample code for this chapter includes the original Word 2003 output as `WordML Example.xml`, the native Word 2007 output as `WordML Example 2.xml`, and the converted Word 2007 output as `WordML Example 3.xml`, so you can compare the differences. (You can find the source code for this example on the Dummies.com site at `http://www.dummies.com/go/vbafd5e`.)

The Word 2003 settings include a few special features you need to know about. When you try to save a standard Word document as pure XML by selecting the Save Data Only check box (lower-left area of Figure 11-3), Word doesn't generate WordML; instead, it generates standard XML. Unfortunately, your Word template file probably doesn't include the entries required to create standard XML. As a result, the output is 0 bytes long. That's right: Nothing is saved because your document isn't tagged for use with standard XML. See the upcoming "Creating a Simple Word XML Document" section for details on creating a template that saves your data to standard XML.

When you don't need to save all the information provided by WordML and you don't want to create a special template to do the job, you can rely on XSLT to transform your data into standard XML. The benefit of using this technique is that it's faster than using a specialized template. The problem with using this technique is that you can't rely on it to provide complete data translation if you don't use the correct tags or if the XSLT file isn't formatted correctly. See the upcoming "Saving your Word document by using XSLT" section for details on using this technique.

Manipulating XML Data

Microsoft is making it easier to create, change, delete, import, and export XML by using Office products. XML makes it easier to manage data on the Internet and also to exchange data with other people. This section demonstrates several ways to work with XML data by using Office.

Writing the data to disk

The easiest way to export your data to disk is to save it as an XML document by using the `SaveAs` method. Here's an example of this method:

```
Public Sub OutputInventory()
    ' Use the standard SaveAs method to export XML.
    Sheet1.SaveAs "ExcelXML.XML", xlXMLSpreadsheet
End Sub
```

You can also accomplish this task by choosing the File⇨Save As command. The advantage of this method is that you can concentrate on a single worksheet, a set of records, or an area of a document rather than save the whole document. The first argument is the filename. The second argument varies by Office application. Excel uses the `xlXMLSpreadsheet` to create XML output, and Word uses the `wdFormatXML` constant.

The only problem with this technique is that it saves only the content and information about the content. Figure 11-2 shows some typical output for Word when using this method. This method works best if you plan to manipulate the data outside Office by using another program, interpret the data by using XSLT, or require portions of the data where interpretation isn't required.

Defining a schema

A *schema* is a definition of the structure of your data. You can look at the data and figure out the structure, but the computer can't — it needs additional information. Database managers such as Access always use a schema (you define it when you create a table), but other Office applications don't because you normally don't need to organize the information by using a schema. Figure 11-4 shows a typical worksheet. The data structure is probably obvious to you because each of the columns is named, but the computer doesn't have a clue to what that data means.

Figure 11-4:
Understanding data formats is easy for you but hard for the computer.

⊿	A	B	C
1	Inventory		
2			
3	**Name** ▾	**Value** ▾	**Total** ▾
4	Coat	$49.99	$49.99
5	Jeans	$19.99	$69.98
6	Shirt	$18.95	$88.93
7	Hat	$10.00	$98.93
8	Glasses	$59.99	$158.92
9	Shoes	$29.95	$188.87
10	Other	$39.00	$227.87

An *XML Schema Definition* (XSD) file contains a description of the information that you want to export from or import to an Office application. It doesn't matter which application you use because, at some point, you have to create an XSD file to perform pure XML data transfers. Listing 11-1 shows an example of an XSD file that describes the data shown in Figure 11-4. (You can find the source code for this example on the Dummies.com site at http://www.dummies.com/go/vbafd5e.)

Listing 11-1   Creating an XSD Description

```
<?xml version="1.0"?>
<xs:schema xmlns:xs="http://www.w3.org/2001/XMLSchema">

<xs:element name="Items">
  <xs:complexType>
    <xs:sequence>
      <xs:element name="Item" maxOccurs="unbounded">
        <xs:complexType>
          <xs:sequence>
            <xs:element name="Name" type="xs:string"/>
            <xs:element name="Value" type="xs:decimal"/>
            <xs:element name="Total" type="xs:decimal"/>
          </xs:sequence>
        </xs:complexType>
      </xs:element>
    </xs:sequence>
  </xs:complexType>
</xs:element>

</xs:schema>
```

This is yet another XML file, so it begins with the standard XML processing instruction. The second line contains the URL for the XSD file definitions. You must include this line in all your XSD files. You can include other information, such as a personal namespace, as part of this header, but it's all optional. See the tutorial at `http://www.w3schools.com/schema/default.asp` for additional information.

The structure of your information comes next. Chapter 9 describes how VBA collections work. The tags that XSD relies on to define your data act much like a collection. The top element, Items, defines the collection name. The `<xs:complexType>` tag tells the XSD parser that you're defining something other than a string or an integer. You use the `<xs:sequence>` tag to tell the XSD parser that the next set of elements must appear in the order shown and that the parser can't skip any of the elements.

The `<xs:element name="Item" maxOccurs="unbounded">` tag shows how to create an individual item within an XSD collection. The two things that set this tag apart from the `<Items>` tag is that it appears within the `<Items>` tag and also uses the special maxOccurs attribute. Notice that the maxOccurs attribute is defined as unbounded (unlimited) so that the Items collection can contain as many individual Item elements as needed.

The `<Item>` tag is also a complex type and requires elements in a specific sequence. This time, the individual elements are simple types. The `<Name>` tag is a string, but the `<Value>` and `<Total>` tags are both in decimal notation. XSD doesn't currently support a currency type, so your best choice is to use a decimal to ensure that the XSD parser preserves the accuracy of the data that you transfer.

Defining XSD to worksheet linkage

Writing the XSD file creates a definition that you can use to work with data in Excel. However, you still haven't created linkage between the XSD file and the Excel document. (You should perform this task by using a document template in Word — see the upcoming "Creating a Simple Word XML Document" section for details.) Here's how to create linkage in Excel 2007:

1. **Open Excel and load the document that you want to export.**

2. **Select the Developer tab on the Ribbon.**

3. **Click XML Source.**

   You see the XML Source task pane.

4. **Click XML Maps in the XML Source task pane.**

   Excel displays the XML Maps dialog box.

5. **Click Add in the XML Maps dialog box.**

   The Select XML Source dialog box appears. This dialog box works the same as any other file-opening dialog box. The filter makes it easy to locate XSD files on your system.

6. **Locate the XSD file you want to use and then click Open.**

   Excel adds the new map to the XML Maps dialog box.

7. **Click OK to close the XML Maps dialog box.**

   Excel displays the new map in the XML Source task pane.

8. **Right-click the element you want to map in the XML Source task pane, and choose Map Element from the context menu.**

9. **Highlight the data you want to map to the element, and press Enter.**

   Excel changes the appearance of the data so that it looks like a database entry, as shown earlier, in Figure 11-4.

10. **Repeat Steps 8 and 9 for every data element in the XSD file.**

Exporting the data to disk

After you create a schema and link it to an Office document, you can perform a true export of the information as XML. There are two separate methods to perform this task. The first, ExportXml, creates a string that you can manipulate by using various XML features built into Office. The second, Export, performs a standard export to a file. Listing 11-2 shows examples of both methods.

Listing 11-2   Two Methods for Exporting XML Data

```
Public Sub OutputInventory2()
    ' Use the ExportXml technique to save data and the
    ' data interpretation.
    MsgBox Workbooks(1).XmlMaps("Items_Map").ExportXml()

    ' Use the standard Export method to create a file.
    Workbooks(1).XmlMaps(1).Export "ExcelXML2.XML", True
End Sub
```

In both cases, you rely on collections to obtain the information. Notice that you can use a number or a string to reference the particular XML map that you want to use for export purposes. Both the ExportXml and Export methods include an optional argument that forces the parser to check the XML for proper form before exporting. When using the Export method, you must supply a string, and you should tell the method to overwrite any existing file of the same name.

Importing the data from disk

Importing data from disk varies in difficulty based on the kind of XML file that you want to import. Excel normally does a good job of figuring out how to import well-formed XML. Listing 11-3 shows the code that you need to import a standard XML file.

Listing 11-3   Importing XML from Disk

```
Public Sub ImportInventory()
    ' Obtain the XML from disk using the XmlImport.
    ThisWorkbook.XmlImport "ExcelXML2.XML", _
                            True, _
                            Sheet2.Range("A1")
End Sub
```

The XmlImport method requires three arguments. The first is the name of the file that you want to import. The second indicates whether you want to overwrite any existing data. Finally, you must supply a location to hold the data.

When you run this program, you see an Error in Schema dialog box. The data exported with the example doesn't include an XSD reference. Excel doesn't know how to interpret the data because it has no data definition. In this case, you can safely click the Infer button to get the correct result.

Creating a Simple Word XML Document

Word automates the process of linking an XSD file to your document by adding this feature through the document templates. When you create a document by using a properly designed template, the XML tags are automatically added according to the XSD schema that you create.

You might want to create searchable letters. One way to do this is to export the letters as XML and to use a standard search engine. Start by creating a letter template file. The example includes the usual features, such as To and From addresses, the date that the letter was written, a greeting, the letter body, and a closing element. Listing 11-4 shows the XSD file used to describe this document. (You can find the source code for this example on the Dummies.com site at http://www.dummies.com/go/vbafd5e.)

Listing 11-4   Creating an XSD File to Export a Letter

```xml
<?xml version="1.0"?>
<xs:schema xmlns:xs="http://www.w3.org/2001/XMLSchema"
 targetNamespace="http://www.mysite.com"
 xmlns="http://www.mysite.com"
 elementFormDefault="qualified">

<xs:element name="MyLetter">
  <xs:complexType mixed="true">
    <xs:sequence>
      <xs:element name="FromAddress" type="xs:string"/>
      <xs:element name="Sent" type="xs:string"/>
      <xs:element name="ToName" type="xs:string"/>
      <xs:element name="ToCompany" type="xs:string"/>
      <xs:element name="ToAddress" type="xs:string"/>
      <xs:element name="ToCity" type="xs:string"/>
      <xs:element name="ToState" type="xs:string"/>
      <xs:element name="ToZIP" type="xs:string"/>
      <xs:element name="Greeting" type="xs:string"/>
      <xs:element name="Body" type="xs:string" maxOccurs="unbounded"/>
      <xs:element name="Closing" type="xs:string"/>
    </xs:sequence>
  </xs:complexType>
</xs:element>

</xs:schema>
```

This example doesn't require a collection of items, such as those found in a database, so it doesn't require a complex structure. Each of the elements appears only one time except for the Body element, which can appear once for each paragraph in the letter. Notice that this XSD file includes a targetNamespace. Think of this as the default namespace for the XSD file. Word requires this entry. Word also requires that you include the mixed="true" attribute for the <xs:complexType> tag. Otherwise, it continually reports that the MyLetter element can't contain text.

After you create the template and the XSD file, you need to link the two. The procedure for accomplishing this task is different from working with an individual file. Here are the steps that you need to follow:

1. **Click the Word button to display the Word options. Click Word Options.**

   Word displays the Word Options dialog box.

2. **Select the Add-Ins folder.**

3. **Choose XML Schemas in the Manage field and click Go.**

   Word displays the XML Schema tab of the Templates and Add-ins dialog box.

4. **Click Add Schema.**

   You see the Add Schema dialog box.

5. **Locate the XSD file that contains the schema you want to use. Click Open.**

   The Schema Settings dialog box appears. The dialog box always contains the Uniform Resource Identifier (URI) of the schema and its physical location on the hard drive. You can optionally assign an alias to the schema.

6. **Type an alias for the schema and click OK.**

7. **Click OK to close the Templates and Add-ins dialog box.**

   Word displays the XML Structure task pane.

8. **Highlight an item and then click the schema entry at the bottom of the task pane.**

   Word asks whether you want to apply the schema to the entire document.

9. **Click Yes.**

   Word applies a beginning tag and an ending tag for the schema to the template.

10. **Highlight each element in turn and click its schema entry in the XML Structure task pane.**

    Word applies individual element tags to each field in the template.

11. **Save the new template.**

After you create a document by using the new template, you can use the Save Data Only check box of the Save As dialog box (refer to Figure 11-3). The new document contains just the data that you created in a true XML format.

Changing the Face of XML with XSLT

Looking at Figure 11-2, earlier in this chapter, shows you that XML by itself is a little tough to read. You might also find that some XML files contain too much information. XSLT helps correct both of these problems. It can format the information so that it's easier to read. You can also use XSLT to limit the amount of information that you see. XSLT transforms XML into something usable.

Note that you might see two definitions for XSLT: eXtensible *Style* Language Transformation and eXtensible *Stylesheet* Language Transformations. Both definitions refer to the same technology. I prefer the second form because it better describes how XSLT works.

This section describes how you can use XSLT to change the way that the output from your applications looks. After you save your document as XML, you can present it on a Web site for someone else to see. XSLT can transform the XML into HTML so that other people can enjoy your work.

XSLT can perform other kinds of transformations, so don't limit yourself to the techniques that you see demonstrated in this chapter. For example, you can use XSLT to create another XML document or even a text file. XSLT is all about transforming your data into the form that you want rather than forcing you to accept data in a less-than-optimal form. There's an excellent XSL tutorial at `http://www.w3schools.com/xsl/default.asp`. You can also find a good XSLT reference at `http://www.zvon.org/xxl/XSLTReference/Output/index.html`.

Saving your Word document by using XSLT

You can use XSLT to work with any XML file generated by an Office application — even the WordML documents created by default with Word (see the earlier "Comparing WordML with Saved XML" section for details). When you use the Save As dialog box (refer to Figure 11-3) to save a Word document as XML, you can choose to use an XSLT file to modify the output. (Although this chapter provides enough information about XSLT to work with the examples, *XSLT For Dummies,* by Richard Wagner, provides additional insights that you might find helpful.) You might want only the document information or only the document content. It's even possible to build a list of all the fonts used in every Word document on your machine. Any information that WordML provides is available.

The example in this section helps you overcome one of the problems with the output options provided with Word. By using XSLT, you can create an HTML page containing any information about your document. (Even though the XML Paper Specification, or XPS, file format creates a Web page for your document, it creates an exact replica of the file and doesn't present just the data you want the viewer to see.) This example shows document information, but the technique works with fonts, options, or the content of the file as well. The main reason I chose document information is that this particular technique works well if you want to create a Web site with a listing of all the documents that you've created. Using this technique creates a searchable Web site that's infinitely easier to mine for data than using the Word documents directly.

Before you can export data from Word by using XSLT, you need an XSLT file containing the proper code. Listing 11-5 shows the XSLT code for this example. (You can find the source code for this example on the Dummies.com site at http://www.dummies.com/go/vbafd5e.)

Listing 11-5   Using XSLT to Save a Word Document

```
<?xml version='1.0'?>
<xsl:stylesheet version='1.0'
xmlns:xsl='http://www.w3.org/1999/XSL/Transform'
xmlns:w="http://schemas.microsoft.com/office/word/2002/8/wordml">
<xsl:output method="html" indent="yes" />
<xsl:template match="/">

<!-- Create the HTML Code for this stylesheet. -->
<HTML>
<HEAD>
    <TITLE>Word Document Properties</TITLE>
</HEAD>

<BODY>
<CENTER><H3>Word Document Property Values</H3></CENTER>

<TABLE BORDER="2">
    <TR>
        <TH>Property</TH>
        <TH>Value</TH>
    </TR>
        <xsl:apply-templates select="//w:title"/>
</TABLE>

</BODY>
</HTML>
</xsl:template>

<!-- XSL template section that describes table content. -->

<xsl:template match="w:title">
    <TR>
        <TD>
            Title
        </TD>
        <TD>
            <xsl:value-of select="@w:val"/>
        </TD>
    </TR>
</xsl:template>

</xsl:stylesheet>
```

The code shows only one of the `o:DocumentProperties` values. This document begins with the standard XSL tags. Notice that it includes a special namespace entry, `xmlns:w="http://schemas.microsoft.com/office/word/2002/8/wordml"`. You must include this namespace to transform WordML documents. Otherwise, you can't interpret them by using XSLT.

Notice that the `<xsl:output>` tag uses the `method="html"` attribute to ensure that the output is in pure HTML. The result is displayed as HTML in Internet Explorer even if you use the `method="xml"` attribute. However, you experience fewer problems with other browsers if you use the `method="html"` attribute.

The `<xsl:apply-templates>` tag is the first place where you notice the effect of working with WordML. This tag references the new namespace added at the beginning of the file. If you don't include the namespace, none of the entries in the WordML file matches, and there isn't any output in the XSLT file.

Look at the template. It also includes the WordML namespace. You must also include it for entries such as attributes. Many `o:DocumentProperties` values rely on the `@w:val` attribute to store their content.

To use the XSLT file to translate a Word file, simply select the Apply Transform check box (see the lower-left area of Figure 11-3) and select the XSLT file by clicking the Transform button. The output that you create has an XML extension. Simply change it to HTM, and you can view the information as a Web page.

Automating the Word XML process

You can easily automate the task of saving your Word document by using various XSLT files. All you need is a form of the program shown in Listing 11-6.

Listing 11-6   Automatically Saving a Word XML Document

```
Public Sub SaveXMLDocumentInfo()
    ' Create a File Open dialog box.
    Dim GetFile As FileDialog
    Set GetFile =
            Application.FileDialog(msoFileDialogOpen)

    ' Modify the settings to show XSLT files.
    GetFile.Filters.Clear
```

```
    GetFile.Filters.Add "XSLT File", "*.XSLT"
    GetFile.Show

    ' Make sure the save process uses the template.
    ThisDocument.XMLSaveThroughXSLT = _
        GetFile.SelectedItems (1)

    ' Re-create GetFile as a File Save dialog box.
    Set GetFile = Nothing
    Set GetFile = _
        Application.FileDialog(msoFileDialogSaveAs)

    ' Modify the settings to show HTM files.
    GetFile.FilterIndex = 4
    GetFile.Show

    ' Save the document.
    ThisDocument.SaveAs GetFile.SelectedItems(1), _
                        wdFormatXML
End Sub
```

The code begins by creating a FileDialog object. You use this object to let the user select files during program execution. When you create a file Open dialog box, you can change the filters to meet specific needs. Use the Clear method to remove the default filters and the Add method to create new filters. A *filter* consists of a description and the file extension that you want to support in the dialog box. A file Save dialog box doesn't allow you to modify the filters, but you can choose a default filter to help the program user choose the correct save file type quickly.

This example shows the two essential steps that you must perform to save a file by using XSLT. They include setting the XMLSaveThroughXSLT property to the name of the template that you want to use and using the Save As dialog box to save the document. Notice the new wdFormatXML file format option. This option doesn't appear in older versions of Word (and wasn't documented at the time this book was written). The example code forces a save to an HTM document, so you don't even need to rename the file afterward.

Part IV
Programming for Applications

The 5th Wave
By Rich Tennant

"Roger! Check the sewing machine's connection to the PC. I'm getting e-mails stitched across my curtains again."

In this part . . .

In this part of the book, I get into the details of using VBA with specific applications. In fact, you discover that VBA can cross application boundaries and perform useful work with more than one application at a time. Office, in general, provides many customization opportunities. Although you can make most Office changes manually, it helps to know how to make them automatically, too.

In Chapter 12, I show a technique for changing the Office environment to meet changing requirements. This chapter emphasizes the differences between the older toolbar-and-menu interface and the new Ribbon interface. This chapter is essential for anyone upgrading applications.

In Chapters 13 through 15, I demonstrate how to add functionality to Word, Excel, and Access, respectively. Each of these host applications provides a unique environment where you can change data and create new information at the click of a button.

When you become more proficient with VBA, you want to build better programs that save you more time. In Chapter 16, I demonstrate how to work with more than one Office application at a time, but you can easily apply what you learn to work with applications from other vendors, too.

Chapter 12

VBA Programming in Office

● ●

In This Chapter

▶ Creating new features in the user environment

▶ Changing menus and tools to meet new requirements

▶ Designing tabs for the Office Ribbon interface

▶ Modifying the Ribbon interface externally

● ●

*Y*ou have the skills required to write any program that you want for your copy of Office. However, you can improve efficiency most by personalizing the user environment. A tenfold increase in computer performance is of little consequence if you can't employ that performance productively. Yet a small change in the user interface that does nothing to improve computer performance can net huge gains in your productivity by enhancing efficiency.

Microsoft tuned the Office interface to meet the needs of faceless crowds of people. Microsoft provides options that help you modify the older menu interface manually, but that's time consuming. (The newer Ribbon interface doesn't even provide manual customization options.) You might find that you need a custom interface to perform each task most efficiently, so manual methods are just counterproductive. VBA is the answer to making these changes automatically as you move from document to document.

This chapter demonstrates two things. First, by using VBA, you can modify the Office user interface to meet your specific needs and not those that Microsoft thinks that you might have. Second, VBA helps you perform these interface changes automatically so that you can have a customized environment for every task that you perform.

Working with the User Environment

The user environment is where you spend most of your time. It's the visible part of any application. Because it's the visible part of any application, the user environment is the basis on which you make a decision about the application. First impressions are important to how you view an application.

Think of a user environment as *immersive* — as a package of features that present you with a view of the application as a whole. Don't assume that the user environment is the same as the user interface. The user environment includes several features:

- ✔ **User interface:** The active portion of the user environment, the *user interface* includes the controls that make the application functional.

- ✔ **Graphics:** The physical appearance of the environment affects how you feel about your program. Helpful graphics can direct your attention to specific application features. Some graphics add aesthetic appeal to the application without making it harder to use.

- ✔ **Colors and aesthetics:** The use of color can affect your mood. If you use the wrong colors, you can also make some program elements difficult for anyone with certain forms of color blindness to see. A program can really be a thing of beauty.

- ✔ **Accessibility:** The difficulty that you encounter using an application affects the way that you view it. An application should include context-sensitive help in addition to the main help. It should also include features that make each control easy to use with either the keyboard or mouse.

- ✔ **Logic and flow:** The work required to locate, evaluate, modify, add, and delete data affects your view of an application. Controls should always flow in a logical order to make typing information easy. Data fields should be large enough to include all the information that you need to see at a glance but not so large that you have to move the cursor to see the entire field.

Beneficial changes that you can make

You can make your program a work of art. The beneficial changes that you make to the user environment mean the difference between a program that makes you efficient and one that actually requires more time to use. When you look at your program initially, you think of practical matters — getting the code to work and putting some essential elements in place. After you get past that stage in development, you need to consider the user environment. Here are some beneficial changes that you should consider:

- ✔ **Menus and toolbars:** Create a special menu for features that you use during every session. Note that a feature isn't necessarily a VBA program. For example, it could also be a shortcut to a document template so that you can simply click a button to start a new document that requires a certain template. You could also use toolbar buttons for quick access to special symbols, such as the section (§) symbol used for legal abbreviations. Menu entries are always visible and quite easy to use. Use a special toolbar for features that you use during some sessions but not others. Toolbars are easy to hide. Use both a menu and a toolbar for features that you always use and that require quick access.

✔ **Balloon help:** Every control should have a `ControlTipText` property entry. This includes any toolbar entries that you add. The balloon help text is helpful for anyone who needs additional information about your program features. It's also the only method that ensures that someone who's using a screen reader or other accessibility aid can use your program successfully.

✔ **Helpful graphics:** A graphic can prove more helpful than text in some cases, especially if the graphic clearly illustrates the intent of a feature better than text can explain (a graphic that's worth a thousand words). You might also want to combine graphics with text to ensure complete understanding.

✔ **Simplified displays:** You might find that a display becomes too complex after you add the special features that you need to the features that Microsoft thinks that you want. A program that configures a display with features needed to perform a specific task is helpful because reduced complexity makes it easier to find what you need. In fact, a series of task buttons, such as one for letters, another for notes, and still another for lists, can be quite helpful.

✔ **User settings:** Any time that you can involve the people using your program in the configuration process, you provide a way for them to express their needs.

Problems that you should consider

Whenever you change something in the user environment, you should consider the problems that such a change can create, as described in the following list. The user environment can make or break any program that you create. It might be tempting to add every feature to a menu, drown the display in color, or add graphics to dress up the display.

✔ **Increased training costs:** Whenever you change the user environment, you add a certain amount of confusion. The new features might cause the user to pause and think, or the user might not understand them at all. Training helps users understand the new features and use them efficiently, but training isn't free.

✔ **Update incompatibility:** A new feature that you introduce might cause compatibility problems with future versions of a product. You need to consider how the change will affect the future use of the program.

✔ **Reduced efficiency:** Too many features, controls, display elements, graphics, and other distractions tend to reduce efficiency. It doesn't matter how skilled you are at using a program, too many display elements slow you down because you have to look for what you need. The most efficient program is one that contains just the features that you use and no others.

✔ **Security holes:** Any change that you make to an application can create security holes that the original vendor didn't anticipate and you can't see because you don't have the application code. The very act of turning on macro support in an application opens it to certain types of virus attack. Adding a feature could also make it easier to circumvent security measures, such as the use of data encryption and passwords. Complete testing is usually the only way to ensure that you haven't introduced a security problem.

Manipulating Toolbars and Menus

Office 2007 now has two interfaces, which means that Microsoft has made it more difficult for users of all types. The toolbar-and-menu interface used by previous versions of Office appears in products such as Visio and Outlook, and the new Ribbon interface appears in the core office applications, such as Word and Excel. This section of the chapter works mainly with the older toolbar and menu interface. The "Working with the New Ribbon Interface" section, later in this chapter, describes the newer interface.

No matter what program you create, you need to provide a way to run it. Using the Tools⇨Macro⇨Macros command to display the Macro dialog box works fine for a program that you don't use very often, but you want to make some programs easier to access. Manually adding a favorite program to a toolbar or menu works fine if you always want to have it available, but sometimes you don't want to see this option.

This section describes how you can change the toolbar and menu content of an Office application to meet your needs. These techniques don't work well with Office 2007 applications such as Excel and Word, but they do work well with Visio 2003/2007, Outlook 2003/2007, Word 2003, Excel 2003, and other Office products that rely on the menu interface. You can modify existing menus and toolbars as well as add new entries for your custom programs. These changes can occur automatically as the result of environmental conditions, as the result of actions on your part, or on command. Office applications change their appearance to match conditions anyway — this is simply an extension of that idea to meet your specific needs.

Don't create a document template with special toolbars and think that you can use it effectively with both the menu and Ribbon interfaces. Toolbars created as part of a template (those you add manually by right-clicking the toolbar area and choosing Customize from the context menu) don't even show up with the new Ribbon interface. However, toolbars that you create programmatically do show up in the new Ribbon interface, albeit in the wrong place. You don't see the actual toolbar any longer, but you see the functionality you added on the Add-Ins tab, shown in Figure 12-1.

Figure 12-1:
Toolbars
you add
program-
matically
appear on
the Add-Ins
tab of the
Ribbon.

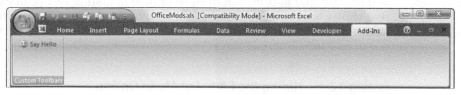

Even though this approach displays all the buttons on the toolbar so that they're usable no matter which interface users require, the buttons are associated with a specific toolbar only when you use the menu interface. Each toolbar appears onscreen with a separator, but that doesn't really help identify it. You see up to three different areas on the Add-Ins tab:

- Menu Commands (associated with any new menus you create)
- Toolbar Commands (associated with any new toolbar commands you create)
- Custom Toolbars (the actual buttons on a toolbar)

Displaying or hiding toolbars and menus

It's helpful to hide or display menus or toolbars as needed. Keeping the display free from clutter is always helpful in improving efficiency and reducing confusion. Both menus and items use the same technique. Working with menus is a little more cumbersome because you have to figure out the name of the menu bar first. It would be nice if Microsoft used the same name for the menu bar in every Office application, but that's just not the case. For example, Excel's menu bar is named Worksheet Menu Bar, but Word uses just Menu Bar. To learn the name of the menu bar for your Office application, simply drag the menu bar from the top and place it somewhere in the editing pane. The name appears on the title bar, as shown in Figure 12-2 for the Word 2003 Menu Bar.

Figure 12-2:
A complete
list of menu
entries
supported
by Word
2003.

After you know the name of the menu or toolbar that you want to change, you can use that information to show or hide it. Listing 12-1 is an example that shows how to work with the Edit⇨Cut menu option. (You can find the source code for this example on the Dummies.com site at http://www. dummies.com/go/vbafd5e.)

Listing 12-1   Hiding the Edit⇨Cut Menu Option

```
Public Sub HideAndShowEditCutMenu()
    ' Create the menu command bar.
    Dim TopMenu As CommandBar
    Set TopMenu = _
        Application.CommandBars("Worksheet Menu Bar")

    ' Access the Edit menu control.
    Dim EditControl As CommandBarControl
    Set EditControl = TopMenu.Controls("Edit")

    ' Use the control to access the command bar.
    Dim EditMenu As CommandBar
    Set EditMenu = _
        TopMenu.Controls(EditControl.Index).CommandBar

    ' Access the Cut submenu.
    Dim EditCut As CommandBarControl
    Set EditCut = EditMenu.Controls("Cut")

    ' Change the visible state according to the current
    ' setting.
    EditCut.Visible = Not EditCut.Visible

    ' Display the current setting.
    If EditCut.Visible Then
        MsgBox "The Cut option is visible."
    Else
        MsgBox "The Cut option isn't visible."
    End If
End Sub
```

This code shows that you need to work your way down to the menu that you want to change. Begin by getting the top-level menu by using the `Application.CommandBars` collection. This collection accepts the name of the toolbar or menu that you want to work with as in index. Because this is an Excel example, the code uses `Worksheet Menu Bar` as input. You can use precisely the same code in Word by using `Menu Bar` instead.

After the code can access the top-level menu, it has to drill down to the Edit⇨Cut option. Don't assume that the person who is using your program hasn't changed things around. You need to ask for the various menu entries by name rather than by numeric value. Consequently, the code must retrieve the Edit menu `CommandBarControl` by using the `Controls` collection. A `CommandBarControl` is the actual menu entry and not the list of items that it contains.

To get the Edit menu `CommandBar`, which is the object that contains the list of items on that menu, the code uses the `EditControl.Index` property. This property contains a number that indicates the position of the Edit menu on the main menu. VBA doesn't return the `CommandBar` unless the code supplies this number. It's a subtle point that will likely cause a lot of errors.

The code can access the `Cut` option of the Edit menu at this point by using the `EditMenu.Controls` collection. The code uses the `Visible` property to hide or show the option as a toggle.

The Ribbon interface displays only those menus or toolbars that you add to the user interface. Because this example hides an existing menu entry, it appears to do nothing when used with Excel 2007 or Word 2007. The code doesn't produce an error either, so you don't need to worry about an older macro like this one displaying an error message, but the user environment might not be set up as you intended because the Ribbon interface simply ignores this code. The "Working with the New Ribbon Interface" section of this chapter describes how you could perform approximately the same task. (Since there isn't an Edit⇨Cut command with the Ribbon, you can't replicate this code completely.)

Modifying the toolbar or menu content

Toolbars and menus have a lot of properties that you can change. Anything that you can change with the Customize feature of the Office application is also available from code. For example, you might want to provide better tooltips for your program or change the wording of the prompt. Here's an example of code that modifies a ToolTip associated with the **B** (bold) button on the Formatting toolbar. (You can find the source code for this example on the Dummies.com site at http://www.dummies.com/go/vbafd5e.)

```
Public Sub ChangeBoldToolTip()
    ' Get the Formatting toolbar.
    Dim FormatBar As CommandBar
    Set FormatBar = Application.CommandBars("Formatting")

    ' Get the Bold control.
    Dim BoldControl As CommandBarControl
    Set BoldControl = FormatBar.Controls("&Bold")

    ' Change the tooltip.
    BoldControl.TooltipText = "Make the text bold!"
End Sub
```

I purposely selected the `TooltipText` property because it's one of the few that's difficult or impossible to change manually. If you want to add ToolTips to common menu or toolbar entries, you have to do it with a program. It's a shame that you have to go to this extreme because many accessibility devices rely on the ToolTips to tell those with special needs about the control. For example, most screen readers used by those with special visual needs rely on these ToolTips, so not adding a ToolTip means that someone with special needs will have difficulty using your program.

The code for this example works much like the earlier "Displaying or hiding toolbars and menus" example. Rather than access the menu, the code accesses the Formatting toolbar that appears in every Office program (so you can move this example to Word or Access unaltered).

After it gains access to the toolbar, the code accesses the **B** button. Notice that the `FormatBar.Controls` collection uses `&Bold` and not just `Bold`. You need to know the `Name` property value of the button that you want to change. Use this procedure to obtain the value:

1. **Right-click anywhere in the toolbar area and then choose Customize from the context menu that appears.**

   The Office application displays the Customize dialog box.

2. **Right-click the menu entry or toolbar control of interest.**

   The Office application displays a list of properties associated with the entry.

3. **Note the Name property value and then click Close in the Customize dialog box.**

Adding and removing toolbars and menus

You might want to add custom toolbars and menus to hold entries for your programs. Using custom setups means that you can show or hide custom programs as needed. This technique also keeps your code separate from the entries that Microsoft has made to ensure that there's little chance of compatibility problems. Listing 12-2 shows one technique for adding a new toolbar. (You can find the source code for this example on the Dummies.com site at http://www.dummies.com/go/vbafd5e.)

Listing 12-2   Adding a New Toolbar

```
Public Sub AddToolbar()
    ' Add the toolbar.
    Dim MyToolbar As CommandBar
    Set MyToolbar = _
        Application.CommandBars.Add("My Toolbar")

    ' Add a control to the toolbar.
    Dim SayHello As CommandBarButton
    Set SayHello = _
        MyToolbar.Controls.Add(msoControlButton)

    ' Configure the control.
    With SayHello
        .Caption = "Say Hello"
        .DescriptionText = "This button displays a
            message."
        .OnAction = "DoSayHello"
        .TooltipText = "This button displays a message."
        .Visible = True
        .Style = msoButtonIconAndCaption
        .FaceId = 59
    End With

    ' Make the toolbar visible.
    MyToolbar.Visible = True
End Sub
```

The entire toolbar structure in Office applications consists of collections. As with any collection, you use the Add method to add a new entry. Because there's only one main menu, any new CommandBar object that you add is treated as a toolbar. When adding a new menu entry, you must retrieve the main menu first and then add your menu to it.

Microsoft supplies a number of controls that you can add to a toolbar. The most common option is a `CommandBarButton` object. You can also choose the `CommandBarComboBox`, `CommandBarControl`, or `CommandBarPopup` object. The Help file doesn't even begin to tell you how many kinds of `CommandBarControl` objects that you can create. Look at the `MsoControl Type` enumeration in Object Browser. However, if you want to stick to the controls that Microsoft recommends, use the `msoControlButton`, `msoControlEdit`, `msoControlDropdown`, `msoControlComboBox`, or `msoControlPopup` types.

After you add a control to your new toolbar, you need to configure it. The new button is blank. The entries that you should always include appear in the code. Make certain that you define an `OnAction` member that reflects an existing Office application command or a `Public Sub` that you've defined. The `FaceId` value, in this case, is the standard smiley face. You do have access to a number of other icon values that are, unfortunately, not documented. Notice also that you must make the individual controls visible by using the `Visible` property as well as the toolbar.

Removing a toolbar isn't nearly as difficult as creating it. Here's the code that you need:

```
Public Sub RemoveToolbar()
    ' Remove the custom toolbar.
    Application.CommandBars("My Toolbar").Delete
End Sub
```

This single command removes the toolbar permanently. Unfortunately, there isn't a good way to save completed toolbars to disk, so hiding the toolbar by using the `Visible` property or deleting it completely are the only two options.

Working with the New Ribbon Interface

Some, but not all, of the Office 2007 applications come with the new Ribbon interface. You probably noticed quite quickly that the Ribbon doesn't provide any simple means of customization. When working with the older menu and toolbar interface, all you needed to do was right-click the toolbar area and choose Customize, but Microsoft doesn't offer this feature in Office 2007. The new interface relies on XML files instead. These XML files describe the structure of the Ribbon.

Understanding the application file content

You can change the Ribbon only when using an Office 2007 file. This means that you must convert any compatibility files (those used with Office 2003 and earlier) before you can make any changes to the Ribbon. The Office 2007 file itself is actually a zip file. In fact, you can change the extension on any Office 2007 file to zip and open it with a product such as WinZIP.

When you open the Office 2007 file as a ZIP file, you see a number of XML files inside. Generally, you don't want to modify these files directly unless you know precisely what they do. In fact, it's better to use tools to modify the content of the Office 2007 file whenever you can. You can use the Office 2007 Custom UI Editor, described later in this section, to do everything you need to do to add or remove tabs, groups, and buttons.

The Office 2007 files contain a number of common elements. The important element for a custom Ribbon is the `customUI.xml` file. This file contains all the definitions for your custom Ribbon. However, just having a list of definitions doesn't do much for you; you must connect the definitions to the document by using the `.rels` (relations) file. Note that this file doesn't have a filename; just an extension. When your custom Ribbon includes icons or other graphics, you also see a `customUI.xml.rels` file that contains pointers to those items. These are all the entries related specifically to your Ribbon.

You also find a few other common elements in the Office 2007 files. The `app.xml` contains application-specific settings for the document, so you may need to interact with it at times. The `core.xml` file contains all the properties for the file, such as the author name and title. Generally, you should access these entries by using the objects discussed in other chapters of this book rather than work with the XML files directly.

Obtaining and using the Office 2007 Custom UI Editor

The official method for modifying the Ribbon has you changing the file extension, extracting the required files, making modifications in an editor, archiving the files again, and, finally, changing the file extension back every time you want to make any change at all. You can see this grueling and error-prone method at `http://msdn2.microsoft.com/en-us/library/ms406046.aspx`. The better way to make changes is to rely on a utility named Office 2007 Custom UI Editor, or Custom UI Editor, for short (`http://openxmldeveloper.org/articles/CustomUIeditor.aspx`). The direct download link is at `http://openxmldeveloper.org/attachment/239.ashx`.

Using the Custom UI Editor is easier than the difficult process that Microsoft suggests. All you do is open your document, template, or add-in, make the required Ribbon additions, and save the file. The next time you open the file in the Office application, it contains the updated Ribbon. Figure 12-3 shows a typical example of the Custom UI Editor in action.

Don't let the XML in this example scare you. As with every XML file, this one starts with an XML processing instruction. The root node, which contains everything else, is <customUI>. The child of interest for this example is <ribbon>, which contains all the Ribbon additions. You can use other child elements on complex setups, such as the <commands> element that lets you change an existing command to do something else.

Most Ribbon additions consist of three elements. First, you need a *tab,* which is the selection you choose to locate a particular Ribbon display. The default tabs have names such as Home and Insert. Second, you need a *group* to hold and organize various controls. For example, the Clipboard group on the Home tab organizes the Cut, Copy, Paste, and Format Painter controls. Third, you need a button or other control to perform an action. Buttons are the easiest controls to use, so that's what this chapter uses as a starting point. Figure 12-3 shows the entries you need in order to add one tab, one group, and one control to the Ribbon.

Figure 12-3:
The Custom UI Editor makes short work of Ribbon changes.

What's a callback?

You see the term *callback* used quite often when you work with the Ribbon. A *callback* is a special kind of an event. When the user clicks a button, the Ribbon receives the event. The event handler for the Ribbon then makes a call to any Sub you define for handling that event in VBA. A callback is more like a function call in VBA than it is an actual event handler. Callbacks can occur for a number of reasons, not just user actions. For example, you can receive a call-back when the application loads.

Anyone who is familiar with older programming languages, such as C or C++, or who worked with the Windows Application Programming Interface (API), is already familiar with call-backs because these environments rely heavily on them. The Ribbon callback may sound like a new idea, but it has been around for quite some time.

This chapter gives you a good starting point for working with the Ribbon. You find, as the book progresses, other information about the Ribbon in specific applications. However, at some point, you need to know information about a Ribbon element that doesn't appear in this book. Microsoft provides detailed Ribbon information at http://msdn2.microsoft.com/en-us/library/ms406047.aspx.

Adding a tab, group, and button

One of the tasks that you commonly perform is creating your own tabs on the Ribbon. However, just creating a tab isn't enough; you must also create a group and a control of some sort. Figure 12-3 shows a typical set-up in the Custom UI Editor. The following steps describe the setup for this example:

1. **Download and install the Custom UI Editor on your system by using the information in the section "Obtaining and using the Office 2007 Custom UI Editor," earlier in this chapter.**

2. **Create a file to hold the new Ribbon tab, group, and button.**

   The example uses Excel, but you can also create the example using Word or any other Office 2007 application that relies on the Ribbon. The Ribbon has certain advantages over the older toolbar and menu setup because it relies on a generic XML file to define the setup.

3. **Close the application you used to create the data file.**

   Always close the host application before you make any changes to the target file using the Custom UI Editor. After you make the changes, save them and reopen the file in the host application. Never make any changes in the Custom UI Editor while you have the host application open. Although your data will remain safe, making changes with both the Custom UI Editor and the host application on the same file can have unpredictable results, including lost VBA code.

4. **Start the Custom UI Editor.**

5. **Open the data file you created. (You may need to set the Files of Type field to All Files (*.*) to see templates and documents.)**

   The Custom UI tab in the editor is blank because you haven't added any custom UI features to this file yet.

6. **Choose Sample⇨Custom Tab in the Custom UI Editor.**

   The Custom UI Editor automatically creates the entries for a custom tab for you.

7. **Modify the entries to look like those shown in Figure 12-3.**

   Notice especially the onAction attribute shown in Figure 12-3. This entry tells the Ribbon to call a Sub with a specific name in your VBA code.

8. **Select the first line of the file. Type** <?xml version="1.0" encoding=" utf-8" ?> **and press Enter.**

   This step adds the XML processing instruction, which is a requirement for every XML file. If you don't add this element, the tab fails to appear as anticipated.

9. **Click Save.**

10. **Open the file in the application you used to create it.**

    You see a new tab like the one shown in Figure 12-4. The tab isn't functional yet, but you can see it.

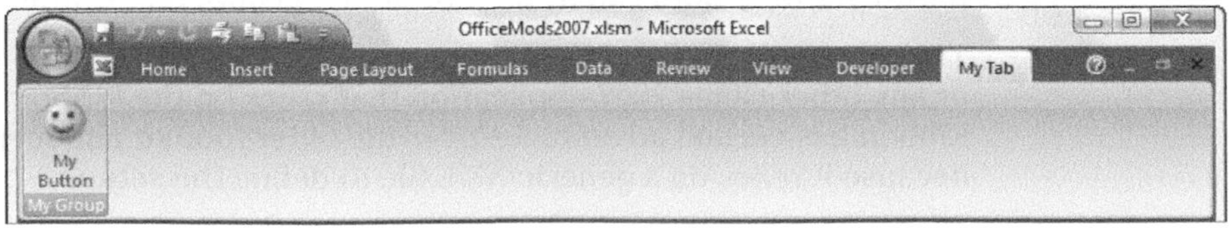

Figure 12-4:
Adding a new tab, group, or control is the first step to programming the Ribbon.

Now that you have a new button you can access, it's time to write some code for it. Writing code for the Ribbon is significantly different from writing code for the menu-and-toolbar setup. Fortunately, the Custom UI Editor can help reduce the difficulty of the coding experience for you.

1. **Open the VBA Editor and add a new module called RibbonX.**

2. **Select the Custom UI Editor again and click Generate Callbacks on the toolbar.**

   You see a Callbacks tab appear with VBA code in it. The code provides precisely what you need to access the button you created. Using this approach takes the guesswork out of creating a Sub for your button. Notice that the callback includes a variable you can use to access the button. You can't access the button directly from VBA.

3. **Highlight all the code and press Ctrl+C.**

4. **Select the VBA Editor. Place the cursor on a new line at the end of the file and press Ctrl+V.**

   You see the VBA code added to the module.

At this point, you can finally add code to interact with your new button. The control variable provides only a few, but essential, values you can use. The following code shows how you can display the control's identifier:

```
'Callback for myButton onAction
Sub myButton_ClickHandler(control As IRibbonControl)
    MsgBox control.ID + " Clicked"
End Sub
```

Add the MsgBox call as shown to display a dialog box. Save the file and click My Button on the My Tab tab. You see a dialog box that contains the My Button identifier.

The same techniques described for a Ribbon addition also work for the application menu. However, rather than use the <tabs> element shown earlier, in Figure 12-3, you use the menu element that you want to change, such as the <fileMenu> element. You can obtain a complete list of all the Ribbon schema elements (the special elements you use to write Ribbon additions) at http://www.microsoft.com/downloads/details.aspx?familyid= 15805380-F2C0-4B80-9AD1-2CB0C300AEF9.

Performing tasks when the Ribbon loads

You have access to a wealth of information about the Ribbon. However, most of this information comes from callbacks. One of the most important callbacks concerns Ribbon loading. You use the `onLoad` attribute for the `<customUI>` element, as shown here:

```
<customUI
    xmlns="http://schemas.microsoft.com/office/2006/01/customui"
    onLoad="RibbonLoaded">
```

This callback looks for a `RibbonLoaded` Sub in your VBA code. As with button and other control events, you can ask the Custom UI Editor to generate the required `Sub` code for you automatically. All you need to do then is fill in the `Sub` with the actions you want to perform. Listing 12-3 shows an example of a common task you could perform in the Ribbon `onLoad` callback. (You can find the source code for this example on the Dummies.com site at `http://www.dummies.com/go/vbafd5e`.)

Listing 12-3   Defining a Callback for Ribbon Loading

```
'Define a global variable to hold the Ribbon reference.
Dim Rib As IRibbonUI

'Callback for customUI.onLoad
Sub RibbonLoaded(ribbon As IRibbonUI)

    'Save the ribbon reference.
    Set Rib = ribbon

    ' Tell the user the Ribbon is loaded.
    MsgBox "Ribbon Loaded"
End Sub
```

This example may not look like much, but you often need the Ribbon reference (`Rib` in this case) when you make changes to the Ribbon. You use the `Invalidate` method to tell the Ribbon to redraw itself to display any features you remove, change, or add.

Modifying existing tabs

You can modify any existing element as long as you know the required identifier. Microsoft provides these identifiers as a download at `http://www.microsoft.com/downloads/details.aspx?familyid=4329d9e9-4d11-46a5-898d-23e4f331e9ae`. You can also view the identifiers by using a special feature of the Office products with the Ribbon interface. The following steps describe how:

1. **Select the Office application's button to display its menu.**

2. **Click the Options button (such as Word Options in Word).**

   You see the Options dialog box for that application.

3. **Select the** `Customization` **folder in the Options dialog box.**

4. **Select an entry in the Choose Command From field.**

5. **Hover the mouse cursor over the control you want to work with.**

   You see a ToolTip that displays the identifier for that control in parentheses after the control name.

Unfortunately, this technique works with controls only. If you want to find the identifiers for tabs or groups, you need to download the Microsoft-supplied documentation.

The example in this section shows how to work with a particular control. It demonstrates two techniques. First, the example adds a new group and control to an existing tab. Second, you see how to change the behavior of an existing control by using a technique called repurposing. You *repurpose* a control when you change its behavior from the default to a custom action and optionally perform the default action afterward.

Creating the custom user interface

Repurposing usually involves two steps. First, you must determine some mechanism to signal the change in behavior. The example uses a simple toggle button for the task, but you could use anything. For example, you might want to disable printing when the user is on the road and doesn't have a printer connected to the system. Second, you must provide the required linkage to repurpose the control. Listing 12-4 shows the code for the simple toggle button used in this example. You would insert this code into the <ribbon> element as shown earlier, in Figure 12-3. (You can find the source code for this example on the Dummies.com site at http://www.dummies.com/go/vbafd5e.)

Listing 12-4   Creating a Toggle Button

```
<tab idMso="TabHome">
   <group id="BehaviorChange"
          label="Behavior"
          insertAfterMso="GroupFont">
     <toggleButton
        id="StopUnderline"
        label="Stop Underlining"
        onAction="StopUnderline_ClickHandler"
        getPressed="StopUnderline_GetPressed"
        size="large"
        imageMso="ColorPickerXLFill"/>
   </group>
</tab>
```

This new group actually appears on the Home tab. Notice that the `<tab>` element uses `idMso` instead of `id` as the identifier. The `idMso` attribute defines an existing identifier — `TabHome` in this case. The `<group>` element defines a new group on the existing tab. The example inserts the new group after the `GroupFont` group, as shown in Figure 12-5.

Figure 12-5:
You can place new groups anywhere within an existing tab.

The toggle button includes a number of new features. Notice that you must provide two callbacks: `onAction` and `getPressed`. The `onAction` callback performs the same task as a standard button by letting you know when the user clicks the toggle button. The `getPressed` callback records the state of the toggle button. Notice that this example uses `ColorPickerXLFill` as the `imageMso` value. You can use the icon from any existing button for controls you create.

The linkage for the repurposing appears as a new child of the `<customUI>` element rather than in the `<ribbon>` element. The `<commands>` provides a list of commands you want to repurpose and the VBA scripts that handle them. Here is the repurposing linkage for this example:

```
<commands>
  <command idMso="Underline" onAction="myUnderline"/>
</commands>
```

Because you're creating linkage to an existing control, you must use the `idMso` attribute with a value that tells which control to repurpose. In this case, the code repurposes the Underline control. The `Sub` used as a callback is `myUnderline`.

Reacting to user input

Now that you have the custom Ribbon changes made, you can create code required to interact with the Ribbon in VBA. Listing 12-5 shows the code required to make this part of the example work. (You can find the source code for this example on the Dummies.com site at `http://www.dummies.com/go/vbafd5e`.)

Listing 12-5   VBA Interaction with the Ribbon

```
'Determines the behavior button state.
Dim lBehavior As Boolean

'Callback for StopUnderline onAction
Sub StopUnderline_ClickHandler( _
   control As IRibbonControl, _
   pressed As Boolean)

   ' Change the behavior state.
   lBehavior = pressed

   ' Update the control.
   Rib.InvalidateControl (control.ID)
End Sub

'Callback for StopUnderline getPressed
Sub StopUnderline_GetPressed( _
   control As IRibbonControl, _
   ByRef returnedVal)

   ' Return the current behavior state.
   returnedVal = lBehavior
End Sub

'Callback for myUnderline onAction
Sub myUnderline(control As IRibbonControl, _
               pressed As Boolean, _
               ByRef fCancelDefault)
   If (lBehavior) Then
       MsgBox "No Underlined Allowed!"
       pressed = False
       fCancelDefault = True
   Else
       fCancelDefault = False
   End If
End Sub
```

The code begins by defining a variable to track the behavioral state of the application. You need this variable to ensure that the Stop Underlining control you added reflects the correct state.

The `StopUnderline_ClickHandler()` Sub receives the current control and its pressed state. Theoretically, you can use the same Sub for all your controls by checking the control's identifier. However, most developers use a separate Sub for each control. The code stores the state of the control in `lBehavior` and then uses `InvalidateControl()` to redraw everything.

Using the Control UI Editor with care

I am showing you this example because the Control UI Editor doesn't always provide the correct arguments for some events, such as `onAction`. When you run this application, you see an error message stating that something has the wrong number of arguments. Unfortunately, VBA doesn't tell you what piece of code has the wrong number of arguments, and troubleshooting doesn't help you find the problem. In this case, the signature (the arguments) for the Underline toggle button callback is incorrect. You can see these signatures at `http://msdn2.microsoft.com/en-us/library/ms406047.aspx`. The correct callback signature looks like this:

```
sub OnAction(control as IRibbonControl, _
             pressed as Boolean, _
             ByRef fCancelDefault)
```

The `StopUnderline_GetPressed()` Sub completes the process of showing the current toggle button state by returning `lBehavior` to the Ribbon. Because the Ribbon calls this Sub when you first load the document, you must also provide a default value for `lBehavior` in `RibbonLoaded()`.

You can repurpose a control to perform any task you want, or you can turn it off completely. In this case, `myUnderline()` performs the default action when `lBehavior` is `False`. However, when the user sets Stop Underlining and `lBehavior` is `True`, the code displays a message telling the user that no underlining is allowed. In addition, the code tells the Ribbon not to depress the Underline toggle button or to perform the default action.

Chapter 13

VBA Programming in Word

● ●

In This Chapter

▶ Working with Word-related objects

▶ Creating access to Word windows and manipulating objects that they contain

▶ Creating access to the Word document

▶ Interacting with the Registry

▶ Modifying document objects in Word

▶ Using shapes effectively

▶ Adding, deleting, moving, and editing text in Word

▶ Creating envelopes and labels

● ●

*W*ord is the Microsoft Office application that you use to create and edit text, which means spending hours typing. All that typing takes time. However, you have at your disposal a personal secretary that can type thousands of words per minute (without error), and you might not even realize it. The programs that you create for Word can do more than simply change the user environment, convert data to text or eXtensible Markup Language (XML), and perform other helpful, nontyping tasks. The fastest typist that you'll ever know is the Word program that you create by using VBA.

Creating a document is more than just typing, though. You also have to consider the formatting of the text and how to divide it into pieces so that it's easy to read. A document might require graphics, and you might want to add special features to make some sections easier to find. Word programs can handle all these needs, too. Simply decide what you want Word to do and write a program to handle the task.

This chapter demonstrates VBA programming techniques that you can use to make your next Word session more enjoyable and productive. Rather than type the same material over and over again, you can concentrate on the creative part of the document. In addition, formatting can become a thing of the past (except for unique situations). A VBA program lets you rely on Word to do the formatting for you.

Understanding the Word-Related Objects

If you've followed the book to this point, you've already created a number of programs by using objects. In fact, you've even looked at Word-specific objects in a few cases. (See the "Creating a Simple Word XML Document" section of Chapter 11 as an example.) Word has three special collections (Documents, Templates, and Windows) that you can use to access the details of the Word environment, which includes any documents that you create.

Using the Documents collection

Documents are the essence of working with Word. They contain the data that you create, format, and print for the world to see. Consequently, the Documents collection is the one that you use most when manipulating content.

The Documents collection contains one copy of each Document object currently opened in Word. If you have more than one copy of the same document open, Word includes a single Document object for each copy.

A Document object isn't the same as a Template object. Word keeps these two object types separate. See the upcoming "Using the Templates collection" section for details on working with templates. A document can include content imported from other files. If you open a TXT file or an XML file, Word treats it as a Document object.

The Documents collection is most useful when you don't know the name of the document that you want to manage. For example, you might create a program that adds contractions to all documents that use the XYZ template. You don't know how many documents use this template or what the user named them, but you know that you need to make the same change to all open documents. Listing 13-1 shows an example that demonstrates how to use a For Each...Next statement to get information about each document that uses the Normal.dot template. (You can find the source code for this example on the Dummies.com site at http://www.dummies.com/go/vbafd5e.)

Listing 13-1   Getting Word Document Information

```
Public Sub MyDocuments()
    ' Create a variable to hold the individual documents.
    Dim MyDocs As Document

    ' Create a variable to hold information about selected
    ' documents.
```

```
    Dim Output As String

    ' Look at each document in the Documents collection.
    For Each MyDocs In Application.Documents

        ' Check for the appropriate template name.
        If UCase(MyDocs.AttachedTemplate) _
            = "NORMAL.DOT" Then

            ' Create a list of information about the
            ' document.
            With MyDocs
            Output = Output + "Name: " + vbTab + vbTab + _
                .Name + vbCrLf + _
                "Window Caption: " + vbTab + _
                .ActiveWindow.Caption + vbCrLf + _
                "Document Type: " + vbTab + _
                IIf(.ActiveWindow.Creator = wdCreatorCode,
            _
                    "Word Document", _
                    "Other Document") + vbCrLf + _
                "Writing Style: " + vbTab + _
                .ActiveWritingStyle(wdEnglishUS) _
                + vbCrLf + "Characters: " + vbTab + _
                CStr(.Characters.Count) + vbCrLf + _
                "Words: " + vbTab + vbTab + _
                CStr(.Words.Count) + vbCrLf + vbCrLf
            End With
        End If
    Next

    ' Output the result.
    MsgBox Output, _
            vbInformation Or vbOKOnly, _
            "Documents that Use the Normal Template"
End Sub
```

The example shows just a few of the properties available with the Document object. The example begins by creating the Document object, MyDocs, and a String, Output, that the code uses to hold the document information. The For Each structure retrieves one Document object at a time from the Documents collection and works with it.

Notice that the template comparison relies on the UCase function. You don't know how the user or Word will capitalize the name of the template, normal.dot, so using the UCase function is the safest way to perform the comparison. The property used, in this case, is MyDocs.AttachedTemplate, which is the individual template used for each document. Word always uses the entry found in the Document Template field on the Templates tab of the Templates and Add-ins dialog box for this property even when a document has more than one template attached to it.

Unlike in previous versions of Windows, where you could count on finding the Normal.dot template, you can actually find one of three templates when working with Word 2007. The Normal.dot template is for compatibility purposes and is purposely used in this example to show that your old macros really will work. The Normal.dotx template provides general support without macros, and the Normal.dotm template provides general support with macros. Consequently, you might actually have to search for three different Normal templates, depending on your application needs. In addition, the Normal.dot template doesn't show up unless you reattach it using the Templates and Add-ins dialog box. Microsoft has hidden this dialog box in Word 2007, but here are the steps to access it:

1. **Click the Office button and click Word Options.**

   You see the Word Options dialog box.

2. **Select the Add-Ins folder.**

3. **Choose Templates in the Manage field and click Go.**

   You see the Templates and Add-ins dialog box.

The code gathers various kinds of input from the document. Some information, such as .ActiveWindow.Caption, is already in text format, so the code doesn't do much more than record the value in Output. Notice the use of the IIf function to perform the .ActiveWindow.Creator = wdCreatorCode inline comparison. Excel uses a similar constant for its documents, xlCreatorCode. The creator code can tell you what kind of document you're working with.

A few of the properties require special handling. For example, because Word is internationalized, you must provide a constant for some properties to ensure that you see the correct value. The .ActiveWritingStyle property value varies by language, so you have to tell VBA which language value to retrieve by using the constant for your country. Because I live in the United States, I used the wdEnglishUS constant.

Many applications maintain statistics for the documents that they maintain, and Word is no exception. The Document object contains a number of statistics that it maintains over the life of the object. The example shows the .Characters.Count and .Words.Count statistics. Figure 13-1 shows the output from this program.

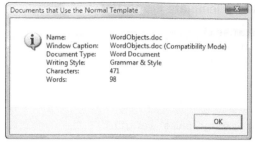

Figure 13-1:
Uncover the mysteries of your data by using the `Document` object.

```
Documents that Use the Normal Template                    X

 (i)    Name:               WordObjects.doc
        Window Caption:     WordObjects.doc (Compatibility Mode)
        Document Type:      Word Document
        Writing Style:      Grammar & Style
        Characters:         471
        Words:              98


                                              OK
```

Using the Templates collection

Word users know that templates provide the information required to give a set of documents the same look and feel. For example, a letter template could include special formatting for the heading and body text. It might include all the text that is the same for each letter, such as your name and address. Specialized templates often include automatic setups so that the initial document is as close as possible to the final product. Templates can use the DOT, DOTX, or DOTM file extensions. Only the DOT and DOTM templates have macros in them. You can still interact with a DOTX template, but you can't store macros in it.

The `Templates` collection contains a list of all the templates in use by your document. Each `Template` object corresponds to a single template file. If you open several documents that rely on the same template, Word creates only one `Template` object. No matter which document you open, Word opens a copy of the Normal template in addition to any special template that the document uses. Word 2007 uses the `Normal.dotx` or `Normal.dotm` template by default. The template that Word 2007 chooses depends on whether you enable macros for the current document. You can also add the `Normal.dot` template for compatibility documents. The special template is still the main template that Word uses, but Word always adds the features found in `Normal.dotm`. Consequently, you should only make changes to `Normal.dotm` that you want to see in every file that you create when using Word.

After you understand how the templates interact with your document, you can change template functionality in a way that makes creating the document easier. In general, you use template programs to make changes to the document as a whole and to all documents affected by that template. Listing 13-2 shows an example of the `Templates` collection in use. (You can find the source code for this example on the Dummies.com site at `http://www.dummies.com/go/vbafd5e`.)

Listing 13-2   Listing Word Template Properties

```
Public Sub MyTemplates()
    ' Holds the current template.
    Dim CurrTemp As Template

    ' Holds the built-in properties.
    Dim CurrProp As DocumentProperty

    ' Holds the property name length.
    Dim PropLen As Integer

    ' Holds the output.
    Dim Output As String

    ' Look at each template in the Templates collection.
    For Each CurrTemp In Application.Templates

        ' Get information about the current template.
        With CurrTemp
            Output = Output + _
                "Name: " + .Name + vbCrLf + _
                "Full Name: " + .FullName + vbCrLf

                ' Check property values for the template.
                For Each CurrProp In _
                    .BuiltInDocumentProperties

                    ' Some entries will fail.
                    On Error Resume Next

                    ' Determine the property name length.
                    PropLen = Len(CurrProp.Name)

                    ' Get the information.
                    Output = Output + _
                        CurrProp.Name + " (" + _
                        CStr(CurrProp.Type) + "): " + _
                        CStr(CurrProp.Value) + vbCrLf
                Next

                ' Add space at the end of the entry.
                Output = Output + vbCrLf + vbCrLf
        End With
    Next

    ' Output the result.
    MsgBox Output, _
        vbInformation Or vbOKOnly, _
        "Templates Currently in Use"
End Sub
```

The code begins by creating `Template` and `DocumentProperty` objects. These two objects hold the information that the program examines during execution. The `PropLen` variable contains the length of the current property name. The `Output` variable contains the output string for this example.

This example uses a double `For Each...Next` statement. The first `For Each...Next` statement controls the selection of a template from the list in the `Application.Templates` collection. The second `For Each...Next` statement controls the selection of properties within the template by using the `.BuiltInDocumentProperties` collection.

Don't assume that Word templates contain only one set of properties. If you want to get a complete list of document properties, you also need to look at the `CustomDocumentProperties` collection. Theoretically, a template could contain custom property collections as well, so you need to check for other additions.

Notice that the code includes both the `.Name` and `.FullName` property values in `Output`. The `.Name` property value includes only the document template name, but the `.FullName` property includes the path information as well. If you want just the path information, use the `Path` property. The seeming replication of information in some Word classes helps you create programs with less work. In this case, you need to know only which property to use instead of having to parse the information from a complex property.

The second loop begins with an `On Error Resume Next` statement. Always include this statement whenever you work with properties. The code calculates the length of the `CurrProp.Name` property next. You could include this calculation in every place that it's needed in the code, but using this technique is more efficient and saves time writing code.

The `Output` variable next receives the name of the property, the property type, and the property value. In previous versions of Word, you could create nicely formatted output by relying on tabs to space the information. The combination of Word 2007 and Vista makes this kind of formatting very difficult. Consequently, rather than use tabs, you need to rely on other forms of formatting for standard message boxes, as shown in the code. Notice that the property type appears in parentheses after the name. If you really do need to create a custom display with columnar formatting, you need to use a custom form with Word 2007. Figure 13-2 shows the output of this program.

Using the Windows collection

The `Windows` collection contains one `Window` object entry for each window that you have open. You use the `Window` object to manage the overall view of a document. For example, you use this object to add or remove scroll bars or the ruler.

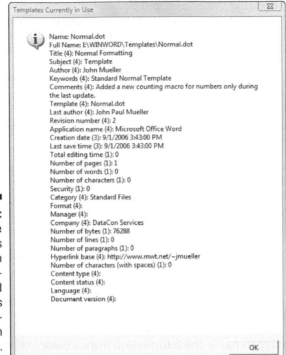

Templates Currently in Use

Name: Normal.dot
Full Name: I:\WINWORD\Templates\Normal.dot
Title (4): Normal Formatting
Subject (4): Template
Author (4): John Mueller
Keywords (4): Standard Normal Template
Comments (4): Added a new counting macro for numbers only during
the last update.
Template (4): Normal.dot
Last author (4): John Paul Mueller
Revision number (4): 2
Application name (4): Microsoft Office Word
Creation date (3): 9/1/2006 3:43:00 PM
Last save time (3): 9/1/2006 3:43:00 PM
Total editing time (1): 0
Number of pages (1): 1
Number of words (1): 0
Number of characters (1): 0
Security (1): 0
Category (4): Standard Files
Format (4):
Manager (4):
Company (4): DataCon Services
Number of bytes (1): 76288
Number of lines (1): 0
Number of paragraphs (1): 0
Hyperlink base (4): http://www.mwt.net/~jmueller
Number of characters (with spaces) (1): 0
Content type (4):
Content status (4):
Language (4):
Document version (4):

OK

Figure 13-2:
Rely on the properties found in both docu- ments and templates for identi- fication information.

Don't confuse a `Window` object with a `Pane` object. A `Window` object can con- tain up to two panes. (Older versions of Word let you create multiple panes; newer versions limit you to two.) The `Window` object is a container for the `Pane` object. You use the `Pane` object to view, add, delete, and otherwise manipulate the current content of a document. A disk file contains the data as of the last save — this object contains the data as it appears in memory.

The panes operate independently of each other. You can select an area of text in one pane and not have it affect the selection in the other pane. However, data changes made in one pane do appear in the other pane. Listing 13-3 shows an example of the `Windows` collection. (You can find the source code for this example on the Dummies.com site at `http://www.dummies.com/go/vbafd5e`.)

Listing 13-3   Determining Window Properties

```
Public Sub MyWindows()
    ' Holds a Window object.
    Dim MyWin As Window

    ' Holds the output.
```

```
    Dim Output As String

    ' Used for loop counting.
    Dim Counter As Integer

    ' Look at each Window in the Windows collection.
    For Each MyWin In Application.Windows

        ' Get the current window information.
        With MyWin
        Output = Output + "Caption: " + .Caption + _
            vbCrLf + "Panes: " + _
            CStr(.Panes.Count) + vbCrLf

        ' Check each of the panes for selected data.
        For Counter = 1 To .Panes.Count
            Output = Output + "Pane " + CStr(Counter) + _
                " Selection: " + _
                CStr(.Panes(Counter).Selection) + _
                vbCrLf
        Next

        ' Add a new pane if possible.
        If .Panes.Count = 1 Then
            .Panes.Add
        End If

        ' Add space to the output.
        Output = Output + vbCrLf

        End With
    Next

    ' Output the result.
    MsgBox Output, _
            vbInformation Or vbOKOnly, _
            "Windows Currently in Use"
End Sub
```

The example shown in Listing 13-3 begins like the other collection examples in this section (see Listings 13-1 and 13-2) by creating an individual object and some associated variables. The Application.Windows contains all the existing windows that are processed one at a time in the code.

Every Window object has a Caption property. This Caption appears as part of the Word title bar text. A Window doesn't have a Name property, like many other objects ,because you never manipulate it by name.

After the code determines the Window caption, it looks at the number of panes associated with that window. In Office 2007, Office 2003, Office XP, and Office 2000, the value is always 1 or 2. The code processes each window in turn. In this case, it retrieves the selected text.

The code shows how you can add another pane to the code. If the user isn't using both panes, you can open a second pane, perform any work that you need to do to the data in that pane, and then close the pane when you finish. This technique lets you work on the data quickly yet return the view to the user's original view. Figure 13-3 shows typical output for this example.

Figure 13-3:
Windows
and panes
work
together to
provide
access to
your data.

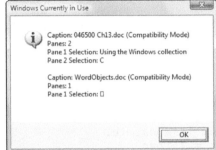

When you run this program a second time, each of the open windows has two panes open even if it had only one pane open to begin with. None of the windows will ever have more than two panes open. If you try to open more than two, VBA generates an error. (The precise error message can vary — sometimes the VBA error messages aren't clear, and you need to look carefully for the cause.)

Accessing the Word Document

Accessing the Word document means accessing specific text elements so that you know what they contain. For example, you might want to process the text one paragraph or one sentence at a time. It's possible to select individual letters in Word along with individual objects, such as pictures. However, sentences are a good place to start because working with sentences exercises many of the calls that you need for other forms of access. Listing 13-4 shows an example that accesses sentences one at a time in the test document. (You can find the source code for this example on the Dummies.com site at http://www.dummies.com/go/vbafd5e.)

Listing 13-4   Retrieving a Specific Sentence from a Document

```
Public Sub AccessTheText()
    ' Holds the current pane.
    Dim CurrPane As Pane

    ' Holds a specific paragraph on the page.
    Dim CurrPara As Paragraph

    ' Holds a single sentence.
    Dim CurrSent As String

    ' Holds the output.
    Dim Output As String

    ' Acts as a loop counter.
    Dim Counter As Integer

    ' Locate the window based on the expected name.
    Dim LocateWindow As Window   ' The current window.
    Dim WinString As String      ' The window caption.
    For Each LocateWindow In Application.Windows
        If Left(LocateWindow.Caption, 15) = _
            "WordObjects.doc" Then

            WinString = LocateWindow.Caption
        End If
    Next

    ' Make sure you can access the pane properly.
    Application.Windows(WinString).View _
        = wdNormalView

    ' Access the test document pane.
    Set CurrPane = _
        Application.Windows(WinString).ActivePane

    ' Access the second paragraph in that pane.
    Set CurrPara = CurrPane.Document.Paragraphs(2)

    ' Access the second sentence in that paragraph.
    For Counter = 1 To CurrPara.Range.Sentences.Count

        ' Get the current sentence content.
        CurrSent = CurrPara.Range.Sentences(Counter)

        ' Add the content to the Output string.
        Output = Output + "Sentence " + CStr(Counter) + _
            ": " + CurrSent + vbCrLf
    Next

    ' Display the sentence.
    MsgBox Output
End Sub
```

The code begins by creating the individual objects needed to hold various document elements. The kind of objects that you create depends on the tasks that you need to perform and on the view option in some cases. For example, if you want to work with the `Pages` collection, the document must appear in Print Layout view.

Because Word 2007 adds the words *Compatibility Mode* to every one of your older documents, macros that relied on a specific document name, such as `WordObjects.doc` in this example, will fail. What you need to do instead is search for the document you want by using a `For Each` loop as shown. After you find the document you want based on a substring, using the `Left()` function in this case, you can store the actual caption in a variable and use the variable in place of the document name you anticipated. This change in coding technique lets the example work without problem with Word 2007 as well as with earlier versions of Word.

To ensure that you can access the document by using the method that you need, you must set the pane or the window to a specific view. The code sets the window to Normal view by setting the `View` property to `wdNormalView`. Also notice that you must use the name and extension of a document to select its window — using just the name isn't enough because you could load multiple documents with the same name and different extensions. Make sure that you add a window number when necessary.

You must use the `Pane` object to access data within the document. It's usually a good idea to create an actual `Pane` object rather than go through the long object hierarchy to access it each time. This program actually takes a microscopic performance hit when using this technique, but the time that you save by not typing is well worth it. Notice that the code uses the `ActivePane` property in this case. You can also use the `Panes` collection.

One of the tricky parts about working in Normal view is that you need to access the document by using paragraphs. If the document has just a few paragraphs, debugging the code isn't difficult. However, life can become interesting for long documents because finding a particular paragraph can become difficult. You can use search techniques to make finding a paragraph easier in many cases.

Collections include a `Count` property that you can use to access individual members by using a `For...Next` loop rather than a `For Each...Next` loop. This example makes use of that feature to create a counter setup that displays the sentence number and the content of that sentence. When you run this program, VBA displays each sentence in the second paragraph of the document in turn. It doesn't display any other sentences.

The document hierarchy continues to words and individual characters. By using Listing 13-4, when you want to select individual words, select the `CurrPara.Range.Sentences(Counter).Words` collection. Use the `CurrPara.Range.Sentences(Counter).Characters` collection to select individual characters in the sentence.

Using the Registry with VBA

Microsoft assumes that you always want to access the Registry to store settings for your program, so it created special functions that let you store settings under one specific key, `\HKEY_CURRENT_USER\Software\VBA`. If you want to store program settings, simply use the `SaveSetting` function. Likewise, the `GetSetting` and `GetAllSettings` functions retrieve information from the Registry. These functions are always safe to use, even when you have User Account Control (UAC) enabled under Vista.

Overcoming UAC problems in Vista

Many Word 2007 applications rely on Registry access, as this one does. Unfortunately, the UAC feature of Vista restricts Registry access. You may find that some of your code doesn't run unless you disable the requisite UAC policy. Rather than disable UAC completely, you can overcome this problem by using the following procedure:

1. **Open the Local Security Policy console, located in the `Administrative Tools` folder of the Control Panel. If necessary, give permission to Vista when asked to open the console (you'll see a dialog box when you have some UAC features enabled).**

2. **Select the `Local Policies\Security Options` folder.**

   You see a list of local policies for the machine.

3. **Locate the policy named User Account Control: Virtualize File and Registry Write Failures to Per-User Locations.**

4. **Right-click the policy and choose Properties.**

   You see the User Account Control: Virtualize File and Registry Write Failures to Per-User Locations Properties dialog box.

5. **Select the Disabled option and click OK.**

6. **Close the Local Security Policy console.**

Accessing any Registry locations in Office

Unfortunately, SaveSetting and GetSetting functions don't provide access to the rest of the Registry. In addition, these functions affect only the current user. The example in the upcoming section "Selecting Objects in a Word Document" shows why this is a problem. You need access to the entire Registry to write functional programs. Consequently, you have to augment the functionality that VBA provides by accessing the Windows 32-bit Application Programming Interface (Win32 API) directly. The *Win32 API* is the entire set of functions that Windows supports. Listing 13-5 shows the code that's required in order to perform the task of reading other parts of the Registry. (You can find the source code for this example on the Dummies.com site at http://www.dummies.com/go/vbafd5e.)

Listing 13-5   Accessing the Registry with VBA

```
' This Windows API function opens a Registry key.
Public Declare Function RegOpenKey _
    Lib "advapi32.dll" _
    Alias "RegOpenKeyA" (ByVal HKey As Long, _
                         ByVal lpSubKey As String, _
                         phkResult As Long) As Boolean

' Use this enumeration for the top-level keys.
Public Enum ROOT_KEYS
    HKEY_CLASSES_ROOT = &H80000000
    HKEY_CURRENT_USER = &H80000001
    HKEY_LOCAL_MACHINE = &H80000002
    HKEY_USERS = &H80000003
    HKEY_PERFORMANCE_DATA = &H80000004
    HKEY_CURRENT_CONFIG = &H80000005
    HKEY_DYN_DATA = &H80000006
End Enum

' This Windows API function reads a value from a key.
Declare Function RegQueryValue _
    Lib "advapi32.dll" _
    Alias "RegQueryValueA" (ByVal HKey As Long, _
                            ByVal lpSubKey As String, _
                            ByVal lpValue As String, _
                            lpcbValue As Long) As Boolean

' This Windows API function closes a Registry key.
Public Declare Function RegCloseKey _
    Lib "advapi32.dll" (ByVal HKey As Long) As Boolean
```

VBA lets you access specific Win32 API functions by using the `Declare` keyword, shown in these three examples. You must give your function a name, as usual. Use the same name as the Win32 API function whenever possible so that you remember the purpose of this function. VBA also requires that you provide the name of the Dynamic Link Library (DLL) file that contains the function by adding the `Lib` keyword. All Registry functions appear in `advapi32.dll`, located in the `\Windows\System32` folder.

Two of these functions use the `Alias` keyword. A Win32 API function might have a common name, such as `RegOpenKey`. However, the DLL might actually hold two or more versions of the function. The `RegOpenKeyA` alias tells VBA to use the ASCII version of the function. You could also use the Unicode (or W) version of the function.

After you provide all the information required to locate the function, you supply a list of arguments. Again, it's a good idea to use the same names that the Microsoft documentation uses so that you remember the purpose of each argument.

Selecting Objects in a Word Document

Complex Word documents often contain objects. An *object* can be any kind of external application data that you wish to associate with the Word document. A report might require that you include information from Excel. You might place Visio drawings in your Word document or use Access when creating a letter. Objects help you create complex documents, which in turn help you better define your data.

Understanding object connectivity

You can link or embed objects into your Word document. Object Linking and Embedding (OLE) is a feature found in most high-end applications. Linking places a pointer to the information within the Word document. Every time Word wants to display that object, it invokes the required OLE server (the application that usually manages the data) and tells it where to find the file on disk. The advantage to this method is that the OLE server updates the data every time that you view the object. Linking also keeps the Word document small because the pointer consumes very little space.

Embedding actually places the data from the file into the Word document. Every time that you view the object, Word passes the data to the OLE server for display and manipulation. The advantage of this method is that the data remains with the document, so you have to send only one file to someone if you want to share the information. Although the individual Word file is larger and doesn't receive updated information, an information package is usually smaller, especially if you compress it using something like WinZip.

Working with embedded objects by using the InlineShape collection

No matter which form of object connectivity you use, Word considers it an InlineShape. The InlineShape collection contains all the objects linked or embedded in the Word document. Because you can use OLE with so many applications, Microsoft had to devise an object-handling strategy that will work with all Word-compatible objects. The example document supplied with the source code, WordObjects, has two embedded objects in it. The first is a picture, and the second is a sound. Listing 13-6 contains some code that demonstrates techniques for working with those two objects. (You can find the source code for this example on the Dummies.com site at http://www.dummies.com/go/vbafd5e.)

Listing 13-6   Using the Registry to Work with Objects

```
Public Sub AccessAnObject()
    ' Holds an indeterminate object.
    Dim AObj As InlineShape

    ' Holds the BMP file class.
    Dim BMPClass As String

    ' Holds picture statistical data.
    Dim Output As String

    ' Holds the Registry key reference.
    Dim RegKeyRef As Long

    ' Holds the length of the Registry data.
    Dim RegLength As Long

    ' Get the BMP file class.
    ' Open the Registry key.
    RegOpenKey ROOT_KEYS.HKEY_CLASSES_ROOT, _
            ".bmp", RegKeyRef

    ' Determine whether the key exists.
    If RegKeyRef = 0 Then

        ' Display an error.
        MsgBox "Couldn't open BMP file Registry setting.", _
```

```
                vbOKOnly Or vbExclamation, _
                "Registry Error"

     ' Exit the sub.
     Exit Sub
  End If

  ' Determine whether the required information exists. If
  ' so, get the data length.
  RegQueryValue RegKeyRef, "", BMPClass, RegLength

  ' Fill the string with the required spaces.
  BMPClass = VBA.String(RegLength, " ")

  ' Retrieve the value.
  RegQueryValue RegKeyRef, "", BMPClass, RegLength
  BMPClass = Left(BMPClass, Len(BMPClass) - 1)

  ' Close the Registry.
  RegCloseKey (RegKeyRef)

  ' Check each inline shape.
  For Each AObj In ThisDocument.InlineShapes

     ' Select the object and show that it is selected.
     AObj.Select
     MsgBox "Object Number " + _
        CStr(AObj.Field.Index) + " is Selected", _
        vbInformation Or vbOKOnly, "Object Select"

     ' If this is a sound object, play it.
     If AObj.OLEFormat.ClassType = "SoundRec" Then
        AObj.OLEFormat.DoVerb wdOLEVerbPrimary
     End If

     ' If this is a picture object, display some
     ' statistics.
     If AObj.OLEFormat.ClassType = BMPClass Then

        ' Get the height and width and then display it.
        Output = "Height: " + CStr(AObj.Height) + _
           vbCrLf + _
           CStr(Application.PointsToInches(AObj.Height))
        _
           + " Inches" + vbCrLf + _
           "Width: " + CStr(AObj.Width) + vbCrLf + _
           CStr(Application.PointsToInches(AObj.Width)) _
           + " Inches"
        MsgBox Output, vbInformation Or vbOKOnly, _
           "Picture Statistics"
     End If
  Next
End Sub
```

The code begins by creating variables to hold the information used in the example. Note the inclusion of an `InlineShape` object to hold each of the objects in the document.

The next section uses the special Registry functions described in the "Using the Registry with VBA" section, earlier in this chapter. This section requires a little more explanation than simply saying what the code does.

Whenever you double-click an icon in Windows Explorer, Windows goes to the Registry and asks what application to use to open that file. Windows stores this information by file extension in the HKEY_CLASSES_ROOT hive of the Registry. (The term *HKEY* stands for *hive key*.) Figure 13-4 shows the entry for the .bmp file extension.

Figure 13-4:
Use the
Registry
Editor to
discover
more about
how OLE
works.

The (Default) value tells Windows which application type to use to open the file. (Other Registry entries contain precise instructions for using this program.) Any file with a .bmp extension on my machine uses Paint Shop Pro as a default, but your machine setup might be different from mine. Because another application creates the objects linked or embedded in a document, Word needs the same kind of information as Windows does to open the OLE server. This information appears in the ClassType property of the InlineShape.OLEFormat object.

When you want to work with an object created by another application in Word, you can't necessarily assume that the program you use to work with that file is the same program used on the machine executing the program. This is the purpose for the Registry code in this example. It shows how you can retrieve the program type information for a particular file extension, such as .bmp.

The code begins by using RegOpenKey to open the Registry and get a reference (also called a *handle*) to a specific Registry key. This function requires the hive key, a *subkey* (the file extension), and a variable to hold the Registry key reference as arguments. You must include code that checks the key for a 0 return value. This value tells you that the key doesn't exist on the target machine. If the key doesn't exist, you can't open that object on that target machine because it lacks the required support.

After the code gets a Registry key reference, it uses it to ask for the program type information by using the RegQueryValue function. To request the information in the (Default) value, you send an empty string as the second argument. Otherwise, you can include a string that has a specific value name in it, such as the PerceivedType value, shown in Figure 13-4. The third argument is a string that holds the name of the program class when the function returns. The RegLength argument tells you how long the BMPClass value is.

The first call to the RegQueryValue function determines only the length of BMPClass. The code uses the VBA.String function to fill BMPClass with spaces. The Win32 API doesn't do this task for you, like the VBA functions do, so it's something that you have to do manually. A second call to the RegQueryValue function fills BMPClass with the program type name.

However, there's still a problem with this string. If you look carefully in the Debugger, you notice that BMPClass has a funny character at the end. This is the 0 termination required by languages such as C. VBA doesn't need a 0 terminator, so the code gets rid of it by using the Left function. The final Registry step is to close the Registry by using the RegCloseKey function.

The code finally begins looking at the individual objects. It begins by selecting the object onscreen and displaying a message box. This code lets you see how the Select method works. It also shows which object the code is working with now.

The example file contains two objects. The WAV file relies on the SoundRec program type, in most cases, so I simply used that value for the example. You can certainly use the Registry technique to look up the program type in your programs. If the object is a sound file, the code plays it by using the DoVerb method with the wdOLEVerbPrimary argument. OLE supports a number of other *verbs* (action words). To see which verbs work with a particular object, right-click the object and see which Object menu entries appear on the context menu. For example, you can play (wdOLEVerbPrimary), edit (wdOLEVerbShow), or open (wdOLEVerbOpen) a sound file.

Notice how the code treats the picture object. In this case, the code compares the picture object with the program type received from the Registry. If the two match, the code displays the height and width of the picture. Notice how this code uses the Application.PointsToInches function to convert to inches the point values that Word normally uses. VBA includes a number of these handy conversion functions that you can use to present data in a format that the viewer understands.

Manipulating Text

The task that you perform most often in Word is manipulating text. The section "Accessing the Word Document," earlier in this chapter, shows how to access the text in your document. You can access every text element, including individual letters, as needed. Selecting text is as easy as using the Select method. (See the section "Selecting Objects in a Word Document," also earlier in this chapter, for an example of how the Select method works.)

After you select the text, you can use simple properties to change its appearance or manipulate it in other ways. For example, you could change the text by making the selection equal to another value. The Font property contains a number of interesting features, including the ability to add special effects, such as strikethrough and underlining. You can also use the Font property to change the font face or size.

The example in Listing 13-7 shows another type of text manipulation. You might need the ability to look for a particular word in a document and just highlight it. It's not necessary to change every occurrence of the word, so a standard search-and-replace doesn't work. All you want to do is find all the occurrences of the target word without a lot of extra work. (You can find the source code for this example on the Dummies.com site at http://www.dummies.com/go/vbafd5e.)

Listing 13-7   Highlighting Text in Word

```
Public Sub HighlightText()
    ' Holds the current pane.
    Dim CurrPane As Pane

    ' Locate the window based on the expected name.
    Dim LocateWindow As Window   ' The current window.
    Dim WinString As String      ' The window caption.
    For Each LocateWindow In Application.Windows
        If Left(LocateWindow.Caption, 15) = _
            "WordObjects.doc" Then

            WinString = LocateWindow.Caption
        End If
    Next

    ' Make sure you can access the pane properly.
    Application.Windows(WinString).View _
        = wdNormalView

    ' Access the test document pane.
    Set CurrPane = _
        Application.Windows(WinString).ActivePane

    ' Get the word to highlight.
    Dim Highlight As String
    Highlight = InputBox("Highlight which word?", _
```

```
                              "Highlight Word", _
                              "document")

    ' Go to the beginning of the document.
    CurrPane.Selection.GoTo wdGoToLine, wdGoToFirst

    ' Creates a search for the word.
    Dim DoSearch As Find
    Set DoSearch = CurrPane.Selection.Find

    ' Perform the search.
    With DoSearch

        ' Clear any existing formatting information.
        .ClearFormatting
        .MatchCase = False

        ' Continue until there is nothing else to search.
        While DoSearch.Execute(FindText:=Highlight)

            ' Highlight any found text in the right color.
            With CurrPane.Selection.FormattedText
               .HighlightColorIndex = wdTurquoise
            End With
        Wend
    End With

    ' Go to the beginning of the document.
    CurrPane.Selection.GoTo wdGoToLine, wdGoToFirst
End Sub
```

The code begins by accessing the current pane. Notice that you must locate the window by using a different technique than in the past because Word 2007 displays the words *Compatibility Mode* with any older file you choose to open. This technique is the same one described earlier, for Listing 13-4. The code then uses the InputBox function to ask what word to search for in the document. Highlight contains the work on return from the call.

Before you begin a search of any kind, you should consider placing the selection point at a known location. The code does this with the .Selection. GoTo method. The arguments for this call literally tell the code to place the selection point on the first line.

Search-and-replace works with the current pane. The code uses the Find property to create DoSearch object. At this point, the code begins setting the search. You must always use the .ClearFormatting function to clear any existing formatting from the search, or else the search is likely to fail. It's also possible to define replacement parameters. The code uses the DoSearch.Execute method to perform the search.

The highlight occurs with the `CurrPane.Selection.FormattedText` object. This object determines the appearance of the text as a whole, including special features, such as highlighting. The code sets the `.HighlightColorIndex` property to `wdTurquoise`, which highlights any selected text onscreen. The text is highlighted automatically as part of the search process.

Unless you want to remove all those highlights by hand, you need a program to remove them for you. The program in Listing 13-8 removes only turquoise highlights. If you have highlights of other colors in the document, the program doesn't remove them.

Listing 13-8   Removing Specific Highlights from a Word Document

```
Public Sub RemoveHighlight()
    ' Holds the current pane.
    Dim CurrPane As Pane

    ' Locate the window based on the expected name.
    Dim LocateWindow As Window   ' The current window.
    Dim WinString As String      ' The window caption.
    For Each LocateWindow In Application.Windows
        If Left(LocateWindow.Caption, 15) = _
            "WordObjects.doc" Then

            WinString = LocateWindow.Caption
        End If
    Next

    ' Make sure you can access the pane properly.
    Application.Windows(WinString).View _
        = wdNormalView

    ' Access the test document pane.
    Set CurrPane = _
        Application.Windows(WinString).ActivePane

    ' Go to the beginning of the document.
    CurrPane.Selection.GoTo wdGoToLine, wdGoToFirst

    ' Creates a search for the word.
    Dim DoSearch As Find
    Set DoSearch = CurrPane.Selection.Find

    ' Perform the search.
    With DoSearch

        ' Clear any existing formatting information.
        .ClearFormatting
```

```
        .Highlight = True
        .MatchCase = False

        ' Continue until there is nothing else to search.
        While DoSearch.Execute()

            ' Remove the highlight as needed.
            With CurrPane.Selection.FormattedText
                If .HighlightColorIndex = wdTurquoise Then
                    .HighlightColorIndex = wdNoHighlight
                End If
            End With
        Wend
    End With

    ' Go to the beginning of the document.
    CurrPane.Selection.GoTo wdGoToLine, wdGoToFirst
End Sub
```

The code for this program works similarly to the text search. However, notice that it searches for a highlight instead, by setting the `.Highlight` to `True`. Unfortunately, `DoSearch` can't look for a specific highlight color, so the code sets up an `If...Then` statement that ensures that only turquoise highlights are removed.

One final point to consider: You can usually perform most tasks in more than one way when working with VBA. In this case, you can substitute the statement `CurrPane.Selection.HomeKey Unit:=wdStory` for `CurrPane.Selection.GoTo wdGoToLine, wdGoToFirst`, if you want, because both statements perform the same task. I used the code shown in Listing 13-8 because I think it's easier to understand. However, you get no performance or other type of advantage when using either statement — both forms of the statement are equally correct.

Working with Envelopes and Labels

One of the items that Word 2007 users commonly want to customize is the output of envelopes and labels. The perceived use for each item is the same — to create a recipient or return address for a package of some sort. Whether the package is an envelope or a box is unimportant. Fortunately, you can create custom code for both envelopes and labels by using built-in VBA features.

Designing the envelope and label form

The example in this section uses a single form for either envelopes or labels. It includes fields for name, address, city, state, and zip code. I purposely kept the form simple so that you can concentrate on technique rather than on customization. The form itself isn't all that special. It includes two command buttons — one for creating the output and another for canceling it. Each of the required fields is a text box. (You can find the source code for this example on the Dummies.com site at http://www.dummies.com/go/vbafd5e.)

After you create a form, you must add a little code to it to make it interact properly with the macro used to perform the actual work. The first addition is an enumeration that tells the caller which button the user clicked. Using an enumeration makes it far simpler to add features to the form later because you don't have to worry about working with actual values in your code — the enumeration makes it simpler to define the values correctly. Here's the enumeration used with this example (simply right-click the form and choose View Code from the context menu to add the enumeration):

```
' A list of click values.
Public Enum DialogResult
    Cancel
    Create
End Enum
```

You also need to define a public variable to hold the button press state. The example uses a value named `Result` of type `DialogResult`. Now it's time to add event handlers. The easy way to perform this task is to double-click the buttons on the front of your form. Here's all you need for the event handler code:

```
Private Sub btnCreate_Click()
    'Set the result value.
    Result = Create

    ' Hide the form.
    Me.Hide
End Sub
```

The event handler sets `Result` to the correct value (`Create` for the Create button and `Cancel` for the Cancel button). It then calls `Me.Hide` to hide the form from view.

Printing envelopes

Word associates envelopes with the document. Consequently, when you work with envelopes, you must have a document in place, it must be active, and you must use the correct document. In addition, you must provide some means for providing input text. The easiest way to do this is to ask the user to select text within the document or to enter it using a form. Because the "Manipulating Text" section, earlier in this chapter, shows how to perform text selections, this example uses the form described in the preceding section. Listing 13-9 shows the code you need in order to interact with the form and print the envelope. (You can find the source code for this example on the Dummies.com site at http://www.dummies.com/go/vbafd5e.)

Listing 13-9   Creating and Printing an Envelope

```
Public Sub CreateEnvelope()
    Dim GetData As frmAddress

    ' Get the recipient's address.
    Set GetData = New frmAddress
    GetData.Show (vbModal)

    ' Determine whether the user wants to
    ' create the envelope.
    If GetData.Result = Cancel Then

        ' Display a result message and exit.
        MsgBox "Envelope Cancelled", _
               vbOKOnly Or vbInformation, _
               "No Envelope Today"
        Exit Sub
    End If

    ' Define the Recipient
    Dim Recipient As String
    Recipient = _
        GetData.txtName + vbCrLf + _
        GetData.txtAddress + vbCrLf + _
        GetData.txtCity + ", " + _
        GetData.txtState + vbTab + _
        GetData.txtZIP

    ' Send the envelope to the printer.
    ActiveDocument.Envelope.PrintOut _
        Address:=Recipient, _
        ReturnAddress:=Application.UserAddress, _
        Size:="Size 10", _
        PrintBarCode:=True
End Sub
```

The example begins by creating the form. You don't want the code to perform any more work until the user has a chance to interact with the form, so the code uses `GetData.Show (vbModal)` to display the form. The code pauses at this point to wait for the user. After the user clicks either Create or Cancel, execution resumes.

At this point, you don't know whether the user clicked Create or Cancel because VBA doesn't provide a convenient method for obtaining this information. Only by testing the public variable `GetData.Result` can you determine the result. When the user clicks Cancel, the code informs the user of the choice and exits without doing anything else.

When the user clicks Create, the code begins by creating a string variable, `Recipient`, to hold the destination address. Notice how the code accesses each of the text boxes in the form in turn to obtain their values. The default property is the value, so you don't need to add a property here. However, you can access other properties by specifying their names.

Now that the code has the destination defined, it calls the `ActiveDocument.Envelope.PrintOut` method. This method has a wealth of input arguments, most of which don't appear in this example. Rather than go through each variable individually, the example uses the named-argument approach to providing input. This method is a handy way of working with some complex VBA methods.

The envelope must include an address and a return address, which are the first two arguments shown. Notice how the code uses the user's address, `Application.UserAddress`, as defined in Word as part of the Mailing Address field in the `Advanced` folder of the Word Options dialog box for Word 2007.

The example also shows how to use optional properties. In this case, the code specifies the envelope size (any of the default sizes that Word provides will do) and the bar code for routing the envelope more quickly. Unfortunately, Word 2007 doesn't provide the bar code feature and Microsoft isn't saying why it took it out. Consequently, even if you set this value to `True`, Word 2007 doesn't provide a bar code as output.

Printing labels

Word associates labels with the application. Consequently, you can print labels at any time, even if you don't have a document loaded. Like the envelope example, this example uses the form described in the "Designing the envelope and label form" section, earlier in this chapter. Listing 13-10 shows the code you need for this example. (You can find the source code for this example on the Dummies.com site at `http://www.dummies.com/go/vbafd5e`.)

Listing 13-10 Creating and Printing a Label

```
Public Sub CreateLabels()
    Dim GetData As frmAddress

    ' Set the form's properties for labels.
    Set GetData = New frmAddress
    GetData.Caption = "Create Labels"
    GetData.btnCreate.ControlTipText = _
        "Create the labels."
    GetData.btnCancel.ControlTipText = _
        "Don't print the labels."

    ' Get the recipient's address.
    GetData.Show (vbModal)

    ' Determine whether the user wants to
    ' create the envelope.
    If GetData.Result = Cancel Then

        ' Display a result message and exit.
        MsgBox "Label Printing Cancelled", _
            vbOKOnly Or vbInformation, _
            "No Labels Today"
        Exit Sub
    End If

    ' Send the labels to the printer.
    Application.MailingLabel.PrintOut _
        Name:="5160", _
        Address:= _
            GetData.txtName + vbCrLf + _
            GetData.txtAddress + vbCrLf + _
            GetData.txtCity + ", " + _
            GetData.txtState + vbTab + _
            GetData.txtZIP
End Sub
```

The default form setup is for envelopes. The first task that the code in this example performs is changing the form content to work with labels. You can use this technique any time you have a form that could serve multiple purposes with just a little adjustment. In this case, the code changes the form's title bar and the ToolTips provided for the two command buttons.

The method for providing user input is the same as when you're working with envelopes. The code displays the form, obtains the user input, checks `Result` to verify that the user hasn't clicked Cancel, and begins processing the label data.

A label doesn't have a return address, so all the code really needs to provide is an address. Now, an address can be anything. Nothing says that you have to print labels that have only addresses on them. However, the `Address` argument always specifies the label content — it can contain anything you choose as long as the content fits on that label.

The `Name` argument contains the label type. Normally, this value is the label number. This example uses an Avery label number, but any number that Word supports works just fine.

Chapter 14

VBA Programming in Excel

● ●

In This Chapter

▶ Working with Excel-related objects

▶ Accessing and using Excel objects

▶ Changing the contents of individual cells

▶ Creating your own functions to use in Excel

▶ Adding pizzazz to your Excel worksheet

▶ Defining your own special-purpose worksheets

● ●

Microsoft Excel provides a wealth of opportunities for custom VBA programs. You can do everything from creating special equations to designing eye-grabbing presentations. With some effort, you can create detailed graphs and charts on the fly. It's also possible to design *self-checking* worksheets, where a press of a button verifies the data you entered.

Of all the Office products, the third-party add-in product market for Excel is the largest and includes a vast array of product types, including add-ins that you can use with your VBA programs. Although you probably wouldn't want to write *War and Peace* with Excel, products are available that you can use to turn it into a simple word processor. Many products provide advanced math modeling and other calculation tasks. You'll also find an assortment of graphics products designed to make charting easier.

You should always check for an existing solution before you write a program that you have to debug and maintain. However, you still need to write programs for Excel because the potential of this program is far from exhausted. This chapter provides the tools that you need in order to write exceptional Excel programs so that you can complete your work quickly and easily. The content focuses on the worksheet instead of on charts because you'll likely spend more time in that area.

Understanding the Excel-Related Objects

Excel relies on some essential objects to provide access to the various data elements. Because of the nature of worksheets, you'll find that each of these objects can actually perform multiple duties. For example, you don't have to access a worksheet through a `Workbook` object unless you don't know the name of the worksheet. Most objects also include links to objects above and below the current position in the hierarchy so that you can use the object of convenience to access a data element.

You also have to consider the way that objects appear in the document. For example, a chart can appear as a separate item, or it can appear within a worksheet. When the chart appears as a separate item, you see it listed in Project Explorer and you can work with the object directly. Always access charts included within a worksheet by using the `Sheet` object.

This section focuses on Excel object issues. The demonstrations show how the various objects interact and what you need to consider while you design and build your Excel program. For example, you need to consider where to add charts and graphs while you build them so that they're most convenient in displaying the data.

Using the Workbooks collection

The `Workbooks` collection contains a list of all the workbooks that are open at any given time. From this list, you can select a single `Workbook` object to use in your program. The `Workbook` object contains general information about the file, such as its name and location. You can also use the `Workbook` object to access any other major object in the document, which includes all `Worksheet` objects and standalone `Chart` objects. Listing 14-1 shows an example of the `Workbooks` collection in use. (You can find the source code for this example on the Dummies.com site at `http://www.dummies.com/go/vbafd5e`.)

Listing 14-1   Using the Workbooks Collection

```
Public Sub WorkbookDemo()
    ' Holds the output data.
    Dim Output As String

    ' Get the test workbook.
    Dim CurrBook As Workbook
```

```
Set CurrBook = _
        Application.Workbooks("ExcelObjects.xls")

' Get the workbook name and location.
Output = "Name: " + CurrBook.Name + vbCrLf + _
        "Full Name: " + CurrBook.FullName + vbCrLf + _
        "Path: " + CurrBook.Path + vbCrLf + vbCrLf

' Holds the current sheet.
Dim CurrSheet As Worksheet

' Look for every sheet.
Output = "Worksheet List:" + vbCrLf
For Each CurrSheet In CurrBook.Worksheets
    Output = Output + CurrSheet.Name + vbCrLf
Next

' Holds the current chart.
Dim CurrChart As Chart

' Look for every chart.
Output = Output + vbCrLf + "Chart List:" + vbCrLf
For Each CurrChart In CurrBook.Charts
    Output = Output + CurrChart.Name + vbCrLf
Next

' Display the output.
MsgBox Output, vbInformation Or vbOKOnly, "Object List"
End Sub
```

The code begins by using the Application.Workbooks collection to
retrieve a single Workbook object. Notice that you must use the full name
of the Excel file, including the file extension, as an index into the collection.
The resulting Workbook object contains the name and path information for
the document. It also contains settings such as the summary information.
You can use this object to control windows and add new main elements,
such as a worksheet.

After the code has access to the workbook, it uses the CurrBook object to
access the list of worksheets. As usual, the code relies on a For Each...Next
statement. You can also use an index to access individual worksheets in your
code. The Worksheet, CurrSheet, contains properties and methods for
manipulating any data that the Worksheet contains, including embedded
objects, such as charts or even pictures. Every worksheet appears in the
CurrBook object list by its object name (not the friendly name that you give
it), so you can access them without using the Worksheets collection.

Unlike worksheets, only independent charts appear as part of `CurrBook`. You use the same technique to access a `Chart` object as a `Worksheet` object. The only difference is that you must use the `Charts` collection. Note that chart names appear in the list of objects presented by `CurrBook`, so you can also access the chart directly as an object without using the `Charts` collection. Figure 14-1 shows typical output from this program.

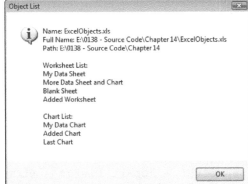

Object List

ⓘ Name: ExcelObjects.xls
Full Name: E:\0138 - Source Code\Chapter 14\ExcelObjects.xls
Path: E:\0138 - Source Code\Chapter 14

Worksheet List:
My Data Sheet
More Data Sheet and Chart
Blank Sheet
Added Worksheet

Chart List:
My Data Chart
Added Chart
Last Chart

OK

Figure 14-1: Retrieving a list of worksheets and charts.

Although you must use the object name to access a worksheet or chart directly in `CurrBook`, the name property used for a collection is actually the friendly name. It's easy to become confused. The Project Explorer window always lists both the friendly name and the object name, so always look to it for guidance when it's unclear which name you should use.

Using the Sheets collection

The `Sheets` collection is the easiest method for accessing worksheets in many situations. You don't have to drill down through the Excel object hierarchy to find the worksheet that you want. However, accessing the worksheets at the top of the hierarchy means that you don't have the objects that exist at lower levels available either, so this technique is a tradeoff.

Designing a basic example

You can use the `Sheets` collection to access all kinds of sheets, not just worksheets. Any standalone `Chart` objects also appear in this collection. Look at the example in the earlier section "Using the Workbooks collection," and you see that it treats charts and worksheets as separate objects. Listing 14-2 shows an example of the `Sheets` collection in use. (You can find the source code for this example on the Dummies.com site at `http://www.dummies.com/go/vbafd5e`.)

Listing 14-2   Using the Sheets Collection

```
Public Sub ListSheets()
    ' An individual entry.
    Dim ThisEntry As Variant

    ' Holds the output data.
    Dim Output As String

    ' Get the current number of worksheets.
    Output = "Sheet Count: " + _
        CStr(Application.Sheets.Count)

    ' List each worksheet in turn.
    For Each ThisEntry In Application.Sheets

        ' Verify there is a sheet to work with.
        If ThisEntry.Type = XlSheetType.xlWorksheet Then
            Output = Output + vbCrLf + ThisEntry.Name
        End If
    Next

    ' Display the result.
    MsgBox Output, _
            vbInformation or vbOKOnly, _
            "Worksheet List"
End Sub
```

The code for this example begins by creating a `Variant` to hold the various sheet types. If you use a `Worksheet` or a `Chart` object, the code fails because the `Sheets` enumeration can return any valid type — not just one valid type. The problem with using a `Variant` is that VBA can't provide balloon help or automatic completion. You must be sure that you type the correct method and property names without the usual help.

After the code creates the required variables, it gets the number of sheets in the workbook. This number includes all the worksheets and charts and not just the worksheets.

A `For Each...Next` loop retrieves each sheet in turn. Notice how the code uses an `If...Then` statement to compare the `Variant` type with the `XlSheetType.xlWorksheet` constant. Using this technique lets you separate the worksheets from other `Sheets` collection types as needed. Figure 14-2 shows the output from this example.

Note that the number of sheets doesn't match the number of names in the list. The `ExcelObjects.xls` example file supplied with the source code contains three worksheets and three charts. I embedded one of the charts on a worksheet, so the total number of `Sheets` collection members is seven.

Figure 14-2:
Retrieving a
list of
worksheets.

Extending test code for practical use

You might look at some of the example programs that you create to discover
something new and then wonder how you can use these examples in an application. Example code (also called *test code*) is often more practical than you
think; you simply have to look at it from another perspective. For example,
the code in the "Designing a basic example" section, earlier in this chapter,
shows how to list a particular type of member from the Sheets collection,
but it might not look that useful. Listing 14-3 contains an example of how you
can extend that example to do something more practical.

Listing 14-3   Determining the Name of the Last Sheet

```
Public Function GetLastSheet() As String
    ' An individual entry.
    Dim ThisEntry As Variant

    ' Holds the output data.
    Dim Output As String

    ' List each worksheet in turn.
    For Each ThisEntry In Application.Sheets

        ' Verify there is a sheet to work with.
        If ThisEntry.Type = XlSheetType.xlWorksheet Then
            Output = ThisEntry.Name
        End If
    Next

    ' Display the result.
    GetLastSheet = Output
End Function
```

The GetLastSheet function performs essentially the same task as the listing
example, but now it tells you the name of the last worksheet in a Sheets collection. The examples in the upcoming sections "Adding and formatting a
worksheet" and "Deleting a worksheet" rely on this function — you can't perform the task with any other technique.

Normally, when you want to add another sheet to the end of the collection, you use the `Application.Sheets.Add After:=Worksheets(Worksheets.Count)` statement. This command adds the new worksheet to the end of the collection, which might not be convenient in many cases. You might prefer to store charts at the end of the list and store worksheets at the beginning of the list.

The example code in the upcoming "Adding and formatting a worksheet" section performs the `Add` method in a special way. It places the new worksheet at the end of the worksheets and not at the end of the list of objects. This code uses the function to add a worksheet by using this statement: `Application.Sheets.Add After:=Worksheets(GetLastSheet)`, `Type:=XlSheetType.xlWorksheet`. See the next section for additional details.

Adding and formatting a worksheet

You might need to use code to add a worksheet to a workbook, for a number of reasons. For example, the information that you need might be a calculated value that Excel doesn't include, or you might need to get the information from an outside source. Listing 14-4 shows some techniques that you can use to add a worksheet to a workbook.

Listing 14-4   Adding a Worksheet to a Workbook

```
Public Sub AddSheetToEnd()
    ' Create a new sheet.
    Dim NewWorksheet As Worksheet
    Set NewWorksheet = _
        Application.Sheets.Add( _
            After:=Worksheets(GetLastSheet), _
            Type:=XlSheetType.xlWorksheet)

    ' Rename the worksheet.
    NewWorksheet.Name = "Added Worksheet"

    ' Place a title in the worksheet.
    NewWorksheet.Cells(1, 1) = "Sample Data"

    ' Add some headings.
    NewWorksheet.Cells(3, 1) = "Label"
    NewWorksheet.Cells(3, 2) = "Data"
    NewWorksheet.Cells(3, 3) = "Sum"

    ' Format the title and headings.
    With NewWorksheet.Range("A1", "B1")
        .Font.Bold = True
        .Font.Size = 12
        .Borders.LineStyle = XlLineStyle.xlContinuous
```

(continued)

Listing 14-4 *(continued)*

```
        .Borders.Weight = XlBorderWeight.xlThick
        .Interior.Pattern = XlPattern.xlPatternSolid
        .Interior.Color = RGB(255, 255, 0)
    End With
    NewWorksheet.Range("A3", "C3").Font.Bold = True

    ' Create some data entries.
    Dim Counter As Integer
    For Counter = 1 To 6

        ' Add some data labels.
        NewWorksheet.Cells(Counter + 3, 1) = _
            "Element " + CStr(Counter)

        ' Add a random integer value between 1 and 10.
        NewWorksheet.Cells(Counter + 3, 2) = _
            CInt(Rnd() * 10)

        ' Add an equation to the third column.
        If Counter = 1 Then
            NewWorksheet.Cells(Counter + 3, 3) = _
                "= B" + CStr(Counter + 3)
        Else
            NewWorksheet.Cells(Counter + 3, 3) = _
                "= C" + CStr(Counter + 2) + _
                " + B" + CStr(Counter + 3)
        End If
    Next
End Sub
```

The code begins by adding a new worksheet to the Sheets collection (and therefore the workbook) by using the Add method. Make sure that you make a variable that is equal to the output of the Add method when you want to add data or format the worksheet after creating it. Notice the Type argument for the Add method. This argument defines the kind of object to add. This feature lets you use the same call to add any legal object to the Sheets collection by changing this one argument.

After the code adds the new worksheet, it uses the NewWorksheet object to perform formatting and add data. The NewWorksheet.Name property affects the name that you see on the tab at the bottom of the page. Note that the example doesn't include code to prevent you from adding this worksheet twice. Make sure that you call the function only one time, or else it fails at the point where VBA attempts to rename the worksheet.

The code adds a title and some headings. These entries appear in the default font and style unless you change them.

You use the `Range` collection to make formatting changes. The code begins by modifying the heading area. It changes the font to bold, makes the font a different size, adds a thick line around the affected boxes, and, finally, makes the inside of the box yellow. Notice the use of various enumerations to make it easier to provide values that VBA understands. Also, notice the use of the `RGB` function to create a color value. The headings appear in bold type but are the same as the other text in all other ways.

The example code shows how to add three kinds of data to an Excel worksheet. The first entry is a simple string that labels the data values. The second entry is an integer value. Notice the use of the `Rnd` function to create a random value between `1` and `10`. The code uses the `CInt` function to convert the value from a `Single` to an `Integer`. The third entry is a *function*, which is a special kind of string that begins with an equals sign. Figure 14-3 shows the output from this program.

Figure 14-3 demonstrates that the code met all its objectives. The `Added Worksheet` appears at the end of the worksheet list but before `Last Chart`. Look at the Formula bar and notice that Excel converted the formula string into an actual formula. The text characteristics of the title and heading are all correct. (Although you can't see the title-block cell color in the book, running the example code shows that it appears in yellow.) The data elements include a label, a random number, and a sum, as expected.

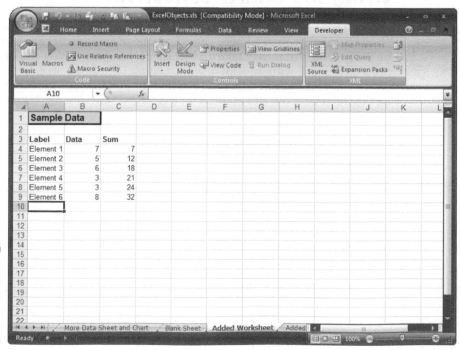

Figure 14-3:
Defining all worksheet elements by using code.

Deleting a worksheet

You don't need to use code to delete a worksheet very often. In fact, you should avoid using this technique to delete a worksheet because your code might not always detect important information that the worksheet contains. However, if you create a temporary worksheet for some quick calculations or you want to perform an automated cleanup of old data, using code can be quite helpful.

Removing a worksheet from a `Sheets` collection is relatively simple. Here's an example of how you can perform this task:

```
Public Sub RemoveLastSheet()
    ' Remove the last worksheet.
    Application.Sheets(GetLastSheet).Delete
End Sub
```

Notice that this code removes the last sheet in the example workbook. This example is generic enough that you can use it to remove the last worksheet in any workbook. However, to see how this example works, you can remove the worksheet added in the section "Adding and formatting a worksheet," earlier in this chapter.

Using the Charts collection

One of the most useful purposes of the `Charts` collection is building a custom chart whenever you need one. The advantage of creating uncommon charts by using code is that they take up less space. In addition, you can create variations on a theme without a lot of work. Listing 14-5 shows an example of the `Charts` collection in action. (You can find the source code for this example on the Dummies.com site at `http://www.dummies.com/go/vbafd5e`.)

Listing 14-5   Creating an Excel Chart

```
Public Sub BuildChart()
    ' Create a new chart.
    Dim NewChart As Chart
    Set NewChart = Charts.Add(After:=Charts(Charts.Count))

    ' Change the name.
    NewChart.Name = "Added Chart"

    ' Create a series for the chart.
    Dim TheSeries As Series
    NewChart.SeriesCollection.Add _
        Source:=Worksheets("My Data Sheet").Range("A$3:B$8")
```

```
Set TheSeries = NewChart.SeriesCollection(1)

' Change the chart type.
TheSeries.ChartType = xl3DPie

' Change the series title.
TheSeries.Name = "Data from My Data Sheet"

' Perform some data formatting.
With TheSeries
    .HasDataLabels = True
    .DataLabels.ShowValue = True
    .DataLabels.Font.Italic = True
    .DataLabels.Font.Size = 14
End With

' Modify the chart's legend.
With NewChart
    .HasLegend = True
    .Legend.Font.Size = 14
End With

' Modify the 3-D view.
With NewChart
    .Pie3DGroup.FirstSliceAngle = 90
    .Elevation = 45
End With

' Format the chart title.
NewChart.ChartTitle.Font.Bold = True
NewChart.ChartTitle.Font.Size = 18
NewChart.ChartTitle.Format.Line.DashStyle _
    = msoLineSolid
NewChart.ChartTitle.Format.Line.Style = msoLineSingle
NewChart.ChartTitle.Format.Line.Weight = 2

' Compute the optimal plot area size.
Dim Size As Integer
If NewChart.PlotArea.Height > NewChart.PlotArea.Width _
        Then
    Size = NewChart.PlotArea.Width
Else
    Size = NewChart.PlotArea.Height
End If

' Reduce the plot area by 10%.
Size = Size - (Size * 0.1)

' Format the plot area.
With NewChart.PlotArea
    .Interior.Color = RGB(255, 255, 255)
```

(continued)

Listing 14-5 *(continued)*

```
        .Border.LineStyle = XlLineStyle.xlLineStyleNone
        .Height = Size
        .Width = Size
        .Top = 75
        .Left = 100
    End With

    ' Format the labels.
    Dim ChartLabels As DataLabel
    Set ChartLabels = TheSeries.DataLabels(0)
    ChartLabels.Position = xlLabelPositionOutsideEnd
End Sub
```

The code begins by creating a new chart. This chart should appear as the last chart in the workbook but not necessarily as the last item in the workbook. Any worksheets that appear after the existing last chart also appear after the new chart. The NewChart.Name property changes the name that appears on the tab at the bottom of the chart — the property doesn't change the chart title.

The chart is blank at this point. To display any data, you must add at least one data series to the chart. A pie chart uses only one data series at a time, but other charts can support (or might even require) multiple data series. For example, a bubble chart requires multiple data series. Consequently, the next task that the code performs is creating a data series based on the My Data Sheet worksheet supplied with the example. Notice that the code can't set TheSeries equal to the output of the Add method in this case, so it uses an extra step to get the new series from the SeriesCollection collection.

Notice that the Range property contains two columns of information. When you're working with Excel 2007, the first column defines the XValues property for the chart. The XValues property determines the entries in the legend for a pie chart. On the other hand, these values appear at the bottom of the display for a bar chart. In both cases, you want to display the labels onscreen so that you can see their effect on the overall display area.

Excel 2007 introduces breaking changes into the creation of charts. Listing 14-5 shows the code you need with the new version. Excel 2003 and older versions use different code to define the XValues property, as shown here:

```
With TheSeries
    .XValues = _
        Worksheets("My Data Sheet").Range("A$3:A$8")
```

If you try to use this code in Excel 2007, you receive an error message. Excel 2007 doesn't separate the series from the XValues information. It uses the first column in the range for the XValues. You can change the column selection programmatically when needed. In addition, when defining a series in Excel 2003 and earlier, you specified only the data values, as shown here:

```
NewChart.SeriesCollection.Add _
    Source:=Worksheets("My Data Sheet").Range("B$3:B$8")
```

It's important to change the ChartType property at the outset if you want to see the correct changes while you build and debug your program. Otherwise, the chart displays the default chart type, and you might not see the changes that you expect. For example, the Legend property works differently when you use a pie chart versus a bar chart.

Notice the appearance of the HasDataLabels and the HasLegend properties in the code. If you don't include these properties, the code displays some rather odd error messages, none of which relates to the problem at hand. When you have problems resolving data-label or legend-formatting errors, always verify that you've added these two property settings to your code.

The 3D property settings appear in several places. Notice the Pie3DGroup object in the code. VBA supports other kinds of objects for other kinds of charts, so you must use the correct object for the type of chart that you want to create. Some global 3-D settings appear as part of the chart. For example, the Elevation property, which affects the angle of presentation, is part of the global settings group. Don't assume that two settings that appear on the same page of a property sheet will also appear in the same object in VBA.

Changing the ChartTitle format is almost a requirement because VBA uses the default font for every entry that the code creates. The example code shows a few of the changes that you might want to make. However, VBA provides a relatively large number of formatting features that you can choose. For example, the larger font size normally used by the ChartTitle lets you use special effects, like Shadow.

Excel 2007 formats the ChartTitle differently than older versions do. Consequently, you need different code between versions — there isn't any way to use the same code for both versions. Although you can format text as you did before, Excel 2007 complains when you attempt to access the Font property from within a With structure, as shown here:

```
With NewChart.ChartTitle
    .Font.Bold = True
    .Font.Size = 18
    .Border.LineStyle = XlLineStyle.xlContinuous
    .Border.Weight = XlBorderWeight.xlMedium
End With
```

In addition, older versions of Excel use the `Border` property. This property doesn't exist in Excel 2007 — use the `Format` property instead, as shown in Listing 14-5. The `Format` property uses different constants than before. For example, the `LineStyle` property value of `XlLineStyle.xlContinuous` is now `msoLineSolid` for the `Line.DashStyle` property.

The plot area is one of the last elements that you should work on because every other setting change that you make affects it. The example shows some of the changes that you always want to make to the plot area. The plot area background begins as gray, which actually makes some chart types difficult to read if you don't change it. It's also a good idea to get rid of the border around some charts. (You want to keep it for bar charts in many cases.) Finally, you generally want to optimize the position and size of the chart to make it as large as possible. Figure 14-4 shows the output from this example.

The Ribbon takes up considerable space. Consequently, chart code you wrote in the past may suddenly appear to stop working. In fact, what you see is the chart flashing onscreen as though a severe error has occurred in Excel. A chart that might have fit fine in a 450-x-450-pixel area in Excel 2003 might cause problems in Excel 2007. Listing 14-5 shows a technique you can use to make the chart fit no matter which version of Excel you use. The downside to this approach is that it's harder to create the custom look that hard coding afforded in previous versions of Excel.

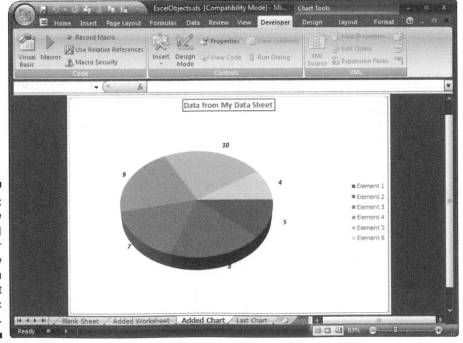

Figure 14-4:
Dynamically created charts offer flexibility that you don't get with static charts.

In addition to having problems in fitting the chart correctly, you find that Excel 2007 uses a best-fit method for placing the data labels. Consequently, a label that used to appear on the outside of the pie chart when working with Excel 2003 may very well appear inside the pie chart with Excel 2007. Because of the effect of the Ribbon, you should probably add label positioning code, as shown in Listing 14-5, to obtain accurate label placement between Excel versions.

Using the Windows collection

Excel records one `Window` object in the `Windows` collection for every file that you open. Consequently, the `Windows` collection doesn't tell you much about the data except at a very high level. For example, you could use the `Window` object to determine the names of files that you have opened. The `Window` object can also determine the active `Sheet` object (see the section "Using the Sheets collection," earlier in this chapter, for details) and tell you about general settings, such as whether Excel displays grids on the worksheets. In general, you don't use the `Windows` collection for low-level data manipulation in Excel because there are easier methods of getting access to what you need. Listing 14-6 shows an example of the `Windows` collection at work. (You can find the source code for this example on the Dummies.com site at `http://www.dummies.com/go/vbafd5e`.)

Listing 14-6   Listing Application Windows

```
Public Sub ListWindows()
    ' Holds a Window object.
    Dim MyWin As Window

    ' Holds the output.
    Dim Output As String

    ' Look at each window in the Windows collection.
    For Each MyWin In Application.Windows

        ' Get the current window information.
        With MyWin
        Output = Output + "Caption: " + .Caption + vbCrLf + _

            "Display Tabs: " + _
            IIf(MyWin.DisplayWorkbookTabs, "Yes", "No") + _
            vbCrLf + "Zoom Factor: " + CStr(MyWin.Zoom) + _
            vbCrLf + "Panes: "

        ' Determine the number of panes.
```

(continued)

Listing 14-6 *(continued)*

```
        If .ActiveSheet.Type = -4167 Then

            ' Store the number of panes.
            Output = Output + CStr(.Panes.Count) + vbCrLf

            ' Add a new pane if possible.
            If .Panes.Count = 1 Then
                .SplitHorizontal = 200
                .SplitVertical = 200

            ' Remove extra panes if possible.
            ElseIf .Panes.Count = 4 Then
                .SplitHorizontal = 0
                .SplitVertical = 0
            End If
        Else
            Output = Output + "No Panes on a Chart" + vbCrLf
        End If

        ' Add space to the output.
        Output = Output + vbCrLf

        End With
    Next

    ' Output the result.
    MsgBox Output, _
            vbInformation Or vbOKOnly, _
            "Windows Currently in Use"
End Sub
```

The code begins by creating a `Window` object from the `Application.`
`Windows` collection. It uses this object to determine some characteristics
about the window, such as

✔ The window name (not the tab name)

✔ Whether the workbook tabs are visible

✔ The current zoom factor

Excel presents a few problems when you use this approach. Notice that the
code looks for a worksheet by using the constant number `-4167`. The
number for charts is equally odd: `-4102`. These aren't the constants used for
other code in this chapter, and this issue points out one reason why you want
to avoid using the `Windows` collection when you can.

Charts don't have panes. However, you can split a worksheet both horizontally and vertically, for a total of four panes. The code shows how to perform both types of splits and also how to close them. Notice that you don't use the standard `Panes.Add` method that other applications, such as Word, use. When you want to split the view, you must tell VBA how many pixels to display on the left or top of the split. Figure 14-5 shows the output from this example.

Figure 14-5: Displaying Excel window statistics.

Selecting Objects within Excel

You can place any object that you want in an Excel worksheet, including pictures and sounds. These kinds of objects work very much the same in Excel as they do in Word. (See the "Selecting Objects in a Word Document" section of Chapter 13.) The main difference is that you use the `OLEObjects` collection of the sheet that holds the object. However, Excel can also embed `Chart` objects in a worksheet. Because this is such a special feature, I show you in this section how to work with embedded `Chart` objects.

The same data can say different things depending on how you present it. A pie chart tells the viewer about parts of a whole, and a bar chart compares individual values. The problem with charts that you create in Excel is that they're static — they continue to say the same thing unless you redesign them. Fortunately, you can control the appearance of an embedded chart just as easily as you can control a standalone chart. The code in Listing 14-7 demonstrates a rotating chart technique. (You can find the source code for this example on the Dummies.com site at `http://www.dummies.com/go/vbafd5e`.)

Listing 14-7   Designing a Rotating Chart Presentation

```
Public Sub SelectObject()
    ' Select the worksheet.
    Sheet2.Select

    ' Select the object.
    Sheet2.ChartObjects(1).Select

    ' Create a chart object.
    Dim EmbeddedChart As Chart
    Set EmbeddedChart = Sheet2.ChartObjects(1).Chart

    ' Make sure the chart has a title.
    EmbeddedChart.HasTitle = True

    ' Look for the chart object.
    With EmbeddedChart

        ' Rotate between chart types. Change the title as
        ' needed to match the chart type.
        Select Case .ChartType
            Case XlChartType.xlPie
                .ChartType = xlArea
                .ChartTitle.Caption = "More Data (Area)"
            Case XlChartType.xlArea
                .ChartType = xlLine
                .ChartTitle.Caption = "More Data (Line)"
            Case XlChartType.xlLine
                .ChartType = xlColumnClustered
                .ChartTitle.Caption = "More Data (Column)"
            Case XlChartType.xlColumnClustered
                .ChartType = xlPie
                .ChartTitle.Caption = "More Data (Pie)"
        End Select
    End With
End Sub
```

The code begins by selecting the correct worksheet and the chart embedded on that worksheet. The `ChartObjects` collection contains one entry for each embedded chart on the worksheet. The `Select` method highlights the chart of interest on the worksheet.

You should notice two significant differences between Excel 2007 and older versions of Excel. First, the Chart Tools tab appears at the top of the Ribbon. Selecting the tab shows you design tools for charts. You can choose from three subtabs, including Design, Layout, and Format. Second, the selection square is far more noticeable. Microsoft made it significantly thicker than in previous versions, so the selected object is more obvious.

Unlike many collections, the ChartObjects collection doesn't return the selected chart by default. You must specifically request the chart by using the Sheet2.ChartObjects(1).Chart property.

After the code gets hold of the chart, it checks the HasTitle property. It's possible that this property is set to False, so you must check it each time; otherwise, changing the ChartTitle object results in an error.

The Select Case statement relies on the current ChartType property value to choose the next chart. The code sets the ChartType property value to one of the standard constants and then changes the chart's caption to match the chart type. Notice that you must use the ChartTitle.Caption property to change the title. The ChartTitle object is self contained and includes a number of other formatting properties. Figure 14-6 shows typical output from this program.

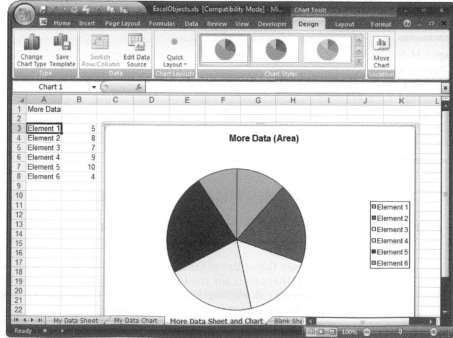

Figure 14-6: Rotating through a number of chart selections.

Developing Custom Functions in Excel

Formulas are the lifeblood of Excel. You can't find too many worksheets that are devoid of formulas because you need formulas to figure out new values based on your existing data. Microsoft includes a wealth of standard formulas in Excel. In fact, it's possible that you'll never need anything more than the Microsoft formulas. However, formulas are extremely important, so it's handy to know how to create one of your own.

All formulas in Excel rely on functions. If you want to create a special formula for your worksheet, all you need is a function to perform the task. The functions that you create appear in the User Defined category of the Insert Function dialog box, which you access by using the following procedure:

1. **Select the Formulas tab of the Ribbon.**

2. **Click Function Wizard.**

   You see the Insert Function dialog box, shown in Figure 14-7.

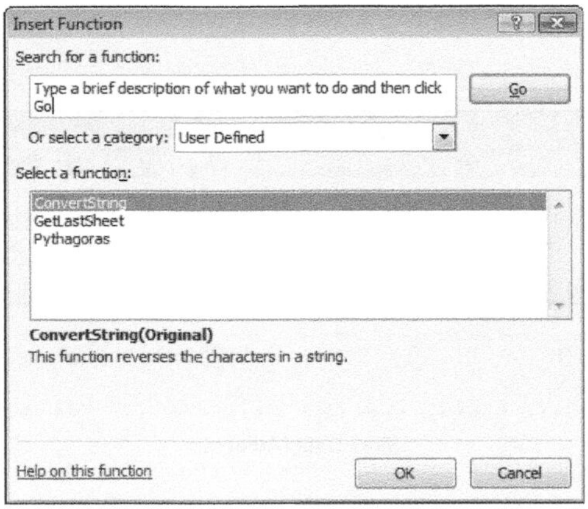

Figure 14-7:
Choosing a user-defined function to insert in a worksheet.

3. **Select User Defined in the Or Select a Category field.**

4. **Highlight the function you want to insert.**

5. **Click OK.**

   You might see the optional Function Arguments dialog box, shown in Figure 14-8 (this one is for the Pythagoras function described in the "Defining math calculations" section, later in this chapter). Notice how the dialog box shows the result of the calculation, which means that you could use this dialog box to perform a what-if analysis without ever inserting the function. Simply click Cancel when you finish working with the function.

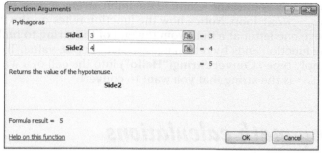

Figure 14-8:
Add any
required
arguments
for the
function you
select.

6. **Type the arguments required for the function, and then click OK.**

Excel inserts the function into the current cell.

Performing data conversion

One of the more interesting uses for specialized formulas is data conversion.
A *data conversion* can convert one type of data to another, or it can manipulate the data in some way. Listing 14-8 shows an example of a function that
reverses the order of letters in a string. (You can find the source code for
this example on the Dummies.com site at http://www.dummies.com/
go/vbafd5e.)

Listing 14-8   Performing a String Conversion

```
Public Function ConvertString(Original As String) As
           String
   ' Used for loops.
   Dim Counter As Integer

   ' Contains the string length.
   Dim StrLen As Integer
   StrLen = Len(Original)

   ' Holds the output string.
   Dim Output As String
   Output = ""

   ' Reverse the string.
   For Counter = StrLen To 1 Step -1
      Output = Output + Mid(Original, Counter, 1)
   Next

   ' Return the result.
   ConvertString = Output
End Function
```

The code begins by getting the length of the input string. It uses this value as part of a `For...Next` loop. Notice how the function relies on the `Mid` function to retrieve one letter at a time from the end of the string to build `Output`. The function ends by returning the final `Output` value. To use this function, simply type =**ConvertString("Hello")** into the cell of a worksheet, where `"Hello"` is the string that you want to convert.

Defining math calculations

Another common type of formula is the math equation. The Pythagoras function, shown in Listing 14-9, computes the length of the hypotenuse of a triangle, given the length of two sides. (You can find the source code for this example on the Dummies.com site at `http://www.dummies.com/go/vbafd5e.`)

Listing 14-9   Calculating the Hypotenuse of a Triangle

```
Public Function Pythagoras(Side1 As Double, _
    Side2 As Double) As Double

    ' Perform the calculation.
    Pythagoras = Math.Sqr((Side1 * Side1) + (Side2 *
            Side2))

End Function
```

Math calculations are usually simple in that you don't have to create any special variables to use them. However, splitting complex calculations into pieces can help you debug them. To use this function, type =**Pythagoras(3,4)**.

Adding comments to your functions

When you open the Insert Function dialog box, Excel displays a message saying that no help is available for your function. You can use one of two techniques to add comments to your functions. Use the following procedure to add the comment with the first technique:

1. **Click the Developer tab and then click Macros.**

   VBA displays the Macro dialog box.

2. **Type the name of your function in the Macro Name field.**

   Notice that VBA doesn't highlight the Create button because it knows that the function exists even though the function doesn't appear in the macro list.

3. **Click Options.**

   Excel displays the Macro Options dialog box.

4. **Type a description of the function in the Description field, but don't change anything else.**

5. **Click OK.**

   The Macro dialog box appears.

6. **Click Cancel.**

   Excel closes the Macro dialog box.

7. **Save the file and close Excel.**

When you open the file again, the functions have a description. Closing and reopening Excel is necessary to reload the file.

The advantage of the second technique, shown in Listing 14-10, is speed. You can use this technique to add descriptions to several functions quickly. Begin by exporting the file from the VBA Integrated Development Environment (IDE). (See the "Exporting a module from a program" section in Chapter 6.) Open the file by using a text editor, such as Notepad. Immediately after the function declaration, type a VB_Description attribute, such as this one.

Listing 14-10   Adding a Comment by Using an Attribute

```
Public Function Pythagoras(Side1 As Double, _
   Side2 As Double) As Double
Attribute Pythagoras.VB_Description = "Returns the value of the hypotenuse."

   ' Perform the calculation.
   Pythagoras = Math.Sqr((Side1 * Side1) + (Side2 * Side2))

End Function
```

Notice the way that the description appears in the file. You must type the keyword Attribute followed by the name of the function and the keyword VB_Description. Type the text that you want to appear as a description for the function in the Insert Function dialog box.

Save the file. Remove the old copy of the file from the modules list and import the new copy. (See the section "Importing a module in a program," in Chapter 6.) You see the description in the Insert Function dialog box even though you can't see it in the VBA IDE.

Chapter 15

VBA Programming in Access

*M*icrosoft Access is a database management system (DBMS) that provides a number of opportunities for developing programs with VBA. In fact, it's safe to say that some people make a good living performing this very task. The kinds of tasks that you can perform by using a database are also varied — everything from writing reports to creating new and better methods for data entry. You can also use Access as a data storage method for everything from scientific needs to your CD collection.

This chapter introduces you to database programming in Access. I'm assuming that you know how to use Access and that you have already used it to create elements such as tables, which are composed of *records* (individual entries in the table) and *fields* (the individual entries in the record). Consider this chapter your doorway to a much larger world. I could easily write an entire book on the topic of database management and still not exhaust the topic. In fact, database management books consume a large part of my personal library. Consequently, this chapter discusses just the VBA portion of Microsoft Access. By using VBA, you can

✔ Make the task of managing your Access data easier by reducing data entry requirements or ensuring that the data the user enters meets certain requirements

✔ Perform data manipulation, such as extracting just the records that you need

✔ Provide customized data output, such as reports

Of course, you might want to know more about database programming in Access than this single chapter can provide. As I've said, I have a bookshelf full of database books, and sometimes find that even all these resources aren't sufficient to meet every need because you can perform so many tasks with databases. With this in mind, you might want to look at *Access 2007 For Dummies* (by John Kaufeld, Laurie Ulrich Fuller, and Ken Cook) for some additional basics. This book is the one to get if you have no idea of how Access works and you really want to know more. If you're ready to have a more significant look at Access development, consider getting *Access 2007 All-in-One Desk Reference For Dummies,* by Alan Simpson, Margaret Levine Young, and Alison Barrows. The *All-in-One* contains about twice as much material as *Access 2007 For Dummies.* To give you some idea of how closely some books examine Access, you should check out *Access 2007 Forms & Reports For Dummies,* by Brian Underdahl. Imagine having an entire book talk solely about the topic of creating great forms and reports. (All three books are published by Wiley.)

Because *database management* (the organized storage of data in one or more tables) is such a large topic, you need to consider just how you'll use database management to answer an immediate need. Small, easy projects are the best way to start with Microsoft Access. However, you should also choose a database project that makes a difference. My first project was a contact management database that I've improved over the years and still use today. This contact management system is a good way to use Access, and it's something I care about, so I understand Access better today — because *I* wrote the contact management system — than if I had chosen an inconsequential project.

This chapter also focuses on some key areas that you can use immediately to increase your personal productivity and to help others in a small group (office) setting. For example, I increased my personal productivity by using an Access database to maintain lists of interesting words that I learn. I also have one that maintains the inventory for my office. Folks can use either of these databases to discover new VBA programming techniques, improve their personal productivity, and help other people in a small office setting.

Microsoft Access is actually a very good database to use for a number of office tasks. It's small, you don't need a server to use it, and it doesn't require complex knowledge that only a computer expert could love. Although Access includes all the support required to work on a server, you can also create databases for personal use. You could create something as simple as a to-do list that will make you more productive, even though you wouldn't necessarily want to share it with anyone else.

Access 2007 supports three file formats: Access 2000, Access 2002–2003, and Access 2007. The Access 2002–2003 format runs with the fewest compatibility problems in the widest range of Access versions currently available. The VBA macros you write don't require conversion even when used in Access 2007. You don't apparently gain any VBA functionality by choosing the Access 2007

format, either, so the choice is relatively easy to make from a purely VBA perspective. Consequently, this book uses the Access 2002–2003 format. You
can't open the files used for the examples in this chapter by using Access
2000 or earlier versions, but you can use the BAS files found with the example
files to create your own Access files, if you want to do so.

Understanding the Access-Related Objects

Microsoft Access provides more objects than just about any other Office
application that you'll use. You can create a database, populate it with information, and print it out without ever using the user interface. In addition,
these objects are interesting because they perform so many tasks well.
Access even has a special object (see the upcoming "Accessing special commands with the DoCmd object" section) that performs little utility tasks.
You need to know about a variety of collections and objects in order to
perform many tasks programmatically. (See the object hierarchy chart
at `http://msdn.microsoft.com/library/en-us/vbaac10/html/
acsumAccessObjHierarchy.asp` for a complete list of Access objects.)

Don't assume that you need to perform every task by using code. In fact, it's
to your advantage to play around with the user interface for some time
before you even consider using VBA with Access. The user interface includes
a wealth of features for creating objects that you need by using the Access
Designer rather than imagining them by using code.

The macro system provided with Access is also superior to (and different
from) other Office applications. Access macros reside separately from VBA,
and you can use them to perform a number of tasks. In fact, you'll find that
macros are a required addition to VBA to create some types of programs.
Access presents some unique problems and opportunities for the VBA user.

Understanding Access and sub-procedure use

When you create a program for Word or Excel, you normally create it by adding
sub-procedures (the `Sub` statement). However, when you work with Access,
you normally use a `Function` statement instead. If you want to execute the
function independently, you need to create a macro with the `RunCode` action.
The Function Name field contains the name of the function and any arguments
that it requires. Figure 15-1 shows an example of such a macro.

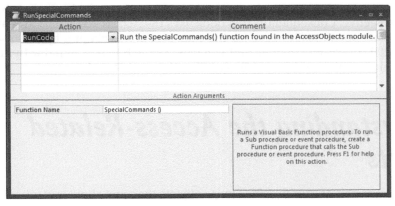

Figure 15-1:
Create
functions in
Access and
run them by
using
macros.

When you do decide to create sub-procedures, you must call the sub-procedure by using a function. Although a sub-procedure executes within the VBA Integrated Development Environment (IDE), it doesn't do you much good outside that environment.

Unlike other Office Applications, Access 2007 provides access to the Visual Basic Editor on the Database Tools tab (rather than on the Developer tab) of the Ribbon. Simply click Visual Basic on the Database Tools tab to display the editor. You'll also find several other interesting buttons on this tab. Click Run Macro to display a list of macros that you can run. Instead of a big green arrow, the icon is smaller and appears near the Visual Basic button. Rather than have to jump through major hoops to add macros to the Ribbon, highlight the macro you want to use and click Create Shortcut Menu from Macro. Finally, you can convert macros to Visual Basic by highlighting the macro and clicking Convert Macros to Visual Basic on the Database Tools tab.

Using the Application object effectively

Access has a number of interesting and useful features in the `Application` object. When you're using other Office applications, the `Application` object tends to provide a means for access collections, such as the `Sheets` collection in Excel. In Access, you can use the `Application` object to perform other tasks. Listing 15-1 shows an example of a few of the features that you should try. (You can find the source code for this example on the Dummies.com site at `http://www.dummies.com/go/vbafd5e`.)

Listing 15-1   Using a Progress Meter in Access

```
Public Function UseApplication()
    ' Create an output string.
    Dim Output As String

    ' Fill it with text version of a numeric error.
    Output = Application.AccessError(14)

    ' Display the result.
    MsgBox "Error number 14 is " + Chr(&H22) + Output + _
        Chr(&H22), vbInformation, "Error Number Text"

    ' Add this database to the favorites list.
    Application.AddToFavorites

    ' Perform some system commands.
    ' Create a progress meter.
    Application.SysCmd acSysCmdInitMeter, "Progress Meter", _
        5
    Dim Counter As Integer

    ' Update the meter until finished.
    For Counter = 1 To 5
        Application.SysCmd acSysCmdUpdateMeter, Counter
        MsgBox "Click to proceed", vbInformation, "Progress"
    Next

    ' Remove the meter.
    Application.SysCmd acSysCmdRemoveMeter

    ' Say you're done by changing the status bar text.
    Application.SysCmd acSysCmdSetStatus, _
                    "Progress meter is done."
End Function
```

The example performs three unique tasks, but you can use many others. The first task is to determine what an error code means. You often receive error numbers from VBA that you then have to look up somewhere (such as online or in a help file or by asking someone online) in hopes of finding a meaning. The `Application.AccessError` method takes the guesswork out of finding a human-readable explanation for a numeric error.

You might want to include the next method in an installation program or as part of the automatic execution sequence. The `Application.AddToFavorites` method places a pointer to the database in your Favorites folder. You can access the database by using the Start➪Favorites menu or from within Internet Explorer.

When you write a program that performs a number of tasks, it could require some time to complete. In fact, you might even begin thinking that the task is taking so long that the computer has failed. A progress meter can help in this situation by providing visual feedback that something is indeed going on with the computer.

The `Application.SysCmd` method can display a progress meter on the status bar when you call it with the `acSysCmdInitMeter` as the first argument. The second argument contains the text that you want to display on the status bar while the progress meter is visible. The third argument tells how many segments the project meter requires. You should include one segment per each major task that the program performs. Figure 15-2 shows a typical example of the progress meter for this program.

Figure 15-2:
A progress
meter.

Notice how the example uses a `For...Next` loop to update the progress meter. You use the `Application.SysCmd acSysCmdUpdateMeter` method call to provide update information. The second argument should contain the amount of the update — a higher number increases the length of the progress meter indicator. You can use this feature to your advantage. Counting down instead of up can show negative progress, such as backing out of an unsuccessful database update.

When you finish using the progress meter, you remove it by calling the `Application.SysCmd acSysCmdRemoveMeter` method. Normally, this act displays the word `Ready` on the status bar. However, you can make the status bar say anything that you want by calling the `Application.SysCmd acSysCmdSetStatus` method. The second argument contains the text that you want to display in this case. The example uses this technique to tell you that the progress meter portion of the example is complete.

Defining your work area with the Workspaces collection

You can use the `Workspaces` collection for a number of tasks. Each `Workspace` object within the collection contains an environment in which you can perform database- or Access-related tasks. The `Workspaces` collection contains a single, default `Workspace` object when you first start Access, which is enough to perform most of the work that you need to do.

Most Access programming tasks never require that you open more than one database at a time, which is why the default `Workspace` is sufficient. You can use this default `Workspace` to perform a number of tasks, such as add a new user or perform database maintenance. Listing 15-2 shows an example of a generic function for adding a user to a database. (You can find the source code for this example on the Dummies.com site at `http://www.dummies.com/go/vbafd5e`.)

Listing 15-2   Adding a User to a Database

```
Public Function ConfigureUser()
    ' Get the default workspace.
    Dim CurWrk As Workspace
    Set CurWrk = DBEngine.Workspaces(0)

    ' Get the username and password.
    Dim Username As String
    Dim Password As String
    Username = InputBox("Type a user name.", "New User")
    Password = InputBox("Type a password.", "New User")

    ' Create a new user.
    Dim NewUser As User
    Set NewUser = CurWrk.CreateUser(Name:=Username, _
                                    Password:=Password, _
                                    PID:=Username)

    ' Add the user to the database.
    CurWrk.Users.Append NewUser

    ' Modify the user setup for a default user.
    Dim AddGroup As Group
    Set AddGroup = NewUser.CreateGroup("Users", "Users")
    NewUser.Groups.Append AddGroup
End Function
```

The code begins by accessing the default `Workspace` object in the `Workspaces` collection. Notice that the code uses the `DBEngine` object as the source of the `Workspaces` collection. Even though you shouldn't have to use this extra reference, the program fails intermittently if you don't. The default `Workspace` object doesn't actually exist until you call on the `Workspaces` collection the first time. Access creates this object automatically during the first request. You can add workspaces to the `Workspaces` collection by calling the `CreateWorkspace` method.

The next step is to get a username and password by calling the `InputBox` function. You can also use a custom form or request the information as part of the calling syntax for the function. The point is to obtain the required user information. In some cases, you might even want to include multiple options to add to the flexibility of your program.

After the code gets the username and password, it creates the `NewUser` object. The `CurWrk.CreateUser` method fills the `NewUser` object with data. You must provide a name, password, and personal identifier (PID) as arguments. This example uses the `Username` value as the PID. You can use any string containing between 4 and 20 characters. The `Username` should be unique, so using it as the `PID` value tends to ensure this fact.

However, creating the `NewUser` object doesn't add the user to the database even though you used the `CurWrk.CreateUser` method to perform the task. The code uses the `CurWrk.Users.Append` method to add the user to the list of users in the database.

At this point, you have a new user without any rights. To add rights, you must assign the user to a group. This three-step task begins by creating a group entry in the `NewUser` object. When the group has the same name as an existing group, Access adds the user to the existing group rather than create a new one. The user has the same rights as everyone else in that group. Consequently, the `NewUser.CreateGroup` method can result in a new group, or it can simply reference an existing group. The code adds the user to the existing group in the database by using the `NewUser.Groups.Append` method.

Working with the DBEngine object

The `DBEngine` object is useful for performing several tasks. You can use it to access the `Workspaces` collection, as shown in the earlier section "Defining your work area with the Workspaces collection." This section presents the most useful features of the `DBEngine` object. See the help topic at `http://msdn.microsoft.com/library/en-us/vbaac11/html/acproDBEngine_HV05187151.asp` for a complete reference.

Vista and Access security

Vista strictly controls access to just about everything related to Access. You'll very likely run into problems with the User Account Control (UAC) feature of Vista when you're working with Access. In fact, some security-related macros in this chapter might not run at all solely because

Vista prevents you from running them. Make sure that you have the proper privileges to use Access when you're working with security features, by ensuring that you set up security in Access as required using the features on the Database Tools tab of the Ribbon.

This object is also useful for some database maintenance tasks. It's important to perform tasks such as compacting the database from time to time (normally accomplished by executing the Office➪Manage➪Compact and Repair Database command). Using the DBEngine.CompactDatabase method helps you perform this task automatically. You can even use this object to register an Open Database Connectivity (ODBC) source automatically by calling the DBEngine.RegisterDatabase method. (You manually register an ODBC source by using the Data Sources [ODBC] applet in the Control Panel.)

You might not realize that Access can work in one of several database modes by using a number of different technologies. When you use the DBEngine approach, you can choose between the *Microsoft Jet Engine* (the set of DLLs that Access uses natively for communicating with the database) or *ODBCDirect* (a special set of DLLs that many programming environments, including Access, can use to communicate with the database) by using the DBEngine. DefaultType property. The Microsoft Jet Engine approach is best suited to situations where you know the location of the MDB file and want to work directly with it. The ODBCDirect approach is best suited for named sources created with the Data Sources (ODBC) applet of the Control Panel.

However, one of the most useful ways to use the DBEngine object is to perform some types of security tasks. For example, you can use the DBEngine object to modify workgroup setups and change the default settings for the database as a whole. Listing 15-3 shows an example of how you can get the default settings. (You can find the source code for this example on the Dummies.com site at http://www.dummies.com/go/vbafd5e.)

Listing 15-3   Getting the Default DBEngine Settings

```
Public Function GetDBEngineProperties()
    ' Create an output string.
    Dim Output As String

    ' Make a place for the property values.
    Dim CurProp As Property

    ' Some properties won't have a value.
    On Error Resume Next

    ' Get the current properties.
    For Each CurProp In DBEngine.Properties
        Output = Output + CurProp.Name + ": " + _
            CStr(CurProp.Value) + vbCrLf
    Next

    ' Display the results.
    MsgBox Output, vbInformation, "DBEngine Properties"
End Function
```

Many of the objects in Access have a `Properties` collection. Each `Property` is a separate object that controls some aspect of the database operation. The properties define a database characteristic or the location of configuration information, as shown in Figure 15-3. This is a standard list of properties for the `DBEngine` when you use it in Microsoft Jet Engine mode.

Figure 15-3:
Use the
`DBEngine`
properties
to determine
the
database
character-
istics.

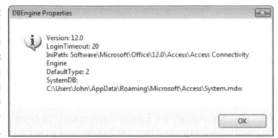

DBEngine Properties

Version: 12.0
LoginTimeout: 20
IniPath: Software\Microsoft\Office\12.0\Access\Access Connectivity Engine
DefaultType: 2
SystemDB:
C:\Users\John\AppData\Roaming\Microsoft\Access\System.mdw

OK

The essential information for Access appears in the `Version` property. This property tells you the version of Data Access Objects (DAO) installed on the host machine. When this value is less than 3.6, you encounter problems getting some DAO features listed in the help file to work. (Access 2002 and Access 2003 use the 3.6 version, and Access 2007 uses the 12.0 version, as shown in the figure.) Consequently, when you run your program on another machine and it fails — even though it worked on your machine — verify the DAO version number.

The `IniPath` property contains the location of the information for Access in the Registry. See the "Using the Registry with VBA" section of Chapter 13 for details on using the Registry. The contents of the Registry vary by machine and installation. However, you can usually find a list of database conversion entries in `HKEY_LOCAL_MACHINE` as well as the path to the security settings for this user under `HKEY_CURRENT_USER`.

Getting the security settings is a little more difficult. Listing 15-4 shows an example of how you can determine the settings for a particular object type, such as a table or a report. These are general settings for the entire class of objects and not for a specific object. (You can find the source code for this example on the Dummies.com site at `http://www.dummies.com/go/vbafd5e`.)

Listing 15-4   Getting DBEngine Security Settings

```
Public Function GetDBEngineSecurity()
   ' Create an output string.
   Dim Output As String

   ' Set the system database value if necessary.
   If DBEngine.SystemDB = "" Then
      DBEngine.SystemDB = "System.mdw"
   End If

   ' Get the current database.
   Dim TheDB As Database
   Set TheDB = DBEngine.Workspaces(0).Databases(0)

   ' Create a container object to hold the security data.
   Dim AContainer As Container

   ' Check each container for data.
   For Each AContainer In TheDB.Containers

      With AContainer

      ' Store the name of the permission object.
      Output = Output + .Name + ":" + vbCrLf

      ' Check the flag values.
      If .AllPermissions And dbSecReadDef Then
         Output = Output + "Can Read Definition" + vbCrLf
      End If

      ... other permissions ...

      If .AllPermissions And dbSecDBOpen Then
         Output = Output + "Can Open" + vbCrLf
      End If
      End With

      ' Display the results.
      MsgBox Output, vbInformation, "DBEngine Security"

      ' Erase the data.
      Output = ""
   Next

End Function
```

The code begins by checking the DBEngine.SystemDB property value.
When this property is blank, the DBEngine object can't retrieve security
information. You must make this check before you do any other work with
the DBEngine object. Generally, setting the property as shown lets you
retrieve the security information.

Access places security information in the `Containers` collection. Each `Container` object has properties, such as the permission object name. One of the more important features is the `AllPermissions` property. This property looks like any `Long` value that you might have seen in the past, but it really consists of a number of individual flag values. A *flag* is an individual bit within the `Long` value. Setting the flag to 1 turns on that entry, and setting it to 0 turns it off. Consequently, if you want to let someone read the definition for a particular property object, you set the `dbSecReadDef` flag on.

The `If...Then` statements perform a logical `And` on the `AllPermissions` property. Each flag entry, such as `dbSecDBOpen`, has one bit set. If this bit is also set in the `AllPermissions` property, the `If...Then` statement expression is true. Figure 15-4 shows some typical output from this example when you use the default configuration or log in as the admin account.

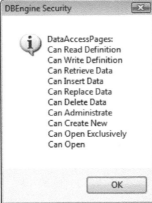

Figure 15-4: Every object type has a separate security container that you can validate.

Setting the flag value in the `AllPermissions` property requires a little different technique. The idea is to perform a Boolean operation that results in the right bit result in the `AllPermissions` property. Here's typical code for setting a flag on or off within the `AllPermissions` property:

```
' Set the flag on.
.AllPermissions = .AllPermissions Or dbSecDBOpen

' Set the flag off.
.AllPermissions =.AllPermissions And Not dbSecDBOpen
```

You can use the Windows Calculator to make this more understandable. When you place the calculator in Bin mode, it displays the individual bits of the number that you type. Combine this utility with either the Immediate or Locals window to work out the effect of the flag changes. The Not, And, Or, and Xor buttons on the Calculator work just like the commands in VBA, so you can check for the results that you want before you commit them to code. (See the "Defining hex and octal values" section of Chapter 4 for details on using the Windows Calculator.)

Using the CurrentDB and related objects

The latest version of Access has new and interesting ways to perform a task. The CurrentDB object originally appeared in Office 2000 as an updated version of the DBEngine.Workspaces(0).Databases(0) object. You should use the CurrentDB object, whenever possible, to perform actual database work because this object includes a few new features that make it a better fit for multi-user environments. However, when you want to use multiple workspaces, you still need to use the DBEngine.Workspaces collection.

You use the CurrentDB object to gain full control over the information contained in the current MDB file. This is a complete database object and not a single table. Listing 15-5 shows an example of how you can use the CurrentDB and its related objects. See the upcoming section "Understanding the Database objects" for details on elements such as the Recordsets and Fields collections. (You can find the source code for this example on the Dummies.com site at http://www.dummies.com/go/vbafd5e.)

Listing 15-5   Getting Database Configuration Information

```
Public Function CheckCurrentDB()
    ' Create an individual table definition.
    Dim CurTblDef As TableDef

    ' Create an individual recordset.
    Dim CurRec As Recordset

    ' Create an individual field.
    Dim CurField As Field

    ' Create an output string.
    Dim Output As String

    ' Check each recordset in the database.
    For Each CurTblDef In CurrentDb.TableDefs

        ' Open a recordset for each table definition.
        Set CurRec = CurrentDb.OpenRecordset(CurTblDef.Name)

        ' Get the recordset name.
        Output = Output + CurRec.Name + vbCrLf

        ' Check for records.
```

(continued)

Listing 15-5 *(continued)*

```
        If CurRec.RecordCount = 0 Then

            ' Tell the user and exit.
            Output = Output + "No Records Available"
            GoTo SkipFields

        End If

        ' Check each field definition in the recordset.
        For Each CurField In CurRec.Fields

            ' Get the field name, type, and current value.
            Output = Output + "Name: " + CurField.Name + _
                vbCrLf + vbTab + "Type: " + _
                CvtType(CurField.Type) + vbCrLf + vbTab + _
                "Value: "

            ' Some values are null.
            If IsNull(CurField.Value) Then
                Output = Output + "Null" + vbCrLf
            Else
                Output = Output + CStr(CurField.Value) +
                vbCrLf
            End If
        Next

SkipFields:
        ' Display the results.
        MsgBox Output, vbInformation, "CurrentDB
            Information"

        ' Erase the data.
        Output = ""

        ' Close each recordset in turn.
        CurRec.Close
    Next
End Function
```

The code begins by creating objects that represent various database elements that you've used in the past. For example, a `TableDef` object is a representation of the table design that you create by using the Access Designer. The `CurrentDB` object contains a `TableDefs` collection with every table that the MDB file contains. It might surprise you to learn that Access has seven or more internal tables that it maintains in addition to the tables that you create. When you run this program on the sample database, you see eight table definitions because there really are eight tables in the database. These internal tables can provide useful information, but you generally don't want to use them.

Although the example code doesn't show them, the `CurrentDB` object also contains a `QueryDefs` collection for queries and a `Containers` collection for security objects. You use these objects in the same way that you use the objects for the `Workspaces` collection. See the earlier section "Working with the DBEngine object" for details.

To work with a particular table or query, you must create a `Recordset` object. The code performs this task by using the `OpenRecordset` method. The first argument for this method contains the name of the table that you want to open or the query that you want to create. The example shows one technique for opening an individual table when you don't know the table name when you write the code.

The presence of a table doesn't necessary indicate that it contains any data. You can check for this condition by using the `RecordCount` property. If this property is `0`, the table lacks records, and you shouldn't attempt to do anything other than add records or determine configuration information. The example code shows one situation where you really do need to use a `GoTo` statement. In this case, you must skip the record-specific code if there are no records to process.

The record processing code works with individual fields, much as you will when writing code to change the information in the database. The code gets the field name, type, and current value. A field can contain a `Null` (or nothing) value. It's important to remember that VBA uses `Null` for values and `Nothing` for objects. The `IsNull` function returns `True` when a field is `Null`. You must use this technique instead of the `Is Nothing` method that is used with objects.

The Type field also requires special processing in this case. When you convert an enumerated value to a string and that value resides in a variable, VBA returns a number and not the string value of the enumeration. If you want to see a string value, you need to write an enumeration conversion function, such as the `CvtType` function, shown in Listing 15-6. (You can find the source code for this example on the Dummies.com site at `http://www.dummies.com/go/vbafd5e`.)

Listing 15-6   Converting a Numeric Type Value into a String

```
Public Function CvtType(DataType As Long) As String
   ' Use a case statement to choose a data type.
   Select Case DataType
      Case DataTypeEnum.dbBigInt
         CvtType = "dbBigInt"
      ... Other Cases ...
      Case DataTypeEnum.dbVarBinary
         CvtType = "dbVarBinary"
      Case Else
         CvtType = "Type Unknown"
   End Select
End Function
```

This function ends up as a giant `Select Case` statement. Always include a `Case Else` clause in case the function receives a nonstandard value. Otherwise, your code could fail. Figure 15-5 shows typical output from this example.

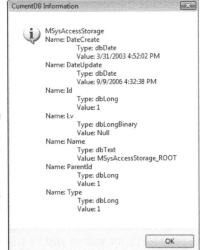

Figure 15-5:
Use
`TableDef`,
`Record`,
and `Field`
objects to
work with
tables.

Figure 15-5 shows one of the hidden Access tables that you encounter when working with the `CurrentDB` object. Notice that the example provides the data types and values for each field, along with the appropriate field name. Although it's fun to poke around a bit, exercise care when working with the `CurrentDB` object because you could damage one of these hidden system tables.

Understanding the Database objects

Access provides a number of `Database` objects that you commonly use to create programs. Here's a list of the common objects and collections that you use for database programs:

> ✔ **Connections collection:** You must create at least one connection for each Access database. The connection determines how the program communicates with the database. However, you can create more than one connection when you're using ADO. By way of contrast, when you're using DAO, the `Connection` object and the `Database` object are the same. The `Connections` collection contains one `Connection` object for each database connection.

✔ **Databases collection:** A Database object is the representation of the physical storage for all the tables, queries, reports, and other database elements. The Database object is the container — not the content. The Databases collection contains one Database object for each database that the program has opened.

✔ **Recordsets collection:** A Recordset object is the representation of one data set. A data set could reference a single table, or it could reference multiple tables by using a query. A *query* is a SQL statement that defines the data that you want to retrieve and what technique to use to combine data from multiple tables. (See the upcoming section "Understanding SQL: A Quick Overview" for details.) The Recordsets collection contains one Recordset object for each query made against a Database object. You can create multiple Recordset objects for each database.

✔ **Command object:** This is the representation of a SQL statement in object form. The Command object also contains any arguments required by the SQL statement. You execute a command against a Connection object to open the query and retrieve a Recordset object for use in your program.

✔ **Fields collection:** A Recordset object contains one or more Field objects that define each record. The Fields collection contains the list of Field objects for a given Recordset.

✔ **TableDefs collection:** Every time that you create a new table by using the Access Table Designer, Access adds a TableDef object to the TableDefs collection of the database. The TableDef object defines every element of the table, including field names and data types.

✔ **QueryDefs collection:** A *query* defines how you want to get data from the database. Access provides the means to create static Query objects by using the Query Designer and stores each QueryDef (query definition) object in the QueryDefs collection.

✔ **Relations collection:** A *table* represents a single set of related data. A *data set* can contain one or more tables that contain data in a particular relationship. For example, a customer record can reference multiple invoice records. The customer record and the invoice records reside in different tables. A Relation object defines the references between two tables. Access stores each of these Relation objects in the Relations collection.

Accessing special commands with the DoCmd object

The DoCmd object provides you with a number of interesting methods that look similar to the list of macros that you find in the Macro dialog box. You can't perform every macro task by calling on DoCmd object services, but this object is exceptionally useful if you want to perform some tasks in code rather than write a macro to do them. Think of the DoCmd object as a means of bypassing the Access macro requirements, in some situations, so that you can make your VBA code easier to read, as shown in Listing 15-7. (You can find the source code for this example on the Dummies.com site at http://www.dummies.com/go/vbafd5e.)

Listing 15-7   Using the DoCmd Object for Special Tasks

```
Public Function SpecialCommands()
    ' Sound a beep.
    MsgBox "Sounding a beep!", vbInformation, "DoCmd Event"
    DoCmd.Beep

    ' Turn echo off and then back on.
    DoCmd.Echo False, "Echo is off!"
    MsgBox "Echo is off!", vbInformation, "DoCmd Event"
    DoCmd.Echo True, "Echo is on!"
    MsgBox "Echo is on!", vbInformation, "DoCmd Event"

    ' Open and close a query.
    DoCmd.OpenQuery "GetWordList", acViewNormal, acReadOnly
    MsgBox "Query is open!", vbInformation, "DoCmd Event"
    DoCmd.Close acQuery, "GetWordList"
    MsgBox "Query is closed!", vbInformation, "DoCmd Event"

    ' Run a macro.
    DoCmd.RunMacro "RunSayHello"
End Function

Public Function SayHello()
    ' Say hello to the user.
    MsgBox "Hello!", vbExclamation, "Say Hello Message"
End Function
```

This code performs a number of interesting tasks. First, it tells the system to beep. In most cases, you want to avoid using the Beep method because it only tells the user that there's an error and doesn't say what error the user made or how to fix it. In some cases, such as when a user reaches the end of the database records, using the Beep method works fine because the meaning of the beep is clear to most users.

Access normally echoes every change to the environment onscreen. An *echo* is the display of a command and its consequences. Having the commands flash onscreen while your program performs its task is distracting and could cause some users problems. Consequently, you might want to turn off the echo by using the DoCmd.Echo method. The first argument is True or False depending on whether you want to turn echo on or off. The second argument is a string that VBA displays on the status bar. It's important to display this information so that the user knows that Access is working in the background.

You can also use the DoCmd object to open and close various kinds of Access objects, such as tables, reports, and queries. For example, you can use it to open and close a query by calling the OpenQuery and general Close methods.

Notice that you can define the query that you want to open, the view that you want to use, and the kind of access to provide. The example opens the GetWordList query in Normal view for read-only access. You could just as easily open a query in Design view for read/write access.

The Close method works for a variety of objects. If you use Close by itself, VBA closes the currently selected object. However, you can also provide the kind of object that you want closed, along with the object name. This second method is safer because you don't close by mistake an object that you really want open. Closing an object means that it's no longer available for any use, so closing an object by mistake could mean that your program experiences an error even if the code is normally correct.

You can also use DoCmd to run a macro by using the RunMacro method. This macro indirectly runs the SayHello function. You could also call the SayHello function directly, but macros often contain a series of instructions that you wouldn't want to include in your code.

A few of the DoCmd object functions seem to have odd results or might not work at all. For example, the AddMenu function doesn't appear to work, and Microsoft has documented this issue on its Web site. Make sure that you test the program by using the same platform that the user will use when you use the DoCmd object in your code. (If you don't know what platform the user will have, you had better research the user to find out.)

Understanding SQL: A Quick Overview

SQL (pronounced "SEE-quel") is a specialized language used by many database management systems (DBMSes) to manipulate data. You normally don't need to use SQL in Access programs because you can create a query by using the Access Query Designer. The Query Designer is one of the first tools that you learn to use because you need it to link tables and create complex data sets. None of the techniques that you use for designing a database changes when you write VBA programs — you can still create queries and use them just as you always have.

Creating a SQL query the easy way

The only time that you need to consider using SQL directly is if you want to get data from an external source, such as SQL Server or SQL Server Express, or you need a temporary query that you don't want cluttering up the Access environment. I don't show you in this book how to gain access to external data sources because using external data sources could fill an entire book. However, the following procedure gives you a very fast and easy method for creating temporary queries:

1. Create a query as you normally do.

Figure 15-6 shows a somewhat complex query for the example database. It includes all the fields from the Word List table. The query has two criteria. Notice that the first criterion uses the VBA Left function.

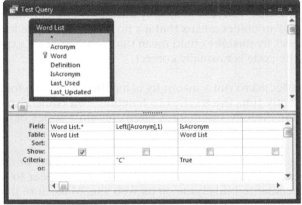

Figure 15-6:
Create a
temporary
SQL query
with the
same
technique
you usually
use.

2. Right-click the upper pane and then choose SQL View from the context menu that appears.

Access displays the SQL for the query that you just created graphically. Figure 15-7 shows the SQL for the test query shown in Figure 15-6.

Figure 15-7:
View the
SQL query
with the SQL
View option.

3. Highlight the SQL query (all the text shown in Figure 15-7) and then click the Copy button on the toolbar.

Access places the query on the Clipboard.

4. **Open the VBA IDE, position the cursor, and then click the Paste button on the toolbar.**

   VBA pastes the query text for you.

5. **Close the SQL query without saving it.**

Note that you can always test your query before you use it in code by using the Datasheet View option. Using this technique ensures that you write the code only once to get the precise results that you want.

Using the SQL query

After you create a SQL query, you can use it in a program to get information from the database. Listing 15-8 shows a short example that uses the test query to get a list of words with acronyms that begin with the letter *C*. (You can find the source code for this example on the Dummies.com site at `http://www.dummies.com/go/vbafd5e.`)

Discovering more about SQL

SQL isn't something that you can understand in a few short lessons. You don't need to spend a lot of time learning SQL to create simple commands, such as retrieving information from a single table, but the commands get more complicated when you ask SQL to do more for you. (The more advanced commands are also product specific, in some cases, so you need to exercise caution.) The best way to build your knowledge of SQL is a little at a time, such as through a newsletter. One such newsletter is SQL Server Professional eXTRA. You can subscribe to it at `http://www.freeenewsletters.com/`.

A number of online sites also make SQL easy and interesting to learn. A Gentle Introduction to SQL (`http://sqlzoo.net/`) provides a number of tutorials and some great how-to links. The advantage of this Web site is that the author provides links for multiple flavors of SQL, which means that you can see how other products use SQL. You get a step-by-step tutorial on standard SQL at `http://www.w3schools.com/sql/default.asp`. The site at `http://`

`www.sqlcourse.com` provides an interactive course where an interpreter tells you how well you do in typing basic commands. Finally, the SQL Tutorial site at `http://www.1keydata.com/sql/sql.html` provides clear demonstrations of individual commands.

When you simply need information about SQL, you should try a few other Web sites. A complete set of reserved words (SQL commands) appears on the Microsoft Web site at `http://msdn.microsoft.com/library/en-us/tsqlref/ts_ra-rz_9oj7.asp`. You can find an outstanding list of SQL resources on the Ocelot Web site at `http://www.ocelot.ca/`. The links and book reviews are especially helpful.

If you want to learn about SQL starting with the basics, check out *SQL For Dummies,* 6th Edition, by Allen G. Taylor (Wiley). This book begins with the basics and then helps you discover advanced techniques, such as working with XML.

Listing 15-8   Performing a Database Query in VBA

```
Public Function QueryCAcronyms()
    ' Create a recordset.
    Dim Rec As Recordset
    Set Rec = _
        CurrentDb.OpenRecordset( _
            "SELECT [Word List].* " + _
            "FROM [Word List] " + _
            "WHERE (((Left([Acronym],1))='C') " + _
            "AND (([Word List].IsAcronym)=True))", _
        Type:=dbOpenDynaset)

    ' Create an output string.
    Dim Output As String

    ' Check each record in the recordset.
    While Not Rec.EOF

        ' Get the information.
        Output = Output + Rec.Fields("Acronym") + vbTab + _
                 Rec.Fields("Word") + vbCrLf

        ' Move to the next record.
        Rec.MoveNext
    Wend

    ' Display the result.
    MsgBox Output, vbInformation, "Words and Acronyms"

    ' Close the recordset.
    Rec.Close
End Function
```

Notice that you still use the `CurrentDb.OpenRecordset` method to get the `Recordset` object. The query is simple text, so you can substitute variables as input. For example, you might add a `Letter` argument to the program that lets you define which letter to use for the search.

A `Recordset` provides the `EOF` property that tells when you reach the end of the file (or recordset). Notice that the code addresses the content of the recordset by using indexed `Fields` collection entries. In this case, the record-set doesn't contain the whole table, just those records that match the criteria.

The `Rec.MoveNext` method is the most important piece of code in this loop. You must provide some means of moving from record to record, or else the code never reaches the end of the recordset. The result of leaving out this piece of code is an endless loop. Whenever you run into this problem, press Ctrl+C to interrupt program execution.

The code uses the `Rec.Close` method to close the recordset. Always close the recordset when you finish using it. Otherwise, you might experience problems using the database later without a machine reboot. For example, when you lock a table for exclusive use and don't close it when you're done, Access keeps the table locked and no one else (not even you) can use it until you reboot the machine.

Adding Form-Related Applications

The example database, queries, data, and associated form in this chapter all come from 1 of about 15 databases that I use personally. This word list is handy because it contains all the words that I've ever had to define in a book. A personal word list is one of the handier database programs that you can maintain because finding the meaning of words (especially jargon related to a specific industry) can prove difficult.

In other examples in this chapter, I show you bits and pieces of the tables and queries that the database contains. In this section, I discuss the form used to query, add, and retrieve words. The form includes a number of helpful buttons and the word information shown in Figure 15-8.

Figure 15-8: Design forms with the idea that you can perform specialized tasks with macros and programs.

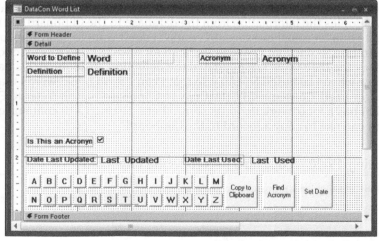

You often need to hide and show fields as needed on a form to reduce clutter and potential confusion. The Is This an Acronym field performs this task by hiding the Acronym field when it isn't needed. Right-click this field and then choose Properties from the context menu that appears. Select the Event tab, and you see a list of events for the check box. Whenever someone marks the check box, the form executes the `AcronymCheck` macro. This macro runs the `SetAcronymLabel` function, shown in Listing 15-9. (You can find the source code for this example on the Dummies.com site at `http://www.dummies.com/go/vbafd5e`.)

Listing 15-9   Hiding or Showing a Form Field As Needed

```
Public Function SetAcronymLabel()
    ' Check the status of the Acronym check box.
    If Forms![DataCon Word List]![IsAcronym] = True Then
        Forms![DataCon Word List]![Acronym Label].Visible = True
        Forms![DataCon Word List]![Acronym].Visible = True
    Else
        Forms![DataCon Word List]![Acronym Label].Visible = False
        Forms![DataCon Word List]![Acronym].Visible = False
    End If
End Function
```

This macro selects the `DataCon Word List` form from the `Forms` collection and locates the `IsAcronym` field on that form. If this field is `True`, which means that the database entry has an acronym, the macro makes the `Acronym` field and its associated label visible. Otherwise, it hides both items.

I set up this program to accept three kinds of entries: An entry can contain a word and a definition, an acronym and a definition, or all three. I often need to send a definition of a word to someone else, so I created a special button that copies the information from the database to the Clipboard so that I can paste it in an e-mail message. Of course, I don't want to send someone an old definition — one that I haven't updated for a while — so this function has to check the date when I last updated the definition. In addition, it's handy to know when I last used an entry so that I can get rid of old words that I no longer need. Consequently, the Copy to Clipboard button (refer to Figure 15-8) has a lot of work to do, as shown here. Listing 15-10 contains code that you can use to copy a record to the Clipboard.

Listing 15-10   Copying a Record to the Clipboard

```
Public Function Create_Record_Copy()
    ' Create some variables.
    Dim strWord As String
    Dim strAcronym As String
    Dim strDefinition As String
    Dim strDate As String
    Dim RecordDate As Date

    ' Some records will start out with a null date that indicates it
    ' hasn't been checked since the check was implemented.
    Forms![DataCon Word List]![Last_Updated].SetFocus
    If Forms![DataCon Word List]![Last_Updated].Text = "" Then
        MsgBox "This definition hasn't been checked before, so ask " _
            "John to check it!", vbOKOnly, "Must Check Definition"
```

```
            Forms![DataCon Word List]![Copy_Text] = " "
            Exit Function
    End If

    ' Get the last updated date from the record.
    strDate = Forms![DataCon Word List]![Last_Updated]
    RecordDate = DateValue(Forms![DataCon Word List]![Last_Updated])

    ' If there is a date, add 366 to it to represent one year.
    RecordDate = RecordDate + 366

    ' The date on some records will be too old, which means it's time
    ' for another check.
    If RecordDate < Now() Then
        MsgBox "The definition dated " + strDate + " is too old, add " _
                "word to the list!", vbOKOnly, "Time to Redefine"
        Forms![DataCon Word List]![Copy_Text] = " "
        Exit Function
    End If

    ' Set the last used field to today.
    Forms![DataCon Word List]![Last_Used] = Now()

    ' Get the values of the word and definition since they'll always be present.
    strWord = Forms![DataCon Word List]![Word]
    strDefinition = Forms![DataCon Word List]![Definition]

    ' Place the data we want to copy on the form.
    Forms![DataCon Word List]![Copy_Text] = strWord + " -- " + strDefinition

    ' Check to see if we need to store the acronym value as well.
    If Forms![DataCon Word List]![IsAcronym] = True Then

        ' If we do need to store the acronym, then place it in a variable.
        strAcronym = Forms![DataCon Word List]![Acronym]

        ' Check to see if there is a definition for this acronym.
        If UCase(strDefinition) = "N/A" Then

            ' If not, then simply place the word and its meaning on the
            ' Clipboard.
            Forms![DataCon Word List]![Copy_Text] = _
                strAcronym + " -- " + strWord
        Else

            ' Otherwise, place the acronym and associated definition on the
            ' Clipboard.
            Forms![DataCon Word List]![Copy_Text] = _
                strAcronym + " -- See " + strWord + Chr(13) + Chr(10) + _
                strWord + " (" + strAcronym + ") -- " + strDefinition
        End If
    End If
End Function
```

The code begins by checking the last date of update. Notice that it sets the focus to the Last_Updated control. When this field is blank, the program displays a message to me saying that I need to update the definition. If the form does contain a Last_Updated value, the code retrieves this value and adds 366 to it. I require that I update my definitions every year, so if it has been more than a year since the last update, the code displays an error message and exits.

After the code knows that the definition isn't too old, it sets the Last_Used field to today's date. This entry lets me know when I last used the definition so that I can remove old entries later.

At this point, the code begins the process of creating the text that it will place on the Clipboard. The simplest case is a word and definition without an acronym, so the code performs that copying process first. The code checks for an acronym next and exits when there isn't one.

When there's an acronym, the code tests to see whether there's a definition. The second case is when there's an acronym and an associated series of words but no definition. A definition of N/A signifies this condition, and the code copies just the acronym and associated words to the Clipboard.

The third condition is one when there's a word, an acronym, and a definition. In this case, the code copies all three entries to the Clipboard.

Creating Automatic Applications

The focus of automatic execution in Access is the Autoexec macro. When you want a database to perform a task automatically after opening, create a macro named Autoexec. Any actions that you add to this macro are executed when you open the database file. This feature works like any other macro, so you can easily add one or more RunCode actions to execute programs associated with the file.

Chapter 16

Applications that Work Together

● ●

In This Chapter

▶ Discovering how working with more than one application makes sense

▶ Working with external applications

▶ Using Word to view Outlook e-mail messages

▶ Creating new e-mail messages with Word

▶ Using Word to create Excel notes

● ●

*Y*ou might never have an interest in using any program other than Word or Excel by itself. It's possible to create some interesting and useful documents with either program. As a database administrator (DBA), you might never need to wander outside the world provided by Access. However, as you move on in your career, you find that you wear more hats and need to manage your data more effectively. Often, this means combining several tools because one tool can't perform a portion of a task effectively. Yes, you can always force Word to create spreadsheets and use Excel as a word processor, but this really isn't efficient.

This chapter shows you how to write programs where a main application such as Word, Excel, or Access calls on a subordinate application to perform some work. In some cases, you need to work with an external program, one that may not even support VBA. The first examples describe how to work in this environment with the idea that you can do anything you might normally do from the command line using VBA. For the remaining examples, I chose to concentrate on Office products because that's what I discuss in most of this book. However, don't limit yourself to the examples in this chapter. Any application that supports VBA can act as a main program. For example, you can just as easily ask CorelDRAW to perform services for Word as ask Excel. Subordinate programs need not support VBA at all when you can work with the result in some way, such as by saving the output to a text file.

Understanding Why You Should Work with More than One Application

Feature bloat (where the vendor adds useless or unnecessary features) is an incredible problem in applications today. Part of the problem is that users ask vendors to keep adding features to programs so that they don't have to leave the comfortable confines of the single program that they know and learn how to use other programs. Another part of the problem is that vendors want to provide you with a good reason to upgrade to the next version of a product. They hope that adding new features will grab your attention as something that you must have. Whether the feature is a request or a marketing idea is beside the point — the problems of feature bloat are numerous.

With feature bloat, a single program consumes more resources, such as memory and disk space. In addition, the added complexity makes the program less stable (it tends to cause errors more often) and increases the program's learning curve. The features are often poorly defined and don't work as well as the same features offered by another program that is dedicated to that purpose. For example, the drawing features in Word can't compare to the drawing features in a program such as CorelDRAW.

The problems with feature bloat addressed by this chapter are functionality and efficiency. Dedicated applications usually provide better functionality than an add-in for an application dedicated to some other purpose. In addition, the dedicated application can usually perform the task faster and with fewer data compatibility problems. Using the dedicated program costs more when you first set up a system, but it pays back the investment by making the system more flexible.

Your main application might not include a feature that you desperately need. For example, when you want to send an e-mail, you need to use a project such as Outlook to do it. Don't assume that *e-mail* means *content*. A program might need to send an e-mail to report an application or a system error to the network administrator. It could also track usage statistics and send them to a central collection point for analysis. You might even want a user to fill out a survey after he uses a new program that you create for a specific length of time.

It would be easy to limit your multi-application programs to simple data exchange or data manipulation. However, you can also use the multiple application technique in a workgroup environment for collaboration. When you complete a task on a project, a program can send your completed data to the next person in line for her additions. The other person might find out about the new file through an e-mail message or an addition to her task list. Your program can interact with the next application in line and also send notifications.

Starting and Stopping External Applications

VBA may not seem particularly powerful when it comes to performing some tasks, such as interacting with external programs, and the truth is that you do need to perform more work than normal to accomplish some tasks. However, VBA offers access to the entire Win32 Application Programming Interface (API) as long as you're willing to create the required *prototypes* (descriptions of the information required for the call you want). Consequently, anything you see listed on the Microsoft MSDN Web site (http://msdn.microsoft.com/library/en-us/winprog/winprog/windows_api_reference.asp) for the Win32 API is also accessible from VBA. You may have already seen one example of such calls, in the section "Accessing any Registry locations in Office" in Chapter 13. However, accessing an external application requires more work. The example in this section is more difficult, but definitely doable.

Deciding how to perform the task

Before you begin working with the Win32 API, you must know which call to use. Accessing an external program is called *creating a process.* Consequently, you must use the CreateProcess() call. However, you must know more. The CreateProcess() call comes in two forms: one for ASCII text named CreateProcessA() and another for Unicode text named CreateProcessW(). In general, you'll find that using ASCII text is much easier in VBA, so this section uses the CreateProcessA() call.

When you create a process using CreateProcessA(), VBA makes the call and immediately begins any other work that you want to perform. This kind of call is an *asynchronous* call, or one that doesn't wait. If you want to perform an asynchronous call, you can use the Shell() function in VBA and not bother with the Win32 API call. However, you're trying to interact with an external application, which means that you must wait for it to complete its task before moving on. In this case, you need to perform a *synchronous* call, one where VBA waits for the results of the external call before it proceeds to the next task. Unfortunately, VBA doesn't provide a way to wait that works well with an external process, so you must again turn to the Win32 API. In this case, the example uses the WaitForSingleObject() call. You make this call after you create the external application to force VBA to wait.

Win32 API calls require that you perform certain housekeeping chores. You don't have to do anything special to free memory and other resources in VBA because VBA does that task for you. However, the Win32 API isn't quite so helpful. When you create a process, the Win32 API returns something called a *handle,* which is a means of grabbing the process and doing something with it, such as waiting for it to end. When you finish using the handle, you must close it by using the `CloseHandle()` call. At this point, you know the three steps that this example must perform:

1. Create a new, external process using the `CreateProcessA()` call.

2. Wait for the external process to finish using the `WaitForSingleObject()` call.

3. Clean up any Win32 API call variables, such as handles, using the required cleanup calls, such as `CloseHandle()`.

In addition to following these three steps, you may need to add code to process the external program results. For example, you might want to execute any of the hundreds of command-line utilities that Windows makes available. You can view the results of these commands in most cases by sending *(redirecting)* their output to a text file using the redirection symbol (>>) on the command line. The "Using Files with the Open Command" section of Bonus Chapter 3 shows one way you can use text file output with your Office applications. (You can find Bonus Chapter 3 on the Dummies.com site at `http://www.dummies.com/go/vbafd5e`.)

Creating the Win32 API calls

The best way to work with the Win32 API in VBA is one step at a time. Define a call, the structures and enumerations to go with that call, and any required cleanup before you move on to the next call. Make sure you understand the sequence of steps you must perform to accomplish the task.

Always create Win32 API calls in a separate module. Because the Win32 API calls are so flexible, you should concentrate on making them modular so that you can use them with other applications. In addition, after you debug the Win32 API calls, you don't want to contaminate the code with application code.

Defining CreateProcessA()

This example uses the `CreateProcessA()` call as a starting point. You can find the actual definition for this call at `http://msdn.microsoft.com/library/en-us/dllproc/base/createprocess.asp`. However, you need a VBA version of this call for the example. Listing 16-1 shows the code you need. (You can find the source code for this example on the Dummies.com site at `http://www.dummies.com/go/vbafd5e`.)

Listing 16-1   Defining CreateProcessA()

```
' This Win32 API call creates an external process.
Private Declare Function CreateProcessA Lib "kernel32" ( _
    ByVal lpApplicationName As String, _
    ByVal lpCommandLine As String, _
    ByVal lpProcessAttributes As Long, _
    ByVal lpThreadAttributes As Long, _
    ByVal bInheritHandles As Long, _
    ByVal dwCreationFlags As Long, _
    ByVal lpEnvironment As Long, _
    ByVal lpCurrentDirectory As String, _
    lpStartupInfo As STARTUPINFO, _
    lpProcessInformation As PROCESS_INFORMATION) _
    As Long

' This structure describes how to start the process. For
' example, it tells what title to give the application
' window and where to display it onscreen. You must tell
' Windows how long this structure is, but Windows uses
' default values for any values you don't supply.
Private Type STARTUPINFO
    cb As Long
    lpReserved As String
    lpDesktop As String
    lpTitle As String
    dwX As Long
    dwY As Long
    dwXSize As Long
    dwYSize As Long
    dwXCountChars As Long
    dwYCountChars As Long
    dwFillAttribute As Long
    dwFlags As Long
    wShowWindow As Integer
    cbReserved2 As Integer
    lpReserved2 As Long
    hStdInput As Long
    hStdOutput As Long
    hStdError As Long
End Type

' This is an output structure. Windows fills this
' structure with useful information about the external
' process that includes a handle to the process, a handle
' to the main thread (because processes can have multiple
' threads), and both the process and thread identifiers.
Private Type PROCESS_INFORMATION
    hProcess As Long
    hThread As Long
    dwProcessID As Long
    dwThreadID As Long
End Type
```

You have many options for defining the `CreateProcessA()` call, but this one seems to work best because it combines maximum flexibility with reduced potential for errors. For example, some people define `lpApplicationName` as a `Long` because they never give an application name. You can then set this value to 0 rather than use `vbNullString`. The data types you choose to represent the various Win32 API call arguments are important because the selection determines how you use the call in your VBA code.

The Win32 API is very inconsistent when it comes to input and output arguments, so you have to exercise care in how you use the functions it supports. In this case, `CreateProcessA()` returns a value of 0 when it fails and a non-zero value when it succeeds. Consequently, you use the return value for error trapping.

The example takes a shortcut with the `lpProcessAttributes` and `lpThreadAttributes` arguments. Normally, you can provide an `LPSECURITY_ATTRIBUTES` (`http://msdn.microsoft.com/library/en-us/secauthz/security/security_attributes.asp`) structure to define security for these arguments. Because of the way you use `CreateProcessA()` in VBA, you don't normally need to provide these data structures. The only time you would need to define these data structures is when the external application you call creates child processes itself and you want to control how those child processes inherit rights from the parent.

How you create the process is important. You tell Windows how you want the process to appear to the user by using the `dwCreationFlags` argument. The MSDN Web site tells you these values at `http://msdn.microsoft.com/library/en-us/dllproc/base/process_creation_flags.asp`. Note that all these values are in hexadecimal. Consequently, you need to define the values using `&H`, as shown here:

```
Private Const NORMAL_PRIORITY_CLASS = &H20&
```

Win32 API calls sometimes require you to provide input, even when you don't use the input as part of the call. The `STARTUPINFO` data structure is one such case. You can use `CreateProcessA()` just fine without it, but you must provide a structure that contains the structure size as a minimum. This argument is also odd because you can provide one of two data structure inputs. The example shows `STARTUPINFO` (`http://msdn.microsoft.com/library/en-us/dllproc/base/startupinfo_str.asp`), but you can also provide `STARTUPINFOEX` (`http://msdn.microsoft.com/library/en-us/dllproc/base/startupinfoex.asp`), which supplies additional information when you need it. It's very unlikely that you'll need to use the added functionality of STARTUPINFOEX with VBA.

The final argument isn't one that you supply; Windows returns it to you. The lpProcessInformation argument tells you about the process that Windows has created when CreateProcessA() returns. This information is helpful for a number of reasons. For example, many Win32 API calls require that you provide a Process Identifier (PID) or a Thread Identifier (TID) as input. The PROCESS_INFORMATION (http://msdn.microsoft.com/library/en-us/dllproc/base/process_information_str.asp) data structure supplies this information.

Defining WaitForSingleObject ( )

You can create specialized processes using CreateProcessA(), but the point of this example is to create a synchronous process; one where VBA waits so that you can do something with the output of the application if you want to do so. The WaitForSingleObject() call (see the details for this call at http://msdn.microsoft.com/library/en-us/dllproc/base/waitforsingleobject.asp) is quite simple in concept: It forces VBA to wait until some event occurs, such as the ending of the application. Listing 16-2 shows the code you need for this part of the example. (You can find the source code for this example on the Dummies.com site at http://www.dummies.com/go/vbafd5e.)

Listing 16-2   Defining WaitForSingleObject()

```
' This function causes VBA to wait for the external
' process and defines how long to wait.
Private Declare Function WaitForSingleObject _
              Lib "kernel32" ( _
    ByVal hHandle As Long, _
    ByVal dwMilliseconds As Long) As Long
```

The input arguments are simple. The handle is the handle returned by CreateProcessA(). The dwMilliseconds argument tells how long to wait in milliseconds. Of course, you might not know how long to wait, so WaitForSingleObject() also provides a special INFINITE value, as described here:

```
Private Const INFINITE = -1&
```

Unlike `CreateProcessA()`, which returns a simple value telling you whether the call failed or succeeded, `WaitForSingleObject()` provides specific return values to indicate levels of success or failure. Many Win32 API calls take this approach, so you always have to check the documentation before you assume specific success or failure values. Here are the values for `WaitForSingleObject()`:

```
' Defines the possible results of the wait.
' The wait was successful.
Private Const WAIT_OBJECT_0 = &H0

' The process was killed for some unknown reason
' before it completed or the wait timed out.
Private Const WAIT_ABANDONED = &H80

' The wait timed out.
Private Const WAIT_TIMEOUT = &H102
```

Defining CloseHandle()

Of the three calls needed for this example, `CloseHandle()` is the easiest. In fact, all you need is a handle to close, as shown here:

```
' Close any Windows handle.
Private Declare Function CloseHandle Lib "kernel32" _
    (ByVal hObject As Long) As Boolean
```

This call always succeeds for a valid handle. The only times you should receive a return value of `False` are when you try to close something other than a handle or the handle you supply is invalid. You can discover more about `CloseHandle()` at `http://msdn.microsoft.com/library/en-us/sysinfo/base/closehandle.asp`.

Encapsulating the process

You can use the Win32 API calls in this example any way you want and in any order you want. The ability to perform tasks any way you see fit makes the Win32 API both flexible and dangerous. Because you'll likely perform some tasks more than once, it pays to encapsulate the process you use into an easy-to-manage function. Listing 16-3 shows the code used for this example. It encapsulates the process of calling an external program and waiting for it to finish. The return value tells the caller what happened during this process. (You can find the source code for this example on the Dummies.com site at `http://www.dummies.com/go/vbafd5e`.)

Listing 16-3   Performing the External Call

```
' This Sub provides specific steps to access external
' programs.
Public Function AccessExternalProgram(CommandAndPath) _
    As Long

    ' Create the required structures.
    Dim StartUp As STARTUPINFO
    Dim ProcessOutput As PROCESS_INFORMATION

    ' Create a variable to check the results of calls
    Dim Result As Long

    ' Because the startup information is input
    ' you must provide at least the data structure
    ' length.
    StartUp.cb = Len(start)

    ' Start the external application.
    Result = CreateProcessA( _
        vbNullString, CommandAndPath, 0&, 0&, 1&, _
        NORMAL_PRIORITY_CLASS, 0&, vbNullString, _
        StartUp, ProcessOutput)

    ' Perform error trapping to ensure the application
    ' started.
    If Result = 0 Then
        AccessExternalProgram = -1
        Exit Function
    End If

    ' Wait for the application to finish.
    AccessExternalProgram = _
        WaitForSingleObject( _
            ProcessOutput.hProcess, INFINITE)

    ' When the call completes, then free the handles.
    ' You must free both the thread and the process
    ' handles.
    Call CloseHandle(ProcessOutput.hThread)
    Call CloseHandle(ProcessOutput.hProcess)
End Function
```

The code begins by creating the variables needed by CreateProcessA().
It also creates a variable to test the return value of CreateProcessA()to
ensure that the system actually created the external process. Notice that
you must initialize StartUp because this structure is provided as input to
CreateProcessA(), but you don't have to do anything with ProcessOutput
because Windows manages this data structure.

After the code calls `CreateProcessA()`, it checks the result. When the result is 0 (the call wasn't successful), the function exits with a value of -1. You can use any method you want to tell the caller that the call isn't successful, but you should provide unique values for each kind of error output. Otherwise, the caller doesn't know how to react to problems.

When the `CreateProcessA()` call is successful, the code calls `WaitFor SingleObject()`. The example uses an `INFINITE` wait because you don't know how long the user will require to perform an external task. It's possible that the system will actually freeze at this point, so you should use an `INFINITE` wait only when you're sure the task will succeed. If you provide a millisecond value, the system can still recover by stopping the waiting period even if the user never responds. Always provide a millisecond value when you can predict the response time with reasonable accuracy.

The final step of the process is to close the handles. You must close both the thread and the process handles. Otherwise, the system experiences a *memory leak;* a condition where Windows can't recover memory that it's using for a particular task when it finishes that task. Memory leaks force you to eventually reboot the system to recover the lost memory.

Calling the AccessExternalProgram function

At this point, you're ready to call the external program. I chose a complex example in this case because external program access is quite powerful; it's more powerful than you might think at first. Listing 16-4 shows the example code in this case. (You can find the source code for this example on the Dummies.com site at `http://www.dummies.com/go/vbafd5e`.)

Listing 16-4   Performing an External Call

```
Sub TestExternalAccess()
    ' Obtains the result of the call.
    Dim Result As Long

    ' Perform the call.
    Result = AccessExternalProgram("CMD.EXE /k " + _
        Chr(34) + _
        "Dir >> Output.TXT | Notepad.EXE Output.TXT" + _
        Chr(34))

    ' Show the call results.
    Select Case Result
```

```
        Case -1
            MsgBox "Couldn't Start Application"
        Case WAIT_OBJECT_0
            MsgBox "Everything Worked!"
        Case WAIT_ABANDONED
            MsgBox "Application Failed to Wait"
        Case WAIT_TIMEOUT
            MsgBox "Application Timed Out"
    End Select
End Sub
```

The code begins by creating a result variable. It then makes the call. In this case, the external program is a command prompt. Using the /k argument is quite powerful because you can tell the command processor to execute any command you want. The example calls the Dir command, which displays a directory of the current location on the hard drive. The Dir command output is redirected to Output.TXT using the redirection symbol. After the Dir call is complete, the command process pipes the information to Notepad.EXE, which displays the content of the Output.TXT file onscreen.

At this point, you see a command prompt, and a copy of Notepad opens on your display. Close Notepad first and then the command prompt. Only after you close both windows does the AccessExternalProgram() function return a result to the test program. The test program displays the result onscreen based on the Result value.

Processing Outlook E-Mail Messages with Word

Outlook is a capable e-mail program. You can use it to get your personal mail or to view newsgroups online. However, you might run into situations when the formatting features that Outlook provides are less than useful. That's the purpose of the example in this case. Word requests the messages that you mark in Outlook and formats them in preparation for printing or just viewing. I use this program to create quick reference resources from my e-mail.

The marking feature of this program is especially helpful because you can mark just some of the messages in a thread instead of outputting them all. This program uses a red flag, but you could modify it to use any flag. In addition, the program automatically marks the message as completed after processing it. This means that you don't have to clear the flags individually.

Unfortunately, the program shown in Listing 16-5 works only with Outlook and not with Outlook Express. You can't work with Outlook Express messages directly with VBA unless you're willing to create your own library or use a third-party COM object, such as DBX2XML (http://www.bizon.org/ilya/dbx2xml.htm). After you translate an Outlook Express DBX (e-mail) file into XML, you can easily import it by using the XML features provided with Office.

Depending on which version of Outlook you use, how you have your security set up, and whether you're running on Vista, you may see one or more warning messages when you run this example. Click OK or Yes to continue running the example; don't compromise your security by changing the application settings. Listing 16-5 shows the code for this example. (You can find the source code for this example on the Dummies.com site at http://www.dummies.com/go/vbafd5e.)

Listing 16-5   Working with Flagged Outlook Messages

```
Public Sub GetFlagged()
    ' Create the Outlook application reference.
    Dim OutlookApp As Outlook.Application
    Set OutlookApp = CreateObject("Outlook.Application")

    ' Create the MAPI namespace reference.
    Dim MAPI_NS As Outlook.NameSpace
    Set MAPI_NS = OutlookApp.GetNamespace("MAPI")

    ' Create a reference to the Inbox.
    Dim Inbox As Outlook.MAPIFolder
    Set Inbox = MAPI_NS.GetDefaultFolder(olFolderInbox)

    ' Holds the current message.
    Dim CurMsg As Outlook.MailItem

    ' Look at all of the messages.
    For Each CurMsg In Inbox.Items

        ' Determine whether this message requires
            processing.
        If CurMsg.FlagStatus = olFlagMarked And _
            CurMsg.FlagIcon = olRedFlagIcon Then

            ' Place the information in the Word document.
            With ActiveWindow.ActivePane.Selection

                ' Create a From header and content.
                .BoldRun
                .TypeText "From: "
```

```
            .BoldRun
            .TypeText CurMsg.SenderName + " <" + _
               CurMsg.SenderEmailAddress + ">"

            ' Go to the next line.
            .InsertParagraph
            .GoTo What:=wdGoToLine, Which:=wdGoToLast

            ' Create a Subject header and content.
            .BoldRun
            .TypeText "Subject: "
            .BoldRun
            .TypeText CurMsg.Subject
            .InsertParagraph
            .GoTo What:=wdGoToLine, Which:=wdGoToLast

            ' Create a Content header and content.
            .BoldRun
            .TypeText "Content: "
            .BoldRun
            .TypeText CurMsg.Body

            ' Create a page separator.
            .InsertParagraph
            .InsertBreak wdPageBreak
            .GoTo What:=wdGoToLine, Which:=wdGoToLast
        End With

        ' Show this action is complete.
        CurMsg.FlagStatus = olFlagComplete

      End If
   Next
End Sub
```

The code begins by creating some Outlook objects, including the application, the namespace, the folder, and an individual message. You might wonder how you gain access to these objects. Add a reference to the Microsoft Outlook Object Library to your program by using the Tools⇨References command.

You can use several techniques to create `OutlookApp`. For example, the code could use `Set OutlookApp = new Outlook.Application`. This technique works fine as long as Outlook is already running. However, using this statement can cause an error when Outlook isn't running, so, whenever possible, you should use the `CreateObject` method shown in the example to ensure reliable program operation.

Outlook might eventually have the ability to use more than one communication technique. For now, Outlook uses Messaging Application Programming Interface (MAPI). You must create a reference to the communication technique or namespace in the program. The code uses the namespace to get a message folder (or other data, such as a contact) by using the method named GetDefaultFolder.

After the code creates the objects that it needs, it uses a For Each...Next loop to check each message in the folder. This program uses the Inbox, but you can use the same technique on any folder. If the message is marked with a red flag, the program processes it. Notice that you must make two checks to see whether the message requires processing. First, you must ensure that the message is marked by using the FlagStatus property. Second, you check the color of the flag by using the FlagIcon property (which seems a tad counterintuitive, even for Microsoft).

The program spends most of its time writing to the document, so the code uses a With ActiveWindow.ActivePane.Selection statement. The formatting in this example is simple: All the headings appear in bold; everything else appears in normal text.

The message format is very predictable, so it performs a minimum of text processing commands. It uses the TypeText method to send text to the current document. Notice the use of the InsertParagraph method. Inserting the paragraph mark doesn't move the selection point. If you don't also use the GoTo method to change the selection point, the program happily continues inserting text at the beginning of the first line. Each message loop ends by inserting a page break after the message by using the InsertBreak wdPageBreak method. I like each message to start on a new page, but you can certainly change this behavior.

The final step in this program is to change the message flag status. Use the CurMsg.FlagStatus = olFlagComplete statement to perform this task. The reason you want to use a completed flag is that it signifies that you've completed working with this message. If you cleared the flag, you might go back later and mark the message for printing again.

Sending E-Mail Messages with Outlook

Creating e-mail with Outlook is straightforward. If you don't like the formatting capabilities of Outlook, you can always create a message in Word and use the Word document as content for the e-mail. However, these two methods of message creation assume that a list of people will receive precisely the same message. When you want to create every message with the same general content and some messages with special content, you need a program.

I often need to send customized announcements by using e-mail, so I created the program shown in the upcoming Listing 16-6. This example is a simplified version of my program, but it presents all the code that you need to create your own custom version. The program relies on a specially formatted Word document that includes tags for particular kinds of information. Figure 16-1 shows the document for this example.

The Word document used for this example has three sections. (You can download it from the Dummies.com Web site at `http://www.dummies.com/go/vbafd5e`.) Using section breaks makes each document area obvious and has advantages when the code processes the document. (See Listing 16-6 and the accompanying code description for details on the advantages of using this technique.) The first section of the example document in Figure 16-1 contains the e-mail subject. Just like in any e-mail message, the subject must appear on a single line.

The second section of the example document in Figure 16-1 contains the general text — the information that you want everyone to see. This section can contain as many or as few lines as you want. The example doesn't process any formatting information, and it doesn't recognize objects, such as pictures.

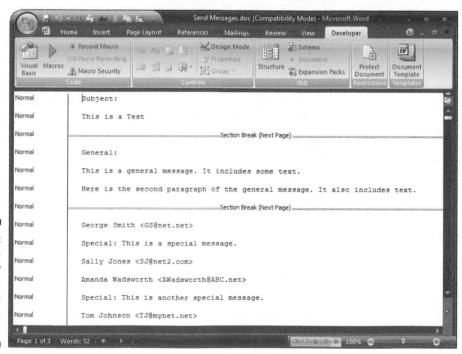

Figure 16-1:
Using a
specially
formatted
document to
create
e-mail.

The third section of the document example shown in Figure 16-1 contains the person's name and e-mail address and any special text. The identification could include just the name or just the address, but the example uses both. Notice that you must include the e-mail address in angle brackets, as shown in the figure. Any special text must appear in a single paragraph. You must mark the paragraph with the `Special` tag, as shown in Figure 16-1. Listing 16-6 shows the code to process this Word document as e-mail messages. Here's the code for this example. (You can find the source code for this example on the Dummies.com site at `http://www.dummies.com/go/vbafd5e`.)

Listing 16-6   Processing a Word Document into an Outlook Message

```
Public Sub CreateMessage()

    With ActiveWindow.Selection

        ' Go to the beginning of the document.
        .GoTo What:=wdGoToLine, Which:=wdGoToFirst

        ' Holds the subject and general text.
        Dim Subject As String
        Dim General As String

        ' Get the subject.
        ' Start by selecting the first word.
        .End = .Start + 8
        ' Make sure it's a subject.
        If .Text = "Subject:" Then
            'Go to the next line and select the subject.
            .GoTo What:=wdGoToLine, Which:=wdGoToNext
            .EndOf Unit:=wdParagraph, Extend:=wdExtend
            .End = .End - 1
            Subject = .Text
        Else
            ' Display an error message.
            MsgBox "You must include a subject line!", _
                vbCritical, "File Formatting Error"
            Exit Sub
        End If

        ' Get the general text.
        ' Start by selecting the keyword.
        .GoTo What:=wdGoToLine, Which:=wdGoToNext
        .Start = .Start + 1
        .End = .Start + 8
        ' Make sure it's the general text.
        If .Text = "General:" Then
            'Go to the next line and select the general text.
            .GoTo What:=wdGoToLine, Which:=wdGoToNext
            .EndOf Unit:=wdSection, Extend:=wdExtend
            .End = .End - 1
            General = .Text
```

```
      End If
End With

' Tracks the end of the text.
Dim EndOfText As Boolean
EndOfText = False

' Holds the user name.
Dim UserName As String

' Holds any special greeting.
Dim Special As String

' Create the Outlook application reference.
Dim OutlookApp As Outlook.Application
Set OutlookApp = CreateObject("Outlook.Application")

' Create the MAPI namespace reference.
Dim MAPI_NS As Outlook.NameSpace
Set MAPI_NS = OutlookApp.GetNamespace("MAPI")

' Create a reference to the Inbox.
Dim Outbox As Outlook.MAPIFolder
Set Outbox = MAPI_NS.GetDefaultFolder(olFolderOutbox)

' Holds the current message.
Dim CurMsg As Outlook.MailItem

' Holds the existing and new start range.
Dim OldStart As Long
Dim MyRange As Range

' Process the next section.
ActiveWindow.Selection.GoTo What:=wdGoToSection, _
   Which:=wdGoToNext

' Keep processing until there is no more text.
While Not EndOfText

   ' Get the user name and e-mail address.
   With ActiveWindow.Selection
      .EndOf Unit:=wdParagraph, Extend:=wdExtend
      UserName = .Text

      ' Determine if the next line is a special
      ' greeting.
      OldStart = .Start
      Set MyRange = .GoTo(What:=wdGoToLine, _
         Which:=wdGoToNext)
      If MyRange.Start = OldStart Then
         EndOfText = True
```

(continued)

Listing 16-6 *(continued)*

```
            End If
            .End = .Start + 8
            ' Make sure it's a subject.
            If .Text = "Special:" Then
                ' Select the Special text.
                .Start = .End + 1
                .EndOf Unit:=wdParagraph, Extend:=wdExtend
                .End = .End - 1
                Special = .Text
                .HomeKey
            Else
                ' Reset the Special text.
                Special = ""

                ' Go back to the previous text.
                .GoTo What:=wdGoToLine, Which:=wdGoToPrevious
            End If

            ' Select the next name in the list. If this is
            ' the end of the text section, set the indicator.
            OldStart = .Start
            Set MyRange = .GoTo(What:=wdGoToLine, _
                Which:=wdGoToNext)
            If MyRange.Start = OldStart Then
                EndOfText = True
            End If
        End With

        Set CurMsg = Outbox.Items.Add()

        ' Add some content.
        CurMsg.Recipients.Add UserName
        CurMsg.Subject = Subject
        CurMsg.Body = General + vbCrLf + vbCrLf + Special

        ' Send the message.
        CurMsg.Send

    Wend

    ' Display the number of messages sent.
    MsgBox CStr(Outbox.Items.Count) + " message sent.", _
        vbInformation, "Messages Sent"
End Sub
```

The code begins by processing the subject and general message. One of the most important considerations is that you have to keep the selection pointer and range in the correct places throughout the processing, or else the messages don't appear correctly.

The reason for the peculiar document format shown in Figure 16-1 becomes a little more obvious when you read the code for this example. The document takes maximum advantage of the text selection features that Word provides. Notice that after the code determines that the Subject tag appears on the first line, it moves to the second line and selects the entire line by calling the EndOf method. Unfortunately, this method also selects the paragraph mark, and you don't want to see that in the message title. (The paragraph mark appears as a square because Outlook can't make it visible.) Consequently, the program uses selection range math to change the selection. The .End = .End - 1 statement simply changes the selection so that it doesn't include the paragraph mark.

Selecting text correctly is a big issue when working with Word. The subject and general text use similar selection techniques. However, the code uses the Unit:=wdSection argument of the EndOf method in the second case to select the rest of the section. Using this technique lets you select an indeterminate number of paragraphs, which makes the program more flexible.

This example uses the same Outlook objects as those used in the earlier section "Processing Outlook E-Mail Messages with Word." See that section for a description of the Application, NameSpace, MAPIFolder, and MailItem objects. The only difference is that this example writes to these objects rather than reads from them.

Processing the names and special text requires a little extra work because you don't know whether every name will have special text associated with it. In addition, the document can contain any number of names, so the code needs to know when it has reached the end of the document (or else it will continue adding names forever). A special variable, EndOfText, tracks the end-of-the-document condition.

The code begins by selecting the username. It doesn't matter whether you provide a name, an e-mail address, or both because Outlook knows how to handle all three conditions.

Checking for a special greeting is the next step. The code doesn't know whether the text exists, so it must make an assumption, validate the results, and take the appropriate action. This example assumes that the special text exists. It selects the text in the next line to see whether it begins with the

Special keyword. If this word is present, the example selects the text that follows the keyword and places it in the Special string. Otherwise, the code clears the Special string and places the cursor on the previous line so that processing continues as though nothing happened.

The code has to track the last line. There are two possibilities. The entry could include a special line of text, or it might simply contain a recipient identity. The first range check that appears as part of the special greeting code checks for a condition where the last line is a recipient identity. The second range check code looks for a condition where the last line is a special greeting. You need both checks to ensure that the code works properly because in the second case, the code won't actually be at the last line until it processes the special message. Leaving out this second check lets the code post an extra e-mail message. However, if you leave out the first check, the code that returns the selection pointer to the previous line prevents the loop from ending.

The loop ends with the code required to send the message that the code creates. The message includes a recipient, the subject, and the text (including a special message). The Send method places the message in the Outlook Outbox.

Sending Notes from Word to Excel

You might find the need to create a utility simply because a task becomes unwieldy in the host program. For example, many of my worksheets contain extensive notes. Editing those notes in Excel can become a real problem after the note gets to a certain size. However, Word provides a great editor, and I can make the notes as long as needed. The example shown in Listing 16-7 includes part of a program that I created for moving notes between Word and Excel so that they're easier to edit. (You can find the source code for this example on the Dummies.com site at http://www.dummies.com/go/vbafd5e.)

Listing 16-7   Moving Notes from Word to Excel

```
Public Sheet As Integer
Public Row As String
Public Column As String

Public Sub SendNote()
    ' The text used as a note.
```

```
   Dim NoteText As String

   With ActiveWindow.Selection

      ' Go to the beginning of the document.
      .GoTo What:=wdGoToLine, Which:=wdGoToFirst

      ' Select the document text.
      .EndOf Unit:=wdSection, Extend:=wdExtend

      ' Get the text.
      NoteText = .Text
   End With

   ' Create a file dialog.
   Dim GetFile As FileDialog
   Set GetFile = Application.FileDialog(msoFileDialogOpen)
   GetFile.AllowMultiSelect = False
   GetFile.Filters.Clear
   GetFile.Filters.Add "Excel Files", "*.XL*"

   ' Get the Excel file.
   GetFile.Show

   ' Get the selected file.
   Dim Filename As String
   Filename = GetFile.SelectedItems(1)

   ' Open the Excel workbook.
   Dim TheBook As Excel.Workbook
   Set TheBook = Excel.Workbooks.Open(Filename)

   ' Request the sheet and cell number for the note.
   NoteSelect.Show

   ' Get the worksheet.
   Dim TheSheet As Excel.Worksheet
   Set TheSheet = TheBook.Sheets(1)

   ' Add the comment.
   TheSheet.Range(Column + Row).AddComment NoteText

   ' Close the workbook.
   TheBook.Close True
End Sub
```

The code begins by getting the note text from the Word document. This
means placing the cursor at the beginning of the document, selecting a range
of text, and copying that text to a local variable.

The next step is to figure out which Excel file to modify. The `GetFile` object is a file dialog box. Unfortunately, the file dialog box filters for Word point to Word documents (not to the Excel documents you need), so the code has to change the filter by using the `Filters.Clear` and `Filters.Add` methods. It's also important to set `GetFile` so that it doesn't allow multiple selections — this program works with only one file at a time.

After the code displays the dialog box and you select a file, `GetFile` contains the name of the selection. This is the full path to the file, so you can select a file anywhere, and the code still works.

It's time to open the Excel file. You don't actually see Excel open — everything takes place in the background. The code uses the value in `Filename` as input to the `Excel.Workbooks.Open` method.

Notice that everything to do with Excel begins with the word *Excel*. Word and Excel often use objects with the same name. Adding the word *Excel* avoids confusion.

This program also requires a custom form. Figure 16-2 shows what this form looks like. The `NoteSelect` form appears onscreen long enough for you to select a sheet, column, and row for the note.

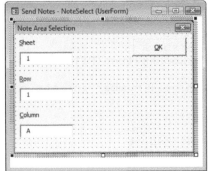

Figure 16-2:
Design forms as needed to get program input.

After the code knows what you want to write and where to place the information, it can open the Excel worksheet by using the `Sheets` collection. Notice how the code combines the `Column` and `Row` values to create a range for the comment. The `AddComment` method accepts the note text. Always make sure that you close the `Workbook` object when you're finished, or else you'll end up with multiple background copies of Excel.

The `NoteSelect` form has a few interesting features. The code shown in Listing 16-8 makes the OK button shown in Figure 16-2 functional.

Listing 16-8   Getting the Sheet, Row, and Column Values

```
Private Sub btnOK_Click()
   ' Add error handling.
   On Error GoTo EntryError

   ' Check the Sheet range.
   If Not CInt(txtSheet.Value) > 0 Then
      MsgBox "Please type a number greater than 0.", _
         vbOKOnly Or vbCritical, "Data Entry Error"
      Exit Sub
   End If

   ' Check the Row range.
   If Not CInt(txtRow.Value) > 0 Then
      MsgBox "Please type a row number greater than 0.", _
         vbOKOnly Or vbCritical, "Data Entry Error"
      Exit Sub
   End If

   ' Check the Column range.
   If Not Asc(txtColumn.Value) > 64 Then
      MsgBox "Please type a letter greater than A.", _
         vbOKOnly Or vbCritical, "Data Entry Error"
      Exit Sub
   End If

   ' Save the data values.
   SendExcelNotes.Sheet = CInt(txtSheet.Value)
   SendExcelNotes.Row = txtRow.Value
   SendExcelNotes.Column = txtColumn.Value

   ' Close the dialog box.
   Me.Hide

   ' Exit the Sub.
   Exit Sub

EntryError:
   ' Tell the user what went wrong.
   MsgBox "You must enter a number for the Sheet and " + _
      "Row fields, and a letter for the Column field.", _
      vbOKOnly Or vbCritical, "Data Entry Error"

   ' Return the fields to appropriate values.
   txtSheet.Value = "1"
   txtRow.Value = "1"
   txtColumn.Value = "A"
End Sub
```

Whenever you need external input from the user, including yourself, it pays to add error trapping. Even I type the wrong text sometimes and find the error trapping helpful in preventing data damage. This form uses two levels of error trapping. First, it checks the data type. When the data type is wrong (such as typing a letter when you really meant to type a number), the program normally goes to the `EntryError` label for standard error handling.

Notice that the code after the `EntryError` label performs two tasks. First, it displays an error message that tells you what went wrong. Second, it returns the three values to default settings. This technique ensures that you can see the correct input, and it reduces the chances of additional errors. Of course, if you have a long form to fill out, this might not be the best solution. You might want to simply say that the data is incorrect and try to point out the problem field (a task that can prove hard to tackle).

The second level of error trapping is *range checking* (making sure that the entry value falls within a specific range of numbers). You can't completely prevent errors, but you can reduce the risk of fatal errors. In this case, the code checks to ensure that the sheet and row numbers are greater than 1 and that you typed as the column value a letter *A* or greater (remember that letters have a numeric value to the computer, as described in Listings 4-2 and 4-3 in Chapter 4). Unfortunately, that's about all the range checking that you can do.

After the code checks the input, it places the information in three global variables found in the `SendExcelNotes` module. These global variables supply the placement information that you can see earlier in this section.

The code ends by hiding the form. Unless you specifically hide the form, it stays visible, and clicking the OK button doesn't appear to have any effect.

Part V
The Part of Tens

In this part . . .

Use Chapter 17 to discover new resources that you can use to build your own VBA library. This chapter contains ten types of resources that you can use to make your VBA programming experience better, easier, faster, or more fun. VBA is a language that lets you decide what you want your host application to do. The VBA resources in this chapter give you ideas of what's possible.

Chapter 18 is a special chapter for anyone upgrading their applications. You'll find that the changes Microsoft made to Office 2007 present special challenges because your code from previous Office versions may not work anymore. These ten helpful tips will make the conversion process easier.

Chapter 17

Ten Kinds of VBA Resources

*Y*ou aren't alone in your quest for the perfect VBA program. Many other companies and individuals produce resources that you can view online or download from the Internet. The resources come in a variety of forms — everything from informational Web sites to newsgroups where you can talk with other people who use VBA to free tools and code. In this chapter, I don't present every VBA resource, but I do present some interesting ideas. The first three sites that you should visit to answer your VBA questions are

✔ **Microsoft Visual Basic for Applications home page:** http://msdn. microsoft.com/isv/technology/vba/default.aspx

✔ **Microsoft Visual Basic home page:** http://msdn.microsoft.com/ vbasic/

✔ **Microsoft Office home page:** http://msdn.microsoft.com/ office/

Using Magazines and Periodicals

Articles come in all shapes, sizes, complexity levels, and forms. Some magazines specialize in a particular reader group, and others tackle a specific product. You can find high-quality articles in both free and paid forms. The length of the articles varies according to the magazine and its goals. In short, you can find one or more magazines that meet particular needs.

Traditional paper magazines and periodicals

Traditional paper magazines and periodicals offer a permanent form of documentation that you can keep on your bookshelf for reference and read just about anywhere. This list is by no means complete but has the advantage of providing a Web reference:

- **Microsoft Certified Professional Magazine Online:** `http://www.mcpmag.com/`

- **Visual Studio Magazine:** `http://www.fawcette.com/vsm/`

- **Access-SQL-VB Advisor Magazine:** `http://accessvbsql advisor.com/`

- **VBUG Magazine:** `http://www.vbug.co.uk/shop/magazines.asp`

Free electronic newsletters

Free newsletters often contain short articles, tips, links, and the occasional coding example. (You might see them listed as *e-newsletters* or *eNewsletters*.) They're a good source of continuous information for building your VBA knowledge base. Here are a few of the better examples:

- **Office Watch:** `http://office-watch.com/`

- **Eli Journals:** `http://www.elementkjournals.com/tips.asp`

- **The Office Experts:** `http://www.theofficeexperts.com/newsletter.htm`

- **Microsoft Office Tips:** `http://www.worldstart.com/msofficetips.htm`

- **DevX.com:** `http://www.windx.com/`

 ✔ **DevSource:** http://www.devsource.com/

 ✔ **InformIT:** http://www.informit.com/articles/

 ✔ **AbleOwl:** http://www4.ableowl.com/ableowl/ablehome.aspx

Many of these sites also provide free downloads. For example, you can find downloads on The Office Experts site at http://www.theofficeexperts.com/downloads.htm. Some sites, such as AbleOwl, provide news about seminars as well as training and support. The reason I list these sites here is that they focus on a newsletter — the other features add to an already great site.

It's important to realize that VBA has a worldwide presence and that not everyone speaks a particular language. For example, one magazine devoted specifically to VBA is *VBA Magazine* (http://www.vba-almere.nl/index.php?id=34), which is produced in the Netherlands. Fortunately, Google provides a solution to this problem. You can use the Google Language Tools (http://www.google.com/language_tools) to translate Web sites from one language to another when Google supports the language. All you need to do is provide the Web site URL in the Translate a Web Site field, choose the desired translation (such as from German to English), and click Translate. Although the translation isn't perfect, it normally works well enough to provide the information you need. Look for the Translate link when you search for Web sites using Google as well.

Using RSS to Obtain the Latest Information

One of the biggest news items today is Rich Site Summary (RSS) (some sources call it Really Simple Syndication and others call it RDF Site Summary — all three terms mean the same thing). The *RSS* technology sends short descriptions of articles to a special application on your machine, called a *reader,* at regular intervals. The summary lets you quickly decide whether you want to read the entire article. All you have to do is click the supplied link when you want to review the material.

Using RSS, you can obtain the latest news within moments after it becomes available. Of course, speed is nice, but knowing that something exists at all is important, which is the real purpose behind using RSS. You subscribe to RSS feeds, and the RSS reader you use provides you with automatic updates. A number of RSS readers exist. For example, you find one supplied with newer versions of Outlook (not Outlook Express).

Most of the magazines described in this chapter now provide RSS feeds. In many cases, all you need to do is click the RSS feed link on the magazine's Web page to subscribe to the RSS feed. You also find a wealth of Microsoft-specific RSS feeds at `http://msdn.microsoft.com/office/rss.xml`. These RSS feeds are the best ones to use when you want to keep in touch with what Microsoft is doing. You should also review the Microsoft suggestions for using RSS at `http://www.microsoft.com/communities/guide/rss.mspx`.

Finding Interesting Newsgroups and List Servers

Most methods of information gathering are *unidirectional:* A vendor or advanced computer user chooses to share code, techniques, or general information through a Web site or newsletter. Although this method of sending information works great for most needs, it's still nice to have two-way communication when you have a question. Newsgroups can really help in this case. All you need to do is point your news reader to the correct group to learn more.

You can also access a newsgroup by typing the news server and newsgroup name in your browser or other Internet address bar like this: `news://news.microsoft.com/microsoft.public.word.vba.addins`. This second technique works well when your ISP doesn't support a particular newsgroup but you know the name of the news server that hosts the newsgroup.

List servers work like newsgroups except that you use your e-mail or a Web site to correspond with other people. You normally have to sign up for a list server, and they're usually moderated to keep conversations on track. You might find that these tightly focused and controlled sources of information help you get what you need quickly, or they might be too confining for words.

This chapter doesn't list the Microsoft or third-party Visual Basic newsgroups; however, because VBA is a true subset of Visual Basic, you can usually find good information in these newsgroups as well. Go to a VBA-specific newsgroup when you can, but look to Visual Basic newsgroups when you can't find what you need.

Microsoft-specific newsgroups

Microsoft provides a number of VBA newsgroups. In fact, you can probably find in this one place everything that you need in order to talk with other VBA users. Most ISPs carry the Microsoft newsgroups. However, you can also access the Microsoft newsgroups directly by using its server at

news.microsoft.com. (If you want to use your browser, you type news://
news.microsoft.com/microsoft.public.access.modulesdaovba, for
example; however, it's usually easier to find the newsgroup in your newsgroup
reader.) Here are some VBA newsgroups that you can visit for additional information. (***Note:*** Most of these sites are product specific, so you need to go to
the VBA site for your particular product, such as Access or Excel.)

- microsoft.public.access.modulesdaovba
- microsoft.public.access.modulesdaovba.ado
- microsoft.public.frontpage.programming.vba
- microsoft.public.office.developer.outlook.vba
- microsoft.public.office.developer.vba
- microsoft.public.outlook.program_vba
- microsoft.public.project.vba
- microsoft.public.visio.developer.vba
- microsoft.public.word.vba.addins
- microsoft.public.word.vba.beginners
- microsoft.public.word.vba.customization
- microsoft.public.word.vba.general
- microsoft.public.word.vba.userforms

Third-party newsgroups

Newsgroups are either news-reader–based or Web-based. The number of
third-party, news-reader–based newsgroups that you find depends on your
ISP and can depend on the vendor. In some cases, you find that the vendor
runs a special news server that you can access by using the same technique
as for the Microsoft newsgroups. Web-based newsgroups rely on a special
Web site interface that you access with your browser. Here are a few of the
third-party newsgroups that you can find without too many problems:

- **AutoDesk AutoCAD newsgroup:** autodesk.autocad.
  customization.vba
- **General VBA help newsgroup:** ingr.cserve.msbbeta.vba-prog
- **Expresso Code Cafe:** http://www.vbdesign.net/expresso/
- **VBWire VB Forums:** http://www.vbforums.com

Some newsgroups, such as Experts Exchange (http://www.
experts-exchange.com/Applications/MS_Office/), require that
you pay a fee to join. In most cases, these groups provide very high-quality

information, but you end up paying a relatively high fee to get it. Whether one of these groups makes sense for your needs depends on how often the site provides information you need that you can't find elsewhere. Generally, you should avoid this kind of Web site unless it becomes apparent that you'll use the service often.

Don't forget to try third-party, general newsgroups, too. For example, you can find various Corel products newsgroups where you can ask about the CorelDRAW or WordPerfect form of VBA at `corel.developers` (and the associated sub-newsgroups). You can also ask general support questions at `corel.support`, which includes a number of sub-newsgroups.

List servers that you access through e-mail and Web sites

List servers have several advantages over newsgroups. For one thing, the *noise level* (unwanted postings) is much lower. These groups are very focused, which means that you normally get good information. A moderator keeps discussions on track, so there's less chance of seeing a discussion entitled Great New VBA Trick that's actually about Uncle Al's birthday party. In many cases, you subscribe by sending the list owner or another special e-mail address an e-mail with the word *Subscribe* as the subject. Here are some list servers that you can try:

- **AccessRabbit:** `mailto:AccessRabbit-subscribe@topica.com`
- **Microsoft Office Tips and Tricks:** `http://lists.topica.com/lists/tutorials-list/`
- **Microsoft Office Freelist Group:** `http://www.freelists.org/cgi-bin/webpage?webpage_id=mso`

Topica is one of the more famous list servers. To find a particular kind of content on Topica, go to `http://www.topica.com/lists/`. Type a search term, such as **Microsoft Office**, in the Search field, choose Lists, and click Search.

Locating Just the Right Code

A number of Web sites cater to the VBA user by proving example code that you can use anywhere in your own code. Most of these sites copyright their code so that you can't use it for profit or as part of a magazine article. The developer provides the code as is, so you might need to debug it a little or modify it to meet your needs. The point is that the code helps you better understand a programming concept, which makes writing your own version of the example much faster. Use these links as your gateway to some great coding examples:

- **VB2theMax:** `http://www.devx.com/vb2themax/Door/18897` (archive) or `http://www.vb2themax.com/` (current material)

- **MVPs.org:** `http://www.mvps.org/`

- **Walker Software:** `http://www.papwalker.com/links.html`

- **Contract CADD Group:** `http://www.contractcaddgroup.com/download/`

- **FreeVBCode:** `http://www.freevbcode.com`

- **VBCode.com:** `http://www.vbcode.com`

- **Word-VBA Code Samples:** `http://www.jojo-zawawi.com/code-samples-pages/code-samples.htm`

Some of these sites include more than just code. For example, the VB2theMax site includes newsletters, articles, tips, and other resources in addition to code downloads. Make sure that you take time to explore these sites fully.

Getting Tools to Make Programming Easier

When you build more programs, you begin to notice that VBA doesn't always provide all the features that you need. In some cases, you might find that the VBA IDE lacks functionality. You might think that Microsoft hasn't really addressed every need and that some tasks require too many steps to complete. Rather than reinvent the wheel and write the addition yourself, consider using one of these third-party products:

- **MZ-Tools (`http://www.mztools.com/`):** An interesting addition to the VBA Integrated Development Environment (IDE) that provides missing functionality. The menu-driven product contains a wealth of features to make your next coding session faster and less error prone.

- **EducationOnlineforComputers.com (`http://www.educationonlineforcomputers.com/`):** A list of interesting links for discovering new facts about VBA in general and Microsoft office products in specific.

- **Add-ins.com (`http://www.add-ins.com/`):** A listing of various add-ins that you can use to enhance your Office experience. Many of these add-ins are also programmable. All these products are shrink wrapped, which means that you must buy before you try.

- **The Spreadsheet Page (`http://www.j-walk.com/ss/`):** A collection of tips, hint, code, and useful downloads. Everything is either *freeware* (no payment required) or *shareware* (try before you buy).

- **ZDNet Downloads (`http://downloads-zdnet.com.com/`):** A site that you need to search carefully for development tools. However, the search is worthwhile because this site contains a wealth of development tools and utilities.

✔ **PRIME Freeware Products (`http://www.primeconsulting.com/freeware/`):** A site that has only free products. You can find everything from a list of VBA annoyances to a bookmark pop-up utility that makes using this feature easier. The site includes a number of other free resource links.

Downloading ActiveX Controls and Third-Party Components

A developer can never have too many controls and components. You don't necessarily have to use them all every time that you write a program. A well-stocked toolbox of controls and components simply makes it easier to find just the tool that you need. Use the following sites as a starting point to building your own control and component toolbox:

✔ **VBA Store at ComponentSource:** `http://www2.componentsource.com/Marketplace/`

✔ **ActiveX.COM:** `http://www.active-x.com/`

✔ **c|net Download.com:** `http://download.com.com/`

✔ **TopShareware:** `http://www.topshareware.com/`

Using the Author As a Resource

The last resource in this chapter is me. That's right — you can call on me at any time to help you with any question that you might have with this book. No, I won't write your next college paper for you, and I don't provide free consulting on projects outside the scope of this book, but I can answer your questions on how collections work.

I also want to hear your thoughts about this book. What do you think I can do to improve it? What would you like to see in the next edition? If you think that I can provide more information in a certain area, feel free to let me know. Any errors or problems that you find are also issues that I want to know about.

You can contact me at `JMueller@mwt.net`. Unless I'm on vacation (rare), I usually answer in around two days. Even if I don't have an answer immediately, I'll let you know that I received your e-mail. Make sure that you check my Web page for updates. Of course, you also find the source code and a few extras on the Dummies.com site at `http://www.dummies.com/go/vbafd5e`.

Chapter 18

Ten Ways to Update Your Old VBA Code Quickly

*M*icrosoft has made some subtle and not-so-subtle changes to Office products that also affect your interactions with them. An example of a subtle, but necessary, change is the size of the variable used to hold the size of a disk drive. Because disk drives have increased in size so dramatically, using a larger variable makes sense, but the change results in an error in your code nonetheless. The best example of a not-so-subtle change is the Ribbon. I'm sure that more than a few VBA programmers are wondering what to do about that. Microsoft has supposedly promised a tool to fix the problem, but might not come out with it very soon.

The focus of this chapter is how to update your code quickly. Not all these tips will be useful in every situation. A search-and-replace fix works only when there's a direct change you can make, when you have a concise way to express the search, and when there are enough places in which you must make the fix to make using search-and-replace viable. For example, if you have a variable that you use in a number of places in a module and the size of that variable is wrong, you can probably fix it using search-and-replace.

Debugging Your Code Before Making Changes

It may sound backward, but the easiest way to find problems in your code is to use the Debugger. If your code is simple enough, you can usually get through a module in a short time. Simply debug the code one message at a time. At some point, the Debugger will report that your code is clean and you can begin working on the less obvious problems (at least to the Debugger), such as missing controls on the Ribbon.

Make sure you record every change you make because you might have the same problems in other modules. By leveraging what you learn from the Debugger, you can further speed the update. For example, you might be able to combine what you learn with the search-and-replace technique. Make sure you employ the techniques described in the "Asking Others About a Fix" section, later in this chapter, as you debug your code. Sometimes you don't need to come up with an answer at all because someone else has already found it.

Using Search-and-Replace to Your Advantage

Search-and-replace is something that just about everyone has used at one time or another. You specify a search term and then ask the computer to look for it and then replace the search term with the new expression you provide. The process seems pretty straightforward, so many people don't give it the thought and consideration it deserves. However, search-and-replace can be an enemy when it comes to code. Replacing some search terms fixes your code; replacing others breaks it. Consequently, I usually don't use the Replace All option and check each change carefully unless there's no doubt that the search term appears only in the places that I think it will.

You display the Replace dialog box by using the Edit⇨Replace command in the Visual Basic Editor. The Find What field contains the search term, and the Replace With field contains the new expression. It's easy to change the scope of the search by using the options in the Search area as follows:

✔ **Current Procedure:** Limits the search to the Sub or Function in which the cursor appears. This option works best when you want to update a single Sub or Function before you move on to the rest of the application. Make sure that the changes you make are to standalone code that doesn't depend on the rest of the module for support.

✓ **Current Module:** Limits the search to the current file. Modules appear as separate items in Project Explorer. Any change you make affects the entire file, but doesn't affect other files in the project. This option works best when you've divided application functionality into individual modules and you want to update the module as a whole.

✓ **Current Project:** Doesn't limit the search at all — the Visual Basic Editor searches all the files in the current project. However, this feature doesn't change other projects that you might have loaded. Consequently, you would need to change a document and its associated template separately when a particular change affects both of them. This option works best after you've located all the required changes and tested the fixes and you want to update your entire application.

✓ **Selected Text:** Limits the search to the text you highlighted before displaying the Replace dialog box. This option works best when you experience problems with a particular area of a procedure and want to update only that part.

It's also possible to limit the search by choosing a search direction (up, down, or all), finding only whole words, or matching the case of the search term. All these filters are common to any application that implements search-and-replace. However, the Visual Basic Editor provides one other search filter: pattern matching. A *pattern* is a combination of standard characters and wildcard characters used to match more than one search term. For example, typing S* would locate all words beginning with the letter *S.* Here is a list of the wildcard character combinations:

✓ *****: Matches any number of characters. For example, R*N would match any word that begins with *R* and ends with *N.* The number of characters between them is unimportant.

✓ **?:** Matches a single character. For example, R?N would match RUN, but not RETURN.

✓ **#:** Matches a single digit, 0 through 9. For example, R#N would match R1N, but not RUN.

✓ **[charlist]:** Matches a single character in a list. For example, R[AU]N would match either RAN or RUN, but not RON.

✓ **[!charlist]:** Matches a single character that doesn't appear in a list. For example, R[AU]N would match RON, but not RAN or RUN.

Asking Others About a Fix

Many people have a tendency to think that they're the only ones experiencing a particular problem. In other cases, the pressures of fixing a problem now, not five minutes from now, keep people from looking for solutions that might help them. However, when it comes to VBA, you have a whole world of people to ask. Unless you're very unlucky, someone out there has experienced a problem that's similar to yours. It may not be precisely the same problem, but the help is there if you want it. The following sections discuss two sources of valuable fixes: Microsoft and third parties.

Finding fixes that Microsoft provides

Microsoft has gotten better about providing fixes in recent years. It isn't the best at it yet, but it has gotten better. Unfortunately, in the usual Microsoft way of doing things, you can't find what you need in a centralized location; the information is usually spread out all over. However, you can use a structured approach to finding the fixes you need.

The first place you should look is in the newsgroups described in Chapter 17. In many cases, people in the know will provide an answer or two that you might have a hard time finding. Make sure you search the newsgroup first for the answer you need, rather than simply assume that no one has asked the question.

Another good place to look is in the Microsoft Knowledge Base. Whenever a problem becomes significant enough to garner major public attention, Microsoft posts a Knowledge Base article about it. When it comes to VBA, Microsoft often posts sample code with the Knowledge Base article, so you might have the fix you need without writing any code yourself. When you perform a search of this type, it pays to use the advance search at `http://support.microsoft.com/search/?adv=1`. Make sure you specify a product (Office in most cases) and the keywords for your problem. Generally, you should include VBA as one of the keywords.

The next place to look is Google. Interestingly enough, you can perform targeted searches with Google that work far better than vendor search engines in many cases. Don't bother with the standard search in this case; use the advanced search at `http://www.google.com/advanced_search?hl=en`. Now, here's the special search technique to remember. You enter your keywords as normal in the Find Results area. However, you filter those results by adding to the Domain field the Microsoft domain you want to search. For example, if you want to search the Microsoft Office content, type **office.microsoft.com** in the Domain field. Likewise, if you want to find technical information, type **msdn.microsoft.com** or **msdn2.microsoft.com** in the Domain field. Don't forget to check the blogs in the `blogs.msdn.com` domain. Lest you think that the blogs aren't helpful, I found over 3,100 blog entries related to VBA while writing this book.

Finding third-party solutions to problems

Third-party sources of fixes abound. Finding them is another matter. The problem is locating what you need in printed or online form without wasting the entire day. Generally, there aren't any one-stop places to find a solution, so don't waste time going to your favorite Web sites and hoping to find an answer. The best solution is to assume that you have an entire world at your disposal and search with that idea.

The problem is to define your search well enough to avoid becoming overwhelmed with hits you can't use. The first two search terms you should use are VBA and the name of your application, such as Word. When a problem is specific to a particular version of a product, include the version as well, such as 2007. When you use a search engine that supports it, such as Google, include the error message as a phrase rather than as individual words. If you have an error number, try including it as well.

Most people don't realize it, but most search engines return different results based on the order of the words you provide. Consequently, if you don't see what you need the first time, try the search terms again, but in a different order.

Searches can sometimes fail when you're too specific. If you don't find what you need in a couple of tries, use fewer search words. Try using individual keywords from the error phrase or eliminate the phrase altogether in favor of an error number. When you don't see what you need, try asking your question on a newsgroup or list server (after searching for your question).

Maintaining a Log

Creating a log of your VBA adventures may seem like a time-consuming task in search of a problem, but it really can work. I set up an Access database for my log. Whenever I encounter a problem, I go to my log first to determine whether I've run into that problem before. It amazes me that I do commonly run into the same problems more than once. Because I've recorded my experience, complete with source code, a fix is usually moments away.

What you put into your log depends on what kind of record you want to create. A good log includes the date, product, and version, along with a short description of the problem and a detailed description. You might also want to include keywords to make searching easier. However, if you use keywords, make sure you use the same keywords consistently so that the search process really is easier.

Grabbing Helpful Code from VBA Help

Microsoft will never tell you that it changed the size of a variable from one version of Office to another. You see a What's New section in the help system, but generally it turns into a sales brochure that tells you how great Office is and why you should recruit others to use it. So, it might seem at first that help is pretty useless when it comes to updating your software. However, the opposite is true.

Let's say you find a bug in your program that appears only in Office 2007 and that you've localized it to a short piece of code using the Debugger. At this point, you have to ask yourself about assumptions you make regarding the code. Compare your code to the example code in help. The comparison process can often help you understand a difference in your code and what Microsoft is expecting. For many developers, the "light" suddenly goes on when they're performing the comparison — the change becomes obvious.

Don't be afraid to set up a test case using that example code and single-stepping through it using the Debugger. In many cases, the act of single-stepping through code and seeing how the variables change can help you recognize a flaw in your own logic.

Getting Your Users to Help You

Users really aren't annoying — at least not all the time. The reason I publish my e-mail address throughout this book is that I depend on readers, people who use my book and its associated code, to help me locate the errors that somehow crept into the book when I wasn't looking. You can do the same thing. Ask users to provide help in locating problems with your application. However, insist that they provide this input in a specific form that answers these questions:

- ✔ What is wrong with the application? (Make sure that this information is specific and not just worded as "It doesn't work.")
- ✔ Why is it wrong?
- ✔ How did you find the problem? (Insist on a set of steps.)
- ✔ Can you reproduce the problem every time you use the application?
- ✔ What do you suggest as a fix?
- ✔ How severe is this problem?
- ✔ Are you willing to test the fix?

Creating an Update Plan

Nothing works well without a plan. You created a plan to build the application, and now you need a plan to update it. Chapter 2 discusses the planning process for a new application, and that part of the process differs very little for an update. You still have to know exactly what the application will do. However, you shouldn't have to start from scratch because you wrote down your original design and can use it as a starting point. (You did, didn't you?)

Updates require several planning steps that you don't face with an original application. The first question you have to ask is what to update. You need to determine which modules and procedures within modules require a change before you can do anything.

After you know what you have to update, you have to prioritize the changes. A non-critical feature should appear lower on the list than a piece of code used by every part of the application. Prioritizing your update makes it easier for you to make the changes that count most first. Users can begin testing these features before you make all the updates, so you'll find potential problems earlier in the process when they're easier to fix. In addition, management knows that you're making progress because they see the updates you're providing.

Make sure you discuss your plan and go over everything on paper before you begin working with the code. It's important that everyone agrees with the changes you want to make and approves of the priority that you assign to each update. In addition, other people may see problems with your plan that you don't see. For example, your application might rely on a module that you can't update properly because of changes that Microsoft has made.

Learning When That Old Code Won't Update

I'm almost positive that I'm not the only one in the world who has Word Basic applications hanging around. Just in case you've never heard about Word Basic, it's an early form of VBA. This code is just about as incompatible as it can get. In fact, unless your Word Basic application runs without a hitch when you try it, you'll probably want to decide between using your old version of Word or updating the macros. That's right: There is a point at which it doesn't pay to update really old code any longer, and for Word Basic applications, that point has come.

However, Word Basic applications aren't the only macros that are ready for the trash heap. Because Office 2007 introduces so many incompatibilities, it might be a good time to review your entire code base. Sometimes, it doesn't pay to update poorly maintained and documented code because there simply isn't any way to make it better. Given the new Office environment, especially for the applications that use the Ribbon, now might be the best opportunity you'll ever have to get a clean start on some of your code.

Before you begin ripping your hair out, it's important to remember that there are many levels of update. You may decide to keep the business logic from your current applications (usually a good decision) and rework the user interface. An update of this sort acknowledges that there were probably problems with the user interface anyway, and the update merely cleans house. Always consider the state of your application before you make the decision to update, stay with your current environment, create a new application based on the old one, or do something in-between.

Using the Code in This Book for Updates

All the examples in this book run well under Office 2007, and they've also been tested to work with Office 2003. In some cases, you can't make the code work in both places, but knowing that is actually an advantage. For example, you need separate code to determine the size of a disk drive in Office 2003 and earlier, and in Office 2007 because the variable sizes are different (and incompatible). Listing 6-1, over in Chapter 6, shows you the technique for determining the amount of space on a drive, and you'll find the information about the new variable size later in that chapter. These little tidbits of information can prove quite helpful as you begin updating your code.

Even when you can't use the information in this book directly, you can use the examples as prototypes. A *prototype* is an example of what you'll do in your code. It's purposely generic so that it can fit a variety of situations. In addition, a prototype is really meant as a model rather than as a precise solution. The idea behind using a prototype is to get an idea of what you want to do from the prototype so that you don't have to reinvent the wheel. The idea is there — now all you need to do is expand it to fit your particular needs.

Index

• P •

BUSINESS, CAREERS & PERSONAL FINANCE

0-7645-9847-3   0-7645-2431-3

Also available:

- Business Plans Kit For Dummies
  0-7645-9794-9
- Economics For Dummies
  0-7645-5726-2
- Grant Writing For Dummies
  0-7645-8416-2
- Home Buying For Dummies
  0-7645-5331-3
- Managing For Dummies
  0-7645-1771-6
- Marketing For Dummies
  0-7645-5600-2

- Personal Finance For Dummies
  0-7645-2590-5*
- Resumes For Dummies
  0-7645-5471-9
- Selling For Dummies
  0-7645-5363-1
- Six Sigma For Dummies
  0-7645-6798-5
- Small Business Kit For Dummies
  0-7645-5984-2
- Starting an eBay Business For Dummies
  0-7645-6924-4
- Your Dream Career For Dummies
  0-7645-9795-7

HOME & BUSINESS COMPUTER BASICS

0-470-05432-8   0-471-75421-8

Also available:

- Cleaning Windows Vista For Dummies
  0-471-78293-9
- Excel 2007 For Dummies
  0-470-03737-7
- Mac OS X Tiger For Dummies
  0-7645-7675-5
- MacBook For Dummies
  0-470-04859-X
- Macs For Dummies
  0-470-04849-2
- Office 2007 For Dummies
  0-470-00923-3

- Outlook 2007 For Dummies
  0-470-03830-6
- PCs For Dummies
  0-7645-8958-X
- Salesforce.com For Dummies
  0-470-04893-X
- Upgrading & Fixing Laptops For Dummies
  0-7645-8959-8
- Word 2007 For Dummies
  0-470-03658-3
- Quicken 2007 For Dummies
  0-470-04600-7

FOOD, HOME, GARDEN, HOBBIES, MUSIC & PETS

0-7645-8404-9   0-7645-9904-6

Also available:

- Candy Making For Dummies
  0-7645-9734-5
- Card Games For Dummies
  0-7645-9910-0
- Crocheting For Dummies
  0-7645-4151-X
- Dog Training For Dummies
  0-7645-8418-9
- Healthy Carb Cookbook For Dummies
  0-7645-8476-6
- Home Maintenance For Dummies
  0-7645-5215-5

- Horses For Dummies
  0-7645-9797-3
- Jewelry Making & Beading For Dummies
  0-7645-2571-9
- Orchids For Dummies
  0-7645-6759-4
- Puppies For Dummies
  0-7645-5255-4
- Rock Guitar For Dummies
  0-7645-5356-9
- Sewing For Dummies
  0-7645-6847-7
- Singing For Dummies
  0-7645-2475-5

INTERNET & DIGITAL MEDIA

0-470-04529-9   0-470-04894-8

Also available:

- Blogging For Dummies
  0-471-77084-1
- Digital Photography For Dummies
  0-7645-9802-3
- Digital Photography All-in-One Desk Reference For Dummies
  0-470-03743-1
- Digital SLR Cameras and Photography For Dummies
  0-7645-9803-1
- eBay Business All-in-One Desk Reference For Dummies
  0-7645-8438-3
- HDTV For Dummies
  0-470-09673-X

- Home Entertainment PCs For Dummies
  0-470-05523-5
- MySpace For Dummies
  0-470-09529-6
- Search Engine Optimization For Dummies
  0-471-97998-8
- Skype For Dummies
  0-470-04891-3
- The Internet For Dummies
  0-7645-8996-2
- Wiring Your Digital Home For Dummies
  0-471-91830-X

* Separate Canadian edition also available
† Separate U.K. edition also available

SPORTS, FITNESS, PARENTING, RELIGION & SPIRITUALITY

0-471-76871-5

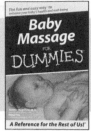

0-7645-7841-3

Also available:

- Catholicism For Dummies
  0-7645-5391-7
- Exercise Balls For Dummies
  0-7645-5623-1
- Fitness For Dummies
  0-7645-7851-0
- Football For Dummies
  0-7645-3936-1
- Judaism For Dummies
  0-7645-5299-6
- Potty Training For Dummies
  0-7645-5417-4
- Buddhism For Dummies
  0-7645-5359-3

- Pregnancy For Dummies
  0-7645-4483-7 †
- Ten Minute Tone-Ups For Dummies
  0-7645-7207-5
- NASCAR For Dummies
  0-7645-7681-X
- Religion For Dummies
  0-7645-5264-3
- Soccer For Dummies
  0-7645-5229-5
- Women in the Bible For Dummies
  0-7645-8475-8

TRAVEL

0-7645-7749-2

0-7645-6945-7

Also available:

- Alaska For Dummies
  0-7645-7746-8
- Cruise Vacations For Dummies
  0-7645-6941-4
- England For Dummies
  0-7645-4276-1
- Europe For Dummies
  0-7645-7529-5
- Germany For Dummies
  0-7645-7823-5
- Hawaii For Dummies
  0-7645-7402-7

- Italy For Dummies
  0-7645-7386-1
- Las Vegas For Dummies
  0-7645-7382-9
- London For Dummies
  0-7645-4277-X
- Paris For Dummies
  0-7645-7630-5
- RV Vacations For Dummies
  0-7645-4442-X
- Walt Disney World & Orlando
  For Dummies
  0-7645-9660-8

GRAPHICS, DESIGN & WEB DEVELOPMENT

0-7645-8815-X

0-7645-9571-7

Also available:

- 3D Game Animation For Dummies
  0-7645-8789-7
- AutoCAD 2006 For Dummies
  0-7645-8925-3
- Building a Web Site For Dummies
  0-7645-7144-3
- Creating Web Pages For Dummies
  0-470-08030-2
- Creating Web Pages All-in-One Desk
  Reference For Dummies
  0-7645-4345-8
- Dreamweaver 8 For Dummies
  0-7645-9649-7

- InDesign CS2 For Dummies
  0-7645-9572-5
- Macromedia Flash 8 For Dummies
  0-7645-9691-8
- Photoshop CS2 and Digital
  Photography For Dummies
  0-7645-9580-6
- Photoshop Elements 4 For Dummies
  0-471-77483-9
- Syndicating Web Sites with RSS Feeds
  For Dummies
  0-7645-8848-6
- Yahoo! SiteBuilder For Dummies
  0-7645-9800-7

NETWORKING, SECURITY, PROGRAMMING & DATABASES

0-7645-7728-X

0-471-74940-0

Also available:

- Access 2007 For Dummies
  0-470-04612-0
- ASP.NET 2 For Dummies
  0-7645-7907-X
- C# 2005 For Dummies
  0-7645-9704-3
- Hacking For Dummies
  0-470-05235-X
- Hacking Wireless Networks
  For Dummies
  0-7645-9730-2
- Java For Dummies
  0-470-08716-1

- Microsoft SQL Server 2005 For Dummies
  0-7645-7755-7
- Networking All-in-One Desk Reference
  For Dummies
  0-7645-9939-9
- Preventing Identity Theft For Dummies
  0-7645-7336-5
- Telecom For Dummies
  0-471-77085-X
- Visual Studio 2005 All-in-One Desk
  Reference For Dummies
  0-7645-9775-2
- XML For Dummies
  0-7645-8845-1

HEALTH & SELF-HELP

0-7645-8450-2

0-7645-4149-8

Also available:

- Bipolar Disorder For Dummies
  0-7645-8451-0
- Chemotherapy and Radiation
  For Dummies
  0-7645-7832-4
- Controlling Cholesterol For Dummies
  0-7645-5440-9
- Diabetes For Dummies
  0-7645-6820-5* †
- Divorce For Dummies
  0-7645-8417-0 †

- Fibromyalgia For Dummies
  0-7645-5441-7
- Low-Calorie Dieting For Dummies
  0-7645-9905-4
- Meditation For Dummies
  0-471-77774-9
- Osteoporosis For Dummies
  0-7645-7621-6
- Overcoming Anxiety For Dummies
  0-7645-5447-6
- Reiki For Dummies
  0-7645-9907-0
- Stress Management For Dummies
  0-7645-5144-2

EDUCATION, HISTORY, REFERENCE & TEST PREPARATION

0-7645-8381-6

0-7645-9554-7

Also available:

- The ACT For Dummies
  0-7645-9652-7
- Algebra For Dummies
  0-7645-5325-9
- Algebra Workbook For Dummies
  0-7645-8467-7
- Astronomy For Dummies
  0-7645-8465-0
- Calculus For Dummies
  0-7645-2498-4
- Chemistry For Dummies
  0-7645-5430-1
- Forensics For Dummies
  0-7645-5580-4

- Freemasons For Dummies
  0-7645-9796-5
- French For Dummies
  0-7645-5193-0
- Geometry For Dummies
  0-7645-5324-0
- Organic Chemistry I For Dummies
  0-7645-6902-3
- The SAT I For Dummies
  0-7645-7193-1
- Spanish For Dummies
  0-7645-5194-9
- Statistics For Dummies
  0-7645-5423-9

Get smart @ dummies.com®

- **Find a full list of Dummies titles**
- **Look into loads of FREE on-site articles**
- **Sign up for FREE eTips e-mailed to you weekly**
- **See what other products carry the Dummies name**
- **Shop directly from the Dummies bookstore**
- **Enter to win new prizes every month!**

* Separate Canadian edition also available
† Separate U.K. edition also available

Available wherever books are sold. For more information or to order direct: U.S. customers visit www.dummies.com or call 1-877-762-2974.
U.K. customers visit www.wileyeurope.com or call 0800 243407. Canadian customers visit www.wiley.ca or call 1-800-567-4797.

Printed and bound by CPI Group (UK) Ltd, Croydon, CR0 4YY

27/10/2024

14580182-0004